THE OFFICIAL®

2011 BLACKBOOK PRICE GUIDE TO UNITED STATES POSTAGE STAMPS

THIRTY-THIRD EDITION

BY MARC HUDGEONS, N.L.G., TOM HUDGEONS JR., AND TOM HUDGEONS SR.

HOUSE OF COLLECTIBLES
Random House Reference • New York

House of Collectibles and colophon are registered trademarks of Random House, Inc.

RANDOM HOUSE is a registered trademark of Random House, Inc.

Please address inquiries about electronic licensing of any products for use on a network, in software, or on CD-ROM to the Subsidiary Rights Department, Random House Information Group, fax 212-572-6003.

This book is available for special discounts for bulk purchases for sales promotions or premiums. Special editions, including personalized covers, excerpts of existing books, and corporate imprints, can be created in large quantities for special needs. For more information, write to Random House, Inc., Special Markets/Premium Sales, 1745 Broadway, MD 6-2, New York, NY 10019 or e-mail specialmarkets@randomhouse.com

Visit the Random House Web site:
www.randomhouse.com

ISBN: 978-0-375-72325-4

ISSN: 0195-3559

Printed in the United States of America

10 9 8 7 6 5 4 3 2 1

Thirty-Third Edition: June 2010

TABLE OF CONTENTS

OFFICIAL BOARD OF CONTRIBUTORS

The author would like to express a special thank-you to:

Peter C. Mastrangelo, Executive Director, Kim Kowalczyk, Education Director, and Judy Johnson, Membership Director at THE AMERICAN PHILATELIC SOCIETY, State College, PA, 16803, for directory listings,

Michael Schreiber and Donna Houseman at LINN'S STAMP NEWS, Sidney, OH, 45365, for their article,

Donald Sundman at MYSTIC STAMP COMPANY, Camden, NY, 13316 for his article and pricing information,

Daisy Ridgway, Public Affairs Manager at THE NATIONAL POSTAL MUSEUM, Smithsonian Institution, Washington, D.C, 20560, for articles,

Alex Bereson at UNITED NATIONS PHILATELIST, San Francisco, CA, 94131, for his pricing information,

Peter Martin of THE AMERICAN FIRST DAY COVER SOCIETY, P.O. Box 791, State College, PA, 16804 for his pricing information,

Robert Dumaine of DUCK STAMP COLLECTORS SOCIETY, Houston, TX, 77282, and

Kelly L. Spinks at THE UNITED STATES POSTAL SERVICE, Washington, D.C., 20260, for permission to reproduce the photography of U.S. stamps. *The designs for the stamps issued from 1978 to date are copyrighted by The U.S. Postal Service and are used with the permission of the U.S. Postal Service.*

NOTE TO READERS

THE OFFICIAL®

2011
BLACKBOOK
PRICE GUIDE TO
UNITED STATES
POSTAGE
STAMPS

LINN'S LOOK AT THE NEW STAMP ISSUES

by George Amick

In 2009, the United States Postal Service issued 170 collectible varieties of stamps and postal stationery, the lowest total since the 161 varieties of 2005. Postal stationery comprised 54 items, or nearly one-third of the 2009 number, an unusually high proportion for the category.

Although 2009, like 2008, saw an increase in the rates for first-class mail, expedited mail, international mail, and postcards, the number of new definitives was only 22, compared to 50 in the preceding year.

There also were fewer special stamps, another category primarily for mail use, with 17 varieties in 2009, compared to 20 In 2008.

In 2010, those totals should decline even further if, as promised, no general rate increase occurs.

Commemoratives in 2009 numbered 77, three fewer than in 2008. Most of these were produced in se-tenant multiple design panes, the largest of which was a 20-stamp Early Television Memories pane featuring photographs of stars of TV shows that originated in the black-and-white-TV era. The pane was six years in the making and was a legacy of Azeezaly Jaffer, the former stamp services and public affairs chief who left USPS In 2006.

One of the year's showcase issues was a block of four marking Abraham Lincoln's 200th anniversary and picturing Lincoln in four historical personas: rail splitter, lawyer, politician, and president. Issued in February, Lincoln's birth month, the stamps had only a three-month life as stand-alone postage before the first-class rate rose from 42¢ to 44¢ May 11.

Two small souvenir sheets contained stamps honoring 12 Civil Rights pioneers (on six stamps) and four U.S. Supreme Court justices. An illustration of a Macy's-type Thanksgiving Day Parade was spread horizontally across four stamps in a continuous-design style first used in 1967 for the 5¢ Space Twins pair (Scott 1331–32).

Because the Postal Service apparently doesn't consider a year complete without stamps featuring imaginary characters, it celebrated the 20th anniversary of the Fox TV cartoon show *The Simpsons* with five stamps in a convertible booklet of 20 depicting Homer, Marge, Bart, Lisa, and Maggie Simpson. These stamps were designed by series creator Matt Groening. The USPS created additional collectibles for the specialist by producing the booklets with four different cover designs.

New stamps in ongoing series honored writer Richard Wright (Literary Arts) and two unrelated Coopers, educator-scholar-feminist Anna Julia Cooper (Black Heritage) and movie star Gary Cooper (Legends of Hollywood); celebrated the second year in the Lunar New Year cycle, the Year of the Ox; depicted five Gulf Coast lighthouses; featured the third group of 10 Flags of Our Nation; and illustrated the flora and fauna of a kelp forest on the 11th and next-to-last Nature of America pane.

The Richard Wright stamp bore a 61¢ denomination covering the first-class rate for letters weighing more than 1 ounce but less than 2 ounces, introducing a new USPS policy in which Literary Arts commemoratives will double as higher-value mail-use stamps in years when the rates increase.

Two singles that could have been included in existing series, but weren't, depicted 19th-century writer Edgar Allan Poe and 20th-century comedian and actor Bob Hope. Three states—Alaska, Oregon and Hawaii—were honored on anniversaries of their statehood, following a tradition dating to the 3¢ Michigan Centenary commemorative of 1935.

A new American Flag design for the 44¢ rate was displayed on six definitive varieties, while the now-familiar Liberty Bell image turned up on four additional nondenominated forever stamp varieties.

The 44¢ rate also brought forth the seventh collectible variety to bear the Purple Heart design so popular with veterans' groups and Congress.

Artist Nancy Stahl's stylized wildlife art appeared on two varieties of a Polar Bear stamp with a 28¢ denomination to cover the new postcard rate, and a 64¢ Dolphin stamp for 1-ounce nonmachinable first-class letters.

A 78¢ Distinguished Americans stamp depicting philanthropist Mary Lasker was issued for the new 3-ounce first-class rate.

For the second consecutive year, no Official mail stamp was issued to cover a new first-class rate, but the USPS did issue a 1¢ Great Seal Official mail stamp in a pane of 20 for use with existing 41¢ Great Seal Official mail stamps and 42¢ Great Seal Official mail stamped envelopes.

New rates for Priority Mail and Express Mail brought forth stamps illustrating a redwood forest and Yellowstone National Park, respectively, in keeping with the tourist attractions design theme currently used for those categories.

Similarly, new rates for international airmail were covered with stamps in the long-running Scenic American Landscapes series bearing photos of Zion National Park and Grand Teton National Park.

The rate change led to a se-tenant pair of love stamps depicting a king and queen of hearts based on a deck of 18th century French playing cards, and wedding-invitation stamps for the 1-ounce and 2-ounce rates with photographs of gold rings and a cake, respectively.

The Postal Service introduced new designs for its 44¢ Hanukkah and Kwanzaa stamps, retiring the designs that had served for four successive first-class rate changes.

However, USPS used the well-established blue-and-gold Eid stamp design for the sixth time, choosing not to create a new image to mark the two major Islamic festivals. USPS also recycled the design of its all-purpose Celebrate stamp, which made its third appearance with a different denomination.

The year's bumper crop of postal stationery included the first forever stamped envelope, which reproduced the Liberty Bell from Tom Engeman's familiar stamp illustration.

The priciest item for stationery was a set of 44¢ letter sheets bearing imprints of the five Gulf Coast Lighthouses stamps that sold for $15.95 for a set of 10, or approximately $1.60 each for 44¢ face-value sheet.

Picture postal cards were issued with imprints of the Gulf Coast Lighthouses, Early Television Memories, Kelp Forest and The Simpsons stamps, 30 in all.

The standard postal card for the 28¢ rate came in two designs, each depicting a pair of koi fish, and the 44¢ standard stamped envelope bore an image of the legendary thoroughbred racehorse Seabiscuit.

As it has done since 1994, the Postal Service's mail-order fulfillment center sold uncut press sheets of selected new commemoratives at face value. Available in that format were Year of the Ox, Abraham Lincoln, Bob Hope, Early Television Memories, Gary Cooper, and Kelp Forest stamps.

America's No. 1 Stamp Album
The Minuteman

The Minuteman album is now available in four parts with a handsome standard 3-ring binder. Now an intermediate, or beginner U.S. collector can have an album to fit their collecting interest.

Item	Description (Pages Only)		Retail
180PMM19	19th Century 1840-99	15 pgs.	$5.99
180PMM20	20th Century 1900-99	362 pgs.	$35.99
180PMM21	21st Century 2000-03	78 pgs.	$12.99
180PMM21A	21st Century 2004-06	56 pgs.	$35.99
180BNDR3	Minuteman 3-Ring Binder		$7.99

Minuteman 20th Century Album Kit

Includes album pages from 1840-2007 and two Minutman binders.

Item	Description	Retail
180MMKIT	20th Century Kit	$109.99

MARKET REVIEW

by Donald Sundman

The stamp market held steady during the 2008-2009 financial crisis. The high-end market is as active as I've seen it in 25 years. Many trends worked together to sustain the vigorous stamp market, and most of these trends will continue.

High-value stamps maintained their value better than other investments—stocks, bonds, and real estate—during the recession. This news made national headlines, prompting collectors and investors alike to purchase valuable stamps. Many record stamp prices were set, including approximately $474,800 for the unreleased 1968 China Large Whole Country Is Red stamp and $299,000 for the imperforate 1851 twelve-penny Queen Victoria stamp. Conversely, four inverted Jenny stamps went unsold in 2009.

More than the normal number of valuable collections were sold during this last year and the market absorbed the material. Several sales were noteworthy for both the quality of the material offered and the prices they realized, including the spectacular Alan B. Whitman collection.

Dealers are now complaining about the lack of "fresh collections" on the market. That is, a collection that was built by a collector over a long period of time—typically 25 to 50 years—and contains stamps and covers that have been off the market for many years. The economy may be a reason for the lack of fresh collections. Demographics show us the typical active collector is 50 and older. This group may have a lot of disposable income because their children are grown. Retired collectors have stable income and can pursue their hobby. Rather than selling them in a weak economy, many actually expand their collections.

Very well-centered U.S. stamps commanded breathtaking prices in 2009. A prime example is the mint, never-hinged #404 that auctioned recently for $105,000. This remarkable realization is more than 50 times its catalogue value. However, the market for graded U.S. stamps softened somewhat, with values of some stamps down 50 percent or more——a sharp drop from *Scott Market Quarterly* values. Graded stamps are a speculative market that sees much greater price swings than non-graded stamps. This makes it a challenge to predict the future.

Historically, stamps are a bargain compared to most collectible markets. Collectors who recognize value are drawn to stamps because they are less expensive. It remains to be seen if the financial crisis attracted new collectors to our hobby, brought back people who enjoyed collecting in their youth, or both.

The future looks bright for stamp collectors and dealers. In 2009, William H. Gross auctioned his collection of Confederate stamps to help fund an $8 million gift to the National Postal Museum. The generous donation will help create a new 12,000-square-foot gallery that will be named in Gross's honor. The new gallery will give the museum space at the street level and provide room for exhibiting national stamp treasures that have been locked away for generations. Scheduled to open in 2012, the gallery will also have room for educational exhibits and public programs. It will make a great museum even better—a valuable destination for stamp and history lovers from around the world.

The election of the first African-American U.S. president and the death of pop star Michael Jackson prompted many nations to issue stamps commemorating these events. While not as popular as Elvis commemorative stamps, the new Obama and Jackson issues generated interest and stimulated sales.

The 2010 U.S. stamp program will also give collectors a reason to cheer. An Olympic Games stamp—a favorite subject for many collectors—will be released to commemorate the 2010 Winter Olympic Games in Vancouver. Entertainment legends Katharine Hepburn and Kate Smith will be honored, along with a highly anticipated Scouting stamp. And the U.S. Postal Service will almost certainly announce its plans to commemorate the 150th anniversary of the Civil War. If done right, it could prove to be as popular as the bicentennial stamps of the 1970s.

This is good news. Fresh stamp designs and interesting subjects can only be good for our hobby. In addition to pleasing those of us who are active collectors, they act as tiny billboards seen by millions of viewers every day—attracting interest and bringing new collectors into the fold.

HOW TO USE THIS BOOK

The main section of this book lists U.S. postage stamps with the exception of special issues such as airmail, revenues, etc. Special issues are grouped separately in sections of their own. Please refer to the Table of Contents.

Identification. Illustrations appear together with stamps. In some cases, two or more stamp issues are similar in appearance, but differ only in minor details, such as watermark or gauge of perforation. They are known as face-identical stamps. Listings of face-identical stamps subsequent to the first variety are cross-referenced to the initial listing and its illustration by use of a tilde and the initial catalogue number in parentheses, e.g. Scott number 18 (~5), which indicates that stamp No. 18 possesses the same design as No. 5.

The denomination and a description are given for each stamp. Denominations for non-denominated stamps are given in parentheses, e.g. (15¢) "A" & Eagle.

The type of gum (water activated or self-adhesive) is given only where necessary to distinguish two similar issues.

Prices. Prices are given in columns for unused and used examples, in the median grade of fine to very fine (F-VF). Those of higher quality sell for more; those of lesser quality sell for less. Stamps with faults or defects are worth only a small fraction of catalogue value.

Prices shown are intended to be actual retail selling prices; however, be aware that prices vary with the market and from dealer to dealer. A dash (—) in place of a price indicates that the item is either seldom available or that it does not exist in the form indicated. It should not be assumed, however, that such items are invariably more valuable than those for which prices are shown.

Prices for unused stamps issued before 1935 are for hinged examples. Never-hinged examples sell for more. The never-hinged premium appears in parentheses where applicable, e.g. (NH add 50%). Prices for unused stamps issued after 1935 are for never-hinged (NH) examples. Stated values are a general guide and do not reflect the price of the occasional superb example, such as an early imperforate with four wide margins.

A minimum price of 14¢ has been assigned to the most common stamps, such as those that you might receive on everyday mail. The minimum price reflects the labor incurred by a stamp dealer when filling an order for an individual example, should one be requested. Common stamps can be obtained in packets and bulk mixtures for much less than the listed minimum price.

No prices are given from multiples of used self-adhesive se-tenants, because once the stamps have been removed from their backing paper they cannot be reattached to form a multiple.

A box is provided to the left of each listing for keeping a record of the stamps in your collection.

Plate Blocks. Prices for plate blocks appear in the column headed "Plate Block." Prices for plate blocks of se-tenant issues appear on the line describing the se-tenant multiple under the heading "Plate Block." Plate blocks are assumed to be blocks of four unless otherwise indicated. When the number of stamps is greater than four, it is shown in parentheses following the price of the plate block.

Line Pairs and Plate Number Coil (PNC) Strips. Prices for line pairs are given in the column headed "Line Pair." Prices for plate number coil strips are given in the column headed "PNC Strip (5)". The numeral "5" in parentheses indicates that the price is for a strip of 5 stamps with the plate number located on the center stamp. The standard length for collecting PNC strips is five stamps, although both longer and shorter strips are sometimes collected. In many cases, prices for longer or shorter strips vary only slightly from those for strips of 5; however, some shorter strips (especially early PNCs) are significantly less valuable than strips of five. Check with a dealer active with PNCs for up-to-the-minute prices.

Mint Sheets. Mints sheets are priced in a separate section following the section for stamps.

Se-tenant Stamps. Listings indicate the minimum number of stamps necessary in each instance for a complete se-tenant multiple (block or strip). It is often possible to obtain blocks or strips containing all the designs necessary for a complete multiple but in an order or sequence other than that listed. Only in those cases where the listed sequence is necessary to form a larger design (e.g. No. 1331-32, the Space Twins issue) is the exact order crucial. In all other cases, it is okay to collect se-tenants in whatever order the individual stamps may occur. Some se-tenants can be collected either as blocks or strips; they are indicated in the listings.

HOW TO GRADE STAMPS

A person need not be an expert to judge the quality or grade of a stamp. All he needs is a discerning eye, possibly a small linear measuring device, and the grading instructions listed below.

The major catalogs traditionally list stamps simply as "Unused" or "Used." Auction houses, however, will describe the stamps for sale in a more informative manner. The greater the value of the stamp, the more thoroughly it is described.

There is no officially accepted system of grading stamps. What we have done in this book is essentially to set up a system of grading stamps using the suggestions and practices of stamp dealers from all over the country. Total agreement was made to the following categories and grades of stamps that are most frequently traded.

CATEGORIES

Mint—The perfect stamp with superb centering, no faults, and usually with original gum (if issued with gum).

Unused—Although unused, this stamp may have a hinge mark or may have suffered some change in its gum since it was issued.

Used—Basically this will be the normal stamp that passed through the government postal system and will bear an appropriate cancellation.

Cancelled to Order—These are stamps that have not passed through the postal system but have been carefully cancelled by the government usually for a commemoration. These are generally considered undesirable by collectors.

GRADE—STAMP CENTERING

Average—The perforations cut slightly into the design.

Fine—The perforations do not touch the design at all, but the design will be off center by 50 percent or more of a superb centered stamp.

Very Fine—The design will be off center by less than 50 percent of a superb stamp. The off-centered design will be noticeable.

Extra Fine—The design will be almost perfectly centered. The margin will be off by less than 25 percent of a superb stamp.

Superb—This design will be perfectly centered with all four margins exactly the same. On early imperforate issues, superb specimens will have four clear margins that do not touch the design at any point.

GRADE—STAMP GUM

Original Gum—This stamp will have the same gum on it that it had the day it was issued.

Regummed—This stamp will have new gum applied to it as compared to an original gummed stamp. Regummed stamps are worth no more than those with gum missing.

No Gum—This stamp will have had its gum removed or it may have not been issued with gum.

Never Hinged—This stamp has never been hinged so the gum should not have been disturbed in any way.

Lightly Hinged—This stamp has had a hinge applied. A lightly wetted or peelable hinge would do very little damage to the gum when removed.

Heavily Hinged—This stamp has had a hinge applied in such a manner as to secure it to the stamp extremely well. Removal of this hinge proves to be disastrous, in most cases, since either part of the hinge remains on the stamp or part of the stamp comes off on the hinge, causing thin spots on the stamp.

GRADE—STAMP FAULTS

Any fault in a stamp such as thin paper, bad perforations, creases, tears, stains, ink marks, pin holes, etc., depending upon the seriousness of the fault, usually results in grading the stamp to a lower condition.

OTHER STAMP CONSIDERATIONS

CANCELLATIONS

Light Cancel—This stamp has been postally cancelled but the wording and lines are very light and almost unreadable.

Normal Cancel—This stamp has been postally cancelled with just the right amount of pressure. Usually the wording and lines are not distorted and can be made out.

Heavy Cancel—This stamp has been postally cancelled. In the process excessive pressure was used, and the wording and lines are extremely dark and sometimes smeared and in most cases unreadable.

PERFORATIONS

Not to be overlooked in the appearance of a stamp are its perforations. The philatelist might examine these "tear apart" holes with a magnifying glass or microscope to determine the cleanliness of the separations. One must also consider that the different types of paper, upon which the stamp was printed, will sometimes make a difference in the cleanliness of the separations. The term "pulled perf" is used to denote a badly separated stamp in which the perforations are torn or ragged.

COLOR

Other important factors such as color affect the appearance and value of stamps. An expert will have a chart of stamp colors. Chemical changes often occur in inks. Modern printing sometimes uses metallic inks. These "printings" will oxidize upon contact with the natural secretions from human skin.

In some cases, the color of a stamp is deliberately altered by chemicals to produce a rare shade. Overprints can be eliminated. Postmarks may be eradicated. Replacing gum is a simple process. Some stamps have been found to bear forged watermarks. The back of the paper was cut away and then the stamps rebacked with appropriately watermarked paper.

There are stamp experts who earn a living in the business of stamp repairing. They are craftsmen of the first order. A thin spot on a stamp can be repaired by gluing it on a new layer of paper. Missing perforations can be added. Torn stamps can be put back together. Pieces of stamps may be joined.

In some countries it is accepted practice for an expert, upon examination of a stamp, to certify the authenticity by affixing his signature to the back of the stamp. If the stamp is not genuine, it is his right and duty to so designate on the stamp; but these signatures can also be faked.

FACTORS THAT DETERMINE
STAMP VALUES

The collector value (or "market value") of any stamp rests with a variety of factors. Philately becomes a bit less mysterious when one understands the forces at work in the stamp marketplace.

A beginner often assumes that expensive stamps are expensive because of rarity. Certainly there is a great deal of talk about stamp rarities within the hobby, and so it is natural enough to ascribe high prices to the phenomenon of rarity. In fact, rarity is only one of several factors that influence stamp prices, and the influence it carries is not particularly clear-cut.

In this book you will note some stamps (mostly among the early regular issues) with values of $1,000, $2,000, and even higher. Obviously these stamps are rarer than those selling for $10 or $15. But having said that, we have virtually summed up our useful knowledge of rarity and its effect on prices. A comparison of prices between stamps in roughly similar ranges of value does not indicate which is the rarer. A stamp selling for $1,000 is not necessarily rarer than one selling for $500. A $10,000 stamp may actually be more abundant than one which commands $5,000. This hard-to-comprehend fact of philatelic life prevails because of the other factors involved in determining a stamp's price. If rarity were the only factor, one could, of course, easily see which stamps are the rarest by the prices they fetch.

The word "rare" is an elixir to many collectors, not only of stamps but other collectors' items. Sellers are well aware of this, and seldom fail to sprinkle the word liberally in their sales literature. There is no law against calling a stamp rare, as this represents a personal opinion more than anything else and opinions are allowable in advertising. Unfortunately, there is no standard definition for rarity. Does "rare" mean just a handful of specimens in existence, with one reaching the sales portals once in five years? Does it mean 100 in existence, or 1,000, or some other number? Since stamps are—today, at any rate—printed in the multimillions, a thousand surviving specimens might seem a very tiny total to some people. Further complicating this situation is the fact that the specific rarity of most stamps cannot be determined, or even estimated, with any hope of accuracy. The quantities printed are recorded for most of our stamps, going back even into the nineteenth century, but the quantity surviving of any particular stamp is anyone's guess. It is obvious that a stamp that goes through the auction rooms once a year is fairly rare, but this provides no sound basis for guessing the number of specimens in existence. That could only be accomplished if some sort of grand census could be taken, and all specimens tallied. This, of course, is nothing but a pipe dream. Some collectors would not participate in such a census; some might be unaware that it was being conducted. Then, too, there are many scarce or rare stamps in hands other than those of collectors, such as dealers and museums. Additionally, there could be (and probably are) existing specimens of rare stamps yet to be discovered, as fresh discoveries are made periodically in the hobby through attic cleaning and the like.

In terms of influence on price, rarity is outdistanced somewhat by popularity. Some stamps, for one reason or other, are simply more popular than others. They have a sort of innate appeal for hobbyists, either through reputation, exquisite designing, circumstances of issue, oddity, or various other potential reasons. These stamps sell out rapidly from the stocks of dealers, while some stamps that are supposedly scarcer will linger in stock albums for ages and ages waiting to tempt a customer. It is no wonder, then, that the prices of popular stamps rise more quickly than those that are scarce but not in brisk demand. The Columbian series typifies the effect of popularity on stamp values. If stamp prices were fixed by scarcity alone, none of the Columbians would be selling for nearly as much. Much of their value derives from their overwhelming popularity with collectors of U.S. stamps. It would be safe to say, in fact, that all of the Columbians, from the lowest face value to the $5, are more plentiful than other U.S. stamps selling for precisely the same sums. Every dealer has Columbians in stock, and quite a few dealers have the high value of the set, too. They are not "hard to get." But they are very costly.

Popularity, of course, does not remain constant forever. There are shifts in philatelic popularity, usually slight but occasionally extreme. The popularity of commemoratives as a whole versus regular issues as a whole can change from time to time. Then, too, there are swings of popularity for airmails, first-day covers, blocks, coil pairs, mint sheets, and all other philatelic material. A climb or decline in the price of any philatelic item is often an indication of the forces of popularity at work. Then there are activities of investors to consider, whose buying habits seldom reflect those of the pure collector. A great deal of buying by investors in any short period of time (such as occurred during 1979 and 1980, and to less extent in 1981) can make prices seem well out of balance.

Also on the subject of prices, it is important for the beginner to realize that arithmetic is usually futile when dealing with stamp values. You cannot determine the price of one philatelic item by knowing the value of a similar one. This can best be shown by the relative values of singles and blocks of four. A block of four is, as one would expect, worth more than four times as much as single specimens of that stamp. It is not just four specimens of the stamp, but four of them attached, which lends added scarcity and appeal. The difficulty lies in trying to use mathematics to determine a block's value. Some blocks are worth five times as much as the single stamp; some six times; some ten times as much or even more. Almost all blocks—except very common ones—will vary somewhat in value, in relation to the value of the individual stamp. There is no satisfactory explanation for this, other than the presumption that some blocks are scarcer than others or just in greater demand than others.

In the case of common philatelic items, the value hinges greatly on the method of sale. If you want to buy one specimen of a common cover, you may have to pay $1.50. But if you were willing to buy a hundred common first-day covers of the dealer's choice, you could very likely get them for $75 or 75¢ each. Buying in quantity, and allowing the dealer to make the selections, can save a great deal of money. Of course one may then ask: What is the real value of those covers? Is it $1.50 or 75¢? The only answer is that it depends on how you buy!

If this article seems to raise a great many questions without supplying many answers, it will, hopefully, serve to show that stamp collecting is not bound to rigid formulas. What happens in the stamp market is largely beyond prediction, or precise explanation. This, indeed, is one of the exciting aspects of the hobby.

REPAIRS, FAKES, AND OTHER UNDESIRABLES

Philately, like most hobbies, is not without its pitfalls. The collector who buys from reputable dealers runs very little risk, as today's stamp pros have high principles and are hard to fool. Buying from auction sales and small dealers, who may not have expert knowledge, is another matter. Here the collector must call into play his own expertise and learn to distinguish the bad from the good.

In the early years of philately, stamps provided a playground for fakers and swindlers. They took advantage of the public's gullibility and the general lack of published information about stamps. Copies were printed of rare stamps, as well as of stamps that never existed in the first place. Cancels were bleached from used specimens to make them appear unused. Fake margins were added to imperforates, to allow ordinary copies to be sold as "superb with jumbo margins." Perforated stamps were reperforated to make them better centered. Thin spots in the paper were filled in, tears closed, missing portions of paper replaced. Stamps were doctored and manipulated in more ways than could be imagined, all in the hope of fooling collectors and making anywhere from a few extra cents to thousands of dollars on them. One of the favorite tricks of fakers was to apply bogus overprints or surcharges. By merely using a rubber handstamp and a pad of ink, they could stamp out a hundred or more "rarities" in a few minutes, turning ordinary British or other issues into varieties not found in any catalogue. It was all a great game and proved very profitable, until collectors and the philatelic public at large became wary of such practices. Even though most of these fakes from the hobby's pioneer years have disappeared out of circulation, a few still turn up and must be guarded against.

U.S. stamps have not been faked nearly so extensively as those of many other nations, notably South America and Japan. Still, the collector should learn to watch for fakes and also for repaired specimens.

Total Fake. The counterfeit stamp always varies somewhat from a genuine specimen, though the difference may be very slight. Detection can usually be made if the suspect stamp is examined alongside one known to be genuine. By using a magnifier, the lines of engraving and paper quality can be compared. The ink on a fake is likely to have a fresher appearance and will lie on the surface as a result of being printed at a later date and on less sophisticated equipment; however, this is not always the case. Experts say that when a stamp appears to be a fake, or a reprint, the odds are very good that it is. Some experience is necessary before anyone can get a first-glance reaction to a stamp. The presence or absence of a cancel has no bearing on the likelihood of a stamp being a fake, as cancels can be faked, too.

Faked Cancel. Faked cancels are very rare on U.S. stamps, as nearly all are worth more unused than used. One notable exception is the 90¢, 1857–1861. These are applied either with a fake hand stamp or simply drawn with pen and ink. Skillfully drawn faked cancels can be very deceptive. Faked cancels are much more numerous on covers than loose stamps.

Removed Cancels. So-called cleaned copies of used stamps, sold as unused, were once very plentiful and are still encountered from time to time. The faker, of course, chooses lightly cancelled specimens from which the obliteration can be removed without leaving telltale evidence. In the case of imperforates he may trim down the margins to remove part of the cancel. Rarely will he attempt to clean a stamp whose cancel falls across the face or any important portion of the stamp. Holding the stamp to a strong light may reveal the cancel lines. X-ray examination provides positive proof.

Added Margin(s). When margins have been added to an imperforate stamp, the paper fibers are woven together (after moistening) along the back and at the front where the margin extends beyond the stamp's design. They can usually be detected by looking closely for a seam or joint at the point where the design ends and the margin begins. A magnifying glass will be necessary for this. When held against a light, the reverse side will probably show evidence of the weaving operation. Sometimes the added margins are of a slightly different grade of paper.

Reperforated. A stamp that has been reperforated to improve its centering will usually be slightly smaller than a normal specimen, and this can be revealed by placing it atop an untampered copy.

Filled Thin Spots. If held to a light and examined with a good magnifier, filled-in thin spots will normally appear darker than the remainder of the stamp. Such spots are often mistaken for discoloration by beginners. Thin spots are filled in by making a paste of paper pulp and glue and applying it gradually to the injured area. After drying, the stamp is placed in a vise so that no telltale hills or valleys are left. This is not really considered forgery but honest repair work; it becomes forgery only if done with the intent of selling the stamp as undamaged.

Closed Tears. These are almost always visible against a light with a magnifier, even if small. A routine examination of any rare stamp should include a check of its margins for possible closed or open tears.

Type Identifier

Types of the 1¢ Franklin 1851–1860.

Type I   Type Ia

Type I. The scrollwork on all sides is complete. The curved lines at top and bottom are complete and unbroken. The curls at the bottom scrollwork are complete.

Type Ia. Similar to Type I at bottom, but the line at the top of the inscription is cut away as are the tops of the ornaments.

Type Ib. Similar to Type I at top, but at bottom the curved line below the denomination is partly cut away and the scrollwork is not as complete. (Not illustrated.)

Type II   **Type III**

Type II. The curls and plumes of the bottom ornaments are incomplete. The curved line below the denomination is complete, as are the side ornaments.

Type III. The center portions of the curved lines at both top and bottom are incomplete. Side ornaments are intact.

Type IIIa. Similar to Type III, but only one of the curved lines, either top or bottom, has been cut away. (Not illustrated.)

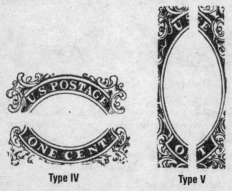

Type IV   **Type V**

Type IV. Similar to Type II, but the curved lines at either top or bottom (or both) are complete and more pronounced, having been reworked.

Type V. Similar to Type III, but the side ornaments are partially cut away.

Types of the 3¢ Washington of 1851–1860 (Scott Nos. 10, 11, 26, 26a, and 41).

Type I. The frame line is complete all around the design.

Type II. No horizontal frame lines along the top and bottom of stamps. Vertical frames at sides, however, are unbroken and continuous.

Type IIa. Similar to Type II except vertical frame lines break between stamps.

Types the 5¢ Jefferson of 1851–1860 (Scott Nos. 12, 27, 28, 28A, 29, 30, 30A and 42).

Type I. The projections at top, bottom and sides are complete.

Type II. The projections at top and bottom are cut away.

Types of the 10¢ Washington of 1851–1860 (Scott Nos. 13, 14, 15, 16, 31, 32, 33, 34, 35 and 43).

Type I. The shells at the lower corners are almost complete. The outer line below the inscription "Ten Cents" is nearly complete. The outer lines at top above "U.S. Postage" and letters "X" at each corner are not complete.

Type II. The outer lines at top above "U.S. Postage" and letters "X" at each corner are complete. The outer line below the inscription "Ten Cents" is broken. The shells at the lower corners are partially cut away.

Type III. The outer lines of the inscriptions at both top and bottom are broken. The outer lines above the letters "X" at top are broken and the shells at the lower corners are partially cut away.

Type IV. The outer lines of the inscriptions at both top and bottom have been recut and appear more pronounced.

Type V. One or two of the three small "pearls" that appear at the sides on the lower part of the design have been cut away. The outer line atop the letter "X" at top right has been cut away.

Secret Marks on the Banknote Issues.

1¢. The secret mark is contained in the ball just to the left of the top of the numeral "1."

2¢. The secret mark is a small diagonal line beneath the scroll above and to left of the letters "U.S."

3¢. The secret mark is additional heavy shading in the ribbon below the letters "RE."

6¢. The secret mark is additional heavy shading of the four vertical lines in the lower left ribbon.

7¢. The secret mark is two semicircles added to the ball ornament at lower right.

10¢. The secret mark is a small semicircle added to the pendant ball at the right end of the denomination tablet.

12¢. The secret mark is the addition of two balls to the numeral "2."

15¢. The secret mark is the strengthening of lines at the "v" at the top left triangle.

Types of the 2¢ Washington of 1894–1898 (Scott Nos. 249, 250, 251, 252, 265, 266 and 267).

| Type I | Type II | Type III |

Type I. Horizontal lines across the triangles at top are of the same thickness throughout.

Type II. Horizontal lines are thin inside the triangles.

Type III. The double frame of the triangles do not contain any lines.

Types of the $1 Perry of 1894–1895 (Scott Nos. 261, 261A, 276 and 276A).

| Type I | Type II |

Type I. Circles around the numeral in the lower corners are broken.

Type II. Circles around the numeral in the lower corners are complete.

Types of the 10¢ Webster of 1898 (Scott Nos. 282C and 283).

Type I   Type II

Type I. Circles around the numerals in the lower corners are complete.

Type II. Circles around the numerals in the lower corners are broken.

Types of the 2¢ Washington of 1912–1920.

Type I   Type II

Type I. The tip of the left ribbon contains a single vertical mark. The second curve in the right ribbon contains a single vertical mark. The top line of the toga is faint. Shading lines on the face that terminate at the ear are not joined. Type I occurs on both flat plate and rotary press printings.

Type Ia. Similar to Type I except that the lines atop the toga and toga button are heavy. (Not illustrated).

Type II. Vertical marks in the ribbons are the same as Type I. The line atop the toga and toga button are heavy. A pronounced vertical line joins the shading lines on the face that terminate at the ear. Type II occurs only on rotary press printings.

Type III

Type IV

Type III. Similar to Type II except that the ribbons contain two vertical marks instead of one. Type III occurs only on rotary press printings.

Type IV. The top line of the toga is broken. The lines inside the button for the letters "ᗡ I D."

Type V

Type Va

Type V. The toga button contains five vertical lines. The top line of the toga is complete. The nose is shaded as illustrated. Type V occurs only on offset printings.

Type Va. Similar to Type V except that the third row of dots from the bottom on the nose contains only four dots rather than six dots. Type Va occurs only on offset printings.

| Type VI | Type VII |

Type VI. Similar to Type V except that the line of shading in the numeral "2" at left is extremely pronounced. Type VI occurs only on offset printings.

Type VII. Contains three vertical rows of dots below the nose. Additional dots of shading have been added to the hair at the top of Washington's head. Type VII occurs only on offset printings.

Types of the 3¢ Washington of 1912–1920.

| Type I | Type II |

Type I. The top of the toga line is weak. The fifth shading line of the toga is partly cut away. The line between the lips is thin. Type I occurs on both flat plate and rotary press printings.

Type II. The top line of the toga is complete and heavy as are the shading lines that join it. Type II occurs on both flat plate and rotary press printings.

Type III   **Type IV**

Type III. Similar to Type II except that the fifth shading line from the left is missing. The letters "P" and "O" in the inscription "Postage" are separated. Type III occurs only on offset printings.

Type IV. Similar to Type III except that the vertical line in the center of the button is a single unbroken vertical line. The letters "P" and "O" in the inscription "Postage" are joined. Type IV occurs only on offset printings.

Types of the 2¢ Washington of 1922 (Scott Nos. 599 and 599A).

Type III   **Type IV**

Type I. Contains thin hair lines atop the head.

Type II. Contains heavy hair lines atop the head.

Watermarks.

USPS

USPS

Double Line Watermark

Single Line Watermark

GENERAL ISSUE

Pricing Note: Prices for unused stamps issued before 1890 are for examples without original gum. Examples with original gum command a premium, which can amount to as much as 50 percent or more. Beware regummed examples. Prices are for sound stamps. Those with faults or defects sell for much less.

1
(3)

2
(4)

Scott No.			Unused	Used
1847.				
❑ 1	5¢	Red Brown	3200.00	550.00
❑ 2	10¢	Black	—	725.00

1875. Reproductions of the 1847 Issue, Issued without Gum.

❑ 3	5¢	Red Brown (~1)	750.00	—
❑ 4	10¢	Black (~2)	875.00	—

NOTE: On originals of the 5¢, the white shirt frill falls well below the top of the numeral "5." On reproductions, the top white shirt frill is even with the top of numeral "5." On originals of the 10¢, the left vertical line of Washington's collar falls below the top of the letter "X." On reproductions, it falls above the top of the "X."

5
(5A, 6, 7, 8, 8A, 9, 18, 19, 20, 21, 22, 23, 24, 40)

1851–1856. Imperforate.

❑ 5	1¢	Blue (~5) (type I)		
❑ 5A	1¢	Blue (~5) (type Ib)	5000.00	3500.00
❑ 6	1¢	Blue (~5) (type Ia)	10000.00	5500.00

10	12	13	17
(11, 25, 26, 26a, 41)	(27, 28, 28A, 29, 30, 30A, 42)	(14, 15, 16, 31, 32, 33, 34, 35, 43)	(36, 36b, 44)

Scott No.			Unused	Used
❑ 7	1¢	Blue (~5) (type II)	665.00	225.00
❑ 8	1¢	Blue (~5) (type III)	3000.00	1750.00
❑ 8A	1¢	Blue (~5) (type IIIa)	2500.00	750.00
❑ 9	1¢	Blue (~5) (type IV)	450.00	150.00
❑ 10	3¢	Orange Brown (type I)	1500.00	100.00
❑ 11	3¢	Dull Red (~10) (type I)	120.00	20.00
❑ 12	5¢	Red Brown (type I)	1125.00	725.00
❑ 13	10¢	Green (type I)	1000.00	400.00
❑ 14	10¢	Green (~13) (type II)	1500.00	245.00
❑ 15	10¢	Green (~13) (type III)	1800.00	225.00
❑ 16	10¢	Green (~13) (type IV)	1500.00	900.00
❑ 17	12¢	Black	2200.00	375.00

1857–1861. Same Designs as the 1851–1856 Issue, Perforated 15.

❑ 18	1¢	Blue (~5) (type I)	1000.00	500.00
❑ 19	1¢	Blue (~5) (type Ia)	6000.00	450.00
❑ 20	1¢	Blue (~5) (type II)	525.00	300.00
❑ 21	1¢	Blue (~5) (type III)	1600.00	1200.00
❑ 22	1¢	Blue (~5) (type IIIa)	1000.00	500.00
❑ 23	1¢	Blue (~5) (type IV)	4000.00	625.00
❑ 24	1¢	Blue (~5) (type V)	115.00	65.00
❑ 25	3¢	Rose (~10) (type I)	1200.00	100.00
❑ 26	3¢	Dull Red (~10) (type II)	75.00	15.00
❑ 26a	3¢	Dull Red (~10) (type IIa)	185.00	125.00
❑ 27	5¢	Brick Red (~10) (type I)	10,000.00	1200.00

NOTE: Refer to the Type Identifier for information on types.

37	**38**	**39**
(45)	(46)	(47)

Scott No.			Unused	Used
☐ 28	5¢	Red Brown (~12) (type I)	2200.00	775.00
☐ 28A	5¢	Indian Red (~12) (type I)	2500.00	1600.00
☐ 29	5¢	Brown (~12) (type I)	1200.00	350.00
☐ 30	5¢	Orange Brown (~12) (type II)	1000.00	575.00
☐ 30A	5¢	Brown (~12) (type II)	725.00	300.00
☐ 31	10¢	Green (~13) (type I)	7200.00	835.00
☐ 32	10¢	Green (~13) (type II)	2000.00	300.00
☐ 33	10¢	Green (~13) (type III)	1800.00	225.00
☐ 34	10¢	Green (~13) (type IV)	1600.00	1000.00
☐ 35	10¢	Green (~13) (type IV)	200.00	115.00
☐ 36	12¢	Black (~17) (type I)	600.00	300.00
☐ 36b	12¢	Black (~17) (type II)	400.00	200.00
☐ 37	24¢	Gray Lilac	625.00	250.00
☐ 38	30¢	Orange	1000.00	325.00
☐ 39	90¢	Blue	1650.00	—

1875. Reprints of the 1857–1861 Issue, Perforated 12, Issued without Gum.

☐ 40	1¢	Bright Blue (~5)	525.00	—
☐ 41	3¢	Scarlet (~10)	3000.00	—
☐ 42	5¢	Orange Brown (~12)	1400.00	—
☐ 43	10¢	Blue Green (~13)	2500.00	—
☐ 44	12¢	Greenish Black (~17)	2500.00	—
☐ 45	24¢	Blackish Violet (~37)	2400.00	—
☐ 46	30¢	Yellow Orange (~38)	3200.00	—
☐ 47	90¢	Deep Blue (~39)	4500.00	—

NOTE: Refer to the Type Identifier for information on types.

63
(63b, 86,
92, 102)

64
(64b, 65, 66, 79, 83,
85, 85C, 88, 94, 104)

67
(75, 76,
95, 105)

68
(62B, 89, 96,
106)

69
(85E, 90,
97, 107)

70
(70b, 70c, 78,
99, 109)

71
(100, 110)

72
(101, 111)

Scott No.			Unused	Used
1861. Perforated 12.				
❑ 62B	10¢	Dark Green (~68)	3200.00	900.00
1861–1862.				
❑ 63	1¢	Blue	175.00	50.00
❑ 63B	1¢	Dark Blue	275.00	100.00
❑ 64	3¢	Pink	3800.00	700.00
❑ 64B	3¢	Rose Pink	400.00	140.00
❑ 65	3¢	Rose	75.00	14.00
❑ 66	3¢	Lake	—	—
❑ 67	5¢	Buff	835.00	625.00
❑ 68	10¢	Yellow Green	400.00	50.00
❑ 69	12¢	Black	700.00	100.00
❑ 70	24¢	Red Lilac	1000.00	235.00
❑ 70b	24¢	Steel Blue	3750.00	625.00
❑ 70c	24¢	Violet	5000.00	1000.00
❑ 71	30¢	Orange	800.00	150.00
❑ 72	90¢	Blue	1275.00	360.00

73
(84, 85B, 87, 93, 103)

77
(91, 98, 108)

Scott No.			Unused	Used
1861–1866. New Values or New Colors.				
❑ 73	2¢	Black	220.00	85.00
❑ 75	5¢	Red Brown (~67)	2000.00	385.00
❑ 76	5¢	Brown (~67)	800.00	140.00
❑ 77	15¢	Black	1000.00	150.00
❑ 78	24¢	Lilac (~70)	625.00	140.00

1867. Same Designs as the 1861–1866 Issue, Grill with Points Up.

A Grill. Grill Covers Entire Stamp.

❑ 79	3¢	Rose (~64)	2500.00	1400.00

C Grill. Grill Measures About 13 x 16 mm.

❑ 83	3¢	Rose (~64)	2200.00	825.00

1867. Same Designs as the 1861–66 Issue, Grill with Points Down.

D Grill. Grill Measures About 12 x 14 mm.

❑ 84	2¢	Black (~73)	8250.00	2800.00
❑ 85	3¢	Rose (~64)	2500.00	875.00

Z Grill. Grill Measures About 11 x 14 mm.

❑ 85B	2¢	Black (~73)	3500.00	1250.00
❑ 85C	3¢	Rose (~64)	4750.00	2450.00
❑ 85E	12¢	Black (~69)	5000.00	1250.00

E Grill. Grill Measures About 11 x 13 mm.

❑ 86	1¢	Blue (~63)	1400.00	425.00
❑ 87	2¢	Black (~73)	625.00	150.00
❑ 88	3¢	Rose (~64)	350.00	40.00
❑ 89	10¢	Green (~68)	2000.00	265.00
❑ 90	12¢	Black (~69)	1850.00	265.00
❑ 91	15¢	Black (~77)	3800.00	475.00

Scott No.			Unused	Used

F Grill. Grill Measures About 9 x 13 mm.

			Unused	Used
❏ 92	1¢	Blue (~63)	500.00	200.00
❏ 93	2¢	Black (~73)	220.00	50.00
❏ 94	3¢	Red (~64)	175.00	25.00
❏ 95	5¢	Brown (~67)	1500.00	600.00
❏ 96	10¢	Yellow Green (~68)	1500.00	220.00
❏ 97	12¢	Black (~69)	1500.00	225.00
❏ 98	15¢	Black (~77)	1500.00	265.00
❏ 99	24¢	Gray Lilac (~70)	1850.00	800.00
❏ 100	30¢	Orange (~71)	2500.00	625.00
❏ 101	90¢	Blue (~72)	4500.00	1500.00

1875. Re-issue of 1861–1866 Issues, without Grill, Perforated 12, Hard White Paper.

			Unused	Used
❏ 102	1¢	Blue (~63)	375.00	225.00
❏ 103	2¢	Black (~73)	1500.00	1000.00
❏ 104	3¢	Brown Red (~64)	1800.00	1400.00
❏ 105	5¢	Light Brown (67)	1500.00	1000.00
❏ 106	10¢	Green (~68)	2200.00	1400.00
❏ 107	12¢	Black (~69)	2500.00	1500.00
❏ 108	15¢	Black (~77)	2500.00	1600.00
❏ 109	24¢	Deep Violet (~70)	2800.00	2200.00
❏ 110	30¢	Brownish Orange (~71)	2400.00	325.00
❏ 111	90¢	Blue (~72)	3800.00	2650.00

112	**113**	**114**	**115**
(123, 133)	(124)	(125)	(126)

1869. Pictorial Issue, with Grill.

❏ 112	1¢	Buff	340.00	150.00
❏ 113	2¢	Brown	270.00	60.00
❏ 114	3¢	Ultramarine	200.00	30.00
❏ 115	6¢	Ultramarine	1500.00	200.00

116
(127)

117
(128)

118
(119, 129)

120
(130)

121
(131)

122
(132)

Scott No.			Unused	Used
❏ 116	10¢	Yellow	950.00	185.00
❏ 117	12¢	Green	950.00	185.00
❏ 118	15¢	Brown & Blue (type I)	3200.00	500.00
❏ 119	15¢	Brown & Blue (~118) (type II)	1250.00	250.00
❏ 120	24¢	Green & Violet	425.00	475.00
❏ 121	30¢	Blue & Carmine	2500.00	450.00
❏ 122	90¢	Carmine & Black	3750.00	220.00

NOTE: Type II (No. 119) contains a small diamond-shaped ornament at center just above the central picture. Type I (No. 118) does not contain the diamond-shaped ornament.

1875. Re-issue of the 1869 Pictorial Issue, Hard White Paper, without Grill.

❏ 123	1¢	Buff (~112)	335.00	275.00
❏ 124	2¢	Brown (~113)	675.00	425.00
❏ 125	3¢	Blue (~114)	2500.00	1500.00
❏ 126	6¢	Blue (~115)	1200.00	525.00
❏ 127	10¢	Yellow (~116)	1500.00	825.00
❏ 128	12¢	Green (~117)	1600.00	1100.00
❏ 129	15¢	Brown & Blue (~118) (type III)	1400.00	725.00
❏ 130	24¢	Green & Violet (~120)	1400.00	825.00
❏ 131	30¢	Blue & Carmine (~121)	1750.00	875.00
❏ 132	90¢	Carmine & Black (~122)	2800.00	1600.00

NOTE: Type III (No. 129) is similar to Type I (No. 118) above except that it does not contain the fringe of brown shading lines around the central picture as does Type I.

134
(145, 156,
182, 206)

135
(146, 157,
178, 183)

136
(147, 158, 184,
207, 214)

137
(148, 159, 186,
208, 208a)

138
(149, 160,
196)

139
(151, 161, 187, 188,
188b, 209, 209b)

140
(151, 162)

141
(152, 163,
189)

142
(153, 164)

143
(154, 165, 190, 217)

144
(155, 166, 191, 218)

Scott No.			Unused	Used
1880. 1869 Pictorial Issue, Soft Porous Paper.				
❏ 133	1¢	Buff (~112)	240.00	200.00
1870–1871. Printed by the National Bank Note Co., with Grill.				
❏ 134	1¢	Ultramarine	1600.00	175.00
❏ 135	2¢	Red Brown	1200.00	125.00
❏ 136	3¢	Green	575.00	40.00
❏ 137	6¢	Carmine	3500.00	425.00
❏ 138	7¢	Vermilion	2600.00	400.00
❏ 139	10¢	Brown	3400.00	450.00
❏ 140	12¢	Light Violet	—	2500.00
❏ 141	15¢	Orange	4750.00	1500.00
❏ 142	24¢	Purple	—	4600.00

Scott No.			Unused	Used
❏ 143	30¢	Black	15,000.00	2000.00
❏ 144	90¢	Carmine	12,500.00	1500.00

1870–1871. Same Designs, without Grill.

❏ 145	1¢	Ultramarine (~134)	425.00	18.00
❏ 146	2¢	Red Brown (~135)	300.00	15.00
❏ 147	3¢	Green (~136)	250.00	8.00
❏ 148	6¢	Carmine (~137)	750.00	22.00
❏ 149	7¢	Vermilion (~138)	800.00	80.00
❏ 150	10¢	Brown (~139)	800.00	25.00
❏ 151	12¢	Dull Violet (~140)	1650.00	165.00
❏ 152	15¢	Bright Orange (~141)	1650.00	165.00
❏ 153	24¢	Purple (~142)	1250.00	165.00
❏ 154	30¢	Black (~143)	4200.00	185.00
❏ 155	90¢	Carmine (~144)	3650.00	250.00

1873. Same Designs as the 1870–1871 Issue, Printed by the Continental Bank Note Co., with Secret Marks, Thin Hard Grayish-White Paper.

❏ 156	1¢	Ultramarine (~134)	240.00	18.00
❏ 157	2¢	Brown (~135)	375.00	18.00
❏ 158	3¢	Green (~136)	150.00	7.00
❏ 159	6¢	Dull Pink (~137)	400.00	25.00
❏ 160	7¢	Orange Vermilion (~138)	1200.00	85.00
❏ 161	10¢	Brown (~139)	700.00	25.00
❏ 162	12¢	Black Violet (~140)	1600.00	125.00
❏ 163	15¢	Yellow Orange (141)	1500.00	125.00
❏ 164	24¢	Purple (~142)	—	125.00
❏ 165	30¢	Gray Black (~143)	2000.00	125.00
❏ 166	90¢	Rose Carmine (~144)	2400.00	225.00

NOTE: Refer to the Type Identifier for information on secret marks.

179
(185)

1875.

❏ 178	2¢	Vermilion (~135)	350.00	18.00
❏ 179	5¢	Blue, Zachary Taylor	2850.00	26.00

Scott No.			Unused	Used

1879. Same Designs as the 1870–1875 Issue, Printed by the American Bank Note Co., Soft Porous Yellowish-White Paper.

			Unused	Used
❏ 182	1¢	Dark Ultramarine (~134)	250.00	6.00
❏ 183	2¢	Vermilion (~135)	125.00	6.00
❏ 184	3¢	Green (~136)	120.00	4.00
❏ 185	5¢	Blue (~179)	425.00	14.00
❏ 186	6¢	Pink (~137)	800.00	20.00
❏ 187	10¢	Brown (~139), without secret mark	2500.00	24.00
❏ 188	10¢	Brown (~139), with secret mark	225.00	24.00
❏ 188b	10¢	Black Brown (~139)	850.00	100.00
❏ 189	15¢	Red Orange (~141)	375.00	25.00
❏ 190	30¢	Full Black (~143)	1000.00	75.00
❏ 191	90¢	Carmine (~144)	1650.00	200.00

NOTE: Refer to the Type Identifier for information on secret marks.

205
(216)

1882.

❏ 205	5¢	Yellow Brown, James Garfield	325.00	18.00

1881–1882. Designs of the 1873 Issue, Re-engraved.

❏ 206	1¢	Gray Blue (~134)	175.00	5.00
❏ 207	3¢	Blue Green (~136)	175.00	5.00
❏ 208	6¢	Rose (~137)	175.00	70.00
❏ 208a	6¢	Brown Red (~137)	175.00	75.00
❏ 209	10¢	Brown (~139)	300.00	18.00
❏ 209b	10¢	Black Brown (~139)	300.00	55.00

NOTE: Re-engraved types can be distinguished as follows: The 1¢ is a milky gray blue and lines of shading have been added to the ornament balls in the upper corners. The 3¢ contains a short horizontal line engraved below the "ts" of "cents." The 6¢ contains three vertical lines at the left of the design instead of four. The 10¢ contains four vertical lines between the outer border and portrait oval instead of five.

210
(213)

211
(215)

212

Scott No.			Unused	Used
1883.				
❑ 210	2¢	Red Brown	65.00	8.00
❑ 211	4¢	Blue Green	145.00	15.00
1887.				
❑ 212	1¢	Ultramarine	120.00	5.00
❑ 213	2¢	Green (~210)	55.00	5.00
❑ 214	3¢	Vermilion (~136)	85.00	50.00
1888.				
❑ 215	4¢	Carmine (~211)	240.00	25.00
❑ 216	5¢	Indigo (~205)	240.00	25.00
❑ 217	30¢	Orange Brown (~143)	350.00	100.00
❑ 218	90¢	Purple (~144)	725.00	235.00

PRICING NOTE: From this point forward, prices for unused stamps are for examples with original gum.

219

219D
(220, 220a, 220c)

1890–1893. (NH Add 100%)				
❑ 219	1¢	Dull Blue	40.00	5.00
❑ 219D	2¢	Lake	335.00	5.00
❑ 220	2¢	Carmine (~219D)	40.00	5.00
❑ 220a	2¢	Carmine (Cap on left 2)	150.00	10.00
❑ 220c	2¢	Carmine (Cap both 2s)	450.00	20.00

221 222 223 224 225

226 227 228 229

Scott No.			Unused	Used
❏ 221	3¢	Purple	140.00	8.00
❏ 222	4¢	Dark Brown	120.00	7.00
❏ 223	5¢	Chocolate	85.00	7.00
❏ 224	6¢	Brown Red	100.00	22.00
❏ 225	8¢	Lilac	80.00	12.00
❏ 226	10¢	Green	235.00	7.00
❏ 227	15¢	Indigo	235.00	18.00
❏ 228	30¢	Black	375.00	35.00
❏ 229	90¢	Orange	500.00	80.00

230 231 232

1893. Columbian Exposition Issue. (NH Add 100–200%)

❏ 230	1¢	Blue	26.00	1.50
❏ 231	2¢	Violet	28.00	1.00
❏ 231c	2¢	"Broken Hat" variety (~231)	85.00	1.50
❏ 232	3¢	Green	85.00	15.00

NOTE: A notch appears at the top of Columbus's hat on the broken hat variety.

Scott No.			Unused	Used
❑ 233	4¢	Ultramarine	80.00	12.00
❑ 234	5¢	Chocolate	135.00	12.00
❑ 235	6¢	Purple	135.00	20.00
❑ 236	8¢	Magenta	100.00	15.00
❑ 237	10¢	Black Brown	140.00	10.00
❑ 238	15¢	Dark Green	250.00	75.00
❑ 239	30¢	Orange Brown	340.00	80.00
❑ 240	50¢	Slate Blue	625.00	200.00
❑ 241	$1	Salmon	1250.00	500.00
❑ 242	$2	Brown Red	1250.00	525.00

NOTE: Refer to the Type Identifier for information on types.

243

244

245

Scott No.			Unused	Used
❑ 243	$3	Yellow Green	3000.00	150.00
❑ 244	$4	Crimson Lake	3200.00	800.00
❑ 245	$5	Black	3000.00	220.00

246
(247, 264, 279)

248
(249, 250, 251, 252, 265,
266, 267, 279B, 279C, 279D)

253
(268)

254
(269, 280)

255
(270, 281)

1894. Similar to the Series of 1890–1893 but with Triangles added in Upper Corners, Unwatermarked. (NH Add 100%)

❑ 246	1¢	Ultramarine	40.00	7.00
❑ 247	1¢	Blue (~246)	75.00	7.00
❑ 248	2¢	Pink (type I)	50.00	7.00
❑ 249	2¢	Carmine Lake (~248) (type I)	145.00	7.00
❑ 250	2¢	Carmine (~248) (type I)	40.00	4.00
❑ 251	2¢	Carmine (~248) (type II)	265.00	7.00
❑ 252	2¢	Carmine (~248) (type III)	140.00	10.00
❑ 253	3¢	Purple	125.00	10.00
❑ 254	4¢	Dark Brown	150.00	8.00
❑ 255	5¢	Chocolate	125.00	8.00

NOTE: Refer to the Type Identifier for information on types.

256 (271, 282, 282a)	**257** (272)	**258** (273, 282C, 283)	**259** (274, 284)

260 (275)	**261** (261A, 276, 276A)	**262** (277)	**263** (278)

Scott No.			Unused	Used
❑ 256	6¢	Dull Brown	175.00	25.00
❑ 257	8¢	Violet Brown	125.00	18.00
❑ 258	10¢	Dark Green	240.00	18.00
❑ 259	15¢	Dark Blue	240.00	60.00
❑ 260	50¢	Orange	600.00	80.00
❑ 261	$1	Black (type I)	825.00	260.00
❑ 261A	$1	Black (~261) (type II)	2000.00	500.00
❑ 262	$2	Blue	2500.00	775.00
❑ 263	$5	Dark Green	4500.00	1750.00

1895. Same Designs as the 1894 Issue, Double Line Watermark.
(NH Add 100%)

❑ 264	1¢	Blue (~246)	12.00	5.00
❑ 265	2¢	Carmine (~248) (type I)	35.00	5.00
❑ 266	2¢	Carmine (~248) (type II)	25.00	6.00
❑ 267	2¢	Carmine (~248) (type III)	12.00	5.00
❑ 268	3¢	Purple (~253)	35.00	5.00
❑ 269	4¢	Dark Brown (~254)	50.00	5.00
❑ 270	5¢	Chocolate (~255)	35.00	5.00
❑ 271	6¢	Dull Brown (~256)	125.00	6.00
❑ 272	8¢	Violet Brown (~257)	75.00	6.00
❑ 273	10¢	Dark Green (~258)	120.00	6.00
❑ 274	15¢	Dark Blue (~259)	200.00	18.00

NOTE: Refer to the Type Identifier for information on types.

Scott No.			Unused	Used
❑ 275	50¢	Dull Orange (~260)	340.00	35.00
❑ 276	$1	Black (~261) (type I)	525.00	80.00
❑ 276A	$1	Black (~261) (type II)	1250.00	160.00
❑ 277	$2	Blue (~262)	1200.00	240.00
❑ 278	$5	Dark Green (~263)	1800.00	375.00

1898. Same Designs as the 1894 Issue but with Changed Colors, Double Line Watermark. (NH Add 100%)

❑ 279	1¢	Deep Green (~246)	20.00	5.00
❑ 279B	2¢	Red (~248)	20.00	5.00
❑ 279C	2¢	Rose Carmine (~248)	350.00	75.00
❑ 279D	2¢	Orange Red (~248)	20.00	2.00
❑ 280	4¢	Rose Brown (~254)	40.00	5.00
❑ 281	5¢	Dark Blue (~255)	55.00	5.00
❑ 282	6¢	Lake (~256)	55.00	7.00
❑ 282a	6¢	Purplish Lake (~256)	55.00	7.00
❑ 282C	10¢	Brown (~258) (type I)	185.00	7.00
❑ 283	10¢	Orange Brown (~258) (type II)	140.00	7.00
❑ 284	15¢	Olive Green (~259)	140.00	9.00

285

286

287

288

289

1898. Trans-Mississippi Exposition Issue. (NH Add 100%)

❑ 285	1¢	Yellow Green	40.00	7.00
❑ 286	2¢	Copper Red	40.00	7.00
❑ 287	4¢	Orange	160.00	28.00
❑ 288	5¢	Dull Blue	160.00	28.00
❑ 289	8¢	Violet Brown	175.00	35.00

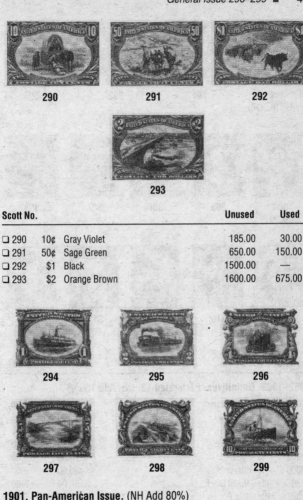

290 **291** **292**

293

Scott No.			Unused	Used
❏ 290	10¢	Gray Violet	185.00	30.00
❏ 291	50¢	Sage Green	650.00	150.00
❏ 292	$1	Black	1500.00	—
❏ 293	$2	Orange Brown	1600.00	675.00

294 **295** **296**

297 **298** **299**

1901. Pan-American Issue. (NH Add 80%)

❏ 294	1¢	Green & Black	60.00	6.00
❏ 295	2¢	Carmine & Black	25.00	6.00
❏ 296	4¢	Chocolate & Black	80.00	12.00
❏ 297	5¢	Ultramarine & Black	100.00	18.00
❏ 298	8¢	Brown Violet Black	120.00	55.00
❏ 299	10¢	Yellow Brown Black	175.00	28.00

300
(314, 316, 318)

301

302

303

304
(315, 317)

305

306

307

308

309

310

311

312
(479)

313
(480)

Scott No.			Unused	Used
1902–1903. Definitives, Perforated 12. (NH Add 100%)				
❏ 300	1¢	Blue Green	14.00	5.00
❏ 301	2¢	Carmine	25.00	5.00
❏ 302	3¢	Violet	70.00	6.00
❏ 303	4¢	Brown	80.00	5.00
❏ 304	5¢	Blue	80.00	5.00
❏ 305	6¢	Claret	80.00	6.00
❏ 306	8¢	Violet Black	50.00	5.00
❏ 307	10¢	Red Brown	75.00	5.00
❏ 308	13¢	Purple Black	75.00	10.00
❏ 309	15¢	Olive Green	175.00	5.00
❏ 310	50¢	Orange	500.00	25.00
❏ 311	$1	Black	850.00	80.00
❏ 312	$2	Dark Blue	1250.00	160.00
❏ 313	$5	Dark Green	2500.00	425.00

Scott No.			Unused	Used

1906–1908. Designs of the 1902–1903 Issue, Imperforate.
(NH Add 80%)

			Unused	Used
❑ 314	1¢	Blue Green (~300)	40.00	25.00
❑ 315	5¢	Blue (~304)	3500.00	550.00

1908. Coil Stamps, Perforated 12 Horizontally.

❑ 316	1¢	Blue Green (~300)	5000.00	—
❑ 317	5¢	Blue (~304)	4500.00	—

1908. Coil Stamp, Perforated 12 Vertically.

❑ 318	1¢	Blue Green (~300)	5000.00	3650.00

319
(319a, 320, 320a)

1903. Perforated 12. (NH Add 85%)

❑ 319	2¢	Carmine	8.00	5.00
❑ 319a	2¢	Lake (~319)	—	—

1906. Imperforate. (NH Add 85%)

❑ 320	2¢	Carmine (~319)	30.00	28.00
❑ 320a	2¢	Lake (~319)	65.00	35.00

323   **324**   **325**

1904. Louisiana Purchase Issue. (NH Add 90%)

❑ 323	1¢	Green	45.00	8.00
❑ 324	2¢	Carmine	42.00	7.00
❑ 325	3¢	Violet	100.00	30.00

326   **327**

Scott No.			Unused	Used
❏ 326	5¢	Dark Blue	140.00	32.00
❏ 327	10¢	Red Brown	200.00	35.00

328   **329**   **330**

1907. Jamestown Exposition Issue. (NH Add 90%)

❏ 328	1¢	Green	40.00	8.00
❏ 329	2¢	Carmine	40.00	8.00
❏ 330	5¢	Blue	120.00	30.00

331	**332**	**333**	**334**
(343, 348, 352, 357, 374, 383, 385, 387, 390, 392)	(344, 349, 353, 358, 375, 384, 386, 388, 391, 393, 519)	(345, 359, 376, 394, 426, 445, 456, 464, 483, 484, 489, 493, 494, 501, 502, 529, 530, 535, 541)	(346, 350, 354, 360, 377, 395, 427, 446, 457, 465, 495, 503)

1908–1909. Washington-Franklin Series, Perforated 12, Double Line Watermark. (NH Add 90%)

❏ 331	1¢	Green	15.00	5.00
❏ 332	2¢	Carmine	10.00	5.00
❏ 333	3¢	Violet	35.00	5.00
❏ 334	4¢	Orange Brown	40.00	5.00

335
(347, 355, 351, 361, 378, 396, 428, 447, 458, 466, 467, 496, 504, 505)

336
(362, 379, 429, 468, 506)

337
(363, 380)

338
(356, 364, 381)

339
(365)

340
(366, 382)

341

342

Scott No.			Line Pair	Unused	Used
❑ 335	5¢	Blue		50.00	7.00
❑ 336	6¢	Red Orange		55.00	7.00
❑ 337	8¢	Olive Green		50.00	7.00
❑ 338	10¢	Yellow		80.00	7.00
❑ 339	13¢	Blue Green		50.00	14.00
❑ 340	15¢	Pale Ultramarine		80.00	10.00
❑ 341	50¢	Violet		275.00	25.00
❑ 342	$1	Violet Black		425.00	80.00

1908–1909. Imperforate, Double Line Watermark. (NH Add 90%)

❑ 343	1¢	Green (~331)		8.00	7.00
❑ 344	2¢	Carmine (~332)		18.00	7.00
❑ 345	3¢	Deep Violet (~333)		20.00	25.00
❑ 346	4¢	Orange Brown (~334)		35.00	25.00
❑ 347	5¢	Blue (~335)		50.00	40.00

1908–1910. Coil Stamps, Perforated 12 Horizontally. (NH Add 90%)

❑ 348	1¢	Green (~331)	235.00	30.00	25.00
❑ 349	2¢	Carmine (~332)	385.00	125.00	25.00
❑ 350	4¢	Orange Brown (~334)	1200.00	200.00	120.00
❑ 351	5¢	Blue (~335)	1200.00	200.00	140.00

Scott No.			Line Pair	Unused	Used

1909. Coil Stamps, Perforated 12 Vertically. (NH Add 90%)

			Line Pair	Unused	Used
❏ 352	1¢	Green (~331)	675.00	80.00	45.00
❏ 353	2¢	Carmine (~332)	675.00	115.00	18.00
❏ 354	4¢	Orange Brown (~334)	825.00	225.00	75.00
❏ 355	5¢	Blue (~335)	850.00	215.00	80.00
❏ 356	10¢	Yellow (~338)	—	2500.00	1000.00

1909. Washington-Franklin Series, Printed on Bluish Gray Paper. (NH Add 90%)

			Unused	Used
❏ 357	1¢	Green (~331)	175.00	140.00
❏ 358	2¢	Carmine (~332)	250.00	140.00
❏ 359	3¢	Violet (~333)	3200.00	1800.00
❏ 360	4¢	Orange Brown (~334)	20000.00	—
❏ 361	5¢	Blue (~335)	8000.00	3500.00
❏ 362	6¢	Orange (~336)	1600.00	3500.00
❏ 363	8¢	Olive Green (~337)	20000.00	—
❏ 364	10¢	Yellow (~338)	4000.00	2400.00
❏ 365	13¢	Blue Green (~339)	4200.00	2600.00
❏ 366	15¢	Pale Ultramarine (~340)	8000.00	1500.00

367
(368, 369)

1909. Lincoln Memorial Issue. (NH Add 85%)

			Unused	Used
❏ 367	2¢	Carmine, perforated 12	15.00	6.00
❏ 368	2¢	Carmine (~367), imperforate	32.00	25.00
❏ 369	2¢	Carmine (~367), perforated 12, on bluish gray paper	400.00	240.00

370
(371)

372
(373)

Scott No.			Line Pair	Unused	Used
1909. Alaska–Yukon Issue. (NH Add 80%)					
❏ 370	2¢	Carmine, perforated 12		15.00	6.00
❏ 371	2¢	Carmine (~370), imperforate		35.00	20.00
1909. Hudson–Fulton Issue. (NH Add 80%)					
❏ 372	2¢	Carmine, perforated 12		18.00	6.00
❏ 373	2¢	Carmine (~372), imperforate		40.00	20.00

1910–1911. Washington-Franklin Series, Perforated 12, Single Line Watermark. (NH Add 90%)

				Unused	Used
❏ 374	1¢	Green (~331)		16.00	5.00
❏ 375	2¢	Carmine (~332)		16.00	5.00
❏ 376	3¢	Deep Violet (~333)		25.00	5.00
❏ 377	4¢	Brown (~334)		45.00	5.00
❏ 378	5¢	Blue (~335)		38.00	5.00
❏ 379	6¢	Red Orange (~336)		50.00	5.00
❏ 380	8¢	Olive Green (~337)		150.00	14.00
❏ 381	10¢	Yellow (~338)		150.00	8.00
❏ 382	15¢	Ultramarine (~340)		275.00	16.00

1910. Washington-Franklin Series, Imperforate, Single Line Watermark. (NH Add 80%)

				Unused	Used
❏ 383	1¢	Green (~331)		9.00	7.00
❏ 384	2¢	Carmine (~332)		9.00	7.00

1910. Coil Stamps, Perforated 12 Horizontally, Single Line Watermark. (NH Add 90%)

			Line Pair	Unused	Used
❏ 385	1¢	Green (~331)	500.00	50.00	18.00
❏ 386	2¢	Carmine (~332)	800.00	80.00	24.00

Scott No.			Line Pair	Unused	Used

1910–1911. Coil Stamps, Perforated 12 Vertically, Single Line Watermark. (NH Add 90%)

❑ 387	1¢	Green (~331)	1200.00	240.00	45.00
❑ 388	2¢	Carmine (~332)	4000.00	875.00	40.00

1910. Coil Stamps, Perforated 8½ Horizontally, Single Line Watermark. (NH Add 90%)

❑ 390	1¢	Green (~331)	42.00	14.00	7.00
❑ 391	2¢	Carmine (~332)	240.00	40.00	15.00

1910–1913. Coil Stamps, Perforated 8½ Vertically, Single Line Watermark. (NH Add 90%)

❑ 392	1¢	Green (~331)	175.00	35.00	25.00
❑ 393	2¢	Carmine (~332)	350.00	50.00	15.00
❑ 394	3¢	Violet (~333)	350.00	65.00	55.00
❑ 395	4¢	Brown (~334)	450.00	80.00	55.00
❑ 396	5¢	Blue (~335)	450.00	80.00	65.00

397
(401)

398
(402)

399
(403)

400
(400A, 404)

1913. Panama–Pacific Issue, Perforated 12. (NH Add 90%)

❑ 397	1¢	Green	30.00	6.00
❑ 398	2¢	Carmine	30.00	6.00
❑ 399	5¢	Blue	85.00	14.00
❑ 400	10¢	Orange Yellow	150.00	25.00
❑ 400A	10¢	Orange	285.00	25.00

Scott No.			Line Pair	Unused	Used

1914–1915. Panama-Pacific Issue, Perforated 10. (NH Add 90%)

❑ 401	1¢	Green (~397)		30.00	8.00
❑ 402	2¢	Carmine (~398)		100.00	7.00
❑ 403	5¢	Blue (~399)		200.00	20.00
❑ 404	10¢	Orange (~400)		140.00	75.00

405
(408, 410, 412, 424, 441, 443, 448, 452, 462, 481, 486, 490, 498, 525, 531, 536, 538, 542, 543, 544, 545)

406
(409, 411, 413, 425, 442, 444, 449, 450, 453, 454, 455, 459, 461, 463, 482, 487, 488, 491, 492, 499, 500, 526, 527, 528, 528A, 528B, 532, 533, 534, 534A, 534B, 539, 540, 546)

407
(430, 469, 507)

1912–1914. Washington-Franklin Series, Perforated 12, Single Line Watermark. (NH Add 90%)

❑ 405	1¢	Green		12.00	4.50
❑ 406	2¢	Carmine		12.00	4.50
❑ 407	7¢	Black		85.00	12.00

1912. Washington-Franklin Series, Imperforate, Single Line Watermark. (NH Add 90%)

❑ 408	1¢	Green (~405)		6.00	4.50
❑ 409	2¢	Carmine (~406)		6.00	4.50

1912. Coil Stamps, Perforated 8½ Horizontally, Single Line Watermark. (NH Add 90%)

❑ 410	1¢	Green (~405)	60.00	12.50	6.50
❑ 411	2¢	Carmine (~406)	75.00	12.50	6.50

1912. Coil Stamps, Perforated 8½ Vertically, Single Line Watermark. (NH Add 90%)

❑ 412	1¢	Green (~405)	175.00	38.00	10.00
❑ 413	2¢	Carmine (~406)	285.00	50.00	6.00

414
(431, 470, 508)

415
(432, 471, 509)

416
(433, 472, 497, 510)

417
(435, 435a, 474, 512)

418
(437, 475, 514)

419
(438, 476, 515)

420
(439, 476A, 516)

421
(422, 440, 477, 517)

423
(460, 478, 518, 518b)

Scott No.			Unused	Used

1912–1914. Washington-Franklin Series, Perforated 12, Single Line Watermark. (NH Add 90%)

			Unused	Used
❏ 414	8¢	Olive Green	75.00	6.00
❏ 415	9¢	Salmon Red	75.00	14.00
❏ 416	10¢	Orange Yellow	65.00	4.50
❏ 417	12¢	Claret Brown	65.00	5.00
❏ 418	15¢	Gray	100.00	4.50
❏ 419	20¢	Ultramarine	230.00	16.00
❏ 420	30¢	Orange Red	165.00	27.50
❏ 421	50¢	Violet	425.00	27.50

1912. Franklin Types, Perforated 12, Double Line Watermark.
(NH Add 90%)

			Unused	Used
❏ 422	50¢	Violet (~421)	325.00	25.00
❏ 423	$1	Violet Black	535.00	80.00

434
(473, 511)

Scott No.			Line Pair	Unused	Used

1914–1915. Washington-Franklin Series, Perforated 10, Single Line Watermark. (NH Add 90%)

			Line Pair	Unused	Used
❑ 424	1¢	Green (~405)		8.00	4.25
❑ 425	2¢	Carmine (~406)		8.00	4.25
❑ 426	3¢	Deep Violet (~333)		18.00	4.25
❑ 427	4¢	Brown (~334)		55.00	4.25
❑ 428	5¢	Blue (~335)		55.00	4.25
❑ 429	6¢	Orange (~336)		65.00	4.25
❑ 430	7¢	Black (~407)		100.00	6.00
❑ 431	8¢	Olive Green (~414)		45.00	4.25
❑ 432	9¢	Salmon Red (~415)		85.00	12.00
❑ 433	10¢	Orange Yellow (~416)		85.00	4.25
❑ 434	11¢	Dark Green		40.00	8.00
❑ 435	12¢	Claret Brown (~417)		40.00	7.50
❑ 435a	12¢	Copper Red (~417)		40.00	7.50
❑ 437	15¢	Gray (~418)		165.00	10.00
❑ 438	20¢	Ultramarine (~419)		250.00	8.00
❑ 439	30¢	Orange Red (~420)		345.00	18.00
❑ 440	50¢	Violet (~421)		700.00	20.00

1914. Coil Stamps, Perforated 10 Horizontally, Single Line Watermark. (NH Add 90%)

			Line Pair	Unused	Used
❑ 441	1¢	Green (~405)	20.00	12.50	7.00
❑ 442	2¢	Carmine (~406)	85.00	12.50	8.00

1914. Coil Stamps, Perforated 10 Vertically, Single Line Watermark. (NH Add 90%)

			Line Pair	Unused	Used
❑ 443	1¢	Green (~405)	225.00	30.00	10.00
❑ 444	2¢	Carmine (~406)	325.00	65.00	6.00
❑ 445	3¢	Violet (~333)	800.00	325.00	125.00
❑ 446	4¢	Brown (~334)	800.00	150.00	55.00
❑ 447	5¢	Blue (~335)	300.00	100.00	38.00

Scott No.			Line Pair	Unused	Used

1914–1916. Rotary Press Coil Stamps, Perforated 10 Horizontally, Single Line Watermark. (NH Add 90%)

❑ 448	1¢	Green (~405)		20.00	12.00
❑ 449	2¢	Red (~406) (type I)		2500.00	450.00
❑ 450	2¢	Carmine (~406) (type III)		175.00	12.00

1914–1916. Rotary Press Coils, Perforated 10 Vertically, Single Line Watermark. (NH Add 90%)

❑ 452	1¢	Green (~405)	100.00	25.00	7.00
❑ 453	2¢	Red (~406) (type I)	800.00	150.00	7.00
❑ 454	2¢	Carmine (~406) (type II)	500.00	120.00	10.00
❑ 455	2¢	Carmine (~406) (type III)	100.00	18.00	6.00
❑ 456	3¢	Violet (~333)	1200.00	300.00	100.00
❑ 457	4¢	Brown (~334)	225.00	35.00	40.00
❑ 458	5¢	Blue (~335)	225.00	55.00	40.00

1914. Imperforate, Single Line Watermark. (NH Add 60%)

❑ 459	2¢	Carmine (~406)		475.00	1000.00

1915. Franklin Type, Perforated 10, Double Line Watermark. (NH Add 90%)

❑ 460	$1	Violet Black (~423)		1200.00	165.00

1915. Washington Type, Flat Plate Printing, Perforated 11, Single Line Watermark, Design Measures 18½–19 x 22 mm. (NH Add 90%)

❑ 461	2¢	Pale Carmine Red (~406)		325.00	250.00

1916–1917. Washington-Franklin Series, Perforated 10, Unwatermarked. (NH Add 90%)

❑ 462	1¢	Green (~405)		17.50	5.00
❑ 463	2¢	Carmine (~406)		17.50	5.00
❑ 464	3¢	Violet (~333)		80.00	13.00
❑ 465	4¢	Orange Brown (~334)		65.00	5.00
❑ 466	5¢	Blue (~335)		100.00	5.00
❑ 467	5¢	Carmine (error) (~335)		800.00	75.00
❑ 468	6¢	Red Orange (~336)		140.00	12.00
❑ 469	7¢	Black (~407)		150.00	15.00
❑ 470	8¢	Olive Green (~414)		80.00	9.00

NOTE: Refer to the Type Identifier for information on types.

Scott No.			Line Pair	Unused	Used
❏ 471	9¢	Salmon Red (~415)		80.00	18.00
❏ 472	10¢	Orange Yellow (~416)		150.00	6.00
❏ 473	11¢	Dark Green (~434)		55.00	18.00
❏ 474	12¢	Claret Brown (~417)		65.00	8.00
❏ 475	15¢	Gray (~418)		350.00	18.00
❏ 476	20¢	Ultramarine (~419)		350.00	18.00
❏ 476A	30¢	Orange Red (~420)		3500.00	—
❏ 477	50¢	Light Violet (~421)		1200.00	75.00
❏ 478	$1	Violet Black (~423)		1000.00	25.00

1916–1917. Designs of 1902–1903, Perforated 10, Unwatermarked. (NH Add 80%)

❏ 479	$2	Dark Blue (~312)		450.00	55.00
❏ 480	$5	Light Green (~313)		375.00	42.00

1916–1917. Washington-Franklin Series, Imperforate, Unwatermarked. (NH Add 90%)

❏ 481	1¢	Green (~405)		7.00	5.00
❏ 482	2¢	Carmine (~406)		7.00	5.00
❏ 483	3¢	Violet (~333) (type I)		20.00	10.00
❏ 484	3¢	Violet (~333) (type II)		16.00	6.00

1916–1922. Rotary Press Coil Stamps, Perforated 10 Horizontally, Unwatermarked. (NH Add 85%)

❏ 486	1¢	Green (~405)	12.00	7.00	5.00
❏ 487	2¢	Carmine (~406) (type II)	125.00	20.00	6.00
❏ 488	2¢	Carmine (~406) (type III)	35.00	6.00	5.00
❏ 489	3¢	Violet (~333)	50.00	7.00	5.00

1916–1922. Rotary Press Coil Stamps, Perforated 10 Vertically, Unwatermarked. (NH Add 90%)

❏ 490	1¢	Green (~405)	15.00	4.00	6.00
❏ 491	2¢	Carmine (~406) (type II)	1200.00	2500.00	80.00
❏ 492	2¢	Carmine (~406) (type III)	80.00	12.00	5.00
❏ 493	3¢	Violet (~333) (type I)	140.00	20.00	6.00
❏ 494	3¢	Violet (~333) (type II)	80.00	15.00	5.00
❏ 495	4¢	Orange Brown (~334)	100.00	15.00	10.00
❏ 496	5¢	Blue (~335)	65.00	10.00	10.00
❏ 497	10¢	Orange Yellow (~416)	150.00	270.00	14.00

513

Scott No.			Unused	Used

1917–1919. Washington-Franklin Series, Flat Plate Printing, Perforated 11, Unwatermarked. (NH Add 90%)

			Unused	Used
❏ 498	1¢	Green (~405)	6.00	5.00
❏ 499	2¢	Rose (~406) (type I)	6.00	5.00
❏ 500	2¢	Deep Rose (~406) (type Ia)	350.00	200.00
❏ 501	3¢	Violet (~333) (type I)	22.00	5.00
❏ 502	3¢	Violet (~333) (type II)	22.00	5.00
❏ 503	4¢	Brown (~334)	20.00	5.00
❏ 504	5¢	Blue (~335)	20.00	5.00
❏ 505	5¢	Rose (error) (~335)	500.00	380.00
❏ 506	6¢	Red Orange (~336)	20.00	5.00
❏ 507	7¢	Black (~407)	25.00	5.00
❏ 508	8¢	Olive Bistre (~414)	22.00	5.00
❏ 509	9¢	Salmon Red (~415)	22.00	5.00
❏ 510	10¢	Orange Yellow (~416)	22.00	5.00
❏ 511	11¢	Light Green (~434)	17.50	5.00
❏ 512	12¢	Claret Brown (~417)	17.50	5.00
❏ 513	13¢	Apple Green	17.50	8.00
❏ 514	15¢	Gray (~418)	60.00	5.00
❏ 515	20¢	Ultramarine (~419)	60.00	5.00
❏ 516	30¢	Orange Red (~420)	45.00	5.00
❏ 517	50¢	Red Violet (~421)	85.00	5.00
❏ 518	$1	Violet Brown (~423)	80.00	5.00
❏ 518b	$1	Deep Brown (~423)	1750.00	1000.00

1917. Washington Type, Perforated 11, Double Line Watermark. (NH Add 80%)

❏ 519	2¢	Carmine (~332)	1000.00	800.00

NOTE: Refer to the Type Identifier for information on types.

523
(547)

524

Scott No.			Unused	Used

1918. Washington-Franklin Series, Perforated 11, Unwatermarked. (NH Add 90%)

			Unused	Used
❏ 523	$2	Orange Red & Black	800.00	250.00
❏ 524	$5	Deep Green & Black	285.00	55.00

1918–1920. Washington-Franklin Series, Offset Printing, Perforated 11, Unwatermarked. (NH Add 90%)

❏ 525	1¢	Gray Green (~405)	8.00	5.50
❏ 526	2¢	Carmine (~406) (type IV)	32.00	5.50
❏ 527	2¢	Carmine (~406) (type V)	26.00	5.50
❏ 528	2¢	Carmine (~406) (type Va)	15.00	5.50
❏ 528A	2¢	Carmine (~406) (type VI)	60.00	5.50
❏ 528B	2¢	Carmine (~406) (type VII)	32.00	5.50
❏ 529	3¢	Violet (333) (type III)	12.00	5.50
❏ 530	3¢	Purple (~333) (type IV)	12.00	5.50

1918–1920. Washington-Franklin Series, Offset Printing, Imperforate, Unwatermarked. (NH Add 90%)

❏ 531	1¢	Gray Green (~405)	20.00	17.50
❏ 532	2¢	Carmine (~406) (type IV)	55.00	35.00
❏ 533	2¢	Carmine (~406) (type V)	200.00	80.00
❏ 534	2¢	Carmine (~406) (type Va)	150.00	17.50
❏ 534A	2¢	Carmine (~406) (type VI)	60.00	30.00
❏ 534B	2¢	Carmine (~406) (type VII)	2100.00	850.00
❏ 535	3¢	Violet (~333)	20.00	12.00

1918–1920. Washington Type, Offset Printing, Perforated 12½, Unwatermarked. (NH Add 90%)

❏ 536	1¢	Gray Green (~405)	40.00	35.00

PLEASE NOTE: Unless otherwise noted, plate blocks are assumed to be blocks of 4. Where the number is more than 4, it appears in parentheses immediately following the price for the plate block. Blocks containing fewer than the appropriate number of stamps are not considered to be plate blocks and sell for much less.

537

Scott No.			Plate Block	Unused	Used

1919. (NH Add 90%)

| ❏ 537 | 3¢ | Victory | 125.00 (6) | 9.00 | 6.00 |

1919–1921. Washington-Franklin Series, Rotary Press Printing, Perforated 11 x 10. (NH Add 90%)

❏ 538	1¢	Green (~405)	140.00	20.00	15.00
❏ 539	2¢	Carmine Rose (~406) (type II)	—	2850.00	4500.00
❏ 540	2¢	Carmine Rose (~406) (type III)	135.00	25.00	20.00
❏ 541	3¢	Violet (~333)	450.00	50.00	35.00

1920. Washington-Franklin Series, Rotary Press Printing, Perforated 10 x 11, Design Measures 19 x 22½–22½ mm. (NH Add 90%)

| ❏ 542 | 1¢ | Green (~405) | 220.00 | 22.00 | 9.00 |

1921. Washington-Franklin Series, Rotary Press Printing, Perforated 10 x 10, Design Measures 19 x 22½ mm. (NH Add 90%)

| ❏ 543 | 1¢ | Green (~405) | 30.00 | 9.00 | 7.00 |

1922. Washington-Franklin Series, Rotary Press Printing, Perforated 11 x 11, Design Measures 19 x 22½ mm. (NH Add 90%)

| ❏ 544 | 1¢ | Green (~405) | — | RARE | 4000.00 |

1921. Washington-Franklin Series, Rotary Press Printing, Perforated 11 x 11, Design Measures 19½–20 x 22 mm. (NH Add 90%)

| ❏ 545 | 1¢ | Green (~405) | 1200.00 | 875.00 | 200.00 |
| ❏ 546 | 2¢ | Carmine Rose (~406) | 800.00 | 200.00 | 140.00 |

1920. Washington-Franklin Series, Flat Press Printing, Perforated 11 x 11. (NH Add 90%)

| ❏ 547 | $2 | Carmine & Black (~523) | 3500.00 | 350.00 | 80.00 |

548 **549** **550**

Scott No.			Plate Block	Unused	Used

1920. Pilgrim Issue. (NH Add 80%)

			Plate Block	Unused	Used
❏ 548	1¢	Green	50.00 (6)	12.00	6.00
❏ 549	2¢	Carmine Rose	75.00 (6)	12.00	6.00
❏ 550	5¢	Deep Blue	500.00 (6)	55.00	22.00

551	**552**	**553**	**554**
(653)	(575, 578, 581, 597, 604, 532)	(557, 582, 598, 605, 631, 633)	(577, 579, 583, 595, 599, 599A, 606, 634, 634A)

555	**556**	**557**	**558**
(584, 600, 635)	(585, 601, 636)	(586, 602, 637)	(587, 638, 723)

1922–1925. Definitives, Flat Press Printing, Perforated 11.
(NH Add 80%)

❏ 551	½¢	Olive Brown	7.00 (6)	6.50	4.50
❏ 552	1¢	Deep Green	25.00 (6)	6.50	4.50
❏ 553	1½¢	Yellow Brown	40.00 (6)	6.50	4.50
❏ 554	2¢	Carmine	25.00 (6)	6.50	4.50
❏ 555	3¢	Violet	225.00 (6)	24.00	4.50
❏ 556	4¢	Yellow Brown	225.00 (6)	24.00	4.50
❏ 557	5¢	Dark Blue	180.00 (6)	25.00	4.50
❏ 558	6¢	Red Orange	420.00 (6)	45.00	4.50

| | | 559 | 560 | 561 | 562 |
| | | (588, 639) | (589, 640) | (590, 641) | (591, 603, 642) |

559 (588, 639)
560 (589, 640)
561 (590, 641)
562 (591, 603, 642)

563 (692)
564 (693)
565 (695)
566 (696)

567 (698)
568 (699)
569 (700)
570 (701)

Scott No.			Plate Block	Unused	Used
❏ 559	7¢	Black	75.00 (6)	15.00	5.50
❏ 560	8¢	Olive Green	600.00 (6)	60.00	5.50
❏ 561	9¢	Rose	175.00 (6)	22.00	5.50
❏ 562	10¢	Orange	250.00 (6)	28.00	4.50
❏ 563	11¢	Blue Green	35.00 (6)	8.00	4.50
❏ 564	12¢	Brown Violet	75.00 (6)	12.00	4.50
❏ 565	14¢	Dark Blue	65.00 (6)	12.00	4.50
❏ 566	15¢	Gray	275.00 (6)	30.00	4.50
❏ 567	20¢	Carmine Rose	265.00 (6)	30.00	4.50
❏ 568	25¢	Green	265.00 (6)	30.00	4.50
❏ 569	30¢	Olive Brown	265.00 (6)	45.00	4.50
❏ 570	50¢	Lilac	675.00 (6)	70.00	4.50

| 571 | 572 | 573 |

Scott No.			Plate Block	Unused	Used
❏ 571	$1	Violet Black	475.00 (6)	75.00	7.00
❏ 572	$2	Deep Blue	850.00 (6)	135.00	9.00
❏ 573	$5	Carmine & Blue	235.00 (8)	200.00	18.00

Series of 1922–1925, Imperforate. (NH Add 60%)

❏ 575	1¢	Green (~552)	85.00 (6)	12.00	8.00
❏ 576	1½¢	Yellow Brown (~553)	40.00 (6)	9.00	7.00
❏ 577	2¢	Carmine (~554)	40.00 (6)	9.00	7.00

1923–1926. Definitives, Rotary Press Printing, Perforated 11 x 10, Designs Measure 19½ x 22½ mm. (NH Add 60%)

❏ 578	1¢	Green (~552)	850.00	115.00	145.00
❏ 579	2¢	Carmine (~554)	770.00	115.00	125.00

1923–1926. Series of 1922–1925, Rotary Press, Perforated 10. (NH Add 60%)

❏ 581	1¢	Green (~552)	125.00	12.00	4.25
❏ 582	1½¢	Brown (~553)	55.00	10.00	4.25
❏ 583	2¢	Carmine (~554)	55.00	10.00	4.25
❏ 584	3¢	Violet (~555)	300.00	35.00	4.25
❏ 585	4¢	Yellow Brown(~556)	275.00	20.00	4.25
❏ 586	5¢	Blue (~557)	250.00	20.00	4.25
❏ 587	6¢	Red Orange (~558)	200.00	18.00	4.25
❏ 588	7¢	Black (~559)	175.00	18.00	6.00
❏ 589	8¢	Olive Green (~560)	250.00	35.00	5.00
❏ 590	9¢	Rose (~561)	100.00	12.00	4.25
❏ 591	10¢	Orange (~562)	550.00	80.00	4.25

Scott No.			Line Pair	Unused	Used

1923–1926. Series of 1922–1925, Rotary Press Coil Stamps, Perforated 11. (NH Add 60%)

❏ 595	2¢	Carmine (~554)	2000.00	375.00	300.00

NOTE: No. 595 is a sheet stamp made from coil waste. Its design measures $19\frac{1}{2} \times 22\frac{1}{2}$ mm.

1923–1929. Series of 1922–1925, Rotary Press Coil Stamps, Perforated 10 Vertically. (NH Add 60%)

❏ 597	1¢	Green (~552)	6.00	5.50	4.50
❏ 598	1½¢	Deep Brown (~553)	6.00	5.50	4.50
❏ 599	2¢	Carmine (~554) (type I)	6.00	5.50	4.50
❏ 599A	2¢	Carmine (~554) (type II)	700.00	150.00	12.00
❏ 600	3¢	Deep Violet (~555)	50.00	8.00	4.50
❏ 601	4¢	Yellow Brown (~556)	35.00	5.50	4.50
❏ 602	5¢	Dark Blue (~557)	15.00	5.50	4.50
❏ 603	10¢	Orange (~562)	35.00	5.50	4.50

NOTE: Refer to the Type Identifier for information on types.

1924–1925. Series of 1922–1925, Coil Stamps, Perforated 10 Horizontally. (NH Add 70%)

❏ 604	1¢	Green (~552)	6.00	4.00	2.50
❏ 605	1½¢	Yellow Brown (~553)	6.00	4.00	2.50
❏ 606	2¢	Carmine (~554)	6.00	4.00	2.50

610
(611, 612)

Scott No.			Plate Block	Unused	Used

1923. Harding Memorial Issue. (NH Add 80%)

❏ 610	2¢	Black, perforated 11	35.00 (6)	5.00	5.00
❏ 611	2¢	Black (~610), imperforate	100.00 (6)	12.00	6.00
❏ 612	2¢	Black (~610), perforated 10	325.00	25.00	6.00

| 614 | 615 | 616 |

Scott No.			Plate Block	Unused	Used

1924. Huguenot–Walloon Issue. (NH Add 80%)

❏ 614	1¢	Green	40.00 (6)	8.00	7.00
❏ 615	2¢	Carmine Rose	80.00 (6)	8.00	7.00
❏ 616	5¢	Dark Blue	425.00 (6)	35.00	25.00

| 617 | 618 | 619 |

1925. Lexington–Concord Sesquicentennial. (NH Add 60%)

❏ 617	1¢	Green	60.00 (6)	10.00	6.00
❏ 618	2¢	Carmine Rose	75.00 (6)	10.00	6.00
❏ 619	5¢	Dark Blue	325.00 (6)	30.00	16.50

| 620 | 621 |

1925. Norse-American Issue. (NH Add 80%)

| ❏ 620 | 2¢ | Carmine & Black | 225.00 (8) | 10.00 | 8.00 |
| ❏ 621 | 5¢ | Dark Blue & Black | 800.00 (8) | 22.00 | 15.00 |

622
(694)

623
(697)

Scott No.			Plate Block	Unused	Used

1925–1926. 1922–1925 Series New Values, Perforated 11.
(NH Add 80%)

❏ 622	13¢	Green	170.00 (6)	42.00	6.00
❏ 623	17¢	Black	50.00 (6)	35.00	6.00

627

628

629
(630)

1926. (NH Add 60%)

❏ 627	2¢	Sesquicentennial Exposition	42.00 (6)	7.00	6.00
❏ 628	5¢	Ericsson Memorial	100.00 (6)	7.00	6.00
❏ 629	2¢	Battle of White Plains	45.00 (6)	6.00	5.00
❏ 630	2¢	White Plains souvenir sheet (~629)	—	600.00	475.00

1926. Series of 1922–1925, Rotary Press Printing, Imperforate. (NH Add 60%)

❏ 631	1½¢	Brown (~553)	75.00	8.00	5.00

1926–1928. Series of 1922–1925, Perforated 11 x 10½.
(NH Add 60%)

❏ 632	1¢	Green (~552)	40.00	6.00	5.00
❏ 633	1½¢	Yellow Brown (~553)	40.00	6.00	5.00
❏ 634	2¢	Carmine (~554) (type I)	20.00	6.00	5.00
❏ 634A	2¢	Carmine (~554) (type II)	600.00	260.00	14.00

Scott No.			Plate Block	Unused	Used
❏ 635	3¢	Violet (~555)	20.00	6.25	4.25
❏ 636	4¢	Yellow Brown (~556)	80.00	6.25	4.25
❏ 637	5¢	Dark Blue (~557)	20.00	6.25	4.25
❏ 638	6¢	Red Orange (~558)	25.00	6.25	4.25
❏ 639	7¢	Black (~559)	25.00	6.25	4.25
❏ 640	8¢	Olive Green (~560)	20.00	6.25	4.25
❏ 641	9¢	Orange Red (~561)	22.00	6.25	4.25
❏ 642	10¢	Orange (~562)	25.00	6.25	4.25

643

644

1927. (NH Add 60%)

❏ 643	2¢	Vermont Sesquicentennial	45.00 (6)	7.00	6.00
❏ 644	2¢	Oriskany - Saratoga	45.00 (6)	7.00	6.00

645

646

647

648

649

650

1928. (NH Add 50–60%)

❏ 645	2¢	Valley Forge	30.00 (6)	8.00	6.00
❏ 646	2¢	Molly Pitcher	40.00	8.00	6.00
❏ 647	2¢	Hawaii	160.00	8.00	6.00
❏ 648	5¢	Hawaii	330.00	18.00	14.00
❏ 649	2¢	Aeronautics Conference	20.00 (6)	8.00	6.00
❏ 650	5¢	Aeronautics Conference	60.00 (6)	8.00	6.00

651

654
(655, 556)

Scott No.			Plate Block	Unused	Used
1929. (NH Add 50%)					
❏ 651	2¢	George Rogers Clark	15.00 (6)	7.00	6.00
❏ 652		**need info**			

1929. Series of 1922–1925, Rotary Press Printing, 11 x 10½.
(NH Add 10–35%)

Scott No.			Plate Block	Unused	Used
❏ 653	½¢	Olive Brown (~551)	8.00	6.50	5.00
❏ 654	2¢	Edison - Light Bulb, perforated 11	35.00 (6)	6.50	5.00
❏ 655	2¢	Edison (~654), perforated 11 x 10½	50.00	6.50	5.00

Scott No.			Line Pair	Unused	Used
1929. Coil Stamp.					
❏ 656	2¢	Edison – Light Bulb (~654)	80.00	20.00	8.00

657

Scott No.			Plate Block	Unused	Used
1929.					
❏ 657	2¢	Sullivan Expedition	38.00 (6)	8.00	6.00

658

669

Scott No.			Plate Block	Unused	Used

1929. Series of 1922–1925, Perforated 11 x 10½, Overprinted "Kans." (NH Add 50%)

			Plate Block	Unused	Used
❏ 658	1¢	Green	55.00	8.00	6.50
❏ 659	1½¢	Brown	55.00	8.00	6.50
❏ 660	2¢	Carmine	55.00	8.00	6.50
❏ 661	3¢	Violet	235.00	35.00	15.00
❏ 662	4¢	Yellow Brown	235.00	35.00	15.00
❏ 663	5¢	Deep Blue	175.00	18.00	15.00
❏ 664	6¢	Red Orange	450.00	45.00	18.00
❏ 665	7¢	Black	525.00	45.00	25.00
❏ 666	8¢	Olive Green	825.00	125.00	65.00
❏ 667	9¢	Light Rose	325.00	36.00	20.00
❏ 668	10¢	Orange Yellow	325.00	36.00	20.00

1929. Series of 1922–1925, Perforated 11 x 10½, Overprinted "Nebr." (NH Add 50%)

			Plate Block	Unused	Used
❏ 669	1¢	Green	65.00	10.00	6.00
❏ 670	1½¢	Brown	65.00	10.00	6.00
❏ 671	2¢	Carmine	65.00	10.00	6.00
❏ 672	3¢	Violet	210.00	28.00	10.00
❏ 673	4¢	Brown	250.00	28.00	18.00
❏ 674	5¢	Blue	325.00	32.00	18.00
❏ 675	6¢	Orange	475.00	50.00	22.00
❏ 676	7¢	Black	325.00	35.00	22.00
❏ 677	8¢	Olive Green	425.00	65.00	30.00
❏ 678	9¢	Rose	525.00	65.00	30.00
❏ 679	10¢	Orange Yellow	1000.00	150.00	30.00

NOTE: Fakes abound, especially on used stamps.

680   **681**   **682**   **683**

Scott No.			Plate Block	Unused	Used
1929. (NH Add 35%)					
☐ 680	2¢	Battle of Fallen Timbers	26.00 (6)	6.50	4.25
☐ 681	2¢	Ohio River Canalization	24.00 (6)	6.50	4.25
1930. (NH Add 35%)					
☐ 682	2¢	Massachusetts Bay Colony	40.00 (6)	6.50	4.25
☐ 683	2¢	Charleston, SC	50.00 (6)	6.50	4.25

684   **685**
(686)   (687)

1930. Series of 1922–1925, Rotary Press Printing, Perforated 11 x 10½. (NH Add 35%)

☐ 684	1½¢	Warren G. Harding (full face)	6.00	5.00	2.50
☐ 685	4¢	William Howard Taft	20.00	5.00	2.50

Scott No.			Line Pair	Unused	Used
1930. Series of 1922–1925, Rotary Press Coil Stamps, Perforated 10 Vertically. (NH Add 40%)					
☐ 686	1½¢	Harding (~684)	12.00	5.00	4.00
☐ 687	4¢	Taft (~685)	12.00	5.00	4.00

688   **689**   **690**

Scott No.			Plate Block	Unused	Used

1930. (NH Add 35%)

❏ 688	2¢	Battle of Braddock's Field	36.00 (6)	6.00	4.25
❏ 689	2¢	Von Steuben	30.00 (6)	6.00	4.25
❏ 690	2¢	Pulaski	14.00 (6)	6.00	4.25

1931. Series of 1922–1925, Rotary Press Printing, Perforated 11 x 10½ or 10½ x 11. (NH Add 40%)

❏ 692	11¢	Light Blue (~563)	18.00	7.00	4.25
❏ 693	12¢	Brown Violet (~564)	26.00	7.00	4.25
❏ 694	13¢	Yellow Green (~622)	20.00	7.00	4.25
❏ 695	14¢	Dark Blue (~565)	30.00	7.00	4.25
❏ 696	15¢	Gray (~566)	40.00	9.00	4.25
❏ 697	17¢	Black (~623)	35.00	9.00	4.25
❏ 698	20¢	Carmine Rose (~567)	42.00	15.00	4.25
❏ 699	25¢	Blue Green (~568)	50.00	15.00	4.25
❏ 700	30¢	Brown (~569)	80.00	20.00	4.25
❏ 701	50¢	Lilac (~570)	185.00	50.00	4.25

702   **703**

1931. (NH Add 25%)

❏ 702	2¢	Red Cross	8.00	6.00	4.25
❏ 703	2¢	Surrender at Yorktown	8.00	6.00	4.25

PLEASE NOTE: Unless otherwise noted, plate blocks are assumed to be blocks of 4. Where the number is more than 4, it appears in parentheses immediately following the price for the plate block. Blocks containing fewer than the appropriate number of stamps are not considered to be plate blocks and sell for much less.

704 705 706 707

708 709 710 711

712 713 714 715

Scott No.			Plate Block	Unused	Used
1932. Washington Bicentennial Set. (NH Add 40%)					
❑ 704	½¢	Olive Brown	6.00	2.00	1.75
❑ 705	1¢	Green	8.00	2.00	1.75
❑ 706	1½¢	Brown	25.00	2.00	1.75
❑ 707	2¢	Carmine	5.00	2.00	1.75
❑ 708	3¢	Purple	20.00	4.25	2.25
❑ 709	4¢	Light Brown	12.00	4.25	2.25
❑ 710	5¢	Blue	20.00	4.25	2.25
❑ 711	6¢	Orange	12.00	4.25	2.25
❑ 712	7¢	Black	12.00	4.25	2.25
❑ 713	8¢	Olive Bistre	75.00	4.25	2.25
❑ 714	9¢	Pale Red	50.00	4.25	2.25
❑ 715	10¢	Orange Yellow	100.00	15.00	2.25
		Set of 12 (704–715)	—	25.00	8.00

716	717	718	719	720
				(721, 722)

Scott No.			Plate Block	Unused	Used
1932. (NH Add 30%)					
❑ 716	2¢	Olympics - Lake Placid	14.00 (6)	5.50	2.25
❑ 717	2¢	Arbor Day	14.00	5.50	2.25
❑ 718	3¢	Olympics - Runner	15.00	5.50	2.25
❑ 719	5¢	Olympics - Discus Thrower	25.00	5.50	2.25
❑ 720	3¢	George Washington	10.00	4.00	2.25

Scott No.			Line Pair	Unused	Used
1932. Coil Stamps. (NH Add 30%)					
❑ 721	3¢	Washington (~720) perf 10 vertically	10.00	5.00	2.50
❑ 722	3¢	Washington (~720) perf 10 horizontally	10.00	5.00	2.50
❑ 723	6¢	Garfield (~558) perf 10 vertically	50.00	18.00	2.50

724	725

Scott No.			Plate Block	Unused	Used
1932. (NH Add 30%)					
❑ 724	3¢	William Penn	20.00 (6)	5.00	2.50
❑ 725	3¢	Daniel Webster	20.00 (6)	5.00	2.50

726

727
(752)

728
(730, 766)

729
(731, 767)

Scott No.			Plate Block	Unused	Used
1933. (NH Add 30%)					
❑ 726	3¢	General Oglethorpe	15.00 (6)	5.25	2.25
❑ 727	3¢	Washington at Newburgh	7.50	5.25	2.25
❑ 728	1¢	Century of Progress - Fort Dearborn	7.50	5.25	2.25
❑ 729	3¢	Century of Progress - Skyscrapers	7.50	5.25	2.25

730

731

1933. A.P.S. Convention Souvenir Sheets, Imperforate, Ungummed.

❑ 730	1¢	Sheet of 25 (~728)	—	48.00	25.00
❑ 730a	1¢	Single stamp	—	7.00	5.00
❑ 731	3¢	Sheet of 25 (~729)	—	32.00	30.00
❑ 731a	3¢	Single stamp	—	7.00	5.00

732

733
(735, 753, 768)

734

Scott No.			Plate Block	Unused	Used
1933. (NH Add 20%)					
❏ 732	3¢	National Recovery Act (NRA)	6.00	2.50	1.50
❏ 733	3¢	Byrd Antarctic Expedition	14.00 (6)	2.50	1.50
❏ 734	5¢	Kosciuszko	40.00 (6)	2.50	1.50

735

1934. National Philatelic Exhibition Souvenir Sheet, Imperforate, Ungummed .

❏ 735	3¢	Sheet of 6 (~733)	—	18.00	12.00
❏ 735a	3¢	Single stamp	—	8.00	6.00

736

737
(738, 754)

739
(755)

Scott No.			Plate Block	Unused	Used
1934. (NH Add 20%)					
❑ 736	3¢	Maryland Tercentenary	10.00 (6)	1.25	.85
❑ 737	3¢	Mother's Day, perf 11 x 10½	4.00	1.25	.85
❑ 738	3¢	Mother's Day (~737), perf 11	5.00 (6)	1.25	.85
❑ 739	3¢	Wisconsin Tercentenary	6.00 (6)	1.25	.85

741
(757)

742
(750, 758, 770)

740
(751, 756, 769)

743
(759)

744
(760)

1934. National Parks Issue, Perforated. (NH Add 25%)

❑ 740	1¢	Yosemite	5.00 (6)	1.25	.85
❑ 741	2¢	Grand Canyon	5.00 (6)	1.25	.85
❑ 742	3¢	Mt. Rainier	5.00 (6)	1.25	.85
❑ 743	4¢	Mesa Verde	12.00 (6)	2.00	1.00
❑ 744	5¢	Yellowstone	12.00 (6)	2.00	1.00

745
(761)

746
(762)

747
(763)

748
(764)

749
(765, 797)

Scott No.			Plate Block	Unused	Used
❏ 745	6¢	Crater Lake	20.00 (6)	7.50	5.25
❏ 746	7¢	Acadia	18.00 (6)	7.50	5.25
❏ 747	8¢	Zion	20.00 (6)	7.50	5.25
❏ 748	9¢	Glacier	20.00 (6)	7.50	5.25
❏ 749	10¢	Smoky Mountains, gray black	30.00 (6)	7.50	5.25
		Set of 10 (740–749)	—	12.00	5.25

750

1934. A.P.S. Convention Souvenir Sheet, Imperforate, Gummed.
(NH Add 25%)

❏ 750	3¢	Sheet of 6 (~742)	—	40.00	35.00
❏ 750a	3¢	Single stamp	—	10.00	7.00

751

Scott No.			Plate Block	Unused	Used

1934. Trans-Mississippi Philatelic Exposition Souvenir Sheet, Imperforate, Gummed. (NH Add 25%)

❏ 751	1¢	Sheet of 6 (~740)	—	18.00	15.00
❏ 751a	1¢	Single stamp	—	6.00	4.50

1935. Farley Special Printing, Perforated, Ungummed.

❏ 752	3¢	Washington at Newburgh (~727)	22.00	6.00	4.50
❏ 753	3¢	Byrd Antarctic Expedition (~733)	18.00 (6)	6.00	4.50

1935. Farley Special Printing, Imperforate, Ungummed.

❏ 754	3¢	Mother's Day (~737)	20.00 (6)	6.00	4.50
❏ 755	3¢	Wisconsin Tercentenary (~739)	20.00 (6)	6.00	4.50

1935. Farley Special Printing, National Parks Set, Imperforate, Ungummed.

❏ 756	1¢	Yosemite (~740)	7.00 (6)	6.00	4.50
❏ 757	2¢	Grand Canyon (~741)	10.00 (6)	6.00	4.50
❏ 758	3¢	Mt. Rainier (~742)	18.00 (6)	6.00	4.50
❏ 759	4¢	Mesa Verde (~743)	20.00 (6)	6.00	4.50
❏ 760	5¢	Yellowstone (~744)	25.00 (6)	6.00	4.50
❏ 761	6¢	Crater Lake (~745)	40.00 (6)	7.00	5.50
❏ 762	7¢	Acadia (~746)	35.00 (6)	7.00	5.50
❏ 763	8¢	Zion (~747)	50.00 (6)	7.00	5.50
❏ 764	9¢	Glacier (~748)	50.00 (6)	7.00	5.50
❏ 765	10¢	Smoky Mountains (~749), gray black	55.00 (6)	7.00	5.50
		Set of 10 (756–765)	—	12.00	8.00

771

Scott No.			Plate Block	Unused	Used

1935. Farley Special Printing, Imperforate, Ungummed.

			Plate Block	Unused	Used
❑ 766	1¢	Souvenir sheet of 25 (~730)	—	28.00	24.00
❑ 767	3¢	Souvenir sheet of 25 (~731)	—	28.00	24.00
❑ 768	3¢	Souvenir sheet of 6 (~735)	—	20.00	15.00
❑ 769	1¢	Souvenir sheet of 6 (~751)	—	20.00	15.00
❑ 770	3¢	Souvenir sheet of 6 (~750)	—	25.00	20.00
❑ 771	16¢	Airmail Special Delivery	80.00 (6)	8.00	6.00

NOTE: Farley Special Printing items (752–771) were issued in uncut press sheets. Position pairs and blocks that include guide lines or interpane gutters help distinguish Farley items from their regularly issued counterparts.

NOTE: Prices for stamps from 1935 forward are for never-hinged (NH) examples.

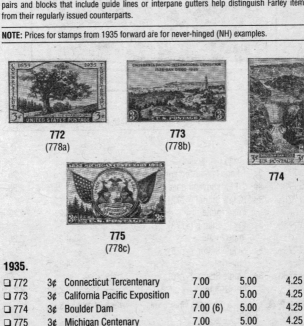

772
(778a)

773
(778b)

774

775
(778c)

1935.

			Plate Block	Unused	Used
❑ 772	3¢	Connecticut Tercentenary	7.00	5.00	4.25
❑ 773	3¢	California Pacific Exposition	7.00	5.00	4.25
❑ 774	3¢	Boulder Dam	7.00 (6)	5.00	4.25
❑ 775	3¢	Michigan Centenary	7.00	5.00	4.25

776
(778d)

777

778

Scott No.			Plate Block	Unused	Used
1936.					
❏ 776	3¢	Texas Centennial	6.00	4.25	2.25
❏ 777	3¢	Rhode Island Tercentenary	6.00	4.25	2.25
❏ 778	3¢	TIPEX souvenir sheet	—	4.25	2.25
❏ 778a	3¢	Single Stamp (~772), imperforate	—	4.25	2.25
❏ 778b	3¢	Single Stamp (~773), imperforate	—	4.25	2.25
❏ 778c	3¢	Single Stamp (~775), imperforate	—	4.25	2.25
❏ 778d	3¢	Single Stamp (~776), imperforate	—	4.25	2.25

NOTE: Prices for stamps from 1935 forward are for never-hinged (NH) examples.

782   **783**    **784**

Scott No.			Plate Block	Unused	Used
❑ 782	3¢	Arkansas Centennial	4.00	1.25	.85
❑ 783	3¢	Oregon Territory Centennial	2.50	1.25	.85
❑ 784	3¢	Susan B. Anthony	2.50	1.25	.85

785    **786**

787    **788**

789    **790**

1936–1937. Army and Navy Issue.

❑ 785	1¢	Washington & Greene	5.00	1.60	.85
❑ 786	2¢	Jackson & Scott	5.00	1.60	.85
❑ 787	3¢	Sherman, Grant & Sheridan	6.00	1.60	.85
❑ 788	4¢	Lee & Stonewall Jackson	12.00	1.60	.85
❑ 789	5¢	West Point	12.00	2.00	1.00
❑ 790	1¢	Jones & Barry	5.00	1.60	.85

791

792

793

794

Scott No.			Plate Block	Unused	Used
❑ 791	2¢	Decatur & McDonough	6.00	1.25	.85
❑ 792	3¢	Farragut & Porter	6.00	1.25	.85
❑ 793	4¢	Sampson, Dewey & Schley	12.00	1.25	.85
❑ 794	5¢	Annapolis	12.00	5.00	1.25
		Set of 10 (785–779)	—	5.00	1.25

795

796

797

1937.

❑ 795	3¢	Ordinance of 1787	5.00	1.25	.85
❑ 796	5¢	Virginia Dare	10.00 (6)	1.25	.85
❑ 797	10¢	SPA souvenir sheet (~749), blue green	—	4.00	1.25

798

799

800

801

802

Scott No.			Plate Block	Unused	Used
☐ 798	3¢	Constitution Sesquicentennial	5.00	.75	.45
☐ 799	3¢	Hawaii	4.00	.75	.45
☐ 800	3¢	Alaska	4.00	.75	.45
☐ 801	3¢	Puerto Rico	4.00	.75	.45
☐ 802	3¢	Virgin Islands	4.00	.75	.45

803

804
(839, 848)

805
(840, 849)

806
(841, 850)

807
(842, 851)

1938. Presidential Series.

☐ 803	½¢	Benjamin Franklin	2.00	.75	.45
☐ 804	1¢	George Washington	2.00	.75	.45
☐ 805	1½¢	Martha Washington	2.00	.75	.45
☐ 806	2¢	John Adams	2.00	.75	.45
☐ 807	3¢	Thomas Jefferson	2.00	.75	.45

808 (843) **809** (844) **810** (845) **811** (846) **812**

813 **814** **815** (847) **816** **817**

818 **819** **820** **821** **822**

Scott No.			Plate Block	Unused	Used
❑ 808	4¢	James Madison	5.00	1.25	.40
❑ 809	4½¢	White House	4.50	1.25	.40
❑ 810	5¢	James Monroe	4.50	1.25	.40
❑ 811	6¢	John Quincy Adams	4.50	1.00	.40
❑ 812	7¢	Andrew Jackson	5.00	1.00	.40
❑ 813	8¢	Martin Van Buren	5.00	1.00	.40
❑ 814	9¢	William Henry Harrison	5.00	1.00	.40
❑ 815	10¢	John Tyler	4.50	1.00	.40
❑ 816	11¢	James Polk	4.50	1.25	.40
❑ 817	12¢	Zachary Taylor	8.00	2.00	.40
❑ 818	13¢	Millard Fillmore	8.00	2.00	.40
❑ 819	14¢	Franklin Pierce	8.00	2.00	.40
❑ 820	15¢	James Buchanan	5.00	1.25	.40
❑ 821	16¢	Abraham Lincoln	8.00	2.00	.55
❑ 822	17¢	Andrew Johnson	8.00	2.00	.40

823 **824** **825** **826** **827**

828 **829** **830** **831**

832
(832b, 832c)

833 **834**

Scott No.			Plate Block	Unused	Used
❏ 823	18¢	Ulysses S. Grant	12.00	5.25	.80
❏ 824	19¢	Rutherford B. Hayes	8.00	5.25	.80
❏ 825	20¢	James A Garfield	8.00	5.25	.80
❏ 826	21¢	Chester A. Arthur	12.00	5.25	.80
❏ 827	22¢	Grover Cleveland	12.00	5.25	1.00
❏ 828	24¢	Benjamin Harrison	20.00	5.25	.80
❏ 829	25¢	William McKinley	10.00	5.25	.80
❏ 830	30¢	Theodore Roosevelt	20.00	5.25	.80
❏ 831	50¢	William Howard Taft	30.00	8.00	.80
❏ 832	$1	Woodrow Wilson, dark violet & black	60.00	14.00	.80
❏ 832b	$1	Wilson (~832), watermarked "USIR"	—	225.00	65.00
❏ 832c	$1	Wilson, (~832), red violet & black	55.00	15.00	.80
❏ 833	$2	Warren G. Harding	140.00	32.00	5.00
❏ 834	$5	Calvin Coolidge	450.00	120.00	5.00

835   836

837   838

Scott No.			Plate Block	Unused	Used
1938.					
❏ 835	3¢	Constitution Ratification	6.00	.80	.40
❏ 836	3¢	Swede-Finn Tercentenary	6.00 (6)	.80	.40
❏ 837	3¢	Northwest Territory	11.00	.80	.40
❏ 838	3¢	Iowa Territory Centennial	8.00	.80	.40

Scott No.			Line Pair	Unused	Used
1939. Presidential Series Coil Stamps, Perforated 10 Vertically.					
❏ 839	1¢	G. Washington (~804)	5.50	.85	.40
❏ 840	1½¢	M. Washington (~805)	5.50	.85	.40
❏ 841	2¢	Adams (~806)	5.50	.85	.40
❏ 842	3¢	Jefferson (~807)	5.50	.85	.40
❏ 843	4¢	Madison (~808)	30.00	6.00	1.00
❏ 844	4½¢	White House (~809)	5.50	4.00	1.00
❏ 845	5¢	Monroe (~810)	28.00	4.00	1.00
❏ 846	6¢	J. Q. Adams (~811)	8.00	4.00	.85
❏ 847	10¢	Tyler (~815)	50.00	10.00	1.00
1939. Presidential Series Coil Stamps, Perforated 10 Horizontally.					
❏ 848	1¢	G. Washington (~804)	4.25	2.00	1.25
❏ 849	1½¢	M. Washington (~805)	4.25	2.00	1.25
❏ 850	2¢	Adams (~806)	7.00	4.00	1.25
❏ 851	3¢	Jefferson (~807)	8.00	4.00	1.25

852   853   854

855   856

857

858

Scott No.			Plate Block	Unused	Used
1939.					
❑ 852	3¢	Golden Gate Exposition	6.25	.85	.40
❑ 853	3¢	New York World's Fair	6.25	.85	.40
❑ 854	3¢	Washington's Inaugural	8.00 (6)	1.00	.40
❑ 855	3¢	Baseball Centennial	10.00	2.00	.40
❑ 856	3¢	Panama Canal	6.25 (6)	.85	.40
❑ 857	3¢	Colonial Printing	6.25	.85	.40
❑ 858	3¢	Washington, Montana & the Dakotas	6.25	.85	.40

NOTE: Prices for stamps from 1935 forward are for never-hinged (NH) examples.

859 860 861 862

863 864 865 866

867 868 869 870

Scott No.			Plate Block	Unused	Used
1940. Famous Americans Series.					
❑ 859	1¢	Washington Irving	5.50	.80	.40
❑ 860	2¢	James Fenimore Cooper	5.50	.80	.40
❑ 861	3¢	Ralph Waldo Emerson	5.50	.80	.40
❑ 862	5¢	Louisa May Alcott	10.00	1.00	.50
❑ 863	10¢	Samuel Clemens	45.00	2.10	2.00
❑ 864	1¢	Henry Wadsworth Longfellow	5.50	.80	.40
❑ 865	2¢	John Greenleaf Whittier	5.50	.80	.40
❑ 866	3¢	James Russell Lowell	5.50	.80	.40
❑ 867	5¢	Walt Whitman	12.00	.80	.40
❑ 868	10¢	James Whitcomb Riley	45.00	3.00	2.00
❑ 869	1¢	Horace Mann	5.50	.80	.40
❑ 870	2¢	Mark Hopkins	5.50	.80	.40

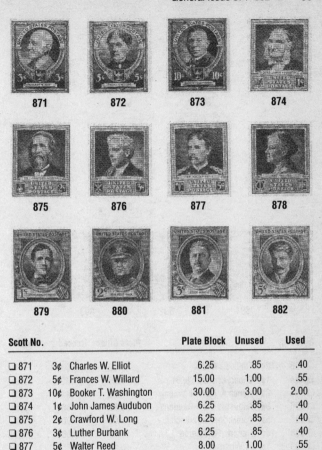

Scott No.			Plate Block	Unused	Used
❏ 871	3¢	Charles W. Elliot	6.25	.85	.40
❏ 872	5¢	Frances W. Willard	15.00	1.00	.55
❏ 873	10¢	Booker T. Washington	30.00	3.00	2.00
❏ 874	1¢	John James Audubon	6.25	.85	.40
❏ 875	2¢	Crawford W. Long	· 6.25	.85	.40
❏ 876	3¢	Luther Burbank	6.25	.85	.40
❏ 877	5¢	Walter Reed	8.00	1.00	.55
❏ 878	10¢	James Adams	26.00	3.00	2.00
❏ 879	1¢	Stephen Collins Foster	6.25	.85	.40
❏ 880	2¢	John Philip Sousa	6.25	.85	.40
❏ 881	3¢	Victor Herbert	6.25	.85	.40
❏ 882	5¢	Edward A. McDowell	12.00	1.00	.40

NOTE: Prices for stamps from 1935 forward are for never-hinged (NH) examples.

883   884   885   886

887   888   889   890

891   892   893

Scott No.			Plate Block	Unused	Used
❑ 883	10¢	Ethelbert Nevin	40.00	4.00	2.00
❑ 884	1¢	Gilbert Charles Stuart	5.25	.85	.40
❑ 885	2¢	James A. McNeill Whistler	5.25	.85	.40
❑ 886	3¢	Augustus Saint-Gaudens	5.25	.85	.40
❑ 887	5¢	Daniel Chester French	8.00	4.00	2.00
❑ 888	10¢	Frederic Remington	35.00	4.00	2.00
❑ 889	1¢	Eli Whitney	5.25	.85	.40
❑ 890	2¢	Samuel F. B. Morse	5.25	.85	.40
❑ 891	3¢	Cyrus McCormick	5.25	.85	.40
❑ 892	5¢	Elias Howe	15.00	4.00	2.50
❑ 893	10¢	Alexander Graham Bell	80.00	14.00	4.00
		Set of 35 (859–893)	—	22.00	6.00

NOTE: Prices for stamps from 1935 forward are for never-hinged (NH) examples.

894

895

896

897

898

899   900   901   902

Scott No.			Plate Block	Unused	Used
1940.					
❑ 894	3¢	Pony Express	5.25	.80	.40
❑ 895	3¢	Pan American Union	5.25	.80	.40
❑ 896	3¢	Idaho Statehood	5.25	.80	.40
❑ 897	3¢	Wyoming Statehood	5.25	.80	.40
❑ 898	3¢	Coronado Expedition	5.25	.80	.40
❑ 899	1¢	Defense – Statue of Liberty	5.25	.80	.40
❑ 900	2¢	Defense – Artillery	5.25	.80	.40
❑ 901	3¢	Defense – Torch of Liberty	5.25	.80	.40
❑ 902	3¢	13th Amendment	5.25	.80	.40

903

Scott No.			Plate Block	Unused	Used

1941.

| ❑ 903 | 3¢ | Vermont Statehood | 2.00 | .80 | .40 |

904    **905**    **906**

1942.

❑ 904	3¢	Kentucky	5.00	.80	.40
❑ 905	3¢	Win the War	5.00	.80	.40
❑ 906	5¢	China	14.00	.80	.40

907    **908**

1943.

| ❑ 907 | 2¢ | Allied Nations | 4.00 | .80 | .40 |
| ❑ 908 | 1¢ | Four Freedoms | 4.00 | .80 | .40 |

NOTE: Prices for stamps from 1935 forward are for never-hinged (NH) examples.

909 910

911 912

913 914

915 916

Scott No.			Plate Block	Unused	Used
1943–1944. Overrun Countries Issue.					
❏ 909	5¢	Poland	7.00	.80	.40
❏ 910	5¢	Czechoslovakia	5.25	.80	.40
❏ 911	5¢	Norway	5.25	.80	.40
❏ 912	5¢	Luxembourg	5.25	.80	.40
❏ 913	5¢	Netherlands	5.25	.80	.40
❏ 914	5¢	Belgium	5.25	.80	.40
❏ 915	5¢	France	5.25	.80	.40
❏ 916	5¢	Greece	15.00	2.00	1.00

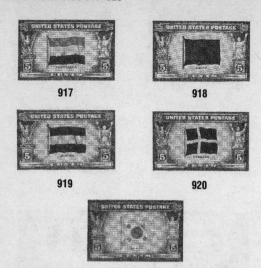

917

918

919

920

921

Scott No.			Plate Block	Unused	Used
❏ 917	5¢	Yugoslavia	8.00	.80	.40
❏ 918	5¢	Albania	8.00	.80	.40
❏ 919	5¢	Austria	6.25	.80	.40
❏ 920	5¢	Denmark	6.25	.80	.40
❏ 921	5¢	Korea	6.25	.80	.40
		Set of 13 (909–921)	—	6.00	4.00

NOTE: Plate blocks of the Overrun Nations Issue are inscribed with the name of country instead of a plate number.

922

923

1944.

❏ 922	3¢	Transcontinental Railroad	5.25	.80	.40
❏ 923	3¢	First Steamship Across Atlantic	5.25	.80	.40

924

925

926

Scott No.			Plate Block	Unused	Used
❑ 924	3¢	Telegraph Centenary	2.25	.80	.40
❑ 925	3¢	Corregidor	2.25	.80	.40
❑ 926	3¢	Motion Pictures	2.25	.80	.40

927

928

929

930

931

1945.

❑ 927	3¢	Florida	2.25	.75	.40
❑ 928	5¢	Toward United Nations	2.25	.75	.40
❑ 929	3¢	Iwo Jima	4.00	.75	.40
❑ 930	1¢	Roosevelt – Hyde Park	4.00	1.00	.50
❑ 931	2¢	Roosevelt – Warm Springs	2.25	.75	.40

Scott No.			Plate Block	Unused	Used
❑ 932	3¢	Roosevelt – White House	2.25	.80	.40
❑ 933	5¢	Roosevelt – Four Freedoms	2.25	.80	.40
❑ 934	3¢	Army – Victory March	2.25	.80	.40
❑ 935	3¢	Navy – Sailors	2.25	.80	.40
❑ 936	3¢	Coast Guard – Landing Craft	2.25	.80	.40
❑ 937	3¢	Alfred E. Smith	2.25	.80	.40
❑ 938	3¢	Texas Centennial	2.25	.80	.40

NOTE: Prices for stamps from 1935 forward are for never-hinged (NH) examples.

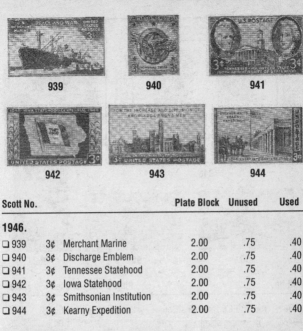

939   940   941

942   943   944

Scott No.			Plate Block	Unused	Used
1946.					
❏ 939	3¢	Merchant Marine	2.00	.75	.40
❏ 940	3¢	Discharge Emblem	2.00	.75	.40
❏ 941	3¢	Tennessee Statehood	2.00	.75	.40
❏ 942	3¢	Iowa Statehood	2.00	.75	.40
❏ 943	3¢	Smithsonian Institution	2.00	.75	.40
❏ 944	3¢	Kearny Expedition	2.00	.75	.40

945

946

947

1947.					
❏ 945	3¢	Thomas A. Edison	2.00	.75	.40
❏ 946	3¢	Joseph Pulitzer	2.00	.75	.40
❏ 947	3¢	U.S. Stamp Centenary	2.00	.75	.40

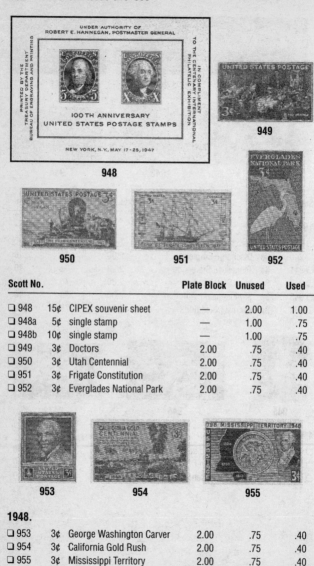

948

949

950

951

952

Scott No.			Plate Block	Unused	Used
❏ 948	15¢	CIPEX souvenir sheet	—	2.00	1.00
❏ 948a	5¢	single stamp	—	1.00	.75
❏ 948b	10¢	single stamp	—	1.00	.75
❏ 949	3¢	Doctors	2.00	.75	.40
❏ 950	3¢	Utah Centennial	2.00	.75	.40
❏ 951	3¢	Frigate Constitution	2.00	.75	.40
❏ 952	3¢	Everglades National Park	2.00	.75	.40

953

954

955

1948.

❏ 953	3¢	George Washington Carver	2.00	.75	.40
❏ 954	3¢	California Gold Rush	2.00	.75	.40
❏ 955	3¢	Mississippi Territory	2.00	.75	.40

Scott No.			Plate Block	Unused	Used
❏ 956	3¢	Immortal Chaplains	4.00	.40	.38
❏ 957	3¢	Wisconsin Centennial	1.25	.40	.38
❏ 958	5¢	Swedish Pioneers	4.00	.40	.38
❏ 959	3¢	Progress of Women	1.25	.40	.38
❏ 960	3¢	William Allen White	4.00	.40	.38
❏ 961	3¢	U.S. Canada Friendship	1.25	.40	.38
❏ 962	3¢	Francis Scott Key	2.00	.40	.38
❏ 963	3¢	Youth Month	1.25	.40	.38
❏ 964	3¢	Oregon Territory	1.25	.40	.38
❏ 965	3¢	Harlan Fiske Stone	4.00	.40	.38
❏ 966	3¢	Mount Palomar	4.00	.40	.38
❏ 967	3¢	Clara Barton	4.00	.40	.38

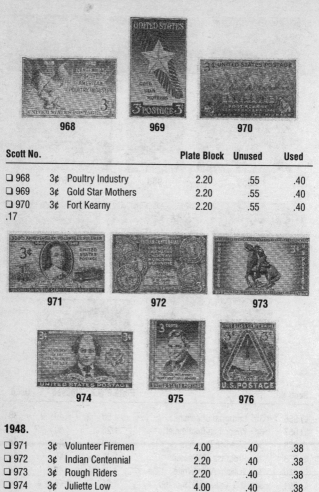

968 **969** **970**

Scott No.			Plate Block	Unused	Used
❏ 968	3¢	Poultry Industry	2.20	.55	.40
❏ 969	3¢	Gold Star Mothers	2.20	.55	.40
❏ 970	3¢	Fort Kearny	2.20	.55	.40

.17

971 **972** **973**

974 **975** **976**

1948.

❏ 971	3¢	Volunteer Firemen	4.00	.40	.38
❏ 972	3¢	Indian Centennial	2.20	.40	.38
❏ 973	3¢	Rough Riders	2.20	.40	.38
❏ 974	3¢	Juliette Low	4.00	.40	.38
❏ 975	3¢	Will Rogers	2.20	.40	.38
❏ 976	3¢	Fort Bliss Centennial	4.00	.40	.38

977   978   979

980

Scott No.			Plate Block	Unused	Used
❑ 977	3¢	Moina Michael	2.20	.40	.34
❑ 978	3¢	Gettysburg Address	4.00	.40	.34
❑ 979	3¢	American Turners	2.20	.40	.34
❑ 980	3¢	Joel Chandler Harris	4.00	.40	.34

981   982

983   984   985

1949.

❑ 981	3¢	Minnesota Centennia	.80	.40	.34
❑ 982	3¢	Washington & Lee University	1.60	.40	.34
❑ 983	3¢	Puerto Rico	1.60	.40	.34
❑ 984	3¢	Annapolis Tercentenary	1.60	.40	.34
❑ 985	3¢	G.A.R.	1.60	.40	.34

986   987   988   989

990   991   992

993   994   995

996   997

Scott No.			Plate Block	Unused	Used
1950.					
❑ 986	3¢	Edgar Allan Poe	2.50	.60	.34
❑ 987	3¢	American Bankers Assn.	4.00	.60	.34
❑ 988	3¢	Samuel Gompers	2.50	.38	.34
❑ 989	3¢	Capitol Dome Statue	2.50	.38	.34
❑ 990	3¢	White House	2.50	.38	.34
❑ 991	3¢	Supreme Court	2.50	.38	.34
❑ 992	3¢	Capitol Building	2.50	.38	.34
❑ 993	3¢	Casey Jones	4.00	.38	.34
❑ 994	3¢	Kansas City Centennial	4.00	.60	.34
❑ 995	3¢	Boy Scouts	4.00	.38	.34
❑ 996	3¢	Indiana Territory	2.50	.60	.34
❑ 997	3¢	California Statehood	2.50	.38	.34

998   999   1000

1001   1002   1003

Scott No.			Plate Block	Unused	Used
1951.					
❑ 998	3¢	United Confederate Vet	1.25	.50	.34
❑ 999	3¢	Nevada Settlement	1.25	.38	.34
❑ 1000	3¢	Cadillac at Detroit	1.25	.38	.34
❑ 1001	3¢	Colorado Statehood	2.00	.38	.34
❑ 1002	3¢	American Chemical Society	1.25	.38	.34
❑ 1003	3¢	Battle of Brooklyn	1.25	.38	.34

1004   1005   1006

1007   1008   1009

1952.					
❑ 1004	3¢	Betsy Ross	2.00	.35	.40
❑ 1005	3¢	4-H Clubs	2.00	.55	.40
❑ 1006	3¢	Baltimore & Ohio Railroad	1.25	.55	.40
❑ 1007	3¢	A.A.A.	1.25	.55	.40
❑ 1008	3¢	NATO	1.25	.38	.40
❑ 1009	3¢	Grand Coulee Dam	1.25	.38	.40

1010

1011

1012

1013

1014

1015

1016

Scott No.			Plate Block	Unused	Used
❑ 1010	3¢	Arrival of Lafayette	2.00	.38	.34
❑ 1011	3¢	Mount Rushmore	1.25	.38	.34
❑ 1012	3¢	Society of Civil Engineers	2.00	.38	.34
❑ 1013	3¢	Women in the Armed Forces	2.00	.38	.34
❑ 1014	3¢	Gutenberg & Printing	2.00	.38	.34
❑ 1015	3¢	Newspaper Boys	1.25	.38	.34
❑ 1016	3¢	International Red Cross	1.25	.38	.34

1017

1018

1019

1953.

❑ 1017	3¢	National Guard	1.25	.38	.34
❑ 1018	3¢	Ohio Statehood	2.00	.38	.34
❑ 1019	3¢	Washington Territory	1.25	.38	.34

1020	1021	1022
1023	1024	1025
1026	1027	1028

Scott No.			Plate Block	Unused	Used
❑ 1020	3¢	Louisiana Purchase	1.65	.38	.34
❑ 1021	5¢	Opening of Japan	2.00	.38	.34
❑ 1022	3¢	American Bar Assn.	1.65	.38	.34
❑ 1023	3¢	Sagamore Hill	1.65	.38	.34
❑ 1024	3¢	Future Farmers	1.65	.38	.34
❑ 1025	3¢	Trucking Industry	1.65	.38	.34
❑ 1026	3¢	George S. Patton	1.65	.38	.34
❑ 1027	3¢	New York City	2.00	.38	.34
❑ 1028	3¢	Gadsden Purchase	1.65	.38	.34

1029

1954.

❑ 1029	3¢	Columbia University	1.25	.38	.34

1030

1031
(1054)

1031A
(1054A)

1032

1033
(1055)

1034
(1056)

1035
(1057)

1036
(1058)

1037
(1059)

1038

1039

1040

1041

Scott No.			Plate Block	Unused	Used
1954–1961. Liberty Series					
❑ 1030	½¢	Benjamin Franklin	1.15	.42	.34
❑ 1031	1¢	George Washington	1.15	.42	.34
❑ 1031A	1¼¢	Palace of Governors	1.15	.42	.34
❑ 1032	1½¢	Mount Vernon	1.15	.42	.34
❑ 1033	2¢	Thomas Jefferson	1.15	.42	.34
❑ 1034	2½¢	Bunker Hill	4.00	.42	.34
❑ 1035	3¢	Statue of Liberty	1.15	.42	.34
❑ 1036	4¢	Abraham Lincoln	1.15	.55	.34
❑ 1037	4½¢	The Hermitage	1.15	.55	.34
❑ 1038	5¢	James Monroe	1.15	.55	.34
❑ 1039	6¢	Theodore Roosevelt	4.00	.55	.34
❑ 1040	7¢	Woodrow Wilson	1.15	.55	.34
❑ 1041	8¢	Statue of Liberty	4.00	.55	.34

1042   **1042A**   **1043**   **1044**

1044A   **1045**   **1046**   **1047**   **1048**
(1059A)

1049   **1050**   **1051**   **1052**   **1053**

Scott No.			Plate Block	Unused	Used
❑ 1042	8¢	Statue of Liberty (re-engraved)	2.15	.80	.34
❑ 1042A	8¢	John J. Pershing	2.15	.80	.34
❑ 1043	9¢	The Alamo	2.15	.80	.34
❑ 1044	10¢	Independence Hall	5.00	.80	.34
❑ 1044A	11¢	Statue of Liberty	2.15	.80	.34
❑ 1045	12¢	Benjamin Harrison	2.15	.80	.34
❑ 1046	15¢	John Jay	5.00	2.20	.34
❑ 1047	20¢	Monticello	5.00	2.20	.34
❑ 1048	25¢	Paul Revere	6.00	2.20	.34
❑ 1049	30¢	Robert E. Lee	8.00	2.20	.34
❑ 1050	40¢	John Marshall	12.00	4.00	.34
❑ 1051	50¢	S. B. Anthony	12.00	2.00	.34
❑ 1052	$1	Patrick Henry	30.00	7.00	2.00
❑ 1053	$5	Alexander Hamilton	400.00	115.00	12.00

Scott No.			Line Pair	Unused	Used
1954–1973. Coil Stamps.					
❏ 1054	1¢	George Washington (~1031)	1.25	.80	.38
❏ 1054A	1¼¢	Palace of Governors (~1031A)	2.00	.80	.38
❏ 1055	2¢	Thomas Jefferson (~1033)	2.00	.80	.38
❏ 1056	2½¢	Bunker Hill (~1034)	4.00	1.00	.38
❏ 1057	3¢	Statue of Liberty (~1035)	1.25	.80	.38
❏ 1058	4¢	Abraham Lincoln (~1036)	1.25	.80	.38
❏ 1059	4½¢	The Hermitage (~1037)	12.00	2.00	1.00
❏ 1059A	25¢	Paul Revere (~1048)	4.00	2.00	1.00

1060

1061

1062

1063

1064

1065

1066

Scott No.			Plate Block	Unused	Used
1954.					
❏ 1060	3¢	Nebraska Territory	1.25	.42	.34
❏ 1061	3¢	Kansas Territory	2.00	.42	.34
❏ 1062	3¢	George Eastman	1.25	.42	.34
❏ 1063	3¢	Lewis & Clark	2.00	.42	.34
1955.					
❏ 1064	3¢	Pennsylvania Academy	2.00	.65	.34
❏ 1065	3¢	Land Grant Colleges	1.25	.65	.34
❏ 1066	8¢	Rotary International	2.00	.65	.34

| 1067 | 1068 | 1069 |

| 1070 | 1071 | 1072 |

Scott No.			Plate Block	Unused	Used
❑ 1067	3¢	Armed Forces Reserves	1.15	.42	.34
❑ 1068	3¢	Old Man of the Mountains	1.50	.55	.34
❑ 1069	3¢	Great Lakes Transportation	1.15	.55	.34
❑ 1070	3¢	Atoms for Peace	1.15	.42	.34
❑ 1071	3¢	Fort Ticonderoga	2.00	.42	.34
❑ 1072	3¢	Andrew Mellon	1.15	.55	.34

| 1073 | 1074 |

1956.

❑ 1073	3¢	Benjamin Franklin	2.20	.42	.34
❑ 1074	3¢	Booker T. Washington	2.20	.42	.34

1075

1076

1077

1078

1079

1080

Scott No.			Plate Block	Unused	Used
❏ 1075	12¢	FIPEX Souvenir Sheet	—	4.00	2.00
❏ 1075a	3¢	single stamp	—	2.00	1.15
❏ 1075b	8¢	single stamp	—	2.00	1.15
❏ 1076	3¢	FIPEX	2.25	.42	.34
❏ 1077	3¢	Wild Turkey	2.25	.42	.34
❏ 1078	3¢	Pronghorn Antelope	2.25	.42	.34
❏ 1079	3¢	King Salmon	2.25	.42	.34
❏ 1080	3¢	Pure Food & Drug Act	4.00	.42	.34

1081

1082

1083

1084

1085

Scott No.			Plate Block	Unused	Used
❑ 1081	3¢	Wheatland	2.00	.55	.34
❑ 1082	3¢	Labor Day	1.15	.55	.34
❑ 1083	3¢	Nassau Hall	1.15	.42	.34
❑ 1084	3¢	Devils Tower	1.15	.42	.34
❑ 1085	3¢	Children's Stamp	1.15	.42	.34

1086

1087

1088

1089

1957.

❑ 1086	3¢	Alexander Hamilton	.85	.40	.34
❑ 1087	3¢	Fight Against Polio	.85	.40	.34
❑ 1088	3¢	Coast & Geodetic Survey	.85	.40	.34
❑ 1089	3¢	Architects	.85	.40	.34

1090

1091

1092

1093

1094

1095

1096

1097

1098

1099

Scott No.			Plate Block	Unused	Used
❏ 1090	3¢	American Steel Industry	1.65	.40	.34
❏ 1091	3¢	International Naval Review	1.65	.40	.34
❏ 1092	3¢	Oklahoma Statehood	1.65	.40	.34
❏ 1093	3¢	Teachers of America	1.65	.40	.34
❏ 1094	4¢	48-Star U.S. Flag	1.65	.40	.34
❏ 1095	3¢	Shipbuilding	2.00	.40	.34
❏ 1096	8¢	Ramon Magsaysay	1.65	.40	.34
❏ 1097	3¢	Lafayette Bicentennial	2.00	.40	.34
❏ 1098	3¢	Whooping Cranes	1.65	.40	.34
❏ 1099	3¢	Religious Freedom	1.65	.40	.34

1100   1104   1105

1106   1107   1108

1109   1110   1111   1112

Scott No.			Plate Block	Unused	Used
1958.					
❏ 1100	3¢	Gardening & Horticulture	.85	.40	.34
❏ 1104	3¢	Brussels Exhibition	.85	.40	.34
❏ 1105	3¢	James Monroe	.85	.40	.34
❏ 1106	3¢	Minnesota Statehood	.85	.40	.34
❏ 1107	3¢	International Geophysical Year	.85	.40	.34
❏ 1108	3¢	Gunston Hall	.85	.40	.34
❏ 1109	3¢	Mackinac Bridge	1.25	.50	.34
❏ 1110	4¢	Simon Bolivar	.85	.40	.34
❏ 1111	8¢	Simon Bolivar	2.00	.50	.34
❏ 1112	4¢	Atlantic Cable Centennial	.85	.40	.34

1113 **1114**

1115

1116

1117 **1118** **1119** **1120**

1121 **1123**

1122

Scott No.			Plate Block	Unused	Used
❑ 1113	1¢	Youthful Lincoln	1.25	.40	.34
❑ 1114	3¢	Bust of Lincoln	1.25	.40	.34
❑ 1115	4¢	Lincoln-Douglas Debates	2.00	.50	.34
❑ 1116	4¢	Statue of Lincoln	1.25	.40	.34
❑ 1117	4¢	Lajos Kossuth	1.25	.40	.34
❑ 1118	8¢	Lajos Kossuth	2.00	.40	.34
❑ 1119	4¢	Freedom of the Press	1.25	.40	.34
❑ 1120	4¢	Overland Mail	2.00	.40	.34
❑ 1121	4¢	Noah Webster	2.00	.40	.34
❑ 1122	4¢	Forest Conservation	1.25	.40	.34
❑ 1123	4¢	Fort Duquesne	1.25	.40	.34

1124

1125

1126

1127

1128

1129

1130

1131

1132

1133

1134

1135

Scott No.			Plate Block	Unused	Used
1959.					
❏ 1124	4¢	Oregon Statehood	1.25	.40	.34
❏ 1125	4¢	Jose de San Martin	.75	.40	.34
❏ 1126	8¢	Jose de San Martin	1.25	.40	.34
❏ 1127	4¢	NATO	.75	.40	.34
❏ 1128	4¢	Arctic Exploration	1.25	.40	.34
❏ 1129	8¢	Peace Through Trade	1.25	.40	.34
❏ 1130	4¢	Silver Centennial	.75	.40	.34
❏ 1131	4¢	St. Lawrence Seaway	1.25	.40	.34
❏ 1132	4¢	49-Star U.S. Flag	.75	.40	.34
❏ 1133	4¢	Soil Conservation	.75	.40	.34
❏ 1134	4¢	Petroleum Industry	1.25	.40	.34
❏ 1135	4¢	Dental Health	1.25	.40	.34

1136 **1137** **1138**

Scott No.			Plate Block	Unused	Used
❏ 1136	4¢	Ernst Reuter	.80	.40	.34
❏ 1137	8¢	Ernst Reuter	2.00	.40	.34
❏ 1138	4¢	Ephraim McDowell	2.00	.40	.34

1139 **1140** **1141**

1142 **1143** **1144**

1145

1960.

❏ 1139	4¢	Credo – Washington	1.25	.40	.34
❏ 1140	4¢	Credo – Franklin	1.25	.40	.34
❏ 1141	4¢	Credo – Jefferson	1.25	.40	.34
❏ 1142	4¢	Credo – Key	2.00	.40	.34
❏ 1143	4¢	Credo – Lincoln	1.25	.40	.34
❏ 1144	4¢	Credo – Henry	1.25	.40	.34
❏ 1145	4¢	Boy Scouts	2.00	.50	.34

1146 **1147** **1148** **1149**

1150 **1151** **1152**

1153 **1154** **1155** **1156**

Scott No.			Plate Block	Unused	Used
❏ 1146	4¢	Winter Olympics	1.60	.40	.34
❏ 1147	4¢	Thomas G. Masaryk	.80	.40	.34
❏ 1148	8¢	Thomas G. Masaryk	1.60	.40	.34
❏ 1149	4¢	World Refugee Year	1.60	.40	.34
❏ 1150	4¢	Water Conservation	.80	.40	.34
❏ 1151	4¢	SEATO	.80	.40	.34
❏ 1152	4¢	American Women	.75	.40	.34
❏ 1153	4¢	50-Star U.S. Flag	4.00	.50	.34
❏ 1154	4¢	Pony Express	.80	.40	.34
❏ 1155	4¢	Employ the Handicapped	1.60	.40	.34
❏ 1156	4¢	World Forestry Congress	.80	.40	.34

1157

1158

1159

1160

1161

1162

1163

1164

1165

1166

1167

Scott No.			Plate Block	Unused	Used
❑ 1157	4¢	Mexican Independence	.80	.40	.34
❑ 1158	4¢	U.S.-Japan Treaty	.80	.40	.34
❑ 1159	4¢	Ignacy Jan Paderewski	4.00	.40	.34
❑ 1160	8¢	Ignacy Jan Paderewski	4.00	.40	.34
❑ 1161	4¢	Robert A. Taft	1.25	.40	.34
❑ 1162	4¢	Wheels of Freedom	.80	.40	.34
❑ 1163	4¢	Boys' Clubs	1.25	.40	.34
❑ 1164	4¢	First Automated P.O.	4.00	.55	.34
❑ 1165	4¢	Gustaf Mannerheim	1.25	.40	.34
❑ 1166	8¢	Gustaf Mannerheim	4.00	.40	.34
❑ 1167	4¢	Campfire Girls	4.00	.40	.34

1168

1169

1170

1171

1172

1173

Scott No.			Plate Block	Unused	Used
❑ 1168	4¢	Guiseppe Garibaldi	.80	.40	.34
❑ 1169	8¢	Guiseppe Garibaldi	4.00	.55	.34
❑ 1170	4¢	Walter F. George	4.00	.55	.34
❑ 1171	4¢	Andrew Carnegie	1.15	.55	.34
❑ 1172	4¢	John Foster Dulles	1.15	.55	.34
❑ 1173	4¢	Echo I Satellite	4.00	.55	.34

1174

1175

1176

1961.

❑ 1174	4¢	Mahatma Gandhi	2.00	.40	.34
❑ 1175	8¢	Mahatma Gandhi	2.00	.40	.34
❑ 1176	4¢	Range Conservation	.85	.40	.34
❑ 1177	4¢	Horace Greeley	2.00	.40	.34

1177

1178

1179

1180

1181

1182

1183

1184

1186

1185

Scott No.			Plate Block	Unused	Used
❑ 1178	4¢	Fort Sumter	4.00	.55	.34
❑ 1179	4¢	Shiloh	4.00	.55	.34
❑ 1180	5¢	Gettysburg	4.00	.55	.34
❑ 1181	5¢	The Wilderness	4.00	.55	.34
❑ 1182	5¢	Appomattox	4.00	.55	.34
❑ 1183	4¢	Kansas Statehood	1.25	.40	.34
❑ 1184	4¢	George W. Norris	1.25	.55	.34
❑ 1185	4¢	Naval Aviation	1.25	.40	.34
❑ 1186	4¢	Workmen's Compensation	1.25	.40	.34

1187 **1188** **1189** **1190**

Scott No.			Plate Block	Unused	Used
❏ 1187	4¢	Frederick Remington	1.25	.75	.34
❏ 1188	4¢	Republic of China	1.25	.75	.34
❏ 1189	4¢	Naismith – Basketball	4.00	.75	.34
❏ 1190	4¢	Nursing	4.00	.75	.34

1191 **1192**

1193 **1194** **1195**

1962.

❏ 1191	4¢	New Mexico Statehood	.85	.40	.34
❏ 1192	4¢	Arizona Statehood	.85	.40	.34
❏ 1193	4¢	Project Mercury	1.15	.40	.34
❏ 1194	4¢	Malaria Eradication	.85	.40	.34
❏ 1195	4¢	Charles Evans Hughes	.85	.40	.34

1196

1197

1198

1199

1200

1201

1202

1203

1204

Scott No.			Plate Block	Unused	Used
❏ 1196	4¢	Seattle World's Fair	.80	.40	.34
❏ 1197	4¢	Louisiana Statehood	2.00	.55	.34
❏ 1198	4¢	The Homestead Act	1.25	.40	.34
❏ 1199	4¢	Girl Scouts	1.25	.40	.34
❏ 1200	4¢	Brien McMahon	1.25	.40	.34
❏ 1201	4¢	Apprenticeship Act	.80	.40	.34
❏ 1202	4¢	Sam Rayburn	1.25	.40	.34
❏ 1203	4¢	Dag Hammarskjold	.80	.40	.34
❏ 1204	4¢	Hammarskjold, yellow inverted	1.25	.40	.34

1205

1206

1207

Scott No.			Plate Block	Unused	Used
❏ 1205	4¢	Christmas Wreath	.80	.40	.34
❏ 1206	4¢	Higher Education	1.25	.40	.34
❏ 1207	4¢	Winslow Homer	1.25	.40	.34

1208

1209
(1225)

1213
(1229)

1962–1963. Definitives.

❏ 1208	5¢	U.S. Flag	.80	.40	.34
❏ 1209	1¢	Andrew Jackson	.80	.40	.34
❏ 1213	5¢	George Washington	.80	.40	.34

Scott No.			Line Pair	Unused	Used

Coil Stamps.

❏ 1225	1¢	Andrew Jackson (~1209)	2.00	1.25	.34
❏ 1229	5¢	George Washington (~1213)	4.00	2.00	.34

1230

1231

1232

1233

1234

1235

1236

1237

1238

Scott No.			Plate Block	Unused	Used
1963.					
❑ 1230	5¢	Carolina Charter	2.00	.55	.34
❑ 1231	5¢	Food for Peace	.75	.40	.34
❑ 1232	5¢	West Virginia Statehood	1.25	.40	.34
❑ 1233	5¢	Emancipation Proclamation	1.25	.40	.34
❑ 1234	5¢	Alliance for Progress	.75	.40	.34
❑ 1235	5¢	Cordell Hull	4.00	.55	.34
❑ 1236	5¢	Eleanor Roosevelt	1.25	.40	.34
❑ 1237	5¢	The Sciences	1.25	.40	.34
❑ 1238	5¢	City Mail Delivery	1.25	.40	.34

1239   **1240**   **1241**

Scott No.			Plate Block	Unused	Used
❑ 1239	5¢	International Red Cross	.80	.38	.32
❑ 1240	5¢	Christmas Tree	1.00	.38	.32
❑ 1241	5¢	John James Audubon	2.00	.38	.32

1243   **1244**

1242

1246

1245   **1247**

1964.

❑ 1242	5¢	Sam Houston	1.25	.55	.34
❑ 1243	5¢	Charles M. Russell	4.00	.55	.34
❑ 1244	5¢	New York World's Fair	1.25	.55	.34
❑ 1245	5¢	John Muir	.80	.42	.34
❑ 1246	5¢	John F. Kennedy	4.25	.85	.34
❑ 1247	5¢	New Jersey Statehood	4.25	.85	.34

1248   **1249**   **1250**

1251   **1252**   **1253**

1254   **1255**   **1256**   **1257**

Scott No.			Plate Block	Unused	Used
❏ 1248	5¢	Nevada Statehood	1.60	.40	.34
❏ 1249	5¢	Register & Vote	.80	.40	.34
❏ 1250	5¢	William Shakespeare	.80	.40	.34
❏ 1251	5¢	The Doctors Mayo	1.60	.40	.34
❏ 1252	5¢	American Music	1.50	.40	.34
❏ 1253	5¢	Homemakers	1.60	.40	.34
❏ 1254	5¢	Holly	—	.70	.40
❏ 1255	5¢	Mistletoe	—	.70	.40
❏ 1256	5¢	Poinsettia	—	.70	.40
❏ 1257	5¢	Conifer	—	.70	.40
		Block of 4 (1254–1257)	10.00	4.00	2.00

1258　　　　**1259**　　　　**1260**

Scott No.			Plate Block	Unused	Used
❑ 1258	5¢	Verrazano Bridge	4.00	.40	.34
❑ 1259	5¢	Modern Art	1.25	.40	.34
❑ 1260	5¢	Amateur Radio	1.25	.50	.34

1261　　　　**1262**　　　　**1263**

1264　　　　**1265**　　　　**1266**

1965.

❑ 1261	5¢	Battle of New Orleans	4.00	.55	.34
❑ 1262	5¢	Fitness – Discus Thrower	1.15	.40	.34
❑ 1263	5¢	Crusade Against Cancer	.80	.40	.34
❑ 1264	5¢	Winston Churchill	1.15	.40	.34
❑ 1265	5¢	Magna Carta	1.15	.40	.34
❑ 1266	5¢	International Cooperation Year	.80	.40	.34

1267

1268

1269

1270

1272

1271

1273

1274

1275   1276

Scott No.			Plate Block	Unused	Used
❑ 1267	5¢	Salvation Army	1.25	.40	.34
❑ 1268	5¢	Dante Alighieri	.80	.40	.34
❑ 1269	5¢	Herbert Hoover	1.25	.40	.34
❑ 1270	5¢	Robert Fulton	1.15	.40	.34
❑ 1271	5¢	Florida Settlement	1.15	.40	.34
❑ 1272	5¢	Traffic Safety	1.15	.40	.34
❑ 1273	5¢	John Singleton Copley	1.25	.40	.34
❑ 1274	11¢	I.T.U.	5.00	.65	.38
❑ 1275	5¢	Adlai E. Stevenson	.80	.40	.34
❑ 1276	5¢	Christmas Angel & Trumpet	.80	.40	.34

1278
(1299)

1279

1280

1281
(1297)

1282
(1303)

1283
(1304)

1283B
(1304C)

1284
(1298)

1285

1286

1286A

1287

Scott No.			Plate Block	Unused	Used
1965–1978. Prominent Americans Series.					
❑ 1278	1¢	Thomas Jefferson	2.25	.40	.34
❑ 1279	1¼¢	Albert Gallatin	10.00	.40	.34
❑ 1280	2¢	Frank Lloyd Wright	.75	.40	.34
❑ 1281	3¢	Francis Parkman	.75	.40	.34
❑ 1282	4¢	Abraham Lincoln	2.00	.50	.34
❑ 1283	5¢	George Washington	.80	.40	.34
❑ 1283B	5¢	Washington ("clean shaven")	.80	.40	.34
❑ 1284	6¢	Franklin D. Roosevelt	1.25	.40	.34
❑ 1285	8¢	Albert Einstein	1.25	.70	.34
❑ 1286	10¢	Andrew Jackson	2.00	.70	.34
❑ 1286A	12¢	Henry Ford	2.00	.70	.34
❑ 1287	13¢	John F. Kennedy	4.00	.85	.34

1288
(1288d, 1288B,
1305E)

1289

1290

1291

1292

1293

1294
(1305C)

1295

Scott No.			Plate Block	Unused	Used
❑ 1288	15¢	Oliver Wendell Holmes (type I)	2.00	.85	.34
❑ 1288d	15¢	Holmes (~1288) (type II)	12.00	1.00	.34

Type I: The tip of the necktie touches the coat. Type II: The tip of the necktie is well clear of the coat.

Scott No.			Plate Block	Unused	Used
❑ 1288B	15¢	Holmes (~1288), perf 10	8.00	.85	.34
		Booklet pane of 8	—	4.00	2.00
❑ 1289	20¢	George C. Marshall	4.00	.80	.34
❑ 1290	25¢	Frederick Douglass	4.00	2.25	.34
❑ 1291	30¢	John Dewey	6.00	2.25	.34
❑ 1292	40¢	Thomas Paine	5.00	2.25	.34
❑ 1293	50¢	Lucy Stone	6.00	2.25	.34
❑ 1294	$1	Eugene O'Neill	15.00	4.00	.34
❑ 1295	$5	John Bassett Moore	60.00	14.00	2.50

Scott No.			Line Pair	Unused	Used

Coil Stamps. Perforated 10 Horizontally.

Scott No.			Line Pair	Unused	Used
❑ 1297	3¢	Francis Parkman (~1281).	2.00	.40	.34
❑ 1298	6¢	Franklin D. Roosevelt (~1284)	2.00	.40	.34

1305

Scott No.			Line Pair	Unused	Used
Coil Stamps. Perforated 10 Vertically.					
❑ 1299	1¢	Thomas Jefferson (~1278)	1.00	.40	.34
❑ 1303	4¢	Abraham Lincoln (~1282)	1.00	.40	.34
❑ 1304	5¢	George Washington (~1283)	.85	.40	.34
❑ 1304C	5¢	Washington ("clean shaven") (~1283B)	2.00	.40	.34
❑ 1305	6¢	Franklin D. Roosevelt	1.00	.40	.34
❑ 1305C	$1	Eugene O'Neill (~1294)	7.00	4.00	2.00
❑ 1305E	15¢	Holmes (~1288)	4.00	2.00	.80

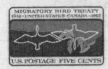

1306

1307

1308

1309

Scott No.			Plate Block	Unused	Used
1966.					
❑ 1306	5¢	Migratory Bird Treaty	.80	.40	.34
❑ 1307	5¢	Humane Treatment of Animals	.80	.40	.34
❑ 1308	5¢	Indiana Statehood	4.00	.50	.34
❑ 1309	5¢	Circus Clown	1.15	.40	.34

1310

1311

1312

1313

1314

Scott No.			Plate Block	Unused	Used
❑ 1310	5¢	SIPEX	1.15	.40	.34
❑ 1311	5¢	SIPEX souvenir sheet	1.15	.55	.34
❑ 1312	5¢	Bill of Rights	.80	.40	.34
❑ 1313	5¢	Polish Millennium	.80	.40	.34
❑ 1314	5¢	National Park Service	1.15	.40	.34

1315

1316

1317

1318

1319

1320

1321

1322

Scott No.			Plate Block	Unused	Used
❏ 1315	5¢	Marine Corps Reserve	.85	.40	.34
❏ 1316	5¢	Women's Clubs	.85	.40	.34
❏ 1317	5¢	Johnny Appleseed	4.00	.40	.34
❏ 1318	5¢	Beautification	1.00	.40	.34
❏ 1319	5¢	Great River Road	.85	.40	.34
❏ 1320	5¢	Servicemen & Savings Bonds	1.00	.40	.34
❏ 1321	5¢	Christmas – Madonna	.85	.40	.34
❏ 1322	5¢	Mary Cassatt	1.00	.40	.34

1323

1324

1325

1326

1327

1328

1329

1330

Scott No.			Plate Block	Unused	Used
1967.					
❑ 1323	5¢	Grange Centenary	2.00	.40	.34
❑ 1324	5¢	Canada Centennial	.80	.40	.34
❑ 1325	5¢	Erie Canal	1.15	.50	.34
❑ 1326	5¢	Search for Peace	4.00	.40	.34
❑ 1327	5¢	Henry David Thoreau	1.15	.50	.34
❑ 1328	5¢	Nebraska Statehood	4.00	.50	.34
❑ 1329	5¢	Voice of America	1.15	.40	.34
❑ 1330	5¢	Davy Crockett	1.15	.50	.34

1331–1332

1333 **1334** **1335**

1336 **1337**

Scott No.			Plate Block	Unused	Used
❑ 1331	5¢	Astronaut EVA	—	1.00	.34
❑ 1332	5¢	Gemini Capsule	—	4.00	.34
		Se-tenant pair (1331–1332)	5.00	2.00	1.50
❑ 1333	5¢	Urban Planning	.85	.40	.34
❑ 1334	5¢	Finland Independence	2.00	.40	.34
❑ 1335	5¢	Thomas Eakins	2.00	.40	.34
❑ 1336	5¢	Christmas – Madonna	.85	.40	.34
❑ 1337	5¢	Mississippi Statehood	4.00	.80	.34

1338
(1338A, 1338D)

1338F
(1338G)

Scott No.			Plate Block	Unused	Used
1968. Definitive.					
☐ 1338	6¢	U.S. Flag, perf 11	1.00	.80	.34

Scott No.			Line Pair	Unused	Used
Coil Stamp.					
☐ 1338A	6¢	U.S. Flag (~1338)	7.00	.40	.34

Scott No.			Plate Block	Unused	Used
1970–1971.					
☐ 1338D	6¢	U.S. Flag (~1338), perf 11x10½	4.00 (20)	.40	.34
☐ 1338F	8¢	U.S. Flag, perf 11 x 10½	5.00	.40	.34

Scott No.			Line Pair	Unused	Used
Coil Stamp.					
☐ 1338G	8¢	U.S. Flag (~1338F)	4.25	.40	.34

1341

1339   **1340**

1342    **1343**   **1344**

Scott No.			Plate Block	Unused	Used
1968.					
❑ 1339	6¢	Illinois Statehood	4.00	.75	.34
❑ 1340	6¢	Hemisfair '68	.80	.75	.34
❑ 1341	$1	Airlift	12.00	2.60	2.00
❑ 1342	6¢	Support Our Youth	1.15	.75	.34
❑ 1343	6¢	Law & Order	1.15	.75	.34
❑ 1344	6¢	Register & Vote	1.15	.25	.34

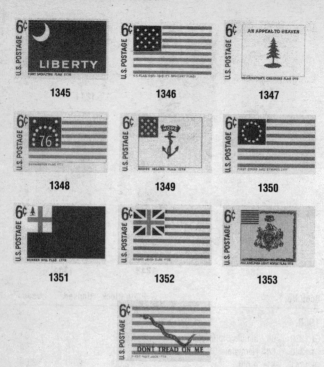

Scott No.			Plate Block	Unused	Used
❑ 1345	6¢	Fort Moultrie Flag	—	.90	.75
❑ 1346	6¢	Fort McHenry Flag	—	.90	.75
❑ 1347	6¢	Washington's Cruisers Flag	—	.90	.75
❑ 1348	6¢	Bennington Flag	—	.90	.75
❑ 1349	6¢	Rhode Island Flag	—	.90	.75
❑ 1350	6¢	First Stars & Stripes	—	.90	.75
❑ 1351	6¢	Bunker Hill Flag	—	.90	.75
❑ 1352	6¢	Grand Union Flag	—	.90	.75
❑ 1353	6¢	Philadelphia Light Horse Flag	—	.90	.75
❑ 1354	6¢	First Navy Jack	—	.90	.75
		Strip of 10 (1345–1354)	12.00 (4)	5.00	4.00

1355

1356

1357

1358

1359

1360

1361

1362

1363

1364

Scott No.			Plate Block	Unused	Used
❑ 1355	6¢	Walt Disney	4.15	2.00	.34
❑ 1356	6¢	Father Marquette	4.15	.80	.34
❑ 1357	6¢	Daniel Boone	4.15	.80	.34
❑ 1358	6¢	Arkansas River Navigation	4.15	.80	.34
❑ 1359	6¢	Leif Erikson	1.25	.80	.34
❑ 1360	6¢	Cherokee Strip Land Rush	4.00	.80	.34
❑ 1361	6¢	John Trumball	4.00	.80	.34
❑ 1362	6¢	Waterfowl Conservation	1.25	.80	.34
❑ 1363	6¢	Christmas – Madonna	6.00 (10)	.80	.34
❑ 1364	6¢	Chief Joseph	2.00	.80	.34

1365–1368

Scott No.			Plate Block	Unused	Used
1969.					
☐ 1365	6¢	Beautification – Cities	—	.75	.34
☐ 1366	6¢	Beautification – Parks	—	.75	.34
☐ 1367	6¢	Beautification – Highways	—	.75	.34
☐ 1368	6¢	Beautification – Streets	—	.75	.34
		Block of 4 (1365–1368)	4.00	2.00	1.00
☐ 1369	6¢	American Legion	.85	.55	.34
☐ 1370	6¢	Grandma Moses	.85	.55	.34
☐ 1371	6¢	Apollo 8	1.25	.55	.34
☐ 1372	6¢	W. C. Handy	4.00	.55	.34

1374

1375

1373

1376–1379

1380

1381

1382

Scott No.			Plate Block	Unused	Used
❑ 1373	6¢	Settlement of California	2.25	.75	.34
❑ 1374	6¢	John Wesley Powell	4.00	.75	.34
❑ 1375	6¢	Alabama Statehood	2.00	.75	.34
❑ 1376	6¢	Pseudotsuga menziesii	—	.90	.34
❑ 1377	6¢	Cypridedium reginae	—	.90	.34
❑ 1378	6¢	Fouquieria splendens	—	.90	.34
❑ 1379	6¢	Franklinia alatamaha	—	.90	.34
		Block of 4 (1376–1379)	4.00	.90	.34
❑ 1380	6¢	Daniel Webster	2.25	.80	.34
❑ 1381	6¢	Professional Baseball	4.00	1.00	.34
❑ 1382	6¢	Intercollegiate Football	4.00	.80	.34

1384

1383

1385

1386

Scott No.			Plate Block	Unused	Used
❏ 1383	6¢	Dwight D. Eisenhower	.80	.40	.34
❏ 1384	6¢	Christmas – Winter Scene	4.00 (10)	.40	.34
❏ 1385	6¢	Hope for the Crippled	.80	.40	.34
❏ 1386	6¢	William Harnett Painting	.80	.40	.34

1376–1379

1970.

❏ 1387	6¢	American Bald Eagle	—	.55	.34
❏ 1388	6¢	African Elephant Herd	—	.55	.34
❏ 1389	6¢	Haida Ceremonial Canoe	—	.75	.34
❏ 1390	6¢	The Age of Reptiles	—	.75	.34
		Block of 4 (1387–1390)	2.00	.80	.60

1391

1392

Scott No.			Plate Block	Unused	Used
❏ 1391	6¢	Maine Statehood	2.00	.80	.34
❏ 1392	6¢	Conservation – Bison	2.00	.80	.34

1393
(1401)

1393D

1394
(1395, 1402)

1396

1970–1974. Definitives.

❏ 1393	6¢	Dwight D. Eisenhower	.80	.65	.32
		Booklet pane of 5 + label	—	1.75	1.25
		Booklet pane of 8	—	2.00	1.25
❏ 1393D	7¢	Benjamin Franklin	2.00	.40	.32
❏ 1394	8¢	Eisenhower, red, black & blue	2.00	.40	.32
❏ 1395	8¢	Eisenhower (~1394), claret	—	.40	.32
		Booklet pane of 4 + 2 labels	—	2.00	.80
		Booklet pane of 6	—	2.00	1.60
		Booklet pane of 7 + 1 label	—	4.00	1.60
		Booklet pane of 8	—	4.00	1.75
❏ 1396	8¢	U.S.P.S. Emblem	5.00	.65	.30

1397

1398

1399

1400

Scott No.			Plate Block	Unused	Used
❑ 1397	14¢	Fiorello LaGuardia	2.00	.65	.34
❑ 1398	16¢	Ernie Pyle	2.00	.65	.34
❑ 1399	18¢	Elizabeth Blackwell	2.00	.65	.34
❑ 1400	21¢	Amadeo P. Giannini	4.00	.80	.34

Scott No.			Line Pair	Unused	Used
Coil Stamps. Perforated 10 Vertically.					
❑ 1401	6¢	Eisenhower (~1393)	.85	.55	.34
❑ 1402	8¢	Eisenhower (~1394) claret	.85	.55	.34

1405

1406

1407

1408

1409

Scott No.			Plate Block	Unused	Used
1970.					
❑ 1405	6¢	Edgar Lee Masters	2.00	.55	.34
❑ 1406	6¢	Women's Suffrage	1.25	.40	.34
❑ 1407	6¢	South Carolina	2.00	.55	.34
❑ 1408	6¢	Stone Mountain	—	.55	.34
❑ 1409	6¢	Fort Snelling	2.00	.40	.34

1410–1413

1414

1414a

1415–1418

Scott No.			Plate Block	Unused	Used
❑ 1410	6¢	Save Our Soil	—	.75	.34
❑ 1411	6¢	Save Our Cities	—	.75	.34
❑ 1412	6¢	Save Our Water	—	.75	.34
❑ 1413	6¢	Save Our Air	—	.75	.34
		Block of 4 (1410–1413)	6.00 (10)	2.00	1.15
❑ 1414	6¢	Christmas – Manger Scene	4.00 (8)	.50	.34
❑ 1414a	6¢	Christmas, precanceled	4.00 (8)	.50	.34
❑ 1415	6¢	Locomotive	—	.75	.34
❑ 1416	6¢	Toy Horse	—	.75	.34
❑ 1417	6¢	Tricycle	—	.75	.34
❑ 1418	6¢	Doll Carriage	—	.75	.34
		Block of 4 (1415–1418)	6.00 (8)	5.00	4.00

1415a–1418a

1419

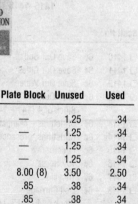

1420

1421   **1422**

Scott No.			Plate Block	Unused	Used
❑ 1415a	6¢	Locomotive, precanceled	—	1.25	.34
❑ 1416a	6¢	Toy Horse, precanceled	—	1.25	.34
❑ 1417a	6¢	Tricycle, precanceled	—	1.25	.34
❑ 1418a	6¢	Doll Carriage, precanceled	—	1.25	.34
		Block of 4 (1415a–1418a)	8.00 (8)	3.50	2.50
❑ 1419	6¢	United Nations	.85	.38	.34
❑ 1420	6¢	Landing of the Pilgrims	.85	.38	.34
❑ 1421	6¢	Disabled Veterans	—	.55	.40
❑ 1422	6¢	Honoring U.S. Servicemen	—	.55	.40
		Se-tenant pair (1421–1422)	2.00	.75	.50

UNITED STATES

AMERICA'S WOOL
1423

DOUGLAS MacARTHUR
1424

1425

Missouri 1821-1971 United States 8c

1426

1427–1430

Scott No.			Plate Block	Unused	Used
1971.					
❏ 1423	6¢	America's Wool	.85	.40	.34
❏ 1424	6¢	Douglas MacArthur	2.00	.40	.34
❏ 1425	6¢	Giving Blood Saves Lives	.85	.40	.34
❏ 1426	8¢	Missouri Statehood	5.00 (12)	.50	.40
❏ 1427	8¢	Trout	—	.50	.40
❏ 1428	8¢	Alligator	—	.50	.40
❏ 1429	8¢	Polar Bear	—	.50	.40
❏ 1430	8¢	California Condor	—	.50	.40
		Block of 4 (1427–1430)	4.00	2.00	1.25

1431

1432

1433

1434–1435

1436

1437

1438

1439

Scott No.			Plate Block	Unused	Used
☐ 1431	8¢	Antarctic Treaty	1.25	.40	.34
☐ 1432	8¢	Revolution Bicentennial	1.25	.40	.34
☐ 1433	8¢	John Sloan	1.25	.40	.34
☐ 1434	8¢	Earth & Lander	1.25	.40	.34
☐ 1435	8¢	Lunar Rover	1.25	.40	.34
		Se-tenant pair (1434–1435)	1.25	.75	.50
☐ 1436	8¢	Emily Dickinson	2.00	.40	.34
☐ 1437	8¢	San Juan, Puerto Rico	1.25	.40	.34
☐ 1438	8¢	Prevent Drug Abuse	2.00 (6)	.40	.34
☐ 1439	8¢	CARE	2.00 (8)	.40	.34

1440–1443

1444

1445

1446

1447

Scott No.			Plate Block	Unused	Used
❑ 1440	8¢	Decatur Home	—	.50	.34
❑ 1441	8¢	The Charles W. Morgan	—	.50	.34
❑ 1442	8¢	San Francisco Cable Car	—	.50	.34
❑ 1443	8¢	San Xavier del Bac Mission	—	.50	.34
		Block of 4 (1440–1443)	2.00	1.00	.75
❑ 1444	8¢	Christmas – Manger Scene	5.25 (12)	.50	.34
❑ 1445	8¢	Christmas – Partridge	5.25 (12)	.50	.34
1972.					
❑ 1446	8¢	Sidney Lanier	2.00	.60	.34
❑ 1447	8¢	Peace Corps	2.00 (6)	.38	.34

1448–1451

1452

1453

1454

1455

Scott No.			Plate Block	Unused	Used
❑ 1448	2¢	Hatteras – Shipwreck in Surf	—	.50	.34
❑ 1449	2¢	Hatteras – Lighthouse	—	.50	.34
❑ 1450	2¢	Hatteras – 3 Shorebirds	—	.50	.34
❑ 1451	2¢	Hatteras – Shorebirds & Dunes	—	.50	.34
		Block of 4 (1448–1451)	1.25	.50	.34
❑ 1452	6¢	Wolf Trap Farm	4.00	.50	.34
❑ 1453	8¢	Old Faithful	1.25	.40	.34
❑ 1454	15¢	Mount McKinley	4.00	.40	.34
❑ 1455	8¢	Family Planning	1.25	.40	.34

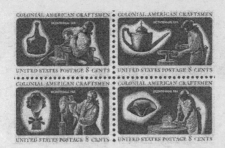

1456–1459

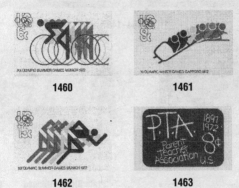

1460   **1461**

1462   **1463**

Scott No.			Plate Block	Unused	Used
❑ 1456	8¢	Craftsmen – Glass Blower	—	.50	.34
❑ 1457	8¢	Craftsmen – Silversmith	—	.50	.34
❑ 1458	8¢	Craftsmen – Wigmaker	—	.50	.34
❑ 1459	8¢	Craftsmen – Hatter	—	.50	.34
		Block of 4 (1456–1459)	2.00	1.00	1.00
❑ 1460	6¢	Cycling	2.00 (10)	.40	.34
❑ 1461	8¢	Bobsledding	4.00 (10)	.40	.34
❑ 1462	15¢	Running	4.00 (10)	.50	.34
❑ 1463	8¢	P.T.A.	1.25	.45	.34
❑ 1463a	8¢	P.T.A., reversed plate number	1.25	—	—

1464–1467

1468

1469

1470

Scott No.			Plate Block	Unused	Used
❏ 1464	8¢	Fur Seal	—	.55	.34
❏ 1465	8¢	Cardinal	—	.55	.34
❏ 1466	8¢	Brown Pelican	—	.55	.34
❏ 1467	8¢	Bighorn Sheep	—	.55	.34
		Block of 4 (1464–1467)	2.00	.75	.50
❏ 1468	8¢	Mail Order	4.25 (12)	.55	.35
❏ 1469	8¢	Osteopathic Medicine	2.00 (6)	.55	.35
❏ 1470	8¢	Tom Sawyer	2.00	.55	.35

1471

1472

1473

1474

Scott No.			Plate Block	Unused	Used
❑ 1471	8¢	Christmas – Angels	4.00 (12)	.40	.34
❑ 1472	8¢	Christmas – Santa	4.00 (12)	.40	.34
❑ 1473	8¢	Pharmacy	2.25	.50	.34
❑ 1474	8¢	Stamp Collecting	2.25	.40	.34

1475

1476

1477

1478

1479

1973.

❑ 1475	8¢	LOVE	2.00 (6)	.40	.34
❑ 1476	8¢	Colonial Printing Press	1.65	.40	.34
❑ 1477	8¢	Posting a Broadside	1.65	.40	.34
❑ 1478	8¢	Post Rider	1.65	.40	.34
❑ 1479	8¢	Drummer	1.65	.40	.34

1480–1483

Scott No.			Plate Block	Unused	Used
❏ 1480	8¢	Tea Party – Dumping Tea	—	.55	.34
❏ 1481	8¢	Tea Party – Ship at Anchor	—	.55	.34
❏ 1482	8¢	Tea Party – Boats & Lantern	—	.55	.34
❏ 1483	8¢	Tea Party – Bystanders on Pier	—	.55	.34
		Block of 4 (1480–1483)	2.00	1.00	.80
❏ 1484	8¢	George Gershwin	4.25 (12)	.55	.34
❏ 1485	8¢	Robinson Jeffers	4.25 (12)	.55	.34
❏ 1486	6¢	Henry O. Tanner	4.25 (12)	.55	.34
❏ 1487	8¢	Willa Cather	5.00 (12)	.55	.34
❏ 1488	8¢	Copernicus	2.00	.55	.34

1489–1492

1493–1496

1497–1498

Scott No.			Plate Block	Unused	Used
❑ 1489	8¢	Window Clerk	—	.75	.34
❑ 1490	8¢	Collecting Mail	—	.75	.34
❑ 1491	8¢	Conveyor Belt	—	.75	.34
❑ 1492	8¢	Bagging Parcels	—	.75	.34
❑ 1493	8¢	Mail in Trays	—	.75	.34
❑ 1494	8¢	Sorting to Pigeonholes	—	.75	.34
❑ 1495	8¢	Keypunch Operators	—	.75	.34
❑ 1496	8¢	Loading Mail Truck	—	.75	.34
❑ 1497	8¢	Carrier Walking Route	—	.75	.34
❑ 1498	8¢	Rural Delivery Carrier	—	.75	.34
		Strip of 10 (1489–1498)	6.00 (20)	4.00	2.00

Harry S. Truman

U.S. Postage 8 cents

1499

Progress in Electronics

1500

Progress in Electronics

1501

Progress in Electronics

1502

Lyndon B. Johnson
United States
8 cents

1503

RURAL AMERICA

1504

RURAL AMERICA

1505

RURAL AMERICA

1506

Scott No.			Plate Block	Unused	Used
❑ 1499	8¢	Harry S. Truman	2.15	.55	.34
❑ 1500	6¢	Spark Coil & Spark Gap	2.15	.40	.34
❑ 1501	8¢	Transistors	2.15	.40	.34
❑ 1502	15¢	Microphone & Speaker	2.15	.40	.34
❑ 1503	8¢	Lyndon B. Johnson	4.00 (12)	.40	.34
❑ 1504	8¢	Angus Cattle	2.15	.40	.34
❑ 1505	10¢	Chautauqua	2.15	.40	.34
❑ 1506	10¢	Winter Wheat	2.15	.40	.34

1507

1508

Scott No.			Plate Block	Unused	Used
❑ 1507	8¢	Madonna & Child	2.75 (12)	.50	.34
❑ 1508	8¢	Christmas Tree	2.75 (12)	.50	.34

1509
(1519)

1510
(1520)

1511

1973–1974. Definitives.

❑ 1509	10¢	Crossed Flags	6.00 (20)	.50	.34
❑ 1510	10¢	Jefferson Memorial	2.25	.50	.34
❑ 1511	10¢	ZIP Code	4.00 (8)	.50	.34

1518

Scott No.			Line Pair	Unused	Used

Coil Stamps.

❑ 1518	6.3¢	Liberty Bell	.85	.38	.34
❑ 1519	10¢	Crossed Flags (~1509)	—	.45	.34
❑ 1520	10¢	Jefferson Memorial (~1510)	.85	.45	.34

1525

1526

1527

1528

1529

Scott No.			Plate Block	Unused	Used

1974.

❑ 1525	10¢	V.F.W.	2.25	.55	.34
❑ 1526	10¢	Robert Frost	2.25	.55	.34
❑ 1527	10¢	Expo '74	4.00 (12)	.40	.34
❑ 1528	10¢	Horse Racing	5.00 (12)	.55	.34
❑ 1529	10¢	Skylab	2.25	.55	.34

1530–1437

Scott No.			Plate Block	Unused	Used
❏ 1530	10¢	UPU – Raphael	—	.55	.40
❏ 1531	10¢	UPU – Hokusai	—	.55	.40
❏ 1532	10¢	UPU – Peto	—	.55	.40
❏ 1533	10¢	UPU – Liotard	—	.55	.40
❏ 1534	10¢	UPU – Terborch	—	.55	.40
❏ 1535	10¢	UPU – Chardin	—	.55	.40
❏ 1536	10¢	UPU – Gainsborough	—	.55	.40
❏ 1537	10¢	UPU – Goya	—	.55	.40
		Block of 8 (1530–1537)	8.00 (16)	4.00	2.25

1538–1441

1542

1543–1446

Scott No.			Plate Block	Unused	Used
❑ 1538	10¢	Minerals – Petrified Wood	—	.40	.34
❑ 1539	10¢	Minerals – Tourmaline	—	.40	.34
❑ 1540	10¢	Minerals – Amethyst	—	.40	.34
❑ 1541	10¢	Minerals – Rhodochrosite	—	.40	.34
		Block of 4 (1538–1541)	4.00	1.50	1.00
❑ 1542	10¢	Fort Harrod Bicentennial	2.25	.50	.34
❑ 1543	10¢	Carpenters' Hall	—	.40	.34
❑ 1544	10¢	We Ask But For Peace	—	.40	.34
❑ 1545	10¢	Deriving Their Just Powers	—	.40	.34
❑ 1546	10¢	Independence Hall	—	.40	.34
		Block of 4 (1543–1546)	2.25	1.50	1.00

1547

1548

1549

1550

1551

1552

Scott No.			Plate Block	Unused	Used
❏ 1547	10¢	Energy Conservation	2.25	.55	.34
❏ 1548	10¢	Legend of Sleepy Hollow	2.25	.55	.34
❏ 1549	10¢	Retarded Children	2.25	.55	.34
❏ 1550	10¢	Christmas – Angel	4.00 (10)	.55	.34
❏ 1551	10¢	Christmas – Currier & Ives	4.00 (12)	.55	.34
❏ 1552	10¢	Christmas – Weather Vane	6.00 (20)	.55	.34

1553   **1554**   **1555**

1556   **1557**

1558   **1559**

1560   **1561**

Scott No.			Plate Block	Unused	Used
1975.					
☐ 1553	10¢	Benjamin West	5.00 (10)	.75	.34
☐ 1554	10¢	Paul Laurence Dunbar	5.00 (10)	.75	.34
☐ 1555	10¢	D. W. Griffith	2.25	.75	.34
☐ 1556	10¢	Pioneer 10	2.25	.55	.34
☐ 1557	10¢	Mariner 10	2.25	.55	.34
☐ 1558	10¢	Collective Bargaining	4.00 (8)	.55	.34
☐ 1559	8¢	Sybil Ludington	4.00 (10)	.55	.34
☐ 1560	10¢	Salem Poor	4.00 (10)	.55	.34
☐ 1561	10¢	Haym Salomon	4.00 (10)	.55	.34

1562

US Bicentennial IOcents

1563

US Bicentennial IOc

1564

1565–1568

1569–1570

Scott No.			Plate Block	Unused	Used
❏ 1562	18¢	Peter Francisco	6.00 (10)	.50	.34
❏ 1563	10¢	Lexington & Concord	4.15 (12)	.50	.34
❏ 1564	10¢	Battle of Bunker Hill	4.15 (12)	.50	.34
❏ 1565	10¢	Continental Army	4.15 (12)	.50	.34
❏ 1566	10¢	Continental Navy	4.15 (12)	.50	.34
❏ 1567	10¢	Continental Marines	4.15 (12)	.50	.34
❏ 1568	10¢	American Militia	4.15 (12)	.50	.34
		Block of 4 (1565–1568)	4.15 (12)	.75	.65
❏ 1569	10¢	Apollo-Soyuz & Earth	4.15 (12)	.50	.34
❏ 1570	10¢	Apollo-Soyuz & Logo	4.15 (12)	.50	.34
		Pair (1569–1570)	4.15 (12)	.75	.65

1571

1576

1572–1575

1577–1578

Scott No.			Plate Block	Unused	Used
❑ 1571	10¢	Int'l Women's Year	2.00 (6)	.55	.34
❑ 1572	10¢	Stagecoach	—	.55	.34
❑ 1573	10¢	Steam Engine	—	.55	.34
❑ 1574	10¢	Biplane	—	.55	.34
❑ 1575	10¢	Satellite	—	.55	.34
		Block of 4 (1572–1575)	4.00 (12)	2.00	.80
❑ 1576	10¢	World Peace Thru Law	2.00	.55	.34
❑ 1577	10¢	Banking	—	.55	.34
❑ 1578	10¢	Commerce	—	.55	.34
		Pair (1577–1578)	2.00	1.25	.55

1579

1580
(1580B)

Scott No.			Plate Block	Unused	Used
❏ 1579	10¢	Madonna & Child	5.50 (12)	.55	.34
❏ 1580	10¢	Prang Card, perf 11	5.50 (12)	.55	.34
❏ 1580B	10¢	Prang Card (~1580), perf 10.5 x 11.3	14.00 (12)	2.00	1.25

1581
(1811)

1582

1584

1585

1590
(1590A, 1591, 1616)

1975–1981. Americana Series.

❏ 1581	1¢	Inkwell	.70	.45	.34
❏ 1582	2¢	Speaker's Lectern	.70	.45	.34
❏ 1584	3¢	Ballot Box	.70	.45	.34
❏ 1585	4¢	Books & Glasses	.75	.45	.34
❏ 1590	9¢	Capitol Dome, white paper, perf 11 x 10½	—	1.15	.75
		Pair (1590 & 1623)	—	1.15	.75
❏ 1590A	9¢	Capitol Dome, white paper, perf 10	—	.55	.40
		Pair (1590A & 1623A)	—	35.00	15.00
❏ 1591	9¢	Capitol Dome (~1590), gray paper	1.00	.80	.40

1592
(1617)

1593

1594
(1816)

1595
(1595a–d, 1618)

1596

1597
(1598, 1618C)

1599
(1619)

Scott No.			Plate Block	Unused	Used
❑ 1592	10¢	Justice	2.15	.40	.34
❑ 1593	11¢	Printing Press	2.15	.70	.34
❑ 1594	12¢	Torch of Liberty	2.15	.70	.34
❑ 1595	13¢	Liberty Bell, from booklet pane	—	.70	.34
❑ 1595a	13¢	Booklet pane of 6	—	2.50	1.60
❑ 1595b	13¢	Booklet pane of 7 + label	—	2.50	1.60
❑ 1595c	13¢	Booklet pane of 8	—	2.50	1.25
❑ 1595d	13¢	Booklet pane of 5 + label	—	2.50	2.00
❑ 1596	13¢	Eagle & Shield	5.00 (12)	.55	.34
❑ 1597	15¢	Stars & Stripes	10.00 (20)	.55	.34
❑ 1598	15¢	Stars & Stripes (~1597)	—	.80	.34
		Booklet pane of 8	—	5.00	1.00
❑ 1599	16¢	Statue of Liberty	4.25	.50	.34

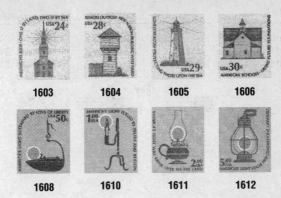

| 1603 | 1604 | 1605 | 1606 |

| 1608 | 1610 | 1611 | 1612 |

Scott No.			Plate Block	Unused	Used
❏ 1603	24¢	Old North Church	5.15	1.60	.34
❏ 1604	28¢	Fort Nisqually	5.15	1.60	.34
❏ 1605	29¢	Sandy Hook Lighthouse	5.15	1.60	.34
❏ 1606	30¢	School House	5.15	1.60	.34
❏ 1608	50¢	Iron Betty Lamp	5.15	2.00	.40
❏ 1610	$1	Rush Lamp	15.00	4.00	.40
❏ 1611	$2	Kerosene Lamp	25.00	6.00	1.25
❏ 1612	$5	Railroad Lantern	50.00	12.00	2.00

| 1613 | 1614 | 1615 | 1615C |

Scott No.			Line Pair	Unused	Used
Americana Series Coil Stamps.					
❏ 1613	3.1¢	Guitar	1.25	.45	.34
❏ 1614	7.7¢	Saxhorns	2.00	.55	.40
❏ 1615	7.9¢	Drum	1.25	.55	.40
❏ 1615C	8.4¢	Piano	4.00	.55	.40

Scott No.			Line Pair	Unused	Used
❑ 1616	9¢	Capitol Dome (~1590)	1.25	.55	.34
❑ 1617	10¢	Justice (~1592)	1.25	.55	.34
❑ 1618	13¢	Liberty Bell (~1595)	1.25	.55	.34

1622
(1622C, 1625)

1623
(1623B)

Scott No.			Plate Block	Unused	Used

1975–1977. Definitives.

Scott No.			Plate Block	Unused	Used
❑ 1622	13¢	Flag & Ind. Hall, perf 11 x 10½	10.00 (20)	2.25	.34
❑ 1622C	13¢	Flag & Ind. Hall (~1622), perf 11½	75.00 (20)	2.25	.75
❑ 1623	13¢	Flag & Capitol, perf 11 x 10½	—	2.25	.34
		Booklet pane of 8 (7 x 1623, 1 x 1590)	—	35.00	—
❑ 1623B	13¢	Flag & Capitol (~1623), perf 10	—	2.00	.34
		Booklet pane of 8 (7 x 1623B, 1 x 1590A)	—	30.00	25.00

Scott No.			Line Pair	Unused	Used

Coil Stamps.

Scott No.			Line Pair	Unused	Used
❑ 1625	13¢	Flag & Independence Hall (~1622)	7.00	.80	.34

1629–1531

1632

Scott No.			Plate Block	Unused	Used
1976.					
❏ 1629	13¢	Youthful Drummer	—	.75	.40
❏ 1630	13¢	Mature Drummer	—	.75	.40
❏ 1631	13¢	Fief Player	—	.75	.40
		Strip of 3, 1629–1631	5.00 (12)	1.00	.65
❏ 1632	13¢	INTERPHIL '76	2.00	.75	.34

1633–1682

Scott No.	Plate Block	Unused	Used
❑ 1633–1682 13¢ Fifty State Flags	32.00 (20)	1.00	.75

❑ 1633 Delaware   ❑ 1637 Connecticut
❑ 1634 Pennsylvania   ❑ 1638 Massachusetts
❑ 1635 New Jersey   ❑ 1639 Maryland
❑ 1636 Georgia   ❑ 1640 South Carolina

- ❏ 1641 New Hampshire
- ❏ 1642 Virginia
- ❏ 1643 New York
- ❏ 1644 North Carolina
- ❏ 1645 Rhode Island
- ❏ 1646 Vermont
- ❏ 1647 Kentucky
- ❏ 1648 Tennessee
- ❏ 1649 Ohio
- ❏ 1650 Louisiana
- ❏ 1651 Indiana
- ❏ 1652 Mississippi
- ❏ 1653 Illinois
- ❏ 1654 Alabama
- ❏ 1655 Maine
- ❏ 1656 Missouri
- ❏ 1657 Arkansas
- ❏ 1658 Michigan
- ❏ 1659 Florida
- ❏ 1660 Texas
- ❏ 1661 Iowa

- ❏ 1662 Wisconsin
- ❏ 1663 California
- ❏ 1664 Minnesota
- ❏ 1665 Oregon
- ❏ 1666 Kansas
- ❏ 1667 West Virginia
- ❏ 1668 Nevada
- ❏ 1669 Nebraska
- ❏ 1670 Colorado
- ❏ 1671 North Dakota
- ❏ 1672 South Dakota
- ❏ 1673 Montana
- ❏ 1674 Washington
- ❏ 1675 Idaho
- ❏ 1676 Wyoming
- ❏ 1677 Utah
- ❏ 1678 Oklahoma
- ❏ 1679 New Mexico
- ❏ 1680 Arizona
- ❏ 1681 Alaska
- ❏ 1682 Hawaii

1683

1684

1685

Scott No.			Plate Block	Unused	Used
❏ 1683	13¢	Telephone Centennial	2.25	.70	.34
❏ 1684	13¢	Commercial Aviation	4.00 (10)	.70	.34
❏ 1685	13¢	Chemistry	5.00 (12)	.70	.34

The Surrender of Lord Cornwallis at Yorktown
From a Painting by John Trumbull

1686

The Declaration of Independence, 4 July 1776 at Philadelphia
From a Painting by John Trumbull

1687

Washington Crossing the Delaware
From a Painting by Emanuel Leutze / Eastman Johnson

1688

Scott No.			Plate Block	Unused	Used
❏ 1686	13¢	Surrender at Yorktown, souvenir sheet	—	5.00	.75
❏ 1686a–e		Any single stamp	—	2.00	1.25
❏ 1687	18¢	Declaration of Independence, souvenir sheet	—	8.00	5.00
❏ 1687a–e		Any single stamp	—	2.25	1.25
❏ 1688	24¢	Crossing the Delaware, souvenir sheet	—	12.00	8.00
❏ 1688a–e		Any single stamp	—	4.00	2.25

Washington Reviewing His Ragged Army at Valley Forge
From a Painting by William T. Trego

1689

1690

Scott No.			Plate Block	Unused	Used
❑ 1689	31¢	Valley Forge, souvenir sheet	—	12.00	8.00
❑ 1689a–e		Any single stamp	—	4.00	2.15
❑ 1690	13¢	Benjamin Franklin	2.15	.80	.65

JULY 4,1776 ┊ JULY 4,1776 ┊ JULY 4,1776 ┊ JULY 4,1776

1691–1694

1695–1698

Scott No.			Plate Block	Unused	Used
❏ 1691	13¢	Delegates Seated & Standing	—	4.25	.85
❏ 1692	13¢	Delegates Seated	—	4.25	.85
❏ 1693	13¢	Delegates at Desk	—	4.25	.85
❏ 1694	13¢	Seated at Large Chair	—	4.25	.85
		Strip of 4 (1691–1694)	15.00 (20)	4.25	2.00
❏ 1695	13¢	Olympics – Diving	—	2.00	1.65
❏ 1696	13¢	Olympics – Skiing	—	2.00	1.65
❏ 1697	13¢	Olympics – Running	—	2.00	1.65
❏ 1698	13¢	Olympics – Skating	—	2.00	1.65
		Block of 4 (1695–1698)	6.00 (20)	4.25	2.00

1701

1699   **1700**

1702

Scott No.			Plate Block	Unused	Used
❏ 1699	13¢	Clara Maass	6.00 (12)	.75	.34
❏ 1700	13¢	Adolph S. Ochs	4.00	.75	.34
❏ 1701	13¢	Christmas – Manger Scene	5.00 (12)	.75	.34
❏ 1702	13¢	Winter Pastimes (overall tagging)	5.00 (10)	.75	.34
❏ 1703	13¢	Winter Pastimes (~1702) (block tagging)	6.00 (10)	.75	.34

1705

US Bicentennial 13c

1704

Scott No.			Plate Block	Unused	Used
1977.					
❏ 1704	13¢	Washington at Princeton	7.00 (10)	.80	.34
❏ 1705	13¢	Sound Recording	5.00	2.00	1.00

Pueblo Art USA 13c

1706–1709

1710

1711

Scott No.			Plate Block	Unused	Used
❑ 1706	13¢	Zia Pot	—	.75	.34
❑ 1707	13¢	San Ildefonso Pot	—	.75	.34
❑ 1708	13¢	Hopi Pot	—	.75	.34
❑ 1709	13¢	Acoma Pot	—	.75	.34
		Block of 4 (1706–1709)	6.00	2.75	1.50
❑ 1710	13¢	Spirit of St. Louis	5.00 (12)	.75	.34
❑ 1711	13¢	Colorado Statehood	5.00	.75	.34

1712–1715

US Bicentennial 13c

1716

1717–1720

1721

Herkimer at Oriskany 1777 by Yohn
US Bicentennial 13 cents

1722

Scott No.			Plate Block	Unused	Used
❏ 1712	13¢	Swallowtail	—	2.25	.75
❏ 1713	13¢	Checkerspot	—	2.25	.75
❏ 1714	13¢	Dogface	—	2.25	.75
❏ 1715	13¢	Orange-Tip	—	2.25	.75
		Block of 4 (1712–1715)	8.00 (12)	2.25	1.00
❏ 1716	13¢	Lafayette	2.00	.70	.34
❏ 1717	13¢	Seamstress	—	.70	.34
❏ 1718	13¢	Blacksmith	—	.70	.34
❏ 1719	13¢	Wheelwright	—	.70	.34
❏ 1720	13¢	Leatherworker	—	.70	.34
		Block of 4 (1717–1720)	5.00 (12)	2.25	1.00
❏ 1721	13¢	Peace Bridge	2.00	.70	.34
❏ 1722	13¢	Battle of Oriskany	4.00 (10)	.70	.34

1723–24

1725

1726

1727

US Bicentennial 13 cents

1728

1729

1730

Scott No.			Plate Block	Unused	Used
❑ 1723	13¢	Energy Conservation	—	.65	.34
❑ 1724	13¢	Energy Development	—	.65	.34
		Se-tenant pair (1723–1724)	5.00 (12)	.75	.50
❑ 1725	13¢	Alta, California	2.25	.45	.34
❑ 1726	13¢	Articles of Confederation	2.25	.65	.34
❑ 1727	13¢	Talking Pictures	2.25	.65	.34
❑ 1728	13¢	Surrender at Saratoga	4.00 (10)	.65	.34
❑ 1729	13¢	Christmas – Valley Forge	7.00 (20)	.65	.34
❑ 1730	13¢	Christmas – Mailbox	4.00 (10)	.65	.34

1731 **1732–1733**

Scott No.			Plate Block	Unused	Used
1978.					
❑ 1731	13¢	Carl Sandburg	5.15	.75	.34
❑ 1732	13¢	Captain James Cook	—	.75	.34
❑ 1733	13¢	Ships at Anchor	—	.75	.34
		Se-tenant pair (1732–1733)	8.00	1.00	.80

1734  **1735**
(1736, 1743)

1978–1980.

❑ 1734	13¢	Indian Head Cent	2.25	.75	.34
❑ 1735	(15¢)	"A" (photogravure)	2.25	.75	.34

Booklet Stamps.

❑ 1736	(15¢)	"A" (~1735) (engraved)	—	.75	.34
		Booklet pane of 8	—	4.00	2.00

1737   **1738–1742**

Scott No.			Plate Block	Unused	Used
❑ 1737	15¢	Roses	—	.60	.30
		Booklet pane of 8	4.00	2.50	1.50
❑ 1738	15¢	Windmill – Virginia	—	.60	.30
❑ 1739	15¢	Windmill – Rhode Island	—	.60	.30
❑ 1740	15¢	Windmill – Massachusetts	—	.60	.30
❑ 1741	15¢	Windmill – Illinois	—	.60	.30
❑ 1742	15¢	Windmill – Texas	—	.60	.30
		Booklet pane of 10 (2 each 1738–1742)	—	5.00	4.00

Scott No.			Line Pair	Unused	Used

Coil Stamp.

Scott No.			Line Pair	Unused	Used
❑ 1743	(15¢)	"A" (~1735) (engraved)	1.00	.60	.22

1744

Scott No.			Plate Block	Unused	Used

1978.

Scott No.			Plate Block	Unused	Used
❑ 1744	13¢	Harriet Tubman	8.00 (12)	.60	.30

1745–1748

1749–1752

Scott No.			Plate Block	Unused	Used
❏ 1745	13¢	Quilt with Flowers	—	.60	.34
❏ 1746	13¢	Red & White Quilt	—	.60	.34
❏ 1747	13¢	Orange Striped Quilt	—	.60	.34
❏ 1748	13¢	Black Plaid Quilt	—	.60	.34
		Block of 4 (1745–1748)	8.00 (12)	2.00	1.25
❏ 1749	13¢	Ballet	—	.60	.34
❏ 1750	13¢	Theater	—	.60	.34
❏ 1751	13¢	Folk Dance	—	.60	.34
❏ 1752	13¢	Modern Dance	—	.60	.34
		Block of 4 (1749–1752)	5.00 (12)	2.00	1.25

1753    **1754**    **1755**    **1756**

1757

Scott No.			Plate Block	Unused	Used
❏ 1753	13¢	French Alliance	2.00	.75	.34
❏ 1754	13¢	Cancer Detection	4.25	.75	.34
❏ 1755	13¢	Jimmie Rodgers	8.00 (12)	.75	.34
❏ 1756	15¢	George M. Cohan	8.00 (12)	.80	.34
❏ 1757	13¢	CAPEX, block of 8	4.25	2.00	1.25
❏ 1757a–h		Any single	—	.75	.40

1758

1759

1760–1763

Scott No.			Plate Block	Unused	Used
❑ 1758	15¢	Photography	6.00 (12)	.75	.34
❑ 1759	15¢	Viking Mission to Mars	2.00	.75	.34
❑ 1760	15¢	Great Gray Owl	—	.75	.34
❑ 1761	15¢	Saw-whet Owl	—	.75	.34
❑ 1762	15¢	Barred Owl	—	.75	.34
❑ 1763	15¢	Great Horned Owl	—	.75	.34
		Block of 4 (1760–1763)	2.00	1.50	1.15

1764–1767

1768

1769

Scott No.			Plate Block	Unused	Used
❏ 1764	15¢	Giant Sequoia	—	.75	.34
❏ 1765	15¢	White Pine	—	.75	.34
❏ 1766	15¢	White Oak	—	.75	.34
❏ 1767	15¢	Gray Birch	—	.75	.34
		Block of 4 (1764–1767).00	7.00 (12)	1.50	1.25
❏ 1768	15¢	Christmas – Madonna	6.00 (12)	.75	.34
❏ 1769	15¢	Christmas – Rocking Horse	6.00 (12)	.75	.34

1770

1771

1772

1979.

❏ 1770	15¢	Robert F. Kennedy	4.00	.95	.34
❏ 1771	15¢	Martin Luther King, Jr.	7.00 (12)	.95	.34
❏ 1772	15¢	Year of the Child	2.00	.95	.34

1773   **1774**

1775–1778

Scott No.			Plate Block	Unused	Used
❏ 1773	15¢	John Steinbeck	4.15	.75	.34
❏ 1774	15¢	Albert Einstein	4.15	.75	.34
❏ 1775	15¢	Toleware – Straight Spout	—	.75	.34
❏ 1776	15¢	Toleware – Tea Caddy	—	.75	.34
❏ 1777	15¢	Toleware – Sugar Bowl	—	.75	.34
❏ 1778	15¢	Toleware – Curved Spout	—	.75	.34
		Block of 4 (1775–1778)	6.00 (10)	2.00	1.15

1779–82

1783–1786

1787

1788

Scott No.			Plate Block	Unused	Used
❑ 1779	15¢	Virginia Rotunda	—	.75	.34
❑ 1780	15¢	Baltimore Cathedral	—	.75	.34
❑ 1781	15¢	Boston State House	—	.75	.34
❑ 1782	15¢	Philadelphia Exchange	—	.75	.34
		Block of 4 (1779–1782)	4.00	2.00	1.50
❑ 1783	15¢	Persistent Trillium	—	.75	.34
❑ 1784	15¢	Hawaiian Wild Broadbean	—	.75	.34
❑ 1785	15¢	Contra Costa Wallflower	—	.75	.34
❑ 1786	15¢	Evening Primrose	—	.75	.34
		Block of 4 (1783–1786)	8.00 (12)	1.75	1.00
❑ 1787	15¢	Seeing for Me	10.00 (20)	.90	.34
❑ 1788	15¢	Special Olympics	4.00 (10)	.90	.34

I have not yet begun to fight

John Paul Jones
US Bicentennial 15c

1789
(1789A, 1789B)

1791–1794

1790

1795–1798

Scott No.			Plate Block	Unused	Used
❏ 1789	15¢	John Paul Jones, perf 11 x 12	5.00 (10)	.75	.34
❏ 1789A	15¢	Jones (~1789), perf 11	4.25 (10)	.80	.50
❏ 1789B	15¢	Jones (~1789), perf 12	14000.00	2000.00	650.00
❏ 1790	10¢	Olympics – Decathlon	4.25 (12)	.75	.34
❏ 1791	15¢	Olympics – Runners	—	.75	.34
❏ 1792	15¢	Olympics – Swimmers	—	.75	.34
❏ 1793	15¢	Olympics – Rowers	—	.75	.34
❏ 1794	15¢	Olympics – Equestrian	—	.75	.34
		Block of 4 (1791–1794)	6.00 (12)	2.00	1.50
❏ 1795	15¢	Olympics – Skater	—	.75	.34
❏ 1796	15¢	Olympics – Skier	—	.75	.34
❏ 1797	15¢	Olympics – Ski Jumper	—	.75	.34
❏ 1798	15¢	Olympics – Hockey	—	.75	.34
		Block of 4 (1795–1795)	6.00 (12)	2.00	1.75

1799    **1800**

1801    **1802**

Scott No.			Plate Block	Unused	Used
❏ 1799	15¢	Christmas – Madonna	6.00 (12)	.75	.34
❏ 1800	15¢	Gingerbread Santa	5.00 (12)	.75	.34
❏ 1801	15¢	Will Rogers	5.00 (12)	.75	.34
❏ 1802	15¢	Vietnam Veterans	5.00 (10)	.75	.34

1803   **1804**

1980.

❏ 1803	15¢	W. C. Fields	6.00 (12)	.80	.34
❏ 1804	15¢	Benjamin Banneker	7.00 (12)	.80	.34

1805–1810

Scott No.			Plate Block	Unused	Used
❑ 1805	15¢	Letters Preserve Memories	—	.75	.34
❑ 1806	15¢	P. S. Write Soon (violet & pink)	—	.75	.34
❑ 1807	15¢	Letters Lift Spirits	—	.75	.34
❑ 1808	15¢	P.S. (green & yellow green)	—	.75	.34
❑ 1809	15¢	Letters Shape Opinions	—	.75	.34
❑ 1810	15¢	P.S. (scarlet & blue)	—	.75	.34
		Strip of 6 (1805–1810)	22.00 (36)	7.00	4.25

1813

Scott No.			Line Pair	Unused	Used
1980. Americana Series Coil Stamps.					
❑ 1811	1¢	Inkwell (~1581)	.60	.55	.34
❑ 1813	3.5¢	Violins	1.00	.55	.34
❑ 1816	12¢	Torch of Liberty (~1594)	2.00	.65	.45

1818
(1819, 1820)

Scott No.	Plate Block	Unused	Used
1981.			
❑ 1818 (18¢) "B" (photogravure)	2.00	.75	.34
❑ 1819 (18¢) "B" (~1818) (engraved)	4.00	.75	.34
Booklet pane of 8	—	5.00	2.50

Scott No.	Line Pair	Unused	Used
Coil Stamp.			
❑ 1820 (18¢) "B" (~1818) (engraved)	1.50	.85	.30

| **1821** | **1822** | **1823** | **1824** |

Scott No.	Plate Block	Unused	Used
1980.			
❑ 1821 15¢ Francis Perkins	2.25	.75	.34
❑ 1822 15¢ Dolley Madison	2.25	.75	.34
❑ 1823 15¢ Emily Bissell	4.00	.85	.34
❑ 1824 15¢ Helen Keller – Anne Sullivan	4.00	.85	.34

1825

1826

1827–1830

1831

Edith Wharton

1832

Glow by Josef Albers USA 15¢
Learning
never ends

1833

Scott No.			Plate Block	Unused	Used
❑ 1825	15¢	Veterans Administration	4.15	.70	.34
❑ 1826	15¢	General Bernardo de Galvez	4.15	.70	.34
❑ 1827	15¢	Brain Coral	—	.70	.34
❑ 1828	15¢	Elkhorn Coral	—	.70	.34
❑ 1829	15¢	Chalice Coral	—	.70	.34
❑ 1830	15¢	Finger Coral	—	.70	.34
		Block of 4 (1827–1830)	6.00 (12)	1.50	1.25
❑ 1831	15¢	Organized Labor	6.00 (12)	.70	.34
❑ 1832	15¢	Edith Wharton	2.00	.70	.34
❑ 1833	15¢	Learning Never Ends	4.15 (6)	.70	.34

1834–1837

1838–1841

Scott No.			Plate Block	Unused	Used
❏ 1834	15¢	Mask – Heiltsuk, Bella Bella	—	.75	.34
❏ 1835	15¢	Mask – Chilkat Tlingit	—	.75	.34
❏ 1836	15¢	Mask – Tlingit	—	.75	.34
❏ 1837	15¢	Mask – Bella Coola	—	.75	.34
		Block of 4 (1834–1837)	12.00 (10)	2.50	1.50
❏ 1838	15¢	Architecture – Smithsonian	—	.75	.34
❏ 1839	15¢	Architecture – Trinity Church	—	.75	.34
❏ 1840	15¢	Architecture – Penn Academy	—	.75	.34
❏ 1841	15¢	Architecture – Lyndhurst	—	.75	.34
		Block of 4 (1838–1841)	5.00	4.00	2.00

Christmas USA 15c

1842

USA 15c
Season's Greetings

1843

Scott No.			Plate Block	Unused	Used
❑ 1842	15¢	Christmas – Madonna & Child	5.00 (12)	.75	.32
❑ 1843	15¢	Christmas – Wreath & Drum	10.00 (20)	.75	.32

1844	**1845**	**1846**	**1847**	**1848**
1849	**1850**	**1851**	**1852**	**1853**

1980–1985. Great Americans Series.

Scott No.			Plate Block	Unused	Used
❑ 1844	1¢	Dorothea Dix	4.00 (20)	.40	.34
❑ 1845	2¢	Igor Stravinsky	.85	.40	.34
❑ 1846	3¢	Henry Clay	.85	.40	.34
❑ 1847	4¢	Carl Schurz	.85	.40	.34
❑ 1848	5¢	Pearl Buck	.85	.40	.34
❑ 1849	6¢	Walter Lippmann	5.00 (20)	.40	.34
❑ 1850	7¢	Abraham Baldwin	5.00 (20)	.40	.34
❑ 1851	8¢	Henry Knox	2.15	.40	.34
❑ 1852	9¢	Sylvanus Thayer	6.00 (20)	.75	.40
❑ 1853	10¢	Richard Russell	7.00 (20)	.75	.40

1854	1855	1856	1857
1858	1859	1860	1861
1862	1863	1864	1865

Scott No.			Plate Block	Unused	Used
❏ 1854	11¢	Alden Partridge	4.25	.80	.34
❏ 1855	13¢	Crazy Horse	2.00	.75	.34
❏ 1856	14¢	Sinclair Lewis	10.00 (20)	.75	.34
❏ 1857	17¢	Rachel Carson	4.25	.75	.34
❏ 1858	18¢	George Mason	4.25	.75	.34
❏ 1859	19¢	Sequoyah	4.25	.75	.34
❏ 1860	20¢	Ralph Bunche	4.25	.80	.34
❏ 1861	20¢	Thomas H. Gallaudet	4.25	.80	.34
❏ 1862	20¢	Harry S. Truman	15.00 (20)	.80	.34
❏ 1863	22¢	John J. Audubon	15.00 (20)	.80	.34
❏ 1864	30¢	Frank C. Laubach	16.00 (20)	.80	.34
❏ 1865	35¢	Charles R. Drew M.D.	6.50	1.15	.34

| **1866** | **1867** | **1868** | **1869** |

Scott No.			Plate Block	Unused	Used
❑ 1866	37¢	Robert Millikan	8.00	2.25	.34
❑ 1867	39¢	Grenville Clark	16.00 (20)	2.25	.34
❑ 1868	40¢	Lillian M. Gilbreth	25.00 (20)	2.25	.34
❑ 1869	50¢	Chester W. Nimitz	12.00	2.25	.34

NOTE: See Nos. 2168–2197 and 2933–2943 for other Great Americans Series stamps.

| **1874** | **1875** |

1876–1879

1981.

❑ 1874	15¢	Everett M. Dirksen	2.25	.75	.34
❑ 1875	15¢	Whitney Moore Young	2.25	.75	.34
❑ 1876	18¢	Rose	—	.75	.34
❑ 1877	18¢	Camellia	—	.75	.34
❑ 1878	18¢	Dahlia	—	.75	.34
❑ 1879	18¢	Lily	—	.75	.34
		Block of 4 (1876–1879)	4.00	2.50	1.50

1880–1889

Scott No.			Plate Block	Unused	Used
Booklet Pane.					
❑ 1880	18¢	Bighorn Sheep	—	.95	.34
❑ 1881	18¢	Mountain Lion	—	.95	.34
❑ 1882	18¢	Harbor Seal	—	.95	.34
❑ 1883	18¢	Bison	—	.95	.34
❑ 1884	18¢	Brown Bear	—	.95	.34
❑ 1885	18¢	Polar Bear	—	.95	.34
❑ 1886	18¢	Elk	—	.95	.34
❑ 1887	18¢	Moose	—	.95	.34
❑ 1888	18¢	White-tailed Deer	—	.95	.34
❑ 1889	18¢	Pronghorn Antelope	—	.95	.34
		Booklet pane of 10 (1880–1889)	—	12.00	8.00

1890

1891

981. Definitive.

Scott No.			Plate Block	Unused	Used
❑ 1890	18¢	Flag – Amber Waves of Grain	6.00 (20)	.85	.60

Scott No.			PNC Strip (5)	Unused	Used
Coil Stamp.					
❑ 1891	18¢	Flag – Sea to Shining Sea	2.00	.85	.34

1892

1893

1894
(1895, 1896)

Scott No.			Plate Block	Unused	Used
1981. Definitives.					
☐ 1892	6¢	Numeral in Circle of Stars	—	2.00	.80
☐ 1893	18¢	Flag – Purple Mountain Majesties	—	.80	.34
		Booklet pane of 8 (two 1892; six 1893)	—	5.00	2.00
☐ 1894	20¢	Flag over Supreme Court	12.00 (20)	1.25	.40

Scott No.			PNC Strip (5)	Unused	Used
1981. Coil Stamp.					
☐ 1895	20¢	Flag over Supreme Court (~1894)	12.00	1.25	.40

Scott No.			Plate Block	Unused	Used
1981. Booklet Stamp.					
☐ 1896	20¢	Flag over Supreme Court (~1894)	—	1.25	.40
		Booklet pane of 6	—	5.00	2.50
		Booklet pane of 10	—	6.50	4.00

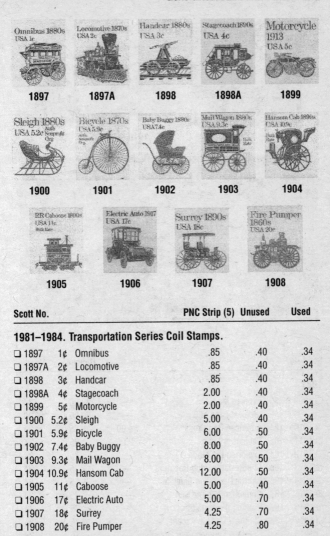

Scott No.			PNC Strip (5)	Unused	Used
1981–1984. Transportation Series Coil Stamps.					
☐ 1897	1¢	Omnibus	.85	.40	.34
☐ 1897A	2¢	Locomotive	.85	.40	.34
☐ 1898	3¢	Handcar	.85	.40	.34
☐ 1898A	4¢	Stagecoach	2.00	.40	.34
☐ 1899	5¢	Motorcycle	2.00	.40	.34
☐ 1900	5.2¢	Sleigh	5.00	.40	.34
☐ 1901	5.9¢	Bicycle	6.00	.50	.34
☐ 1902	7.4¢	Baby Buggy	8.00	.50	.34
☐ 1903	9.3¢	Mail Wagon	8.00	.50	.34
☐ 1904	10.9¢	Hansom Cab	12.00	.50	.34
☐ 1905	11¢	Caboose	5.00	.40	.34
☐ 1906	17¢	Electric Auto	5.00	.70	.34
☐ 1907	18¢	Surrey	4.25	.70	.34
☐ 1908	20¢	Fire Pumper	4.25	.80	.34

NOTE: Some values of the above exist Bureau precanceled. Prices are the same as unprecanceled examples. See Nos. 2123–2136, 2225–2231, 2252–2266, and 2451–2468 for other Transportation Series coil stamps.

1909

1910

1911

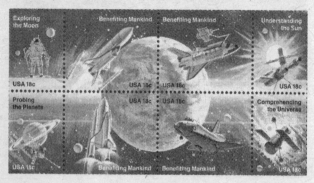

1912–1919

Scott No.			Plate Block	Unused	Used
1981.					
❏ 1909	$9.35	Express Mail	—	30.00	.34
		Booklet pane of 3	—	80.00	4.00
❏ 1910	18¢	American Red Cross	4.00	.85	.34
❏ 1911	18¢	Savings & Loan	2.00	.85	.34
❏ 1912	18¢	Exploring the Moon	—	.75	.34
❏ 1913	18¢	Shuttle Jettisoning Boosters	—	.75	.34
❏ 1914	18¢	Shuttle Deploying Satellite	—	.75	.34
❏ 1915	18¢	Understanding the Sun	—	.75	.34
❏ 1916	18¢	Probing the Planets	—	.75	.34
❏ 1917	18¢	Shuttle – Vertical Ascent	—	.75	.34
❏ 1918	18¢	Shuttle – Landing Gear Down	—	.75	.34
❏ 1919	18¢	Comprehending the Universe	—	.75	.34
		Block of 8 (1912–1919)	10.00 (8)	6.00	4.25

1920

1921–1924

1925   **1926**   **1927**

Scott No.			Plate Block	Unused	Used
☐ 1920	18¢	Professional Management	4.00	.95	.34
☐ 1921	18¢	Save Wetland Habitats	—	.95	.34
☐ 1922	18¢	Save Grassland Habitats	—	.95	.34
☐ 1923	18¢	Save Mountain Habitats	—	.95	.34
☐ 1924	18¢	Save Woodland Habitats	—	.95	.34
		Block of 4 (1921–1924)	4.00	2.00	1.50
☐ 1925	18¢	Disabled Persons	2.50	.95	.34
☐ 1926	18¢	Edna St. Vincent Millay	2.50	.95	.34
☐ 1927	18¢	Alcoholism	32.00 (20)	.95	.34

1928–1931

1932

1933

1934

Scott No.			Plate Block	Unused	Used
❑ 1928	18¢	NYU Library – New York	—	.95	.34
❑ 1929	18¢	Biltmore – Asheville, NC	—	.95	.34
❑ 1930	18¢	Palace of Arts – San Francisco	—	.95	.34
❑ 1931	18¢	Bank – Owatonna, MN	—	.95	.34
		Block of 4 (1928–1931)	4.25	2.00	1.80
❑ 1932	18¢	Babe Zaharias	4.25	.75	.34
❑ 1933	18¢	Bobby Jones	6.00	1.25	.34
❑ 1934	18¢	Frederick Remington	4.00	2.00	.34

1935

1936

1937–1938

1939

1940

1941

Scott No.			Plate Block	Unused	Used
❏ 1935	18¢	James Hoban	4.25	.90	.34
❏ 1936	20¢	James Hoban	4.25	.90	.34
❏ 1937	18¢	Yorktown Map	—	.75	.34
❏ 1938	18¢	Virginia Capes Map	—	.75	.34
		Se-tenant pair (1937–1938)	4.25	1.50	.80
❏ 1939	(20¢)	Christmas – Madonna & Child	4.25	.90	.34
❏ 1940	(20¢)	Christmas – Teddy Bear	4.25	.90	.34
❏ 1941	20¢	John Hanson	4.25	.90	.34

1942–1945

1946
(1947, 1948)

Scott No.			Plate Block	Unused	Used
❑ 1942	20¢	Cactus – Barrel Cactus	—	.75	.34
❑ 1943	20¢	Cactus – Agave	—	.75	.34
❑ 1944	20¢	Cactus – Beavertail Cactus	—	.75	.34
❑ 1945	20¢	Cactus – Saguaro	—	.75	.34
		Block of 4 (1942–1945)	4.00	2.00	1.50
❑ 1946	(20¢)	"C" & Eagle	2.00	.75	.34

Scott No.			Line Pair	Unused	Used
Coil Stamp.					
❑ 1947	(20¢)	"C" & Eagle (~1946)	1.75	.95	.34

Scott No.			Plate Block	Unused	Used
Booklet Stamps.					
❑ 1948	(20¢)	"C" & Eagle (~1946)	—	.95	.34
		Booklet pane of 10	—	8.00	4.00

1949

Scott No.			Plate Block	Unused	Used
❏ 1949	20¢	Bighorn Sheep	—	1.00	.35
		Booklet pane of 10	—	7.00	4.15

1950

1951
(1951A)

1952

1982.

❏ 1950	20¢	Franklin D. Roosevelt	4.25	.95	.35
❏ 1951	20¢	Love – Flowers	2.00	.95	.35
❏ 1952	20¢	George Washington	4.25	.95	.35

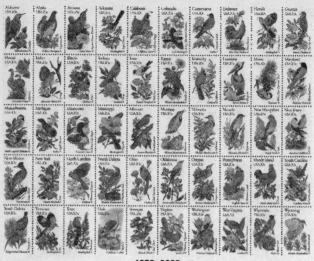

1953–2002

Scott No.			Plate Block	Unused	Used
❑ 1953– 2002	20¢	State Birds & Flowers, perf 10½ x 11¼	—	37.50	—
❑ 1953– 2002	20¢	Any single stamp	—	4.50	.85
❑ 1953A– 2002A	20¢	State Birds & Flowers, perf 11¼ x 11	—	25.00	—
❑ 1953A– 2002A	20¢	Any single stamp	—	1.25	.45

❑ 1953 Alabama
❑ 1954 Alaska
❑ 1955 Arizona
❑ 1956 Arkansas
❑ 1957 California
❑ 1958 Colorado
❑ 1959 Connecticut
❑ 1960 Delaware
❑ 1961 Florida

❑ 1962 Georgia
❑ 1963 Hawaii
❑ 1964 Idaho
❑ 1965 Illinois
❑ 1966 Indiana
❑ 1967 Iowa
❑ 1968 Kansas
❑ 1969 Kentucky
❑ 1970 Louisiana

❑ 1971 Maine	❑ 1987 Ohio
❑ 1972 Maryland	❑ 1988 Oklahoma
❑ 1973 Massachusetts	❑ 1989 Oregon
❑ 1974 Michigan	❑ 1890 Pennsylvania
❑ 1975 Minnesota	❑ 1991 Rhode Island
❑ 1976 Mississippi	❑ 1992 South Carolina
❑ 1977 Missouri	❑ 1993 South Dakota
❑ 1978 Montana	❑ 1994 Tennessee
❑ 1979 Nebraska	❑ 1995 Texas
❑ 1980 Nevada	❑ 1996 Utah
❑ 1981 New Hampshire	❑ 1997 Vermont
❑ 1982 New Jersey	❑ 1998 Virginia
❑ 1983 New Mexico	❑ 1999 Washington
❑ 1984 New York	❑ 2000 West Virginia
❑ 1985 North Carolina	❑ 2001 Wisconsin
❑ 1986 North Dakota	❑ 2002 Wyoming

2003

2004

Scott No.			Plate Block	Unused	Used
❑ 2003	20¢	Netherlands	15.00 (20)	1.25	.34
❑ 2004	20¢	Library of Congress	4.00	1.25	.34

2005

Scott No.			PNC Strip (5)	Unused	Used
Coil Stamp.					
❑ 2005	20¢	Consumer Education	30.00	2.25	.35

2006–2009

2010

2011

THE BARRYMORES

Performing Arts USA 20¢

2012

Dr. Mary Walker
Army Surgeon

Medal of Honor
USA 20c

2013

2014

Scott No.			Plate Block	Unused	Used
1982.					
❑ 2006	20¢	Solar Energy	—	.95	.34
❑ 2007	20¢	Synthetic Fuels	—	.95	.34
❑ 2008	20¢	Breeder Reactor	—	.95	.34
❑ 2009	20¢	Fossil Fuels	—	.95	.34
		Block of 4 (2006–2009)	4.00	2.50	1.50
❑ 2010	20¢	Horatio Alger	4.00	.95	.34
❑ 2011	20¢	Aging Together	2.75	.95	.34
❑ 2012	20¢	The Barrymores	2.75	.95	.34
❑ 2013	20¢	Dr. Mary Walker	2.75	.95	.34
❑ 2014	20¢	International Peace Garden	2.75	.95	.34

2015

2016

2017

2018

2019–2022

Scott No.			Plate Block	Unused	Used
❑ 2015	20¢	America's Libraries	4.25	.95	.34
❑ 2016	20¢	Jackie Robinson	8.00	1.60	.50
❑ 2017	20¢	Touro Synagogue	20.00 (20)	.95	.34
❑ 2018	20¢	Wolf Trap Farm Park	4.25	.95	.34
❑ 2019	20¢	Architecture – Frank Lloyd Wright	—	.95	.34
❑ 2020	20¢	Architecture – Mies van der Rohe	—	.95	.34
❑ 2021	20¢	Architecture – Walter Gropius	—	.95	.34
❑ 2022	20¢	Architecture – Eero Saarinen	—	.95	.34
		Block of 4 (2019–2022)	5.00	4.00	1.50

2023

2024

2025

2026

2027–2030

2031

Scott No.			Plate Block	Unused	Used
❏ 2023	20¢	Francis of Assisi	4.25	.95	.34
❏ 2024	20¢	Ponce de Leon	14.00 (20)	.95	.34
❏ 2025	13¢	Christmas – Kitten & Puppy	2.00	.95	.34
❏ 2026	20¢	Christmas – Madonna & Child	14.00 (20)	.95	.34
❏ 2027	20¢	Christmas – Sledding	—	.95	.34
❏ 2028	20¢	Christmas – Snowman	—	.95	.34
❏ 2029	20¢	Christmas – Ice Skating	—	.95	.34
❏ 2030	20¢	Christmas – Trimming Tree	—	.95	.34
		Block of 4 (2027–2030)	5.00	4.00	1.60
❏ 2031	20¢	Science & Industry	4.25	.95	.34

2032–2035

Scott No.			Plate Block	Unused	Used
❑ 2032	20¢	Ballooning – Intrepid	—	.95	.34
❑ 2033	20¢	Ballooning – Hot Air Balloon	—	.95	.34
❑ 2034	20¢	Ballooning – Hot Air Balloon	—	.95	.34
❑ 2035	20¢	Ballooning – Explorer II	—	.95	.34
		Block of 4 (2032–2035)	6.00	4.00	2.15

2036

2037

2038

2039

2040

1983.

❑ 2036	20¢	USA – Sweden	5.25	.95	.34
❑ 2037	20¢	Civilian Conservation Corps	5.25	.95	.34
❑ 2038	20¢	Joseph Priestley	5.25	.95	.34
❑ 2039	20¢	Volunteer – Lend a Hand	12.00 (20)	.95	.34
❑ 2040	20¢	German Immigration	2.50	.90	.34

2041

2042

2043

2044

2045

2046

2047

Scott No.			Plate Block	Unused	Used
❑ 2041	20¢	Brooklyn Bridge	6.00	.95	.34
❑ 2042	20¢	Tennessee Valley Authority	14.00 (20)	.95	.34
❑ 2043	20¢	Physical Fitness	12.00 (20)	.95	.34
❑ 2044	20¢	Scott Joplin	6.00	.95	.34
❑ 2045	20¢	Medal of Honor	6.00	.95	.34
❑ 2046	20¢	Babe Ruth	12.00	3.00	.34
❑ 2047	20¢	Nathaniel Hawthorne	6.00	.95	.34

2048–2051

2052

2053

2054

Scott No.			Plate Block	Unused	Used
❑ 2048	13¢	Olympics – Discus	—	.95	.34
❑ 2049	13¢	Olympics – High Jump	—	.95	.34
❑ 2050	13¢	Olympics – Archery	—	.95	.34
❑ 2051	13¢	Olympics – Boxing	—	.95	.34
		Block of 4 (2048–2051)	4.25	2.50	1.50
❑ 2052	20¢	Treaty of Paris	4.25	.95	.34
❑ 2053	20¢	Civil Service	12.00 (20)	.95	.34
❑ 2054	20¢	Metropolitan Opera	4.25	.95	.34

2055–2058

2059–2062

Scott No.			Plate Block	Unused	Used
❏ 2055	20¢	Charles Steinmetz	—	.95	.34
❏ 2056	20¢	Edwin Armstrong	—	.95	.34
❏ 2057	20¢	Nikola Tesla	—	.95	.34
❏ 2058	20¢	Philo T. Farnsworth	—	.95	.34
		Block of 4 (2055–2058)	6.00	2.50	2.00
❏ 2059	20¢	Streetcars – First American	—	.95	.34
❏ 2060	20¢	Streetcars – Electric Trolley	—	.95	.34
❏ 2061	20¢	Streetcars – Bobtail Horsecar	—	.95	.34
❏ 2062	20¢	Streetcars – St. Charles Coach	—	.95	.34
		Block of 4 (2059–2062)	6.00	4.00	2.50

NOTE. Prices for stamps from 1935 to date are for never-hinged (NH) examples.

2063   **2064**   **2065**

Scott No.			Plate Block	Unused	Used
❏ 2063	20¢	Christmas – Madonna	4.00	.95	.34
❏ 2064	20¢	Christmas – Santa Claus	12.00 (20)	.95	.34
❏ 2065	20¢	Martin Luther	4.00	.95	.34

2066

2067–70

1984.

❏ 2066	20¢	Alaska Statehood	5.00	.95	.34
❏ 2067	20¢	Olympics – Ice Dancing	—	.95	.34
❏ 2068	20¢	Olympics – Downhill Skiing	—	.95	.34
❏ 2069	20¢	Olympics – Cross Country Skiing	—	.95	.34
❏ 2070	20¢	Olympics – Hockey	—	.95	.34
		Block of 4 (2067–2070)	5.00	3.00	2.50

2071 **2072** **2073** **2074**

2075

2076–2079

2080

Scott No.			Plate Block	Unused	Used
❏ 2071	20¢	FDIC	4.25	.95	.34
❏ 2072	20¢	Love	18.00 (20)	.95	.34
❏ 2073	20¢	Carter G. Woodson	4.25	.95	.34
❏ 2074	20¢	Soil & Water Conservation	4.25	.95	.34
❏ 2075	20¢	Credit Union	4.25	.95	.34
❏ 2076	20¢	Orchids – Wild Pink	—	.95	.34
❏ 2077	20¢	Orchids – Yellow Lady Slipper	—	.95	.34
❏ 2078	20¢	Orchids – Spreading Pogonia	—	.95	.34
❏ 2079	20¢	Orchids – Pacific Calypso	—	.95	.34
		Block of 4 (2076–2079)	5.00	4.00	2.50
❏ 2080	20¢	Hawaii Statehood	4.25	.95	.34

2081

2082–2085

2086

2087

2088

Scott No.			Plate Block	Unused	Used
❑ 2081	20¢	National Archives	4.25	.95	.34
❑ 2082	20¢	Olympics – Men's Diving	—	.95	.34
❑ 2083	20¢	Olympics – Long Jump	—	.95	.34
❑ 2084	20¢	Olympics – Wrestling	—	.95	.34
❑ 2085	20¢	Olympics – Kayaking	—	.95	.34
		Block of 4 (2081–2084)	5.00	4.00	3.00
❑ 2086	20¢	Louisiana World's Exposition	4.25	1.00	.34
❑ 2087	20¢	Health Research	4.25	.95	.34
❑ 2088	20¢	Douglas Fairbanks	16.00 (20)	.95	.34

2091

2089

2090

2092

2093

2094

2095

2096

2097

Scott No.			Plate Block	Unused	Used
❏ 2089	20¢	Jim Thorpe	4.25	1.25	.34
❏ 2090	20¢	John McCormack	4.25	.90	.34
❏ 2091	20¢	St. Lawrence Seaway	4.25	.90	.34
❏ 2092	20¢	Preserving Wetlands	4.25	1.00	.34
❏ 2093	20¢	Roanoke Voyages	4.25	.90	.34
❏ 2094	20¢	Herman Melville	4.25	.90	.34
❏ 2095	20¢	Horace Moses	18.00 (20)	1.25	.34
❏ 2096	20¢	Smokey the Bear	4.25	1.25	.34
❏ 2097	20¢	Roberto Clemente	12.00	4.00	.34

2098–2101

2102

2103

2104

2105

Scott No.			Plate Block	Unused	Used
❏ 2098	20¢	Beagle & Boston Terrier	—	.95	.34
❏ 2099	20¢	Retriever & Cocker Spaniel	—	.95	.34
❏ 2100	20¢	Malamute & Collie	—	.95	.34
❏ 2101	20¢	Coonhound & Foxhound	—	.95	.34
		Block of 4 (2098–2101)	5.00	4.00	2.50
❏ 2102	20¢	Crime Prevention	4.25	.95	.34
❏ 2103	20¢	Hispanic Americans	4.25	.95	.34
❏ 2104	20¢	Family Unity	20.00 (20)	.95	.34
❏ 2105	20¢	Eleanor Roosevelt	4.25	.95	.34

2106

2107

2108

Vietnam Veterans Memorial USA 20c

2109

Scott No.			Plate Block	Unused	Used
❏ 2106	20¢	Nation of Readers	4.25	.95	.34
❏ 2107	20¢	Christmas – Madonna & Child	4.25	.95	.34
❏ 2108	20¢	Christmas – Santa Claus	4.25	.95	.34
❏ 2109	20¢	Vietnam Veterans Memorial	4.25	1.25	.34

2110

2111
(2112, 2113)

1985.

❏ 2110	22¢	Jerome Kern	4.25	.95	.34
❏ 2111	(22¢)	"D" & Eagle	32.00 (20)	1.25	.34

Scott No.		PNC Strip (5)	Unused	Used

1985. Coil Stamp.

❏ 2112 (22¢) "D" & Eagle (~2111)	14.00	2.00	.34

2114
(2115)

Scott No.		Plate Block	Unused	Used

1985.

❏ 2113 (22¢) "D" & Eagle (~2111)	—	1.00	.34
Booklet pane of 10	—	10.00	4.00
❏ 2114 22¢ Flag over Capitol	4.00	1.00	.34

Scott No.		PNC Strip (5)	Unused	Used

1985. Coil Stamps.

❏ 2115 22¢ Flag over Capitol (~2114)	4.00	.50	.40
❏ 2115b With small letter "T" at bottom	4.00	.80	.65

2116

Scott No.		Plate Block	Unused	Used

1985.

❏ 2116 22¢ Flag over Capitol	—	2.00	.40
Booklet pane of 5	—	4.00	2.25

2117–2121

2122

Scott No.			Plate Block	Unused	Used
❏ 2117	22¢	Seashells – Frilled Dogwinkle	—	.95	.34
❏ 2118	22¢	Seashells – Reticulated Dogwinkle	—	.95	.34
❏ 2119	22¢	Seashells – New England Neptune	—	.95	.34
❏ 2120	22¢	Seashells – Calico Scallop	—	.95	.34
❏ 2121	22¢	Seashells – Lightning Whelk	—	.95	.34
		Booklet pane of 10 (2 each 2117–2121)	—	5.00	2.00
❏ 2122	$10.75	Express Mail (type I)	—	30.00	8.00
		Booklet pane of 3	—	80.00	14.00
❏ 2122b	$10.75	Express Mail (~2122) (type II)	—	50.00	16.00
		Booklet pane of 3	—	125.00	—

NOTE: Type I (Plate No. 11111) appears washed-out. Type II (Plate No. 22222) appears brighter and more intensely colored.

Scott No.			PNC Strip (5)	Unused	Used

Transportation Series Coil Stamps.

			PNC Strip (5)	Unused	Used
☐ 2123	3.4¢	School Bus	2.00	.40	.34
☐ 2124	4.9¢	Buckboard	2.00	.40	.34
☐ 2125	5.5¢	Star Route Truck	4.00	.40	.34
☐ 2126	6¢	Tricycle	2.00	.40	.34
☐ 2127	7.1¢	Tractor	4.00	.75	.34
☐ 2128	8.3¢	Ambulance	2.00	.75	.34
☐ 2129	8.5¢	Tow Truck	4.00	.75	.34
☐ 2130	10.1¢	Oil Wagon	4.00	.75	.34
☐ 2131	11¢	Stutz Bearcat	2.00	.75	.34
☐ 2132	12¢	Stanley Steamer	4.00	.75	.34
☐ 2133	12.5¢	Pushcart	4.00	.75	.34
☐ 2134	14¢	Iceboat	4.00	.75	.34
☐ 2135	17¢	Dogsled	4.00	.80	.34
☐ 2136	25¢	Breadwagon	5.00	.80	.34

NOTE: Some values of the above exist Bureau precanceled. Prices are the same as unprecanceled examples.

See Nos. 1897–1908, 2225–2231, 2252–2266, and 2451–2468 for other Transportation Series coil stamps.

2137

2138–2141

2142   **2143**   **2144**

Scott No.			Plate Block	Unused	Used
1985.					
❏ 2137	22¢	Mary McLeod Bethune	4.25	1.25	.34
❏ 2138	22¢	Broadbill Decoy	—	2.00	.34
❏ 2139	22¢	Mallard Decoy	—	2.00	.34
❏ 2140	22¢	Canvasback Decoy	—	1.25	.34
❏ 2141	22¢	Redhead Decoy	—	1.25	.34
		Block of 4 (2138–2141)	14.00	8.00	5.00
❏ 2142	22¢	Winter Special Olympics	4.25	1.25	.34
❏ 2143	22¢	Love	4.25	1.25	.34
❏ 2144	22¢	Rural Electrification	30.00 (20)	1.25	.34

| | 2145 | 2146 | 2147 |

Scott No.			Plate Block	Unused	Used
❑ 2145	22¢	AMERIPEX	5.00	1.00	.34
❑ 2146	22¢	Abigail Adams	5.00	1.00	.34
❑ 2147	22¢	F. A. Bartholdi	5.00	1.00	.34

| 2149 | 2149a | 2150 | 2150a |

Scott No.			PNC Strip (5)	Unused	Used

Coil Stamps.

Scott No.			PNC Strip (5)	Unused	Used
❑ 2149	18¢	George Washington	6.00	1.25	.34
❑ 2149a	18¢	Washington & "Presorted First-Class"	4.25	.80	.34
❑ 2150	21.1¢	Envelopes	5.00	1.25	.34
❑ 2150a	21.1¢	Envelopes & "ZIP + 4"	6.00	1.25	.34

2152

2153

2154

2159

2155–2158

Scott No.			Plate Block	Unused	Used
1985.					
☐ 2152	22¢	Korean War Veterans	4.25	2.25	.34
☐ 2153	22¢	Social Security	4.25	2.25	.34
☐ 2154	22¢	World War I Veterans	4.25	2.25	.34
☐ 2155	22¢	Quarter Horse	—	2.25	.34
☐ 2156	22¢	Morgan Horse	—	2.25	.34
☐ 2157	22¢	Saddlebred Horse	—	2.25	.34
☐ 2158	22¢	Appaloosa	—	2.25	.34
		Block of 4 (2155–2158)	18.00	12.00	8.00
☐ 2159	22¢	Public Education	8.00	4.25	2.00

2160–2163

2164

2165

2166

2167

Scott No.			Plate Block	Unused	Used
❑ 2160	22¢	Youth Year – YMCA	—	1.25	.34
❑ 2161	22¢	Youth Year – Boy Scouts	—	1.25	.34
❑ 2162	22¢	Youth Year – Big Brothers	—	1.25	.34
❑ 2163	22¢	Youth Year – Campfire Girls	—	1.25	.34
		Block of 4 (2160–2163)	8.00	5.00	3.15
❑ 2164	22¢	Help End Hunger	4.25	1.00	.34
❑ 2165	22¢	Christmas – Madonna & Child	4.25	1.00	.34
❑ 2166	22¢	Christmas – Poinsettia	4.25	1.00	.34

1986.

❑ 2167	22¢	Arkansas Statehood	4.25	2.00	.34

2168	2169	2170	2171	2172

2173	2175	2176	2177	2178

2179	2180	2181	2182 (2197)	2183

Scott No.			Plate Block	Unused	Used
1986–1993. Great Americans Series.					
❑ 2168	1¢	Margaret Mitchell	.80	.40	.34
❑ 2169	2¢	Mary Lyon	.80	.40	.34
❑ 2170	3¢	Paul Dudley White M.D.	2.00	.40	.34
❑ 2171	4¢	Father Flanagan	2.00	.40	.34
❑ 2172	5¢	Hugo L. Black	2.00	.40	.34
❑ 2173	5¢	Luis Munoz Marin	2.00	.40	.34
❑ 2175	10¢	Red Cloud	2.00	.40	.40
❑ 2176	14¢	Julia Ward Howe	4.25	.50	.40
❑ 2177	15¢	Buffalo Bill Cody	7.00	1.00	.40
❑ 2178	17¢	Belva Ann Lockwood	4.25	1.00	.40
❑ 2179	20¢	Virginia Apgar	4.25	1.00	.34
❑ 2180	21¢	Chester Carlson	4.25	1.00	.34
❑ 2181	23¢	Mary Cassatt	4.25	1.00	.34
❑ 2182	25¢	Jack London	4.25	1.00	.34
❑ 2183	28¢	Sitting Bull	6.00	1.15	.34

Scott No.			Plate Block	Unused	Used
❏ 2184	29¢	Earl Warren	4.25	1.25	.34
❏ 2185	29¢	Thomas Jefferson	4.25	1.25	.34
❏ 2186	35¢	Dennis Chavez	5.00	2.50	.34
❏ 2187	40¢	Claire Chenault	7.00	1.15	.40
❏ 2188	45¢	Dr. Harvey Cushing	7.00	2.50	.34
❏ 2189	52¢	Hubert Humphrey	8.00	2.50	.40
❏ 2190	56¢	John Harvard	8.00	2.50	.40
❏ 2191	65¢	H. H. "Hap" Arnold	8.50	2.50	.40
❏ 2192	75¢	Wendell Wilkie	10.00	2.50	.40
❏ 2193	$1	Bernard Revel	20.00	4.25	.70
❏ 2194	$1	Johns Hopkins	15.00	4.25	.70
❏ 2195	$2	William Jennings Bryan	25.00	5.00	.90
❏ 2196	$5	Bret Harte	50.00	12.00	4.00
❏ 2197	25¢	Jack London (~2182)	—	1.00	.32
		Booklet pane of 6	—	5.00	4.00

NOTE: See Nos. 1844–1869 and 2933–2943 for other Great Americans Series stamps.

2198–2201

| 2202 | 2203 | 2204 |

Scott No.			Plate Block	Unused	Used
1986.					
❏ 2198	22¢	AMERIPEX – Vintage Hand Cancel	—	1.00	.34
❏ 2199	22¢	AMERIPEX – Boy Stamp Collector	—	1.00	.34
❏ 2200	22¢	AMERIPEX – Magnifying Glass	—	1.00	.34
❏ 2201	22¢	AMERIPEX – Modern Hand Cancel	—	1.00	.34
		Booklet pane of 4 (2198–2201)	—	4.00	2.00
❏ 2202	22¢	Love – Puppy	4.25	.95	.34
❏ 2203	22¢	Sojourner Truth	4.25	.95	.34
❏ 2204	22¢	Republic of Texas	4.25	.95	.34

2205–2209

2210

2211

Scott No.			Plate Block	Unused	Used
❏ 2205	22¢	Fish – Muskellunge	—	1.00	.34
❏ 2206	22¢	Fish – Atlantic Cod	—	1.00	.34
❏ 2207	22¢	Fish – Largemouth Bass	—	1.00	.34
❏ 2208	22¢	Fish – Bluefin Tuna	—	1.00	.34
❏ 2209	22¢	Fish – Catfish	—	1.00	.34
		Booklet pane of 5 (2205–2209)	—	9.00	2.75
❏ 2210	22¢	Public Hospitals	4.25	1.00	.34
❏ 2211	22¢	Duke Ellington	4.25	1.00	.34

2216

2217

2218

2219

Scott No.			Plate Block	Unused	Used
❏ 2216	22¢	AMERIPEX – Presidents I	—	8.00	.34
❏ 2216a-i		Any single stamp	—	4.50	.90
❏ 2217	22¢	AMERIPEX – Presidents II	—	5.00	.34
❏ 2217a-i		Any single stamp	—	4.50	.90
❏ 2218	22¢	AMERIPEX – Presidents III	—	5.00	.34
❏ 2218a-i		Any single stamp	—	4.50	.90
❏ 2219	22¢	AMERIPEX – Presidents IV	—	5.00	.34
❏ 2219a-i		Any single stamp	—	4.50	.90

2220–2223

2224

Scott No.			Plate Block	Unused	Used
❑ 2220	22¢	Elisha Kane Kent	—	1.00	.34
❑ 2221	22¢	Adolphus W. Greely	—	1.00	.34
❑ 2222	22¢	Vilhjalmur Stefansson	—	1.00	.34
❑ 2223	22¢	Peary & Henson	—	1.00	.34
		Block of 4 (2220–2223)	6.00	4.00	3.50
❑ 2224	22¢	Statue of Liberty	4.00	2.25	.34

2225   **2226**   **2228**

Scott No.			PNC Strip (5)	Unused	Used
1986–1987. Transportation Series Coil Stamps.					
❑ 2225	1¢	Omnibus, no ¢ symbol	1.00	.40	.34
❑ 2226	2¢	Locomotive, no ¢ symbol	1.00	.40	.34
❑ 2228	4¢	Stagecoach (~1898A)	2.00	.40	.34
❑ 2231	8.3¢	Ambulance (~2128)	10.00	.40	.34

NOTE: See Nos. 1897–1897A for designs similar to Nos. 2225–2226 except with ¢ symbol,

2235–2238

2239

2240–2243

Scott No.			Plate Block	Unused	Used
1986.					
❏ 2235	22¢	Navajo Carpet – Four Crosses	—	1.00	.34
❏ 2236	22¢	Navajo Carpet – Vertical Diamonds	—	1.00	.34
❏ 2237	22¢	Navajo Carpet – Lowe Art Museum	—	1.00	.34
❏ 2238	22¢	Navajo Carpet – Eight Diamonds	—	1.00	.34
		Block of 4 (2235–2238)	5.00	4.00	3.00
❏ 2239	22¢	T. S. Eliot	4.25	2.00	.34
❏ 2240	22¢	Highlander Figure	—	1.00	.34
❏ 2241	22¢	Ship Figurehead	—	1.00	.34
❏ 2242	22¢	Nautical Figure	—	1.00	.34
❏ 2243	22¢	Cigar Store Figure	—	1.00	.34
		Block of 4 (2240–2243)	5.00	2.50	2.00

2244    **2245**

Scott No.			Plate Block	Unused	Used
❑ 2244	22¢	Christmas – Madonna & Child	4.25	1.00	.34
❑ 2245	22¢	Christmas – Village Scene	4.25	1.00	.34

2247    **2248**

2246

2249    **2250**    **2251**

1987.

❑ 2246	22¢	Michigan Statehood	4.25	1.00	.34
❑ 2247	22¢	Pan American Games	4.25	1.00	.34
❑ 2248	22¢	Love	4.25	1.00	.34
❑ 2249	22¢	Jean Baptiste Pointe du Sable	4.25	1.00	.34
❑ 2250	22¢	Enrico Caruso	2.50	1.00	.34
❑ 2251	22¢	Girl Scouts	4.25	1.00	.34

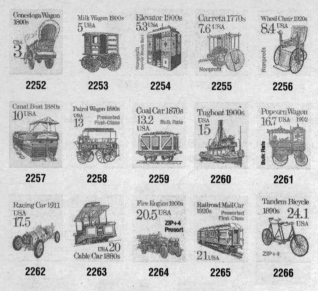

Scott No.			PNC Strip (5)	Unused	Used
1987–1993. Transportation Series Coil Stamps.					
❏ 2252	3¢	Conestoga Wagon	4.25	.40	.34
❏ 2253	5¢	Milk Wagon	4.25	.40	.34
❏ 2254	5.3¢	Elevator	4.25	.40	.34
❏ 2255	7.6¢	Carreta	4.25	.70	.34
❏ 2256	8.4¢	Wheelchair	4.25	.70	.34
❏ 2257	10¢	Canal Boat	4.25	.70	.34
❏ 2258	13¢	Police Wagon	6.00	.80	.34
❏ 2259	13.2¢	Coal Car	5.00	.70	.34
❏ 2260	15¢	Tug Boat	4.25	.70	.34
❏ 2261	16.7¢	Popcorn Wagon	4.25	.70	.34
❏ 2262	17.5¢	Racing Car	6.00	.70	.34
❏ 2263	20¢	Cable Car	5.00	1.00	.34
❏ 2264	20.5¢	Fire Engine	12.00	2.00	.85
❏ 2265	21¢	Railroad Mail Car	8.00	1.00	.70
❏ 2266	24.1¢	Tandem Bicycle	8.00	1.00	.70

See Nos. 1897–1908, 2123–2136, 2225–2231, and 2451–2468 for other
Transportation Series coil stamps.

2267–2274

Scott No.			Plate Block	Unused	Used
1987.					
❏ 2267	22¢	Congratulations!	—	1.50	.34
❏ 2268	22¢	Get Well!	—	1.50	.34
❏ 2269	22¢	Thank You!	—	1.50	.34
❏ 2270	22¢	Love You, Dad!	—	1.50	.34
❏ 2271	22¢	Best Wishes!	—	1.50	.34
❏ 2272	22¢	Happy Birthday!	—	1.50	.34
❏ 2273	22¢	Love You, Mother!	—	2.00	.34
❏ 2274	22¢	Keep in Touch!	—	2.00	.34
		Booklet pane of 10 (2267–2271)	—	16.00	4.25

	2275	2276	2277	2278
			(2279, 2282)	(2285A)

Scott No.			Plate Block	Unused	Used
❑ 2275	22¢	United Way	4.25	1.00	.34
❑ 2276	22¢	Flag & Fireworks	4.25	1.00	.34
		Booklet pane of 20	—	11.00	.60
❑ 2277	(25¢)	"E" & Earth	4.25	1.00	.40
❑ 2278	25¢	Flag & Clouds, perf 10	4.25	1.00	.40

2280	2281	2283	2284	2285

Scott No.			PNC Strip (5)	Unused	Used

Coil Stamps.

❑ 2279	(25¢)	"E" & Earth (~2277)	4.25	1.00	.34
❑ 2280	25¢	Flag over Yosemite	5.00	1.00	.34
❑ 2281	25¢	Honey Bee	6.00	1.00	.34

Booklet Stamps.

❑ 2282	(25¢)	"E" & Earth (~2277)	—	1.25	.40
		Booklet pane of 10	—	8.00	4.00
❑ 2283	25¢	Pheasant	—	1.25	.30
		Booklet pane of 10	—	8.00	4.00
❑ 2284	25¢	Grosbeak	—	1.25	.34
❑ 2285	25¢	Owl	—	1.25	.34
		Booklet pane of 10, (5 each 2284 & 2285)	—	7.00	5.00
❑ 2285A	25¢	Flag & Clouds (2278), perf 10x11		1.25	.34
		Booklet pane of 6		5.00	4.00

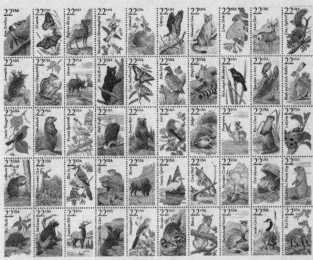

2286–2335

Scott No.	Plate Block	Unused	Used

1987.

❏ 2286–
　2335　22¢　Wildlife, pane of 50　　　—　　100.00　　—
❏ 2286–2335　Any single stamp　　　—　　4.00　　.45

❏ 2286　Barn Swallow
❏ 2287　Monarch Butterfly
❏ 2288　Bighorn Sheep
❏ 2289　Broad-tailed Hummingbird
❏ 2290　Cottontail
❏ 2291　Osprey
❏ 2292　Mountain Lion
❏ 2293　Luna Moth
❏ 2294　Mule Deer
❏ 2295　Gray Squirrel
❏ 2296　Armadillo
❏ 2297　Eastern Chipmunk
❏ 2298　Moose

❏ 2299　Black Bear
❏ 2300　Tiger Swallowtail
❏ 2301　Bobwhite
❏ 2302　Ringtail
❏ 2303　Red-wing Blackbird
❏ 2304　Lobster
❏ 2305　Black-tailed Jack Rabbit
❏ 2306　Scarlet Tanager
❏ 2307　Woodchuck
❏ 2308　Roseate Spoonbill
❏ 2309　Bald Eagle
❏ 2310　Alaskan Brown Bear
❏ 2311　Iiwi

❑ 2312 Badger
❑ 2313 Pronghorn
❑ 2314 River Otter
❑ 2315 Ladybug
❑ 2316 Beaver
❑ 2317 White-tail Deer
❑ 2318 Blue Jay
❑ 2319 Pika
❑ 2320 Buffalo
❑ 2321 Snowy Egret
❑ 2322 Gray Wolf
❑ 2323 Mountain Goat

❑ 2324 Deer Mouse
❑ 2325 Black-tailed Prairie Dog
❑ 2326 Box Turtle
❑ 2327 Wolverine
❑ 2328 Elk
❑ 2329 California Sea Lion
❑ 2330 Mockingbird
❑ 2331 Raccoon
❑ 2332 Bobcat
❑ 2333 Black-footed Ferret
❑ 2334 Canada Goose
❑ 2335 Red Fox

2336

2337

2338

2339

2340

2341

2342

Scott No.			Plate Block	Unused	Used
❑ 2336	22¢	Delaware	5.75	1.25	.34
❑ 2337	22¢	Pennsylvania	5.75	1.25	.34
❑ 2338	22¢	New Jersey	5.75	1.25	.34
❑ 2339	22¢	Georgia	5.75	1.25	.34
❑ 2340	22¢	Connecticut	5.75	1.25	.34
❑ 2341	22¢	Massachusetts	5.75	1.25	.34
❑ 2342	22¢	Maryland	5.75	1.25	.34

May 23, 1788
South Carolina

2343

June 21, 1788
New Hampshire

2344

June 25, 1788   USA
Virginia   25

2345

July 26, 1788   USA
New York   25

2346

November 21, 1789
North Carolina

2347

May 29, 1790
Rhode Island

2348

Friendship
with Morocco
1787-1987

USA 22

2349

William Faulkner

USA 22

2350

Scott No.			Plate Block	Unused	Used
❏ 2343	22¢	South Carolina	5.75	1.25	.34
❏ 2344	22¢	New Hampshire	5.75	1.25	.34
❏ 2345	22¢	Virginia	5.75	1.25	.34
❏ 2346	22¢	New York	5.75	1.25	.34
❏ 2347	22¢	North Carolina	5.75	1.25	.34
❏ 2348	22¢	Rhode Island	5.75	1.25	.34
❏ 2349	22¢	Friendship with Morocco	5.75	1.25	.34
❏ 2350	22¢	William Faulkner	5.75	1.25	.34

2351–2354

2355–2359

Scott No.			Plate Block	Unused	Used
❑ 2351	22¢	Lace	—	1.00	.34
❑ 2352	22¢	Lace	—	1.00	.34
❑ 2353	22¢	Lace	—	1.00	.34
❑ 2354	22¢	Lace	—	1.00	.34
		Block of 4 (2351–2354)	7.00	3.00	2.00
❑ 2355	22¢	Constitution – "Bicentennial"	—	1.00	.34
❑ 2356	22¢	Constitution – "We the People"	—	1.00	.34
❑ 2357	22¢	Constitution – "Establish Justice"	—	1.00	.34
❑ 2358	22¢	Constitution – "And Secure"	—	1.00	.34
❑ 2359	22¢	Constitution – "Do Ordain"	—	1.00	.34
		Booklet pane of 5 (1255–2359)	—	6.00	2.00

2360

2361

2362–2366

2367

2368

Scott No.			Plate Block	Unused	Used
❏ 2360	22¢	U. S. Constitution	5.00	1.25	.34
❏ 2361	22¢	CPAs	14.00	4.00	.34
❏ 2362	22¢	Stourbridge Lion	—	1.25	.34
❏ 2363	22¢	Best Friend of Charleston	—	1.25	.34
❏ 2364	22¢	John Bull	—	1.25	.34
❏ 2365	22¢	Brother Jonathan	—	1.25	.34
❏ 2366	22¢	Gowan & Marx	—	1.25	.34
		Booklet pane of 5 (2362–2367)	—	5.00	4.00
❏ 2367	22¢	Christmas – Madonna & Child	4.25	1.00	.75
❏ 2368	22¢	Christmas – Ornament	4.25	1.00	.75

2369 **2370** **2371**

2372–2375

Scott No.			Plate Block	Unused	Used
1988.					
❏ 2369	22¢	Olympics – Downhill Skier	4.25	1.00	.34
❏ 2370	22¢	Australia Bicentennial	4.25	1.00	.34
❏ 2371	22¢	James Weldon Johnson	4.25	1.00	.34
❏ 2372	22¢	Cats – Siamese & Exotic Short Hair	—	1.00	2.00
❏ 2373	22¢	Cats – Abyssinian & Himalayan	—	1.00	2.00
❏ 2374	22¢	Cats – Maine Coon & Burmese	—	1.00	2.00
❏ 2375	22¢	Cats – American Shorthair & Persian	—	1.00	2.00
		Block of 4 (2372–2375)	5.00	3.00	2.00

2376

2377

2378

2379

2380

2381–2385

Scott No.			Plate Block	Unused	Used
❏ 2376	22¢	Knute Rockne	4.25	1.25	.32
❏ 2377	25¢	Francis Ouimet	5.00	1.25	.32
❏ 2378	25¢	Love – Rose	4.00	1.25	.32
❏ 2379	45¢	Love – Rose	6.00	1.50	.32
❏ 2380	25¢	Olympics – Gymnast on Rings	5.00	1.00	.32
❏ 2381	25¢	Autos – Locomobile	—	1.00	.32
❏ 2382	25¢	Autos – Pierce Arrow	—	1.00	.32
❏ 2383	25¢	Autos – Cord	—	1.00	.32
❏ 2384	25¢	Autos – Packard	—	1.00	.32
❏ 2385	25¢	Autos – Dusenberg	—	1.00	.32
		Booklet pane of 5 (2381–2385)	—	12.00	2.00

2386–2389

2390–2393

2394

Scott No.			Plate Block	Unused	Used
❏ 2386	25¢	Nathaniel Palmer	—	1.00	.34
❏ 2387	25¢	Lt. Charles Wilkes	—	1.00	.34
❏ 2388	25¢	Richard E. Byrd	—	1.00	.34
❏ 2389	25¢	Lincoln Ellsworth	—	1.00	.34
		Block of 4 (2386–2389)	8.00	4.00	2.00
❏ 2390	25¢	Carousel – Deer	—	1.25	.34
❏ 2391	25¢	Carousel – Horse	—	1.25	.34
❏ 2392	25¢	Carousel – Camel	—	1.25	.34
❏ 2393	25¢	Carousel – Goat	—	1.25	.34
		Block of 4 (2390–2393)	8.00	5.00	4.15
❏ 2394	$8.75	Express Mail	100.00	25.00	10.00

2395

2396

2397

2398

2399

2400

Scott No.			Plate Block	Unused	Used
❏ 2395	25¢	Happy Birthday	—	1.25	.34
❏ 2396	25¢	Best Wishes	—	1.25	.34
		Booklet pane of 6 (3 each 2395 & 2396)	—	5.00	4.00
❏ 2397	25¢	Thinking of You	—	1.00	.34
❏ 2398	25¢	Love You	—	1.00	.34
		Booklet pane of 6 (3 each 2397 & 2398)	—	4.50	3.50
❏ 2399	25¢	Christmas – Madonna & Child	4.25	1.00	.34
❏ 2400	25¢	Christmas – Winter Scene	4.25	1.00	.34

2401

2402

2403

2404

2405–2409

Scott No.			Plate Block	Unused	Used
1989.					
❑ 2401	25¢	Montana	4.25	1.25	.34
❑ 2402	25¢	A. Philip Randolph	4.25	1.25	.34
❑ 2403	25¢	North Dakota Statehood	4.25	1.25	.34
❑ 2404	25¢	Washington Statehood	4.25	1.25	.34
❑ 2405	25¢	Steamboats – Experiment	—	1.00	.34
❑ 2406	25¢	Steamboats – Phoenix	—	1.00	.34
❑ 2407	25¢	Steamboats – New Orleans	—	1.00	.34
❑ 2408	25¢	Steamboats – Washington	—	1.00	.34
❑ 2409	25¢	Steamboats – Walk in the Water	—	1.00	.34
		Booklet pane of 5 (2404–2409)	—	5.00	4.25

2410   2411

2412   2413   2414   2415

2416

Scott No.			Plate Block	Unused	Used
❑ 2410	25¢	World Stamp Expo '89	4.25	1.00	.34
❑ 2411	25¢	Arturo Toscanini	4.25	1.00	.34
❑ 2412	25¢	Bicentennial – House of Representatives	5.00	1.00	.34
❑ 2413	25¢	Bicentennial – U. S. Senate	5.00	1.00	.34
❑ 2414	25¢	Bicentennial – Executive Branch	5.00	1.00	.34
❑ 2415	25¢	Bicentennial – Supreme Court	4.25	1.00	.34
❑ 2416	25¢	South Dakota Statehood	4.25	1.00	.34

2417

2418

2419

2420

2421

2422–2425

Scott No.			Plate Block	Unused	Used
❏ 2417	25¢	Lou Gehrig	5.00	1.25	.34
❏ 2418	25¢	Ernest Hemingway	5.00	1.25	.34
❏ 2419	$2.40	Moon Landing	32.00	7.00	3.00
❏ 2420	25¢	Letter Carriers	4.25	.75	.34
❏ 2421	25¢	Bill of Rights	4.50	1.25	.34
❏ 2422	25¢	Dinosaurs – Tyrannosaurus	—	1.25	.34
❏ 2423	25¢	Dinosaurs – Pteranodon	—	1.25	.34
❏ 2424	25¢	Dinosaurs – Stegosaurus	—	1.25	.34
❏ 2425	25¢	Dinosaurs – Brontosaurus	—	1.25	.34
		Block of 4 (2421–2425)	8.00	5.00	4.25

2426

2427

2428
(2429)

2431

2433

Scott No.			Plate Block	Unused	Used
❑ 2426	25¢	Southwest Carving	4.25	1.00	.34
❑ 2427	25¢	Christmas – Madonna	4.25	1.00	.34
❑ 2428	25¢	Christmas – Sleigh	4.25	1.00	.34
❑ 2429	25¢	Christmas – Sleigh (~2428)	—	1.00	.34
		Booklet pane of 10	—	12.90	4.00
❑ 2431	25¢	Eagle & Shield	—	.75	.34
		Booklet pane of 18	—	20.00	—
❑ 2433	$3.60	Lincoln Essays, souvenir sheet	—	20.00	7.00
❑ 2433a-d		Any single stamp	—	4.25	2.20

2434–2437

2438

Scott No.			Plate Block	Unused	Used
❏ 2434	25¢	Stagecoach	—	1.00	.34
❏ 2435	25¢	Paddlewheel Steamer	—	1.00	.34
❏ 2436	25¢	Biplane	—	1.00	.34
❏ 2437	25¢	Automobile	—	1.00	.34
		Block of 4 (2434–2437)	7.00	6.00	4.25
❏ 2438	$1	Souvenir sheet (~2434–2437)	—	5.00	2.00
❏ 2438a-d		Any single stamp	—	6.00	4.25

2440
(2441)

2439

2442

2443

2444

2445–2448

Scott No.			Plate Block	Unused	Used
1990.					
❏ 2439	25¢	Idaho Statehood	4.25	1.00	.34
❏ 2440	25¢	Love	4.25	1.00	.34
❏ 2441	25¢	Love (~2440)	—	1.00	.34
		Booklet pane of 10	—	10.00	6.00
❏ 2442	25¢	Ida B. Wells	4.25	1.00	.34
❏ 2443	25¢	Beach Umbrella	—	1.00	.34
		Booklet pane of 10	—	5.00	4.15
❏ 2444	25¢	Wyoming Statehood	4.25	2.20	.34
❏ 2445	25¢	Films – Wizard of Oz	—	2.20	.34
❏ 2446	25¢	Films – Gone with the Wind	—	2.20	.34
❏ 2447	25¢	Films – Beau Geste	—	2.20	.34
❏ 2448	25¢	Films – Stagecoach	—	2.20	.34
		Block of 4 (2445–2448}	12.00	7.00	4.15

2449

Scott No.			Plate Block	Unused	Used
❏ 2449	25¢	Marianne Moore	4.25	.90	.32

2451   **2452**   **2452D**   **2453**   **2457**
(2452B)   (2454)   (2458)

Scott No.			PNC Strip (5)	Unused	Used
1990. Transportation Series Coil Stamps.					
❏ 2451	4¢	Steam Carriage	2.15	.55	.34
❏ 2452	5¢	Circus Wagon (05) (engraved)	2.15	.55	.34
❏ 2452B	5¢	Circus Wagon (~2452) (05) (photogravure)	2.15	.55	.34
❏ 2452D	5¢	Circus Wagon (~2452) (5¢)	2.15	.55	.34
❏ 2453	5¢	Canoe, brown (engraved)	2.15	.55	.34
❏ 2454	5¢	Canoe, red (~2453) (photogravure)	4.25	.55	.34
❏ 2457	10¢	Tractor Trailer (engraved)	4.25	.55	.34
❏ 2458	10¢	Tractor Trailer (~2457) (photogravure)	4.25	.55	.34

| **2463** | **2464** | **2466** | **2468** |

Scott No.			PNC Strip (5)	Unused	Used
❑ 2463	20¢	Cog Railway	6.00	1.25	.34
❑ 2464	23¢	Lunch Wagon	5.00	1.25	.34
❑ 2466	32¢	Ferryboat	8.00	1.25	.34
❑ 2468	$1	Seaplane	20.00	4.25	.85

NOTE: Some values of the above exist Bureau precanceled. Prices are the same as unprecanceled examples.

See Nos. 1897–1908, 2123–2136, and 2225–2231 for other Transportation Series coil stamps.

2470–2474

Scott No.			Plate Block	Unused	Used
1990.					
❑ 2470	25¢	Lighthouses – Admiralty Head	—	1.00	.65
❑ 2471	25¢	Lighthouses – Cape Hatteras	—	1.00	.34
❑ 2472	25¢	Lighthouses – West Quoddy Head	—	1.00	.34
❑ 2473	25¢	Lighthouses – American Shoals	—	1.00	.34
❑ 2474	25¢	Lighthouses – Sandy Hook	—	1.00	.34
		Booklet pane of 5 (2470–2474)	—	8.00	4.00

2475

2476

2477
(3031, 3031A,
3044)

2478

2479

2480

2481

2482

Scott No.			Plate Block	Unused	Used
❏ 2475	25¢	Stylized Flag	—	1.25	.34
		Booklet pane of 12	—	9.00	—
❏ 2476	1¢	Kestrel ("01" numeral)	1.00	.75	.34
❏ 2477	1¢	Kestrel ("1¢" numeral)	1.00	.75	.34
❏ 2478	3¢	Bluebird ("03" numeral)	2.25	.75	.34
❏ 2479	19¢	Fawn	2.25	1.00	.34
❏ 2480	30¢	Cardinal	4.00	1.00	.34
❏ 2481	45¢	Sunfish	6.00	2.00	.55
❏ 2482	$2	Bobcat	20.00	4.00	2.00

2483
(3048, 3053)

1991–1995. Booklet Stamps.

❏ 2483	20¢	Blue Jay	—	1.25	.38
		Booklet pane of 10	—	7.00	2.00

2484

2486

2487
(2493, 2495)

2488
(2494, 2495A)

2489

2490

2491

2492

Scott No.			Plate Block	Unused	Used
❏ 2484	29¢	Wood Duck, black numerals	—	2.25	.34
		Booklet pane of 10	—	8.00	6.00
❏ 2485	29¢	Wood Duck, red numerals	—	4.00	.34
		Booklet pane of 10	—	7.00	5.25
❏ 2486	29¢	African Violets	—	1.25	.34
		Booklet pane of 10	—	8.00	5.50
❏ 2487	32¢	Peach	—	1.25	.34
❏ 2488	32¢	Pear	—	1.25	.34
		Booklet pane of 10 (5 each of 2487–2488)	—	8.00	6.30
❏ 2489	29¢	Red Squirrel	—	1.25	.34
		Booklet pane of 18	—	15.00	—
❏ 2490	29¢	Red Rose	—	1.25	.34
		Booklet pane of 18	—	14.00	—
❏ 2491	29¢	Pine Cone	—	1.25	.40
		Booklet pane of 18	—	15.00	—
❏ 2492	32¢	Pink Rose	—	2.00	.30
		Booklet pane of 20	—	16.00	—
		Booklet pane of 18	—	15.00	—
		Booklet pane of 16	—	15.00	—
		Booklet pane of 14	—	18.00	—
❏ 2493	32¢	Peach (~2487)	—	2.25	.38
❏ 2494	32¢	Pear (~2488)	—	2.25	.34
		Booklet pane of 20 (10 each 2493–2494)	—	18.00	—

Scott No.			PNC Strip (5)	Unused	Used

1995. Coil Stamps.

Scott No.			PNC Strip (5)	Unused	Used
❏ 2495	32¢	Peach (~2487)	—	4.25	.34
❏ 2495A	32¢	Pear (~2488)	—	4.25	.34
		Se-tenant pair (2495–2495A)	15.00	5.00	—

2496–2500

Scott No.			Plate Block	Unused	Used

1990.

Scott No.			Plate Block	Unused	Used
❏ 2496	25¢	Olympians – Jesse Owens	—	1.00	.34
❏ 2497	25¢	Olympians – Ray Ewry	—	1.00	.34
❏ 2498	25¢	Olympians – Hazel Wightman	—	1.00	.34
❏ 2499	25¢	Olympians – Eddie Eagan	—	1.00	.34
❏ 2500	25¢	Olympians – Helene Madison	—	1.00	.34
		Strip of 5 (2496–2500)	12.00 (10)	5.00	4.25

2501–2505

2506–2507

Scott No.			Plate Block	Unused	Used
❏ 2501	25¢	Headdress – Assiniboine	—	1.25	.40
❏ 2502	25¢	Headdress – Cheyenne	—	1.25	.40
❏ 2503	25¢	Headdress – Comanche	—	1.25	.40
❏ 2504	25¢	Headdress – Flathead	—	1.25	.40
❏ 2505	25¢	Headdress – Shoshone	—	1.25	.40
		Booklet pane of 10 (5 each 2501–2505)	—	12.00	6.00
❏ 2506	25¢	Micronesia	—	2.25	.75
❏ 2507	25¢	Marshall Islands	—	2.25	.75
		Se-tenant pair (2506–2507)	6.00	4.00	1.25

2508–2511

2512

2513

Scott No.			Plate Block	Unused	Used
❑ 2508	25¢	Killer Whale	—	1.00	.34
❑ 2509	25¢	Northern Sea Lion	—	1.00	.34
❑ 2510	25¢	Sea Otter	—	1.00	.34
❑ 2511	25¢	Dolphin	—	1.00	.34
		Block of 4 (2508–2511)	5.00	4.00	1.75
❑ 2512	25¢	Grand Canyon	4.00	1.25	.34
❑ 2513	25¢	Dwight D. Eisenhower	5.00	1.25	.34

2514

2515
(2516)

2517
(2518–2520)

2522

2521

Scott No.			Plate Block	Unused	Used
❑ 2514	25¢	Christmas – Madonna	4.25	1.00	.34
❑ 2515	25¢	Christmas Tree	4.25	1.00	.34
❑ 2516	25¢	Christmas Tree	—	1.00	.34
		Booklet pane of 10	—	8.00	4.00
❑ 2517	(29¢)	"F" & Flower	4.25	1.25	.34

Scott No.			PNC Strip (5)	Unused	Used
Coil Stamp.					
❑ 2518	(29¢)	"F" & Flower (~2517)	5.00	1.25	.34

Scott No.			Plate Block	Unused	Used
1991.					
❑ 2519	(29¢)	"F" & Flower (~2517)	—	1.25	.34
		Booklet pane of 10	—	25.00	14.00
❑ 2520	(29¢)	"F" & Flower (~2517)	—	1.25	.34
		Booklet pane of 10	—	24.00	14.00

NOTE: No. 2519 has a pale green leaf; No. 2520, a bright green leaf.

❑ 2521	(4¢)	Make Up Rate	2.00	.75	.34
❑ 2522	(29¢)	"F" & Stylized Flag	—	1.25	.34
		Booklet pane of 10	—	10.00	—

2523	**2524**	**2528**	**2529**
(2523A)	(2524A, 2525–2527)		(2529C)

Scott No.	PNC Strip (5)	Unused	Used

1991. Coil Stamps.

			PNC Strip (5)	Unused	Used
❑ 2523	29¢	Flag over Mt. Rushmore (engraved)	7.00	2.25	.34
❑ 2523A	29¢	Flag over Mt. Rushmore (photogravure)	6.00	2.25	.34

Scott No.	Plate Block	Unused	Used

1991. Sheet Stamps.

			Plate Block	Unused	Used
❑ 2524	29¢	Tulip, perforated 11	4.00	2.25	.34
❑ 2524A	29¢	Tulip, perforated 13 x 12½	5.00	2.25	.34

Scott No.	PNC Strip (5)	Unused	Used

1991. Coil Stamps.

			PNC Strip (5)	Unused	Used
❑ 2525	29¢	Tulip (~2524), rouletted	6.50	2.25	.34
❑ 2526	29¢	Tulip (~2524), perforated 10	7.00	2.25	.34

Scott No.	Plate Block	Unused	Used

1991. Booklet Stamps.

			Plate Block	Unused	Used
❑ 2527	29¢	Tulip (~2524)	—	2.25	.34
		Booklet pane of 10	—	8.00	4.00
❑ 2528	29¢	Flag & Olympic Rings	—	2.00	.34
		Booklet pane of 10	—	10.00	4.00

Scott No.	PNC Strip (5)	Unused	Used

1991. Coil Stamps.

			PNC Strip (5)	Unused	Used
❑ 2529	19¢	Fishing Boat	5.00	.95	.34
❑ 2529C	19¢	Fishing Boat (~2529)	10.00	2.00	.34

NOTE: No. 2529C contains only one loop of rope on the dock pole.

2530 **2531** **2531A** **2532**

2533 **2534** **2535** **2537**
  (2535A, 2536)

Scott No.			Plate Block	Unused	Used
1991. Booklet Stamp.					
❑ 2530	19¢	Ballooning	—	1.25	.80
		Booklet pane of 10	—	5.00	4.00
1991.					
❑ 2531	29¢	Flags on Parade	4.25	1.25	.34
❑ 2531A	29¢	Torch of Liberty	—	1.25	.34
❑ 2532	50¢	Switzerland	7.00	2.00	.34
❑ 2533	29¢	Vermont Statehood	7.00	2.00	.34
❑ 2534	29¢	Savings Bonds	4.25	1.25	.34
❑ 2535	29¢	Love, perforated 12½ x 13	4.25	1.25	.34
❑ 2535A	29¢	Love, perforated 11 (all sides)	5.00	1.25	.34
❑ 2536	29¢	Love, perforated 11 (2 or 3 sides)	—	1.25	.34
		Booklet pane of 10	—	8.00	4.00
❑ 2537	52¢	Love Birds	7.00	2.00	.34

2538 2539

2540

2541 2542

2543 2544 2544A

Scott No.			Plate Block	Unused	Used
❑ 2538	29¢	William Saroyan	4.00	2.25	.34
❑ 2539	$1	Olympic Rings	12.00	4.00	.90
❑ 2540	$2.90	Eagle & Olympic Rings	35.00	8.00	4.25
❑ 2541	$9.95	Express Mail	100.00	30.00	12.00
❑ 2542	$14	Express Mail	140.00	30.00	20.00
❑ 2543	$2.90	Futuristic Spacecraft	35.00	12.00	6.00
❑ 2544	$3	Space Shuttle "Enterprise"	32.00	12.00	6.00
❑ 2544A	$10.75	Shuttle Blasting Off	100.00	26.00	10.00

2545–2549

2550

2551
(2552)

Scott No.			Plate Block	Unused	Used
❑ 2545	29¢	Fishing Flies – Royal Wulff	—	1.40	.34
❑ 2546	29¢	Fishing Flies – Jock Scott	—	2.00	.34
❑ 2547	29¢	Fishing Flies – Apte Tarpon Fly	—	1.40	.34
❑ 2548	29¢	Fishing Flies – Lefty's Deceiver	—	2.00	.34
❑ 2549	29¢	Fishing Flies – Muddler Minnow	—	1.40	.34
		Booklet pane of 5 (2545–2549)	—	8.00	4.50
❑ 2550	29¢	Cole Porter	4.25	2.00	.34
❑ 2551	29¢	Desert Storm	4.25	1.40	.34
❑ 2552	29¢	Desert Storm, booklet stamp	—	1.40	.34
		Booklet pane of 5	—	5.00	4.00

2553–2557

2558

Scott No.			Plate Block	Unused	Used
❑ 2553	29¢	Olympics – High Jump	—	2.25	.34
❑ 2554	29¢	Olympics – Discus	—	2.25	.34
❑ 2555	29¢	Olympics – Sprint	—	1.25	.34
❑ 2556	29¢	Olympics – Javelin	—	2.25	.34
❑ 2557	29¢	Olympics – Hurdles	—	1.25	.34
		Strip of 5 (2553–2557)	10.00 (10)	4.00	3.50
❑ 2558	29¢	Numismatics	7.50	1.25	.34

2559

2560

2561

Scott No.			Plate Block	Unused	Used
❑ 2559	29¢	World War II, 1941, pane of 10	—	8.00	6.00
❑ 2559a–j	29¢	Any single stamp	—	1.25	.34
❑ 2560	29¢	Basketball	5.25	1.25	.34
❑ 2561	29¢	District of Columbia	5.25	1.25	.34

2562–2566

2567

Scott No.			Plate Block	Unused	Used
1991.					
❑ 2562	29¢	Comedians – Laurel & Hardy	—	1.00	.34
❑ 2563	29¢	Comedians – Bergen & McCarthy	—	1.00	.34
❑ 2564	29¢	Comedians – Jack Benny	—	1.00	.34
❑ 2565	29¢	Comedians – Fanny Brice	—	1.00	.34
❑ 2566	29¢	Comedians – Abbott & Costello	—	1.00	.34
		Booklet pane of 10 (2 each 1561–2566)	—	6.00	4.00
❑ 2567	29¢	Jan E. Matzeliger	4.25	1.00	.34

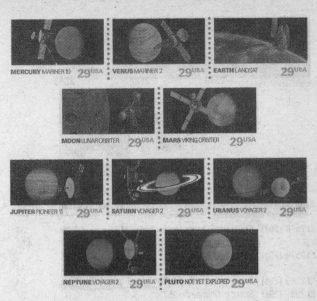

2568–2577

Scott No.			Plate Block	Unused	Used
❑ 2568	29¢	Mercury	—	2.00	.34
❑ 2569	29¢	Venus	—	2.00	.34
❑ 2570	29¢	Earth	—	2.00	.34
❑ 2571	29¢	Moon	—	1.25	.34
❑ 2572	29¢	Mars	—	1.25	.34
❑ 2573	29¢	Jupiter	—	2.00	.34
❑ 2574	29¢	Saturn	—	1.25	.34
❑ 2575	29¢	Uranus	—	2.00	.34
❑ 2576	29¢	Neptune	—	2.00	.34
❑ 2577	29¢	Pluto	—	1.25	.34
		Booklet pane of 10 (2568–2577)	—	12.00	5.00

2578

2579
(2580–2581)

2582

2583

2584

2585

Scott No.		Plate Block	Unused	Used
❏ 2578 (29¢)	Christmas – Madonna & Child	4.25	1.25	.34
	Booklet pane of 10	—	7.50	4.00
❏ 2579 (29¢)	Santa in Chimney, perforated all sides	4.25	1.25	.34
❏ 2580 (29¢)	Santa in Chimney (~2579)	—	2.00	.34
❏ 2581 (29¢)	Santa in Chimney (~2579)	—	2.00	.34
	Booklet pane of 4 (2 each of 2580–2581)	—	10.00	2.00

NOTE: Examples of 2580 contain part of an extra brick on the left side of the top row of bricks; examples of 2581 do not. Nos. 2580–2581 are booklet stamps and contain perforations on only 2 or 3 sides.

❏ 2582 (29¢)	Santa with List	—	1.00	.34
	Booklet pane of 4	—	5.00	1.00
❏ 2583 (29¢)	Santa and Package	—	1.00	.34
	Booklet pane of 4	—	5.00	1.00
❏ 2584 (29¢)	Santa and Fireplace	—	1.00	.34
	Booklet pane of 4	—	5.00	1.00
❏ 2585 (29¢)	Santa and Sleigh	—	1.00	.34
	Booklet pane of 4	—	5.00	1.00

2587

2590

2592

Scott No.			Plate Block	Unused	Used
1994–1995.					
❑ 2587	32¢	James Polk	4.25	2.00	.34
❑ 2590	$1	Surrender of General Burgoyne	12.00	4.00	1.25
❑ 2592	$5	Washington & Jackson	40.00	10.00	4.25

2593
(2593B, 2594)

2595
(2596–2597)

1992–1993. Booklet Stamps.

			Plate Block	Unused	Used
❑ 2593	29¢	Flag, black numeral, perforated 10	—	2.25	.35
		Booklet pane of 10	—	8.00	5.00
❑ 2593B	29¢	Flag (~2593), black numeral, perforated 11 x 10	—	2.25	1.00
		Booklet pane of 10	—	18.00	6.00
❑ 2594	29¢	Flag (~2593, red numeral	—	1.25	.40
		Booklet pane of 10	—	7.00	3.50
❑ 2595	29¢	Eagle & Shield, brown numeral	—	1.25	.55
		Booklet pane of 17	—	15.00	—
❑ 2596	29¢	Eagle & Shield (~2595), green numeral	—	1.25	.55
		Booklet pane of 17	—	12.00	—
❑ 2597	29¢	Eagle & Shield (~2595), red numeral	—	2.00	.55
		Booklet pane of 17	—	14.00	—

2598　　　**2599**

Scott No.			Plate Block	Unused	Used
❏ 2598	29¢	Eagle with Wings Upraised	—	2.25	.55
		Booklet pane of 18	—	15.00	—
❏ 2599	29¢	Statue of Liberty	—	2.25	.45
		Booklet pane of 18	• —	15.00	—

2602　　**2603**　　**2605**　　**2606**　　**2609**
　　　　(2604)　　　　　　(2607–2608)

Scott No.			PNC Strip (5)	Unused	Used

1991–1993. Coil Stamps.

			PNC Strip (5)	Unused	Used
❏ 2602	(10¢)	Bulk Rate USA, "USA" in red	4.25	.55	.34
❏ 2503	(10¢)	USA Bulk Rate, "USA" in blue, bright gold	4.25	.55	.34
❏ 2504	(10¢)	USA Bulk Rate (~2504), "USA" in blue & dull gold	4.25	.55	.34

NOTE: See Nos. 3270–3271 for Eagle & Shield stamps inscribed "USA Presort Std."

❏ 2605	23¢	Flag Presorted First–Class	6.25	1.00	.34
❏ 2606	23¢	Flag & Chrome, bright blue	6.25	1.00	.34
❏ 2607	23¢	Flag & Chrome (~2606), dark blue	6.25	1.00	.34
❏ 2608	23¢	Flag & Chrome (~2606), violet blue	6.25	1.00	.34
❏ 2609	29¢	Flag & White House	6.25	1.00	.34

2611–2615

2618

2616   **2617**

Scott No.			Plate Block	Unused	Used
1992.					
❑ 2611	29¢	Olympics – Hockey	—	1.00	.34
❑ 2612	29¢	Olympics – Figure Skating	—	1.00	.34
❑ 2613	29¢	Olympics – Speed Skating	—	1.00	.34
❑ 2614	29¢	Olympics – Downhill Skiing	—	1.00	.34
❑ 2615	29¢	Olympics – Bobsledding	—	1.00	.34
		Strip of 5 (2611–2615)	12.00 (10)	6.00	4.00
❑ 2616	29¢	World Columbian Stamp Expo	4.25	1.00	.34
❑ 2617	29¢	W. E. B. DuBois	4.25	1.00	.34
❑ 2618	29¢	Love	4.25	1.00	.34

2619

2620–2623

Scott No.			Plate Block	Unused	Used
❑ 2619	29¢	Olympic Baseball	5.25	1.40	.34
❑ 2620	29¢	Seeking Isabella's Support	—	1.40	.34
❑ 2621	29¢	Crossing the Atlantic	—	1.40	.34
❑ 2622	29¢	Approaching Land	—	1.40	.34
❑ 2623	29¢	Coming Ashore	—	1.40	.34
		Block of 4 (2620–2623)	5.25	4.00	2.00

2624   2625

2626   2627

Scott No.		Plate Block	Unused	Used

1992. Columbian Souvenir Sheets.

Scott No.		Plate Block	Unused	Used
❑ 2624 $1.05	Sheet of 3 (1¢, 4¢ & $1 denominations)	—	4.75	2.40
❑ 2625 $4.05	Sheet of 3 (2¢, 3¢ & $4 denominations)	—	4.75	2.40
❑ 2626 85¢	Sheet of 3 (5¢, 30¢ & 50¢ denominations)	—	4.75	2.40
❑ 2627 $3.14	Sheet of 3 (6¢, 8¢ & $3 denominations)	—	8.00	5.00

| | 2628 | | | 2629 | |

Scott No.			Plate Block	Unused	Used
☐ 2628	$2.25	Sheet of 3			
		(10¢, 15¢ & $2 denominations)	—	7.00	2.50
☐ 2629	$5	Sheet of 1 ($5 denomination)	—	15.00	12.00
		Set of 6 sheets	—	40.00	—

2630

2631–2634

2635

2636

Scott No.			Plate Block	Unused	Used
❑ 2630	29¢	N. Y. Stock Exchange	4.25	1.00	.34
❑ 2631	29¢	Cosmonaut	—	1.00	.34
❑ 2632	29¢	Astronaut	—	1.00	.34
❑ 2633	29¢	Apollo Spacecraft	—	1.00	.34
❑ 2634	29¢	Soyuz Spacecraft	—	1.00	.34
		Block of 4 (2631–2634)	4.25	2.25	1.50
❑ 2635	29¢	Alaska Highway	4.25	2.25	.34
❑ 2636	29¢	Kentucky Statehood	4.25	2.25	.34

2637–2641

2642–2646

Scott No.			Plate Block	Unused	Used
❏ 2637	29¢	Olympics – Soccer	—	1.00	.34
❏ 2638	29¢	Olympics – Gymnastics	—	1.00	.34
❏ 2639	29¢	Olympics – Volleyball	—	1.00	.34
❏ 2640	29¢	Olympics – Boxing	—	1.00	.34
❏ 2641	29¢	Olympics – Diving	—	1.00	.34
		Strip of 5 (2637–2641)	15.00 (10)	5.00	4.00
❏ 2642	29¢	Ruby-throated Hummingbird	—	1.00	.34
❏ 2643	29¢	Broad-billed Hummingbird	—	1.00	.34
❏ 2644	29¢	Costa's Hummingbird	—	1.00	.34
❏ 2645	29¢	Rufous Hummingbird	—	1.00	.34
❏ 2646	29¢	Calliope Hummingbird	—	1.00	.34
		Booklet pane of 5 (2642–2646)	—	5.00	4.00

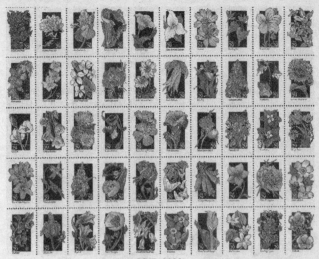

2647–2696

Scott No.		Plate Block	Unused	Used
❑ 2647–2696	29¢ Wildflowers, pane of 50	—	40.00	—
❑ 2647–2696	Any single stamp	—	2.25	1.00

❑ 2647 Indian Paintbrush
❑ 2648 Fragrant Water Lily
❑ 2649 Meadow Beauty
❑ 2650 Jack-in-the-Pulpit
❑ 2651 California Poppy
❑ 2652 Large Flower Trillium
❑ 2653 Tickseed
❑ 2654 Shooting Star
❑ 2655 Stream Violet
❑ 2656 Bluets
❑ 2657 Herb Robert
❑ 2658 Marsh Marigold
❑ 2659 Sweet White Violet
❑ 2660 Claret Cup Cactus
❑ 2661 White Mountain Avens

❑ 2662 Sessile Bellwort
❑ 2663 Blue Flag
❑ 2664 Harlequin Lupine
❑ 2665 Twin Flower
❑ 2666 Common Sunflower
❑ 2667 Sego Lily
❑ 2668 Virginia Bluebells
❑ 2669 Ohi'a Lehua
❑ 2670 Rosebud Orchid
❑ 2671 Showy Evening Primrose
❑ 2672 Fringed Gentian
❑ 2673 Yellow Lady's Slipper
❑ 2674 Passion Flower
❑ 2675 Bunch Berry
❑ 2676 Pasque Flower

- ❏ 2677 Round-Lobed Hepatica
- ❏ 2678 Wild Columbine
- ❏ 2679 Firewood
- ❏ 2680 Indian Pond Lily
- ❏ 2681 Turk's Cap Lily
- ❏ 2682 Dutchman's Breeches
- ❏ 2683 Trumpet Honeysuckle
- ❏ 2684 Jacob's Ladder
- ❏ 2685 Plains Prickly Pear
- ❏ 2686 Mots Campion

- ❏ 2687 Bearberry
- ❏ 2688 Mexican Hat
- ❏ 2689 Harebell
- ❏ 2690 Desert Five Spot
- ❏ 2691 Smooth Solomon's Seal
- ❏ 2692 Red Maids
- ❏ 2693 Yellow Skunk Cabbage
- ❏ 2694 Rue Anemone
- ❏ 2695 Standing Cypress
- ❏ 2696 Wild Flax

2697

Scott No.			Plate Block	Unused	Used
❏ 2697	29¢	World War II, 1942, pane of 10	—	15.00	8.25
❏ 2697a–j	29¢	Any single stamp	—	2.25	.75

2698

2699

2700–2703

2704

Scott No.			Plate Block	Unused	Used
❏ 2698	29¢	Dorothy Parker	4.25	1.00	.34
❏ 2699	29¢	Theodore von Kármán	4.25	1.00	.34
❏ 2700	29¢	Minerals – Azurite	—	1.00	.34
❏ 2701	29¢	Minerals – Copper	—	1.00	.34
❏ 2702	29¢	Minerals – Variscite	—	1.00	.34
❏ 2703	29¢	Minerals – Wulfenite	—	1.00	.34
		Block of 4 (2700–2703)	5.00	3.50	2.50
❏ 2704	29¢	Juan Rodríguez Cabrillo	4.25	1.00	.34

Giraffe

Giant Panda

Flamingo

King Penguins

White Bengal Tiger

2705–2709

CHRISTMAS

Bellini 1480 National Gallery

2710

Scott No.			Plate Block	Unused	Used
❑ 2705	29¢	Giraffe	—	1.00	.38
❑ 2706	29¢	Giant Panda	—	1.00	.38
❑ 2707	29¢	Flamingo	—	1.00	.38
❑ 2708	29¢	King Penguins	—	1.00	.38
❑ 2709	29¢	White Bengal Tiger	—	1.00	.38
		Booklet pane of 5 (2705–2709)	—	5.00	4.00
❑ 2710	29¢	Christmas – Madonna & Child	—	1.00	.38
		Booklet pane of 10	—	8.00	6.00

2711–2714
(2715–2718)

GREETINGS

2719

2720

Scott No.			Plate Block	Unused	Used
❏ 2711	29¢	Christmas – Horse, perf 11½ x 11	—	1.25	.34
❏ 2712	29¢	Christmas – Locomotive, perf 11½ x 11	—	2.00	.34
❏ 2713	29¢	Christmas – Fire Pumper, perf 11½ x 11	—	2.00	.34
❏ 2714	29¢	Christmas – Boat, perf 11½ x 11	—	1.25	.34
		Block of 4 (2711–2714)	—	4.00	2.75

1992. Booklet Stamps.

❏ 2715	29¢	Christmas – Horse (~2711), perf 11	—	2.00	.34
❏ 2716	29¢	Christmas – Locomotive (~2712), perf 11	—	2.00	.34
❏ 2717	29¢	Christmas – Fire Pumper (~2713), perf 11	—	1.25	.34
❏ 2718	29¢	Christmas – Boat (~2714), perf 11	—	1.25	.34
		Booklet pane of 4 (2715–2718)	—	5.00	1.50
❏ 2719	29¢	Christmas – Locomotive (~2712), self-adhesive	—	.80	.34
		Booklet pane of 18	—	18.00	.34
❏ 2720	29¢	Year of the Rooster	4.00	1.25	.34

2721

2722

2723
(2723A)

Scott No.			Plate Block	Unused	Used
1993.					
❏ 2721	29¢	Elvis (no "Presley")	5.25	1.00	.40
❏ 2722	29¢	Oklahoma! (no black frameline)	5.25	1.00	.40

NOTE: See also No. 2769.

❏ 2723	29¢	Hank Williams, perf 10	5.25	2.00	.40
❏ 2723A	29¢	Hank Williams, perf 11.2 x 11.4	150.00	25.00	10.00

NOTE: The inscription on Nos. 2723 and 2723A measures 27½ mm. See also Nos. 2771 and 2775.

2724–2730
(2731–2737)

Scott No.			Plate Block	Unused	Used
❑ 2724	29¢	Elvis (with "Presley")	—	1.50	.34
❑ 2725	29¢	Bill Haley	—	1.50	.34
❑ 2726	29¢	Clyde McPhatter	—	1.50	.34
❑ 2727	29¢	Ritchie Valens	—	1.50	.34
❑ 2728	29¢	Otis Redding	—	1.50	.34
❑ 2729	29¢	Buddy Holly	—	1.50	.34
❑ 2730	29¢	Dinah Washington	—	1.50	.34
		Strip of 7 (2724–2730)	20.00 (10)	12.00	4.25

NOTE: Nos. 2724–2730 lack a black frameline around stamps. See also No. 2731–2737.

Scott No.			Plate Block	Unused	Used
❏ 2731	29¢	Elvis (~2724) (with "Presley")	—	1.25	.40
❏ 2732	29¢	Bill Haley (~2725)	—	1.25	.40
❏ 2733	29¢	Clyde McPhatter (~2726)	—	1.25	.40
❏ 2734	29¢	Ritchie Valens (~2727)	—	1.25	.40
❏ 2735	29¢	Otis Redding (~2728)	—	1.25	.40
❏ 2736	29¢	Buddy Holly (~2729)	—	1.25	.40
❏ 2737	29¢	Dinah Washington (~2730)	—	1.25	.40
		Booklet pane of 8 (1 x 2731; 2 each 2737)	—	7.00	5.00
		Booklet pane of 4 (2731 & 2735–2737)	—	5.00	4.25

NOTE: Nos. 2731–2737 have a black frameline around stamps.

2741–2745

❏ 2741	29¢	Planet & Rings	—	1.00	.34
❏ 2742	29¢	Flying Saucers	—	1.00	.34
❏ 2743	29¢	Jet Backpacks	—	1.00	.34
❏ 2744	29¢	Winged Spacecraft	—	1.00	.34
❏ 2745	29¢	Stubby-winged Spacecraft	—	1.00	.34
		Booklet pane of 5 (2741–2745)	—	5.00	4.25

2747

2748

2746

2749

2754

2750–2753

Scott No.			Plate Block	Unused	Used
❑ 2746	29¢	Percy Lavon Julian	5.25	1.00	.34
❑ 2747	29¢	Oregon Trail	5.25	1.00	.34
❑ 2748	29¢	World University Games	5.25	1.00	.34
❑ 2749	29¢	Grace Kelly	5.25	1.00	.34
❑ 2750	29¢	Clown	—	1.00	.34
❑ 2751	29¢	Ringmaster	—	1.00	.34
❑ 2752	29¢	Trapeze Artist	—	1.00	.34
❑ 2753	29¢	Elephant	—	1.00	.34
		Block of 4 (2750–2753)	10.00 (6)	5.00	4.00
❑ 2754	29¢	Cherokee Strip	5.25	1.00	.34

2755

2756–2759

2760–2764

Scott No.			Plate Block	Unused	Used
❏ 2755	29¢	Dean Acheson	4.00	1.25	.34
❏ 2756	29¢	Steeplechase	—	2.00	.34
❏ 2757	29¢	Thoroughbred Racing	—	2.00	.34
❏ 2758	29¢	Harness Racing	—	1.25	.34
❏ 2759	29¢	Polo	—	1.25	.34
		Block of 4 (2554–2557)	5.00	4.00	2.70
❏ 2760	29¢	Hyacinth	—	1.00	.34
❏ 2761	29¢	Daffodil	—	1.00	.34
❏ 2762	29¢	Tulip	—	1.00	.34
❏ 2763	29¢	Iris	—	1.00	.34
❏ 2764	29¢	Lilac	—	1.00	.34
		Booklet pane of 5 (2760–2764)	—	4.25	2.00

2765

2766

Scott No.			Plate Block	Unused	Used
❏ 2765	29¢	World War II, 1943, pane of 10	—	14.00	6.00
❏ 2765a–j	29¢	Any single stamp	—	2.25	.45
❏ 2766	29¢	Joe Louis	4.50	2.25	.45

2767–2770

Scott No.			Plate Block	Unused	Used
❏ 2767	29¢	Show Boat	—	1.00	.34
❏ 2768	29¢	Porgy & Bess	—	1.00	.34
❏ 2769	29¢	Oklahoma! (~2722) (black frameline)	—	1.00	.34
❏ 2770	29¢	My Fair Lady	—	1.00	.34
		Booklet pane of 4 (2767–2770)	—	6.00	4.25

2771–2774
(2775–2778)

2779–2782

Scott No.			Plate Block	Unused	Used
❏ 2771	29¢	Hank Williams (~2723) (no frameline)	—	1.00	.34
❏ 2772	29¢	Patsy Cline (no frameline)	—	1.00	.34
❏ 2773	29¢	Carter Family (no frameline)	—	1.00	.34
❏ 2774	29¢	Bob Wills (no frameline)	—	1.00	.34
		Block or strip of 4 (2771–2774)	8.00	6.00	4.25

NOTE: The inscription on No. 2771 measures 27mm. See also Nos. 2723, 2723A and 2778.

❏ 2775	29¢	Hank Williams (~2723) (black frameline)	—	1.00	.34
❏ 2776	29¢	Patsy Cline (~2772) (black frameline)	—	1.00	.34
❏ 2777	29¢	Carter Family (~2773) (black frameline)	—	1.00	.34
❏ 2778	29¢	Bob Wills (~2774) (black frameline)	—	1.00	.34
		Booklet pane of 4 (2775–2778)	—	4.00	1.25

NOTE: The inscription on No. 2775 measures 22mm. See also Nos. 2723, 2723A and 2771.

❏ 2779	29¢	Benjamin Franklin	—	1.00	.34
❏ 2780	29¢	Drummer	—	1.00	.34
❏ 2781	29¢	Charles Lindbergh	—	1.00	.34
❏ 2782	29¢	Rare Stamps	—	1.00	.34
		Block of 4 (2779–2782)	8.00	6.00	4.25

2783–84

2785–2788

Scott No.			Plate Block	Unused	Used
❏ 2783	29¢	Deafness – Mother & Child	—	1.00	.34
❏ 2784	29¢	American Sign Language	—	1.00	.34
		Se-tenant pair (2783–2784)	4.00	1.00	.70
❏ 2785	29¢	Rebecca of Sunnybrook Farm	—	.75	.34
❏ 2786	29¢	Little House on the Prairie	—	.75	.34
❏ 2787	29¢	Huckleberry Finn	—	.75	.34
❏ 2788	29¢	Little Women	—	.75	.34
		Block of 4 (2785–2788)	6.00	5.00	4.25

2789

2791–2794
(2795–2803)

Scott No.			Plate Block	Unused	Used
❑ 2789	29¢	Christmas – Madonna & Child	5.00	1.00	.34
❑ 2790	29¢	Madonna & Child (~2789)	—	1.00	.34
		Booklet pane of 4	—	4.00	2.00

NOTE: The design of No.2789 is slightly cropped in No. 2790, the booklet version.

❑ 2791	29¢	Christmas – Jack in the Box	—	1.00	.34
❑ 2792	29¢	Christmas – Reindeer	—	1.00	.34
❑ 2793	29¢	Christmas – Snowman	—	1.00	.34
❑ 2794	29¢	Christmas – Toy Soldier	—	1.00	.34
		Block or strip of 4 (2791–2794)	6.00	5.00	4.00
❑ 2795	29¢	Toy Soldier (~2794)	—	1.25	.34
❑ 2796	29¢	Snowman (~2793)	—	1.25	.34
❑ 2797	29¢	Reindeer (~2792)	—	1.25	.34
❑ 2798	29¢	Jack in the Box (~2791)	—	1.25	.34
		Booklet pane of 10 (2 or 3 of each design)	—	5.00	4.00
❑ 2799	29¢	Snowman (~2793) self-adhesive	—	1.00	.34
❑ 2800	29¢	Toy Soldier (~2794) self-adhesive	—	1.00	.34
❑ 2801	29¢	Jack in the Box (~2791) self-adhesive	—	1.00	.34
❑ 2802	29¢	Reindeer (~2792) self-adhesive	—	1.00	.34
		Booklet pane of 12 (3 each 2799–2802)	—	5.00	—

NOTE: Nos. 2799–2802 measure 19½ x 26½ mm.

Scott No.			Plate Block	Unused	Used
❑ 2803	29¢	Snowman (~2793)			
		self-adhesive	—	1.00	.34
		Booklet pane of 18	—	15.00	—

NOTE: No. 2803 measures 17 x 20 mm.

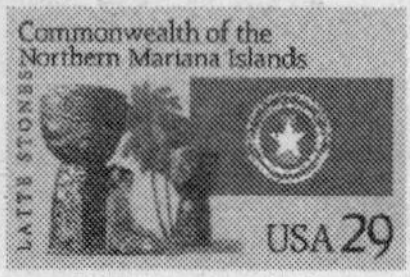

2804

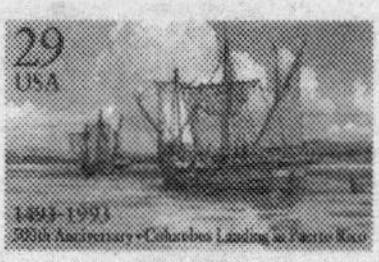

2805

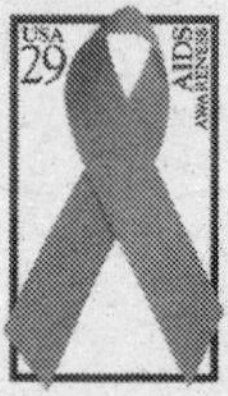

2806

❑ 2804	29¢	Mariana Islands	4.25	1.00	.34
❑ 2805	29¢	Columbus Landing	4.25	1.00	.34
❑ 2806	29¢	AIDS Awareness	4.25	1.00	.34
❑ 2806b	29¢	Booklet pane of 5 (~2806)	—	4.00	2.50

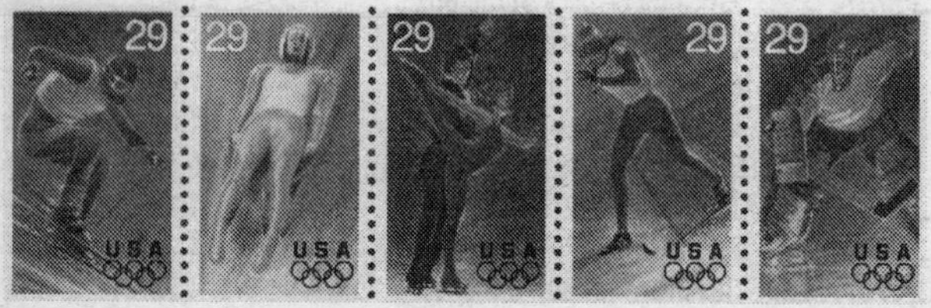

2807–2811

1994.

❑ 2807	29¢	Slalom	—	1.00	.34
❑ 2808	29¢	Luge	—	1.00	.34
❑ 2809	29¢	Ice Dancing	—	1.00	.34
❑ 2810	29¢	Skiing	—	1.00	.34
❑ 2811	29¢	Hockey	—	1.00	.34
		Strip of 5 (2807–2811)	7.00 (10)	6.00	4.25

2812

2813

2814
(2814C)

2815

2816

2817

2818

Scott No.			Plate Block	Unused	Used
❑ 2812	29¢	Edward R. Murrow	4.25	1.00	.34
❑ 2813	29¢	Love – Sunshine Heart	6.00	1.00	.34
		Booklet pane of 18	—	14.00	.34
❑ 2814	29¢	Love – Dove (photogravure)	—	1.00	.34
		Booklet pane of 10	—	8.00	4.00
❑ 2814C	29¢	Love (~2814) (lithographed & engraved)	4.25	1.00	.34
❑ 2815	52¢	Love – Doves	5.00	1.00	.34
❑ 2816	29¢	Dr. Allison Davis	4.25	1.00	.34
❑ 2817	29¢	Year of the Dog	5.00	1.00	.34
❑ 2818	29¢	Buffalo Soldiers	4.25	1.00	.34

2819–2828

Scott No.			Plate Block	Unused	Used
❏ 2819	29¢	Rudolph Valentino	—	1.00	.34
❏ 2820	29¢	Clara Bow	—	1.00	.34
❏ 2821	29¢	Charlie Chaplin	—	1.00	.34
❏ 2822	29¢	Lon Chaney	—	1.00	.34
❏ 2823	29¢	John Gilbert	—	1.00	.34
❏ 2824	29¢	Zasu Pitts	—	1.00	.34
❏ 2825	29¢	Harold Lloyd	—	1.00	.34
❏ 2826	29¢	Keystone Cops	—	1.00	.34
❏ 2827	29¢	Theda Bara	—	1.00	.34
❏ 2828	29¢	Buster Keaton	—	1.00	.34
		Block of 10 (2819–2828)	12.00 (10)	8.00	6.25

2829–2833

2837

Scott No.			Plate Block	Unused	Used
❏ 2829	29¢	Lily	—	1.00	.34
❏ 2830	29¢	Zinnia	—	1.00	.34
❏ 2831	29¢	Gladiola	—	1.00	.34
❏ 2832	29¢	Marigold	—	1.00	.34
❏ 2833	29¢	Rose	—	1.00	.34
		Booklet pane of 5 (2830–2833)	—	4.00	.34
❏ 2834	29¢	World Cup Soccer	4.00	1.25	.34
❏ 2835	40¢	World Cup Soccer	5.00	1.25	.34
❏ 2836	50¢	World Cup Soccer	6.00	1.50	.34
❏ 2837	$1.19	Souvenir Sheet of 3 (2834–2836)	—	5.00	4.25

2838

Scott No.			Plate Block	Unused	Used
❏ 2838	29¢	World War II, 1944, pane of 10	—	8.00	6.00
❏ 2838a–j		Any single stamp	—	2.75	.40

2839

2840

Scott No.			Plate Block	Unused	Used
❏ 2839	29¢	Norman Rockwell	5.00	2.00	.34
❏ 2840	50¢	Rockwell souvenir sheet	—	6.00	3.00
❏ 2840a–d	50¢	Any single stamp	—	1.25	.34

2841

2842

2843–2847

2848

Scott No.			Plate Block	Unused	Used
❏ 2841	29¢	Moon Landing	—	2.25	.34
❏ 2842	$9.95	Moon Landing	80.00	25.00	8.00
❏ 2843	29¢	Hudson's General	—	1.25	.34
❏ 2844	29¢	McQueen's Jupiter	—	1.25	.34
❏ 2845	29¢	Eddy's No. 242	—	2.25	.34
❏ 2846	29¢	Ely's No. 10	—	1.25	.34
❏ 2847	29¢	Buchanan's No. 999	—	2.25	.34
		Booklet pane of 5 (2843–2847)	—	5.00	4.00
❏ 2848	29¢	George Meany	35.00	1.25	.40

2849–2853

Scott No.			Plate Block	Unused	Used
1995.					
❑ 2849	29¢	Al Jolson	—	1.25	.40
❑ 2850	29¢	Bing Crosby	—	1.25	.40
❑ 2851	29¢	Ethel Waters	—	2.00	.40
❑ 2852	29¢	Nat "King" Cole	—	1.25	.40
❑ 2853	29¢	Ethel Merman	—	2.00	.40
		Strip of 5 (2849–2853)	7.00 (10)	4.00	2.00

2854–2861

Scott No.			Plate Block	Unused	Used
❏ 2854	29¢	Bessie Smith	—	1.00	.34
❏ 2855	29¢	Muddy Waters	—	1.00	.34
❏ 2856	29¢	Billie Holiday	—	1.00	.34
❏ 2857	29¢	Robert Johnson	—	1.00	.34
❏ 2858	29¢	Jimmy Rushing	—	1.00	.34
❏ 2859	29¢	"Ma" Rainey	—	1.00	.34
❏ 2860	29¢	Mildred Bailey	—	1.00	.34
❏ 2861	29¢	Howlin' Wolf	—	1.00	.34
		Block of 9 (2854–3861 + any 1 extra stamp)	15.00 (10)	10.00	7.25

2862

2863–2866

2867–2868

Scott No.			Plate Block	Unused	Used
❑ 2862	29¢	James Thurber	4.00	1.00	.34
❑ 2863	29¢	Motorboat & Diver	—	1.00	.34
❑ 2864	29¢	Three–masted Ship	—	1.00	.34
❑ 2865	29¢	Diver & Sunken Wheel	—	1.00	.34
❑ 2866	29¢	Fish & Coral	—	1.00	.34
		Block of 4 (2863–2866)	5.00	4.00	2.50
❑ 2867	29¢	Black-necked Crane	—	2.25	.34
❑ 2868	29¢	Whooping Crane	—	2.25	.34
		Se-tenant pair (2867–2868)	5.00	4.00	2.00

2869

2869g

2870g

Scott No.			Plate Block	Unused	Used
❑ 2869	29¢	Legends of the West	—	20.00	16.00
❑ 2869a–j	29¢	Any single stamp	—	5.00	.34
❑ 2870	29¢	Recalled Legends	—	200.00	—
❑ 2870a–j	29¢	Any single stamp	—	16.00	14.00

NOTE: The Bill Pickett stamps in Nos. 2869 and 2870 differ. The Pickett stamp in No. 2870 shows a handkerchief in the vest pocket. Other stamps in the two panes are similar except that the framelines on No. 2869 are thicker than on No. 2870.

2871
(2871A)

2872

2873

2874

2875

Scott No.			Plate Block	Unused	Used
❑ 2871	29¢	Madonna & Child, perf 11½	5.00	1.25	.34
❑ 2871A	29¢	Madonna & Child (~2871), perf 9½ x 11	—	1.25	.40
		Booklet pane of 10	—	10.00	4.00
❑ 2872	29¢	Teddy Bear in Stocking	5.00	2.50	.34
❑ 2872a	29¢	Booklet pane of 20	—	14.00	8.00
❑ 2873	29¢	Santa Claus	—	2.50	.34
		Booklet pane of 12	—	12.00	6.50
❑ 2874	29¢	Cardinal	—	5.00	.75
		Booklet pane of 18	—	18.00	—
❑ 2875	$2	B.E.P. souvenir sheet	—	20.00	—
		Single stamp	—	5.00	2.25

2876	2877 (2878)	2879 (2880)	2881 (2882–2887, 2889–2892)

Scott No.			Plate Block	Unused	Used
❏ 2876	29¢	Year of the Boar	5.00	1.25	.40
❏ 2877	(4¢)	G Rate Make-up Stamp	2.00	.35	.34
❏ 2878	(4¢)	G Rate Make-up Stamp (~2877)	2.00	.35	.34

NOTE: No. 2877 is printed with bright blue; No. 2878 is printed with dark blue.

			Plate Block	Unused	Used
❏ 2879	(20¢)	Yellow with Black G	5.00	1.25	.34
❏ 2880	(20¢)	Yellow with Red G (~2879)	10.00	1.25	.34
❏ 2881	(32¢)	White with Black G, perf 11.2 x 11.1	12.00	1.25	.34
		Booklet pane of 10	—	8.00	4.00
❏ 2882	(32¢)	White with Red G (~2881)	5.00	1.25	.34

Booklet Stamps.

			Plate Block	Unused	Used
❏ 2883	(32¢)	White with Black G (~2881), perf 10 x 9.9	—	2.00	.34
		Booklet pane of 10	—	12.00	4.00
❏ 2884	(32¢)	White with Blue G (~2881)	—	2.00	.34
		Booklet pane of 10	—	10.00	5.00
❏ 2885	(32¢)	White with Red G (~2881)	—	2.00	.34
		Booklet pane of 10	—	12.00	4.00
❏ 2886	(32¢)	White with Black G (~2881), self-adhesive	—	2.00	.34
		Booklet pane of 18	—	18.00	—
		PNC strip of 5 (see note)	5.00	—	—

NOTE: No.2886 also exists as a coil stamp. Booklet examples and coil examples alike possess straight die cutting and, therefore, are indistinguishable once removed from their backing paper.

Scott No.		Plate Block	Unused	Used
❑ 2887 (32¢)	White with Black G (~2881),			
	self-adhesive	—	2.25	.38
	Booklet pane of 18	—	18.00	—

NOTE: No. 2887 contains noticeable blue shading in the white stripes below the field of stars; No. 2886 does not.

2888

2893

Scott No.		PNC Strip (5)	Unused	Used

Coil Stamps.

❑ 2888 (25¢)	Blue with Black G	10.00	1.25	.60
❑ 2889 (32¢)	White with Black G (~2881)	12.00	4.00	.32
❑ 2890 (32¢)	White with Blue G (~2881)	8.00	1.25	.55
❑ 2891 (32¢)	White with Red G (~2881)	8.00	1.25	.55
❑ 2892 (32¢)	White with Red G (~2881),			
	rouletted	10.00	1.25	.55
❑ 2893 (5¢)	Green with Black G	4.00	.80	.55

2897
(2913–2915, 2920, 3113)

Scott No.		Plate Block	Unused	Used

1995.

❑ 2897	32¢	Flag over Porch, perforated	5.00	2.25	.34

2902	**2903**	**2905**	**2908**	**2911**
(2902B)	(2904, 2904A)	(2906)	(2909–2910)	(2912, 2912A, 3132)

Scott No.		PNC Strip (5)	Unused	Used

Coil Stamps.

☐ 2902	(5¢)	Butte, Non-Profit, perforated	2.00	.55	.34
☐ 2902B	(5¢)	Butte, Non-Profit, die cut	4.00	.55	.34
☐ 2903	(10¢)	Mountain, purple cast, perforated	4.00	.55	.34
☐ 2904	(10¢)	Mountain, bluish cast (~2903), perforated	4.00	.55	.34
☐ 2904A	(10¢)	Mountain, purple cast (~2903), die cut	4.00	.55	.34
☐ 2905	(10¢)	Automobile, Bulk rate, perforated	4.00	.70	.34
☐ 2906	(10¢)	Automobile (~2905), die cut	3.00	.70	.34
☐ 2908	(15¢)	Tail Fin, orange-yellow cast, perforated	5.00	.70	.34
☐ 2909	(15¢)	Tail Fin (~2908), buff cast, perforated	4.00	.70	.34
☐ 2910	(15¢)	Tail Fin (~2908), self-adhesive	4.00	.90	.34
☐ 2911	(25¢)	Juke Box, perforated	6.00	1.25	.55
☐ 2912	(25¢)	Juke Box (~2911), perforated	6.00	1.25	.55
☐ 2912A	(25¢)	Juke Box (~2911), die cut	6.00	1.25	.55
☐ 2913	32¢	Flag over Porch (~2897), perforated	7.00	1.25	.55
☐ 2914	32¢	Flag over Porch (~2897), perforated	8.00	1.25	.55

NOTE: The tan color on No. 2913 appears tan; it appears yellow brown on No. 2914.

☐ 2915	32¢	Flag over porch, die cut (~2897)	14.00	2.25	.55

2919

Scott No.			Plate Block	Unused	Used

Booklet Stamps.

❑ 2916	32¢	Flag over Porch (~2897), water-activated gum	—	1.25	.34
		Booklet pane of 10	—	8.00	4.00
❑ 2919	32¢	Flag over Field, self adhesive	—	4.00	.50
		Booklet pane of 18	—	15.00	.34
❑ 2920	32¢	Flag over Porch (~2897), self-adhesive	—	2.00	.50
		Booklet pane of 20	—	18.00	—

2933   **2934**   **2935**   **2936**   **2938**

1995–1996. Great Americans Series.

❑ 2933	32¢	Milton Hershey	4.00	1.25	.40
❑ 2934	32¢	Cal Farley	4.00	1.25	.34
❑ 2935	32¢	Henry R. Luce	4.00	1.25	.40
❑ 2936	32¢	Lila & DeWitt Wallace	4.00	1.25	.40
❑ 2938	46¢	Ruth Benedict	4.50	2.00	.40

| **2940** | **2941** | **2942** | **2943** |

Scott No.			Plate Block	Unused	Used
❑ 2940	55¢	Alice Hamilton M.D.	7.00	2.25	.80
❑ 2941	55¢	Justin S. Morrill	6.00	2.25	.80
❑ 2942	77¢	Mary Breckinridge	7.00	2.25	.80
❑ 2943	78¢	Alice Paul	8.00	2.25	.80

| **2948** | **2949** | **2950** |

1995.

❑ 2948	(32¢)	Love – Cherub, perforated	4.00	1.25	.40
❑ 2949	(32¢)	Love – Cherub, self-adhesive	—	1.25	.40
		Booklet pane of 20	—	15.00	—
❑ 2950	32¢	Florida Statehood	5.00	1.25	.34

2951–2954

2955	2956	2957	2958
		(2959)	(2960)

Scott No.			Plate Block	Unused	Used
❑ 2951	32¢	Globe in a Tub	—	1.00	.34
❑ 2952	32¢	Sun & Electrical Cord	—	1.00	.34
❑ 2953	32¢	Planting a Tree	—	1.00	.34
❑ 2954	32¢	Clean-up at the Beach	—	1.00	.34
		Block of 4 (2952–2954)	5.00	4.00	2.00
❑ 2955	32¢	Richard M. Nixon	4.25	1.25	.34
❑ 2956	32¢	Bessie Coleman	4.25	1.25	.34
❑ 2957	32¢	Love – Cherub, perforated	4.25	1.25	.34
❑ 2958	55¢	Love – Cherubs, perforated	4.25	2.00	.34
❑ 2959	32¢	Love – Cherub, self-adhesive	—	1.25	.34
		Booklet pane of 10	—	8.00	—
❑ 2960	55¢	Love – Cherubs, self-adhesive	—	4.00	.34
		Booklet pane of 20	—	22.00	—

2966

2967

2961–2965

2968

Scott No.			Plate Block	Unused	Used
❑ 2961	32¢	Volleyball	—	1.25	.34
❑ 2962	32¢	Softball	—	2.00	.34
❑ 2963	32¢	Bowling	—	1.25	.34
❑ 2964	32¢	Tennis	—	2.00	.34
❑ 2965	32¢	Golf	—	1.25	.34
		Strip of 5 (2961–2965)	8.00 (10)	4.00	2.00
❑ 2966	32¢	POW – MIA	4.00	1.25	.40
❑ 2967	32¢	Marilyn Monroe	6.00	1.25	.40
❑ 2968	32¢	Texas Statehood	4.00	1.25	.40

2969–2973

2974

Scott No.			Plate Block	Unused	Used
☐ 2969	32¢	Split Rock Lighthouse	—	2.00	.40
☐ 2970	32¢	St. Joseph Lighthouse	—	1.25	.40
☐ 2971	32¢	Spectacle Reef Lighthouse	—	2.00	.40
☐ 2972	32¢	Marblehead Lighthouse	—	1.25	.40
☐ 2973	32¢	Thirty Mile Point Lighthouse	—	1.25	.40
		Booklet pane of 5 (2969–1973)	—	5.00	2.00
☐ 2974	32¢	United Nations	5.00	1.25	.34

2975

Scott No.			Plate Block	Unused	Used
❏ 2975	32¢	Civil War, pane of 20	—	28.00	16.00
❏ 2975a–t		Any single stamp	—	2.25	.34

2976–2979

2980

Scott No.			Plate Block	Unused	Used
❑ 2976	32¢	Carousel Horse – Gold	—	1.25	.34
❑ 2977	32¢	Carousel Horse – Black & Gold	—	2.00	.34
❑ 2978	32¢	Carousel Horse – Silver	—	1.25	.34
❑ 2979	32¢	Carousel Horse – Brown	—	1.25	.34
		Block of 4 (2976–2979)	8.00	6.00	4.00
❑ 2980	32¢	Women's Suffrage	4.00	1.25	.34

2981

2982

Scott No.			Plate Block	Unused	Used
❑ 2981	32¢	World War II ,1945, pane of 10	—	12.00	7.00
❑ 2981a–j	32¢	Any single stamp	—	2.25	.34
❑ 2982	32¢	Louis Armstrong (white "32¢")	5.00	2.25	.40

2983–2992

Scott No.			Plate Block	Unused	Used
❑ 2983	32¢	Coleman Hawkins	—	1.25	.34
❑ 2984	32¢	Louis Armstrong (black "32¢")	—	1.25	.34
❑ 2985	32¢	James P. Johnson	—	2.00	.34
❑ 2986	32¢	Jelly Roll Morton	—	1.25	.34
❑ 2987	32¢	Charlie Parker	—	2.00	.34
❑ 2988	32¢	Eubie Blake	—	2.00	.34
❑ 2989	32¢	Charles Mingus	—	1.25	.34
❑ 2990	32¢	Thelonious Monk	—	1.25	.34
❑ 2991	32¢	John Coltrane	—	1.25	.34
❑ 2992	32¢	Errol Garner	—	1.25	.34
		Block of 10 (2983–2992)	15.00 (10)	12.00	7.00

2993–2997

2998   **2999**

Scott No.			Plate Block	Unused	Used
❏ 2993	32¢	Aster	—	1.25	.34
❏ 2994	32¢	Chrysanthemum	—	2.00	.34
❏ 2995	32¢	Dahlia	—	2.00	.34
❏ 2996	32¢	Hydrangea	—	1.25	.34
❏ 2997	32¢	Rudbeckia	—	1.25	.34
		Booklet pane of 5 (2993–2997)	—	5.00	2.00
❏ 2998	60¢	Eddie Rickenbacker	8.00	2.00	1.00
❏ 2999	32¢	Republic of Palau	4.00	1.25	.34

3000

3001

3002

Scott No.			Plate Block	Unused	Used
❑ 3000	32¢	Comic Strip Classics	—	20.00	14.00
❑ 3000a–t	32¢	Any single stamp	—	1.25	.34
❑ 3001	32¢	U.S. Naval Academy	4.25	1.25	.34
❑ 3002	32¢	Tennessee Williams	6.00	2.00	.34

3003
(3003A)

3004–3007
(3008–3011, 3014–3017)

3012
(3018)

3013

Scott No.			Plate Block	Unused	Used
❏ 3003	32¢	Madonna & Child, perf 11.2	4.00	1.25	.34
❏ 3003A	32¢	Madonna & Child, perf 9.8 x 11.9	—	1.25	.34
		Booklet pane of 10	—	8.50	4.10
❏ 3004	32¢	Santa & Chimney, perforated	—	1.25	.34
❏ 3005	32¢	Jack-in-the-Box, perforated	—	1.25	.34
❏ 3006	32¢	Boy & Christmas Tree, perforated	—	1.25	.34
❏ 3007	32¢	Santa in Workshop, perforated	—	1.25	.34
		Block or strip of 4	4.00	1.25	.34
		Booklet pane of 10 (2 or 3 each 3004–3007)	—	8.00	5.50
❏ 3008	32¢	Santa in Workshop (~3007), self-adhesive	—	2.00	.34
❏ 3009	32¢	Jack-in-the-Box (~3005), self-adhesive	—	1.25	.34
❏ 3010	32¢	Santa & Chimney (~3004), self-adhesive	—	1.25	.34
❏ 3011	32¢	Boy & Christmas Tree (~3006), self-adhesive	—	1.25	.34
		Booklet pane of 20 (5 each 3008–3011)	—	20.00	.34
❏ 3012	32¢	Christmas – Midnight Angel	—	1.25	.34
		Booklet pane of 20	—	14.00	.34
❏ 3013	32¢	Christmas – Children Sledding	—	2.00	.34
		Booklet pane of 18	—	16.00	—

Scott No.			PNC Strip (5)	Unused	Used

Coil Stamps.

❑ 3014	32¢	Santa in Workshop (~3007), self-adhesive	—	1.25	.34
❑ 3015	32¢	Jack-in-the-Box (~3005), self-adhesive		1.25	.34
❑ 3016	32¢	Santa & Chimney (~3004), self-adhesive	—	1.25	.34
❑ 3017	32¢	Boy & Christmas Tree (~3006), self-adhesive	—	1.25	.34
		Strip of 4 (3014–3017)	10.00	4.25	.34
❑ 3018	32¢	Christmas – Midnight Angel, self-adhesive	12.00	4.25	.34

3019–3023

Scott No.			Plate Block	Unused	Used

1995.

❑ 3019	32¢	1893 Duryea	—	1.25	.34
❑ 3020	32¢	1894 Haynes	—	2.00	.34
❑ 3021	32¢	1898 Columbia	—	2.00	.34
❑ 3022	32¢	1899 Winton	—	1.25	.34
❑ 3023	32¢	1901 White	—	1.25	.34
		Strip of 5 (3019–3023)	12.00 (10)	6.00	.34

3024

3025–3029

3030

Scott No.			Plate Block	Unused	Used
1996.					
❏ 3024	32¢	Utah Statehood	4.00	1.25	.40
❏ 3025	32¢	Crocus	—	2.00	.40
❏ 3026	32¢	Winter Aconite	—	2.00	.40
❏ 3027	32¢	Pansy	—	1.25	.40
❏ 3028	32¢	Snowdrop	—	1.25	.40
❏ 3029	32¢	Anemone	—	1.25	.40
		Booklet pane of 5 (3024–3029)	—	6.00	4.00
❏ 3030	32¢	Love – Cherub, self adhesive	—	18.00	—
		Booklet pane of 15	—	18.00	—
		Booklet pane of 20	—	20.00	—

3032
(3045)

3033

3036

Scott No.			Plate Block	Unused	Used
❏ 3031	1¢	Kestrel, die cut 10½ ("1¢")	1.00	.40	.34
❏ 3031A	1¢	Kestrel, die cut 11½ ("1¢")	1.00	.40	.34
❏ 3032	2¢	Woodpecker	1.00	.45	.34
❏ 3033	3¢	Blue Bird ("3¢")	1.00	.40	.34
❏ 3036	$1	Red Fox	10.00	4.00	.34

NOTE: See Nos. 2476 and 2478 for 1¢ and 3¢ stamps denominated "01" and "03."

Scott No.			PNC Strip (5)	Unused	Used
Coil Stamps.					
❏ 3044	1¢	Kestrel ("1¢")	1.00	.40	.34
❏ 3045	2¢	Woodpecker	1.00	.40	.34

3048

3049
(3054)

Scott No.			Plate Block	Unused	Used
1996. Booklet Stamps.					
❏ 3048	20¢	Blue Jay (~2483), self-adhesive	—	1.00	.34
		Booklet pane of 10	—	7.00	.34
❏ 3049	32¢	Yellow Rose (~2490), self-adhesive	—	2.00	.34
		Booklet pane of 20	—	18.00	—

3050
(3051, 3055)

3052
(3052E)

Scott No.			Plate Block	Unused	Used
❑ 3050	20¢	Pheasant, die cut 11½	—	.90	.34
		Booklet pane of 10	—	6.00	.34
❑ 3051	20¢	Pheasant (~3050), die cut 10½ x 11	—	2.25	.34
		Booklet pane of 5 (& one 3051a)	—	5.00	.34
❑ 3051a	20¢	Pheasant, die cut 10½	—	2.25	.34
❑ 3052	32¢	Coral Pink Rose, die cut 11½ x 11½	—	2.25	.34
		Booklet pane of 20	—	14.00	.34
❑ 3052E	32¢	Coral Pink Rose (~3052), die cut 10½ x 10½	—	2.25	.34
		Booklet pane of 20	—	16.00	—

Scott No.			PNC Strip (5)	Unused	Used

Coil Stamps.

❑ 3053	20¢	Blue Jay (~2483), die cut 11½	6.00	2.25	.34
❑ 3054	32¢	Yellow Rose (~2490), die cut 9½	8.00	1.25	.34
❑ 3055	20¢	Pheasant (~3051), die cut 9½	5.00	1.25	.34

Ernest E. Just

3058

3061–3064

3059

3060

3065

3066

3067

Scott No.			Plate Block	Unused	Used
1996.					
❏ 3058	32¢	Ernest E. Just	4.00	1.25	.40
❏ 3059	32¢	Smithsonian Institution	4.00	1.25	.40
❏ 3060	32¢	Year of the Rat	5.00	2.00	.40
❏ 3061	32¢	Edweard Muybridge	—	.90	.34
❏ 3062	32¢	Ottmar Mergenthaler	—	.90	.34
❏ 3063	32¢	Frederick E. Ives	—	.90	.34
❏ 3064	32¢	William Dickson	—	.90	.34
		Block of 4 (3061–3064)	6.00	4.00	2.50
❏ 3065	32¢	Fulbright Scholarships	4.00	2.25	.40
❏ 3066	50¢	Jacqueline Cochran	6.00	2.25	.40
❏ 3067	32¢	Marathon	4.00	2.25	.40

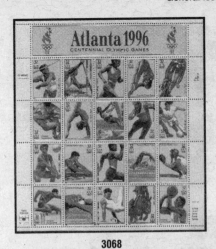

3068

3069

3070
(3071)

3072–3076

Scott No.			Plate Block	Unused	Used
❏ 3068	32¢	Olympics 1996, pane of 20	—	18.00	14.00
		Any single stamp	—	1.25	.34
❏ 3069	32¢	Georgia O'Keeffe	5.00	2.00	.40
❏ 3070	32¢	Tennessee, perforated	4.00	2.00	.40
❏ 3071	32¢	Tennessee (~3070), self-adhesive	—	1.25	.50
		Booklet pane of 20	—	14.00	—
❏ 3072	32¢	Fancy Dance	—	1.00	.34
❏ 3073	32¢	Butterfly Dance	—	1.00	.34
❏ 3074	32¢	Traditional Dance	—	1.00	.34
❏ 3075	32¢	Raven Dance	—	1.00	.34
❏ 3076	32¢	Hoop Dance	—	1.00	.34
		Strip of 5 (3072–3076)	14.00 (10)	6.00	4.00

3077–3080

3081

3082

Scott No.			Plate Block	Unused	Used
❏ 3077	32¢	Eohippus	—	1.25	.34
❏ 3078	32¢	Woolly Mammoth	—	1.25	.34
❏ 3079	32¢	Mastodon	—	1.25	.34
❏ 3080	32¢	Saber-tooth Cat	—	1.25	.34
		Block of 4 (3077–3080)	5.00	4.00	2.00
❏ 3081	32¢	Breast Cancer Awareness	6.00	2.50	.40
❏ 3082	32¢	James Dean	6.00	2.50	.40

3087

3088
(3089)

3083–3086

3089

Scott No.			Plate Block	Unused	Used
❏ 3083	32¢	Mighty Casey	—	1.25	.34
❏ 3084	32¢	Paul Bunyan	—	2.00	.34
❏ 3085	32¢	John Henry	—	1.25	.34
❏ 3086	32¢	Pecos Bill	—	1.25	.34
		Block of 4 (3083–3086)	6.00	4.00	1.80
❏ 3087	32¢	Discus Thrower	4.25	1.25	.40
❏ 3088	32¢	Iowa Statehood, water activated	4.25	1.25	.40
❏ 3089	32¢	Iowa (~3088), self-adhesive	—	.85	.34
		Booklet pane of 20	—	20.00	—
❏ 3090	32¢	RFD – Rural Free Delivery	4.25	1.25	.40
Scott No.		**Plate Block**	**Unused**	**Used**	

3091–3095

❏ 3091	32¢	Riverboat – Robert E. Lee	—	1.00	.34
❏ 3092	32¢	Riverboat – Sylvan Dell	—	1.00	.34
❏ 3093	32¢	Riverboat – Far West	—	1.00	.34
❏ 3094	32¢	Riverboat – Rebecca Everingham	—	1.00	.34
❏ 3095	32¢	Riverboat – Bailey Gatzert	—	1.00	.34
		Strip of 5 (3091–3096)	12.00 (10)	7.00	—

3096–3099

3100–3103

Scott No.			Plate Block	Unused	Used
❑ 3096	32¢	Count Basie	—	1.25	.34
❑ 3097	32¢	Tommy & Jimmy Dorsey	—	2.25	.34
❑ 3098	32¢	Glenn Miller	—	2.25	.34
❑ 3099	32¢	Benny Goodman	—	1.25	.34
		Block or strip of 4 (3096–3099)	5.00	4.00	2.00
❑ 3100	32¢	Harold Arlen	—	1.25	.34
❑ 3101	32¢	Johnny Mercer	—	2.00	.34
❑ 3102	32¢	Dorothy Fields	—	1.25	.34
❑ 3103	32¢	Hoagy Carmichael	—	1.25	.34
		Block or strip of 4 (3100–3103)	8.00	6.00	4.00

3104

3105

Scott No.			Plate Block	Unused	Used
❏ 3104	23¢	F. Scott Fitzgerald	4.00	1.00	.34
❏ 3105	32¢	Endangered Species, pane of 15	—	14.00	9.00
❏ 3105a–o		Any single stamp	—	2.25	.55

3106

3107
(3112)

3108–3111
(3113–3116)

Scott No.			Plate Block	Unused	Used
❏ 3106	32¢	Computer Technology	4.00	1.25	.40
❏ 3107	32¢	Christmas – Madonna & Child	4.00	2.00	.40
❏ 3108	32¢	Family & Fireplace	—	2.00	.40
❏ 3109	32¢	Decorating Christmas Tree	—	1.25	.40
❏ 3110	32¢	Dreaming of Santa	—	1.25	.40
❏ 3111	32¢	Christmas Shopping	—	1.25	.40
		Block or strip of 4 (3108–3111)	5.00	4.00	2.00
❏ 3112	32¢	Madonna & Child (~3107), self-adhesive	—	1.25	.34
		Booklet pane of 20	—	16.00	—
❏ 3113	32¢	Family & Fireplace (~3108), self-adhesive	—	1.25	.40
❏ 3114	32¢	Decorating Tree (~3109) , self-adhesive	—	2.00	.40
❏ 3115	32¢	Dreaming of Santa (~3110) , self-adhesive	—	1.25	.40
❏ 3116	32¢	Christmas Shopping (~3111) , self-adhesive	—	1.25	.40
		Booklet pane of 20 (5 each of 3113–3116)	—	18.00	—

3117

3118

3119

Scott No.			Plate Block	Unused	Used
❑ 3117	32¢	Christmas – Skaters	—	1.25	.34
		Booklet pane of 18	—	16.00	.34
❑ 3118	32¢	Hanukkah	4.00	1.25	.34
❑ 3119	$1	Cycling, souvenir sheet of 2	—	4.00	2.00
		Either single stamp	—	3.00	1.25

3120

3121

3122

3123

3124

3125

Scott No.			Plate Block	Unused	Used
1997.					
❏ 3120	32¢	Year of the Ox	4.25	1.25	.40
❏ 3121	32¢	Benjamin O. Davis, Sr.	4.25	2.00	.40
❏ 3122	32¢	Statue of Liberty	—	1.25	.40
		Booklet pane of 20	—	15.00	—
❏ 3123	32¢	Swans	—	2.00	.55
		Booklet pane of 20	—	15.00	.55
❏ 3124	55¢	Swans	—	2.00	.55
		Booklet pane of 20	—	28.00	—
❏ 3125	32¢	Helping Children Learn	4.25	1.25	.40

3126
(3128)

3127
(3129)

3130

3131

Scott No.			Plate Block	Unused	Used
❏ 3126	32¢	Citron	—	1.25	.55
❏ 3127	32¢	Flowering Pineapple	—	1.25	.55
		Booklet pane of 20 (10 each 3126–3127)	—	16.00	—
❏ 3128	32¢	Citron (~3126)	—	2.00	.75
❏ 3129	32¢	Flowering Pineapple (~3127)	—	1.25	.75
		Booklet pane of 5 (2 of 3128; 3 of 3129)	—	7.50	—

NOTE: Nos. 3126–3127 measure 19½ x 26½ mm; Nos. 3128–3129 measure 18½ x 24 mm.

❏ 3130	32¢	Pacific 97 – Ship	—	1.25	.34
❏ 3131	32¢	Pacific 97 – Stagecoach	—	1.25	.34
		Se-tenant pair (3130–3131)	6.00	2.00	.34

Scott No.		PNC Strip (5)	Unused	Used

Coil Stamps. Linerless Self-Adhesive.

❏ 3132	(25¢)	Jukebox (~2911)	16.00	2.25	.70
❏ 3133	32¢	Flag over Porch (~2897)	7.00	2.25	.50

NOTE: Nos. 3121 and 3122 are not mounted on backing paper (liner) as are other self-adhesive coil stamps.

3134   **3135**

3136

Scott No.			Plate Block	Unused	Used
1997.					
❏ 3134	32¢	Thornton Wilder	4.25	1.25	.42
❏ 3135	32¢	Raoul Wallenberg	4.25	1.25	.50
❏ 3136	32¢	Dinosaurs, pane of 15	—	12.00	—
❏ 3136a–o		Any single stamp	—	—	.42

3137
(3138)

Scott No.			Plate Block	Unused	Used
❏ 3137	32¢	Bugs Bunny		1.00	.34
		Pane of 10	—	12.00	—

NOTE: Die cutting on No. 3137 does not cut into backing.

❏ 3138	32¢	Bugs Bunny (~3137)	—	5.00	.40
		Pane of 10	—	175.00	—

NOTE: Die cutting on No. 3138 cuts through the backing. Used examples of Nos. 3137 and 3138 are identical in appearance. Once removed from backing paper they cannot be distinguished from one another.

❏ 3138c		Booklet pane of 10, right stamp w/o die cut	—	250.00	—

3139

3140

Scott No.			Plate Block	Unused	Used
❏ 3139	50¢	Franklin, pane of 12	—	18.00	—
❏		Single stamp	—	4.25	2.40
❏ 3140	60¢	Washington, pane of 12	—	20.00	—
		Single stamp	—	4.25	2.40

3141

3142

Scott No.			Plate Block	Unused	Used
❏ 3141	32¢	Marshall Plan	4.00	2.50	.40
❏ 3142	32¢	Classic Aircraft, pane of 20	—	18.00	15.00
❏ 3142a–t		Any single stamp	—	2.50	.35

3143–3146

Scott No.			Plate Block	Unused	Used
❏ 3143	32¢	Bear Bryant	—	1.25	.34
❏ 3144	32¢	Pop Warner	—	2.00	.34
❏ 3145	32¢	Vince Lombardi	—	1.25	.34
❏ 3146	32¢	George Halas	—	1.25	.34
		Block of 4 (3143–3146)	5.00	4.00	2.25
❏ 3147	32¢	Vince Lombardi	4.25	1.00	.55
❏ 3148	32¢	Bear Bryant	4.25	1.00	.55
❏ 3149	32¢	Pop Warner	4.25	—	.55
❏ 3150	32¢	George Halas	4.25	—	.55

NOTE: Nos. 3147–3150 were issued in individual (not se-tenant) panes and stamps contain a red stripe above the coach's name. Nos. 3143–3146 were issued in se-tenant panes and do not contain a red stripe above the coach's name.

3151

Scott No.			Plate Block	Unused	Used
❏ 3151	32¢	American Dolls, pane of 15	—	16.00	15.00
❏ 3151a–o		Any single stamp	—	2.50	.55

3152   3153

3154–3157

Scott No.			Plate Block	Unused	Used
❏ 3152	32¢	Humphrey Bogart	4.25	1.25	.40
❏ 3153	32¢	Stars & Strips Forever	4.25	1.25	.40
❏ 3154	32¢	Lily Pons	—	.38	.34
❏ 3155	32¢	Richard Tucker	—	.38	.34
❏ 3156	32¢	Lawrence Tibbett	—	.38	.34
❏ 3157	32¢	Rosa Ponselle	—	.38	.34
		Block or strip of 4 (3154–3157)	8.00	6.00	4.25

3158–3165

3166

3167

Scott No.			Plate Block	Unused	Used
☐ 3158	32¢	Leopold Stokowski	—	1.25	.34
☐ 3159	32¢	Arthur Fiedler	—	1.25	.34
☐ 3160	32¢	George Szell	—	2.00	.34
☐ 3161	32¢	Eugene Ormandy	—	2.00	.34
☐ 3162	32¢	Samuel Barber	—	1.25	.34
☐ 3163	32¢	Ferde Grofé	—	1.25	.34
☐ 3164	32¢	Charles Ives	—	1.25	.34
☐ 3165	32¢	Louis Moreau Gottschalk	—	1.25	.34
		Block of 8 (3158–3163)	10.00 (8)	8.50	4.00
☐ 3166	32¢	Padre Félix Varela	5.00	2.00	.40
☐ 3167	32¢	U.S. Air Force	5.00	1.25	.50

3168–3172

3173   **3174**   **3175**

3176   **3177**

Scott No.			Plate Block	Unused	Used
☐ 3168	32¢	Phantom of the Opera	—	1.25	.34
☐ 3169	32¢	Dracula	—	2.00	.34
☐ 3170	32¢	Frankenstein	—	1.25	.34
☐ 3171	32¢	The Mummy	—	1.25	.34
☐ 3172	32¢	Wolf Man	—	1.25	.34
		Strip of 5 (3168–3172)	12.00	5.00	4.00
☐ 3173	32¢	Supersonic Flight	5.50	1.25	.40
☐ 3174	32¢	Women in the Military	5.50	1.25	.40
☐ 3175	32¢	Kwanzaa	5.50	2.00	.40
☐ 3176	32¢	Christmas – Madonna & Child	—	1.25	.40
		Booklet pane of 20	—	15.00	.40
☐ 3177	32¢	Christmas – Holly	—	2.00	.40
		Booklet pane of 20	—	15.00	—

3178

3179

3180

3181

Scott No.			Plate Block	Unused	Used
❑ 3178	$3	Mars Rover, souvenir sheet	—	7.00	4.25
1998.					
❑ 3179	32¢	Year of the Tiger	4.00	2.40	.60
❑ 3180	32¢	Alpine Skiing	5.00	2.40	.60
❑ 3181	32¢	Madam C.J. Walker	4.00	2.40	.60

3182

3183

3184

3185

Scott No.			Plate Block	Unused	Used

Celebrate the Century.

Scott No.			Plate Block	Unused	Used
❏ 3182	32¢	1900s, pane of 15	—	12.00	8.00
❏ 3182a–o		Any single stamp	—	2.25	.34
❏ 3183	32¢	1910s, pane of 15	—	12.00	10.00
❏ 3183a–o		Any single stamp	—	2.25	.34
❏ 3184	32¢	1920s, pane of 15	—	12.00	10.00
❏ 3184a–o		Any single stamp	—	2.25	.34
❏ 3185	32¢	1930s, pane of 15	—	12.00	9.00
❏ 3185a–o		Any single stamp	—	2.25	.34

3186

3187

3188

3189

Scott No.			Plate Block	Unused	Used
❑ 3186	33¢	1940s, pane of 15	—	14.00	10.00
❑ 3186a–o		Any single stamp	—	2.00	1.25
❑ 3187	33¢	1950s, pane of 15	—	14.00	10.00
❑ 3187a–o		Any single stamp	—	1.25	.40
❑ 3188	33¢	1960s, pane of 15	—	14.00	10.00
❑ 3188a–o		Any single stamp	—	2.00	.40
❑ 3189	33¢	1970s, pane of 15	—	14.00	10.00
❑ 3189a–o		Any single stamp	—	1.25	.40

3190

3191

Scott No.			Plate Block	Unused	Used
❏ 3190	33¢	1980s, pane of 15	—	15.00	10.00
❏ 3190a–o		Any single stamp	—	2.25	.40
❏ 3191	33¢	1990s, pane of 15	—	14.00	10.00
❏ 3191a–o		Any single stamp	—	2.25	.40

3192

3193–3197

3198–3202

Scott No.			Plate Block	Unused	Used
1998.					
❑ 3192	32¢	Remember the Maine	5.00	1.25	.40
❑ 3193	32¢	Southern Magnolia	—	2.00	.40
❑ 3194	32¢	Blue Paloverde	—	2.00	.40
❑ 3195	32¢	Yellow Poplar	—	1.25	.40
❑ 3196	32¢	Prairie Crab Apple	—	1.25	.40
❑ 3197	32¢	Pacific Dogwood	—	1.25	.40
		Strip of 5 (3193-3197)	12.00 (10)	4.00	.40
❑ 3198	32¢	Black Cascade, 13 Verticals, 1959	—	1.25	.40
❑ 3199	32¢	Untitled, 1965	—	1.25	.40
❑ 3200	32¢	Rearing Stallion, 1928	—	1.25	.40
❑ 3201	32¢	Portrait of a Young Man, c. 1945	—	1.25	.40
❑ 3202	32¢	Un Effet du Japonais, 1945	—	1.25	.40
		Strip of 5 (3198-3202)	12.00	4.00	2.00

3203

3204
(3205)

Scott No.			Plate Block	Unused	Used
❏ 3203	32¢	Cinco de Mayo	5.00	2.50	.40
❏ 3204	32¢	Sylvester & Tweety	—	2.50	.40
		Pane of 10	—	5.00	.40
❏ 3205	32¢	Sylvester & Tweety	—	1.25	.40
		Pane of 10	—	7.00	—

NOTE: The stamp in the right panel of No. 3204 contains a die cut; the stamp in the right panel of No. 3205 does not.

3206

Scott No.			Plate Block	Unused	Used
❑ 3206	32¢	Wisconsin Statehood	4.00	1.50	.38

3207
(3207A)

3208
(3208A)

Scott No.			PNC Strip (5)	Unused	Used
Coil Stamps.					
❑ 3207	(5¢)	Wetlands—Nonprofit Org.	4.15	.50	.34
❑ 3207A	(5¢)	Wetlands (~3207), self-adhesive	4.15	.50	.34
❑ 3208	(25¢)	Diner—Presorted First-Class	7.00	1.25	.34
❑ 3208A	(25¢)	Diner (3208), self-adhesive	7.00	1.25	.34

3209

Scott No.			Plate Block	Unused	Used
1998.					
❏ 3209		1989 Trans-Mississippi reissue			
		Sheet of 9	—	10.00	8.00
❏ 3209a	1¢	Marquette on the Mississippi	—	.40	.34
❏ 3209b	2¢	Farming in the West	—	.40	.34
❏ 3209c	4¢	Indian Hunting Buffalo	—	.40	.34
❏ 3209d	5¢	Fremont on Rocky Mountains	—	.40	.34
❏ 3209e	8¢	Troops Guarding Train	—	.40	.34
❏ 3209f	10¢	Hardships of Emigration	—	.40	.34
❏ 3209g	50¢	Western Mining Prospector	—	2.00	.60
❏ 3209h	$1	Western Cattle in Storm	—	4.15	1.25
❏ 3209I	$2	Mississippi Bridge	—	4.15	2.00

NOTE: The reissued stamps are bicolor and contain the date "1998" in the lower right corner. Stamps of the original issue of 1898 are monocolor and contain no date at lower right. Once separated from their respective sheets, Nos. 3209h and 3210 are indistinguishable.

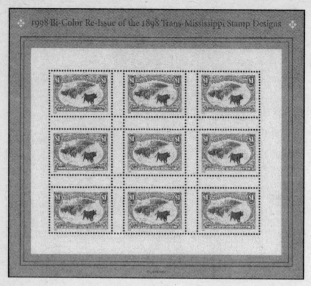

1998 Bi-Color Re-Issue of the 1898 Trans-Mississippi Stamp Designs

3210

Scott No.			Plate Block	Unused	Used
❑ 3210	$1	Cattle in Storm, sheet of 9	—	22.00	15.00

3211

3212–3215

Scott No.			Plate Block	Unused	Used
❏ 3211	32¢	Berlin Airlift	4.00	1.25	.40
❏ 3212	32¢	Leadbelly	—	1.25	.40
❏ 3213	32¢	Woody Guthrie	—	1.25	.40
❏ 3214	32¢	Sonny Terry	—	1.25	.40
❏ 3215	32¢	Josh White	—	1.25	.40
		Block or strip of 4 (3212-3215)	5.00	4.00	2.25

3216–3219

3220

3221

Scott No.			Plate Block	Unused	Used
❑ 3216	32¢	Mahalia Jackson	—	1.25	.40
❑ 3217	32¢	Roberta Martin	—	2.00	.40
❑ 3218	32¢	Clara Ward	—	2.00	.40
❑ 3219	32¢	Sister Rosetta	—	1.25	.40
		Block or strip of 4 (3216–3219)	5.00	4.00	2.00
❑ 3220	32¢	Spanish Settlement	4.00	1.25	.40
❑ 3221	32¢	Stephen Vincent Benét	—	1.25	.40

3222–3225

3226

3227

3228
(3229)

Scott No.			Plate Block	Unused	Used
❑ 3222	32¢	Antillean Euphonia	—	1.25	.34
❑ 3223	32¢	Green-throated Carib	—	1.25	.34
❑ 3224	32¢	Crested Honeycreeper	—	1.25	.34
❑ 3225	32¢	Cardinal Honeyeater	—	1.25	.34
		Block of 4 (3222–3225)	5.00	4.00	2.00
❑ 3226	32¢	Alfred Hitchcock	4.00	1.25	.40
❑ 3227	32¢	Organ & Tissue Donation	4.00	1.25	.40

Scott No.			PNC Strip (5)	Unused	Used
Coil Stamps.					
❑ 3228	(10¢)	Bicycle Handlebar, self-adhesive	6.00	.85	.34
❑ 3229	(10¢)	Bicycle (~3228), water-activated gum	6.00	.85	.34

3230–3234

3235

Scott No.			Plate Block	Unused	Used
1998.					
❑ 3230	32¢	Bright Eyes - Dog	—	1.25	.34
❑ 3231	32¢	Bright Eyes - Fish	—	2.00	.34
❑ 3232	32¢	Bright Eyes - Cat	—	2.00	.34
❑ 3233	32¢	Bright Eyes - Parakeet	—	1.25	.34
❑ 3234	32¢	Bright Eyes - Hamster	—	1.25	.34
		Strip of 5 (3230–3234)	10.00 (10)	4.00	—
❑ 3235	32¢	Klondike Gold Rush	5.00	1.25	.40

3236

Scott No.			Plate Block	Unused	Used
❏ 3236	32¢	American Art, pane of 20	—	20.00	15.00
❏ 3236a–t		Any single stamp	—	2.50	.34

3237

3238–3242

3243   **3244**

Scott No.			Plate Block	Unused	Used
❏ 3237	32¢	Ballet	5.00	1.25	.40
❏ 3238	32¢	Futuristic Truck	—	1.25	.40
❏ 3239	32¢	Pod-craft in Flight	—	1.25	.40
❏ 3240	32¢	Observer in Space Suit	—	1.25	.40
❏ 3241	32¢	Planet Rover	—	1.25	.40
❏ 3242	32¢	Spaceport Dome	—	1.25	.40
		Strip of 5 (3238-3242)	—	4.00	2.00
❏ 3243	32¢	Giving & Sharing	5.00	1.00	.34
❏ 3244	32¢	Christmas - Madonna & Child	—	1.00	.34
		Booklet pane of 20	—	14.00	—

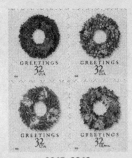

3245–3248
(3249–3252)

3257
(3258)

Scott No.			Plate Block	Unused	Used
❑ 3245	32¢	Evergreen Wreath	—	1.25	.34
❑ 3246	32¢	Victorian Wreath	—	2.00	.34
❑ 3247	32¢	Chili Pepper Wreath	—	2.00	.34
❑ 3248	32¢	Tropical Wreath	—	1.25	.34
		Booklet pane of 20 (3245-3248)	—	6.00	.34
❑ 3249	32¢	Evergreen Wreath (~3245)	—	1.00	.34
❑ 3250	32¢	Victorian Wreath (~3246)	—	1.00	.34
❑ 3251	32¢	Chili Pepper Wreath (~3247)	—	1.00	.34
❑ 3252	32¢	Tropical Wreath (~3248)	—	1.00	.34
		Block or strip of 4 (3249–3252)	5.00	4.00	—

NOTE: Nos. 3249–3252 measure 23 x 30 mm.

Scott No.			Plate Block	Unused	Used
❑ 3257	(1¢)	Weather Vane, white "U.S.A."	1.00	.40	.34
❑ 3258	(1¢)	Weather Vane, blue "U.S.A."	1.00	.40	.34

3259
(3263, 3353)

3260
(3264–3269)

3261

3262

Scott No.			Plate Block	Unused	Used
❏ 3259	22¢	Uncle Sam	5.00	1.00	.40
❏ 3260	(33¢)	Uncle Sam's Hat	5.00	1.00	.40
❏ 3261	$3.20	Space Shuttle	30.00	7.00	5.00
❏ 3262	$11.75	Space Shuttle Piggyback	110.00	25.00	10.00

Scott No.			PNC Strip (5)	Unused	Used
Coil Stamps.					
❏ 3263	22¢	Uncle Sam (~3259)	6.00	1.00	.34
❏ 3264	(33¢)	Uncle Sam's Hat (~3260), water-activated gum	8.00	2.50	.34
❏ 3265	(33¢)	Hat (~3260), self-adhesive, square corners	8.00	2.50	.40
❏ 3266	(33¢)	Hat (~3260), self-adhesive, rounded corners	9.00	2.50	.50

Scott No.			Plate Block	Unused	Used
Booklet Stamps.					
❏ 3267	(33¢)	Hat (~3260), die cut 9.9	—	4.25	.38
		Booklet pane of 10	—	8.00	—
❏ 3268	(33¢)	Hat (~3260), die cut 11 or 11½	—	4.25	.38
		Booklet pane of 10	—	10.00	—
		Booklet pane of 20	—	15.00	—

Scott No.		Plate Block	Unused	Used
❏ 3269 (33¢)	Hat (~3260), die cut 8	—	2.25	.38
	Booklet pane of 10	—	10.00	—
	Booklet pane of 18	—	18.00	—

3270
(3271)

Scott No.		PNC Strip (5)	Unused	Used
Coil Stamps.				
❏ 3270 (10¢)	Eagle & Shield, water-activated gum, perforated	4.00	.55	.40
❏ 3271 (10¢)	Eagle & Shield, self-adhesive, die cut	5.00	.55	.40

NOTE: See Nos. 2602–2604 for Eagle & Shield stamps inscribed "USA Bulk Rate" or "Bulk Rate USA."

3272

3273

Scott No.			Plate Block	Unused	Used
1999.					
❏ 3272	33¢	Year of the Rabbit	4.00	2.25	.42
❏ 3273	33¢	Malcolm X	5.00	2.25	.42

3274   **3275**   **3276**   **3277**
(3278,
3279–3282)

Scott No.			Plate Block	Unused	Used
❑ 3274	33¢	Love - Lacy Valentine	—	1.25	.40
		Booklet pane of 20	—	16.00	.40
❑ 3275	55¢	Love - Lacy Valentine	—	2.00	.40
❑ 3276	33¢	Hospice Care	5.00	1.25	.40
❑ 3277	33¢	Flag & City, water-activated gum, perforated	8.00	1.25	.40
❑ 3278	33¢	Flag & City (~3277), self-adhesive, black date	—	1.25	.40
		Booklet pane of 10	—	10.00	.40
		Booklet pane of 20	—	15.00	.40
❑ 3279	33¢	Flag & City (~3277), self-adhesive, red date	—	1.25	.40
		Booklet pane of 10	—	8.00	—

Scott No.			PNC Strip (5)	Unused	Used

Coil Stamps.

			PNC Strip (5)	Unused	Used
❑ 3280	33¢	Flag & City (~3277), water-activated gum, perforated	8.00	1.25	.40
❑ 3281	33¢	Flag & City (~3277), self-adhesive, square corners	8.00	1.25	.40
❑ 3282	33¢	Flag & City (~3277), self-adhesive, rounded corners	9.00	1.25	.40

3283　　　**3286**　　　**3287**

3288–3292

Scott No.			Plate Block	Unused	Used
1999.					
❑ 3283	33¢	Flag & Chalkboard, self-adhesive	—	1.25	.40
		Booklet pane of 18	—	15.00	—
❑ 3286	33¢	Irish Immigration	5.00	1.25	.40
❑ 3287	33¢	Alfred Lunt & Lynn Fontanne	5.00	2.00	.40
❑ 3288	33¢	Arctic Hare	—	1.25	.40
❑ 3289	33¢	Arctic Fox	—	2.00	.40
❑ 3290	33¢	Snowy Owl	—	2.00	.40
❑ 3291	33¢	Polar Bear	—	1.25	.40
❑ 3292	33¢	Gray Wolf	—	1.25	.40
		Strip of 5 (3288-3293)	8.00 (10)	5.00	2.25

3293

Scott No.		Plate Block	Unused	Used
❑ 3293 33¢	Sonoran Desert, pane of 10	—	10.00	—
❑ 3293a–j	Any single stamp	—	1.25	.45

3294–3297
(3298–3301, 3302–3305)

Scott No.			Plate Block	Unused	Used
❑ 3294	33¢	Blueberries	—	1.25	.34
❑ 3295	33¢	Raspberries	—	2.00	.34
❑ 3296	33¢	Strawberries	—	2.00	.34
❑ 3297	33¢	Blackberries	—	1.25	.34
		Booklet pane of 20 (3294-3297)	—	15.00	—

NOTE: Nos. 3294–3297 exist dated either 1999 or 2000. Prices are the same for both. Nos. 3294–3297 are die cut 11½ x 11½. Nos. 3298–3301 are die cut 9½ x 10.

❑ 3298	33¢	Blueberries (~3294)	—	1.25	.34
❑ 3299	33¢	Raspberries (~3295)	—	2.00	.34
❑ 3300	33¢	Strawberries (~3296)	—	2.00	.34
❑ 3301	33¢	Blackberries (~3297)	—	1.25	.34
		Booklet pane (3298-3301)	—	6.00	—

Scott No.			PNC Strip (5)	Unused	Used

Coil Stamps.

❑ 3302	33¢	Blueberries (~3294)	—	1.25	.34
❑ 3303	33¢	Raspberries (~3295)	—	2.00	.34
❑ 3304	33¢	Strawberries (~3296)	—	1.25	.34
❑ 3305	33¢	Blackberries (~3297)	—	1.25	.34
		Strip of 4 (3302-3305)	5.00	4.00	—

NOTE: See also Nos. 3404–3407. Nos. 3302–3305 contain straight edges at top and bottom; Nos. 3404–3407 contain straight edges at sides.

3306
(3307)

Scott No.			Plate Block	Unused	Used
1999.					
❑ 3306	33¢	Daffy Duck	—	2.50	.34
		Pane of 10	—	8.00	.34
❑ 3307	33¢	Daffy Duck	—	2.50	.34
		Pane of 10, right stamp w/o die cut	—	8.00	—

3308   **3309**

3310–3313

Scott No.			Plate Block	Unused	Used
❏ 3308	33¢	Ayn Rand	5.00	1.50	.40
❏ 3309	33¢	Cinco de Mayo	5.00	1.50	.40
❏ 3310	33¢	Bird of Paradise	—	2.00	.40
❏ 3311	33¢	Royal Poinciana	—	2.00	.40
❏ 3312	33¢	Gloriosa	—	2.00	.40
❏ 3313	33¢	Chinese Hibiscus	—	1.50	.40
		Booklet pane of 20 (3310-3315)	—	15.00	—

3314   **3315**

3316

3317–3320

Scott No.			Plate Block	Unused	Used
❏ 3314	33¢	John & William Bartram	5.00	1.25	.40
❏ 3315	33¢	Prostate Cancer Awareness	5.00	2.00	.40
❏ 3316	33¢	California Gold Rush	5.00	2.00	.40
❏ 3317	33¢	Fish - Yellow & Red Fish	—	1.25	.40
❏ 3318	33¢	Fish - Fish & Thermometer	—	2.00	.40
❏ 3319	33¢	Fish - Blue Fish	—	1.25	.40
❏ 3320	33¢	Fish - Hermit Crab	—	1.25	.40
		Strip of 4 (3317-3320)	—	4.00	—

3321–3324

3325–3328

Scott No.			Plate Block	Unused	Used
❑ 3321	33¢	Extreme Sports – Skateboarding	—	1.25	.34
❑ 3322	33¢	Extreme Sports – BMX Biking	—	2.00	.34
❑ 3323	33¢	Extreme Sports – Snowboarding	—	2.00	.34
❑ 3324	33¢	Extreme Sports – Inline Skating	—	1.25	.34
		Block of 4 (3321–3324)	5.00	4.00	.34
❑ 3325	33¢	Free-blown Glass	—	1.25	.34
❑ 3326	33¢	Mold-blown Glass	—	1.25	.34
❑ 3327	33¢	Pressed Glass	—	1.25	.34
❑ 3328	33¢	Art Glass	—	1.25	.34
		Block or strip of 4 (3225–3228)	5.00	4.00	2.00

Scott No.			Plate Block	Unused	Used
❏ 3329	33¢	James Cagney	4.00	1.25	.40
❏ 3330	33¢	General Billy Mitchell	6.00	2.00	.40
❏ 3331	33¢	Honoring Those Who Served	5.00	2.00	.40
❏ 3332	45¢	Universal Postal Union	6.00	1.25	.70
❏ 3333	33¢	Trains – the "Daylight"	—	2.00	.40
❏ 3334	33¢	Trains – the "Congressional"	—	1.25	.34
❏ 3335	33¢	Trains – the "20th Century Limited"	—	1.25	.34
❏ 3336	33¢	Trains – the "Hiawatha"	—	1.25	.34
❏ 3337	33¢	Trains – the "Super Chief"	—	1.25	.34
		Strip of 5 (3333–3337)	12.00 (10)	5.00	2.00

3338

3339–3344

Scott No.			Plate Block	Unused	Used
❏ 3338	33¢	Frederick Law Olmsted	4.00	1.25	.40
❏ 3339	33¢	Max Steiner	—	2.00	.40
❏ 3340	33¢	Dmitri Tiomkin	—	2.00	.40
❏ 3341	33¢	Bernard Herrmann	—	1.25	.40
❏ 3342	33¢	Franz Waxman	—	2.00	.40
❏ 3343	33¢	Alfred Newman	—	1.25	.40
❏ 3344	33¢	Erich Wolfgang Korngold	—	1.25	.40
		Block of 6 (3339–3344)	8.00 (6)	6.00	4.00

3345–3350

Scott No.			Plate Block	Unused	Used
❏ 3345	33¢	Ira & George Gershwin	—	1.25	.34
❏ 3346	33¢	Lerner & Loewe	—	1.25	.34
❏ 3347	33¢	Lorenz Hart	—	1.25	.34
❏ 3348	33¢	Rodgers & Hammerstein	—	1.25	.34
❏ 3349	33¢	Meredith Willson	—	1.25	.34
❏ 3350	33¢	Frank Loesser	—	1.25	.34
		Block of 6 (3345–3350)	8.00 (6)	5.00	4.00

INSECTS & SPIDERS

3351

Scott No.			Plate Block	Unused	Used
❏ 3351	33¢	Insects & Spiders, pane of 20	—	18.00	12.00
❏ 3351a–t		Any single stamp	—	2.50	.55

3352

Scott No.			Plate Block	Unused	Used
❏ 3352	33¢	Hanukkah	4.00	2.00	.45

Scott No.			PNC Strip (5)	Unused	Used

Coil Stamp.

❏ 3353	22¢	Uncle Sam (~3259), water-activated gum, perforated	6.00	2.50	.38

3354    **3355**

Scott No.			Plate Block	Unused	Used

1999.

❏ 3354	33¢	NATO 50th Anniversary	5.00	1.50	.40
❏ 3355	33¢	Christmas – Madonna & Child	—	1.50	.40
		Booklet pane of 20	—	16.00	—

3356–3359
(3360–3363, 3364–3367)

Scott No.			Plate Block	Unused	Used
❑ 3356	33¢	Leaping Stag, maroon & gold	—	1.25	.40
❑ 3357	33¢	Leaping Stag, blue & gold	—	2.00	.40
❑ 3358	33¢	Leaping Stag, violet & gold	—	2.00	.40
❑ 3359	33¢	Leaping Stag, green & gold	—	1.25	.40
		Block or strip of 4			
		(3356–3359)	7.00	4.00	.40
❑ 3360	33¢	Stag, maroon & gold (~3356)	—	1.25	.40
❑ 3361	33¢	Stag, blue & gold (~3357)	—	1.25	.40
❑ 3362	33¢	Stag, violet & gold (~3358)	—	1.25	.40
❑ 3363	33¢	Stag, green & gold (3359)	—	1.25	.40
		Booklet pane of 20			
		(3360–3363)	—	18.00	.40

NOTE: The frameline on Nos. 3356–3369 is narrower than the frameline on Nos. 3360–3363.

❑ 3364	33¢	Stag, maroon & gold (~3356)	—	2.00	.40
❑ 3365	33¢	Stag, blue & gold (~3357)	—	2.00	.40
❑ 3366	33¢	Stag, violet & gold (~3358)	—	1.25	.40
❑ 3367	33¢	green & gold (3359)	—	1.25	.40
		Booklet pane of 20			
		(3364–3367)	—	15.00	—

NOTE: Nos. 3364–3367 measure 21 x 18 mm.

3368   **3369**   **3370**

3371

Scott No.			Plate Block	Unused	Used
❏ 3368	33¢	Kwanzaa	5.25	1.25	.40
❏ 3369	33¢	Infant New Year	5.25	1.25	.40
❏ 3370	33¢	Year of the Dragon	5.25	1.25	.40
❏ 3371	33¢	Patricia Roberts Harris	5.25	1.25	.40

3372

3373–3377

Scott No.			Plate Block	Unused	Used
❑ 3372	33¢	Los Angeles Class Submarine	5.00	1.25	.40
❑ 3373	22¢	S Class Submarine	—	1.25	.40
❑ 3374	33¢	Los Angeles Class Submarine	—	1.25	.40
❑ 3375	55¢	Ohio Class Submarine	—	2.50	.75
❑ 3376	60¢	USS Holland	—	2.50	.75
❑ 3377	$3.20	Gato Class Submarine	—	4.00	2.75
		Booklet pane of 5 (3373–3377)	—	15.00	2.75
		Intact booklet with 2 panes (3373–3377)		18.00	—

NOTE: No. 3372 contains microprinted letters "USPS" at the base of its conning tower; No. 3374 does not. Each of the two booklet panes in the booklet contain a different marginal text.

3378

3379–3383

Scott No.			Plate Block	Unused	Used
☐ 3378	33¢	Rain Forest, pane of 10	—	9.00	—
☐ 3378a–j		Any single stamp	—	2.00	.40
☐ 3379	33¢	Nevelson – Silent Music I	—	1.25	.40
☐ 3380	33¢	Nevelson – Royal Tide I	—	2.00	.40
☐ 3381	33¢	Nevelson – Black Chord	—	1.25	.40
☐ 3382	33¢	Nevelson – Nightsphere Light	—	1.25	.40
☐ 3383	33¢	Nevelson – Wedding Chapel I	—	1.25	.40
		Strip of 5 (3379–3381)	18.00 (10)	4.00	2.00

3384–3388

3389

3390

Scott No.			Plate Block	Unused	Used
❏ 3384	33¢	Eagle Nebula	—	1.25	.40
❏ 3385	33¢	Ring Nebula	—	2.00	.40
❏ 3386	33¢	Lagoon Nebula	—	2.00	.40
❏ 3387	33¢	Egg Nebula	—	2.00	.40
❏ 3388	33¢	Galaxy NGC 1316	—	1.25	.40
		Strip of 5 (3384–3388)	12.00 (5)	4.00	2.00
❏ 3389	33¢	American Samoa	5.00	1.25	.40
❏ 3390	33¢	Library of Congress	5.00	1.25	.40

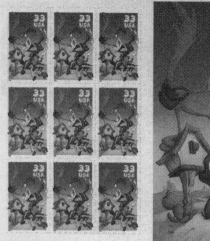

3391
(3392)

Scott No.			Plate Block	Unused	Used
❏ 3391	33¢	Roadrunner & Wile E. Coyote	—	2.50	.60
		Pane of 10	—	8.00	—
❏ 3392	33¢	Roadrunner & Wile E. Coyote	—	2.50	.40
		Pane of 10, right stamp			
		w/o die cut	—	10.00	—

3393–3396

3397

3398

Scott No.			Plate Block	Unused	Used
❑ 3393	33¢	Major General John Hines	—	1.25	.40
❑ 3394	33¢	General Omar Bradley	—	2.00	.40
❑ 3395	33¢	Sergeant Alvin York	—	2.00	.40
❑ 3396	33¢	Second Lt. Audie Murphy	—	1.25	.40
		Block or strip of 4 (3393–3396)	5.00	4.00	2.00
❑ 3397	33¢	Summer Sports – Runners	—	1.25	.40
❑ 3398	33¢	Adoption	—	1.25	.40

3399–3402

Scott No.			Plate Block	Unused	Used
❏ 3399	33¢	Basketball	—	1.25	.34
❏ 3400	33¢	Football	—	1.25	.34
❏ 3401	33¢	Soccer	—	1.25	.34
❏ 3402	33¢	Baseball	—	1.25	.34
		Block or strip of 4			
		(3399–3402)	6.00	4.00	2.50

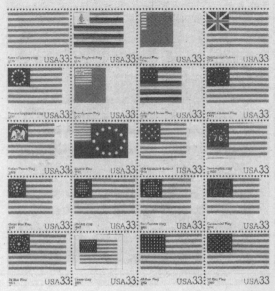

3403

Scott No.			Plate Block	Unused	Used
❏ 3403	33¢	American Flags, pane of 20	—	16.00	12.00
❏ 3403a–t	33¢	Any single stamp	—	4.25	.40

Scott No.			PNC Strip (5)

Coil Stamps.

❏ 3404	33¢	Blueberries (~3294)	—	1.20	.40
❏ 3405	33¢	Strawberries (~3296)	—	1.20	.40
❏ 3406	33¢	Blackberries (~3297)	—	4.25	.40
❏ 3407	33¢	Raspberries (~3295)	—	4.25	.40
		Strip of 4 (3404–3407)	—	5.00	—

NOTE: Nos. 3404–3407 contain straight edges at sides; Nos. 3302–3305 contain straight edges at top and bottom.

3408

Scott No.			Plate Block	Unused	Used
2000.					
❏ 3408	33¢	Baseball, pane of 20	—	16.00	—
❏ 3408a–t	33¢	Any single stamp	—	2.50	.40

3409

3410 **3411**

Scott No.			Plate Block	Unused	Used
❏ 3409	60¢	Probing the Vastness of Space, souvenir sheet of 6	—	10.00	—
		Any single stamp	—	1.25	.40
❏ 3410	$1.00	Exploring the Solar System, souvenir sheet of 5	—	12.00	—
		Any single stamp	—	2.25	1.25
❏ 3411	$3.20	Escaping the Gravity of Earth, souvenir sheet of 2	—	15.00	—
		Any single stamp	—	5.00	2.25

3412

3413

Scott No.		Plate Block	Unused	Used
❑ 3412 $11.75	Space Achievement & Exploration, souvenir sheet of 1	—	35.00	25.00
❑ 3413 $11.75	Landing on the Moon, souvenir sheet of 1	—	35.00	25.00

3414–3417

Scott No.			Plate Block	Unused	Used
❏ 3414	33¢	Space Figures	—	1.25	.34
❏ 3415	33¢	Heart	—	1.25	.34
❏ 3416	33¢	Mommy Are We There Yet	—	1.25	.34
❏ 3417	33¢	Space Dog	—	1.25	.34
		Strip of 4 (3414–3417)	8.00 (8)	4.00	—

3420　　**3426**　　**3431**　　**3432**

Distinguished Americans Series.

❏ 3420	10¢	General Joseph W. Stillwell	2.00	.50	.40
❏ 3426	33¢	Claude Pepper	4.00	1.25	.40
❏ 3431	76¢	Hattie W. Caraway	7.00	2.50	.40
❏ 3432	83¢	Edna Ferber	8.00	2.50	1.00

3438

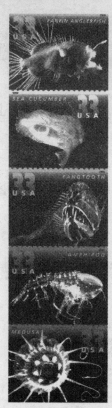

3439–3443

Scott No.			Plate Block	Unused	Used
2000.					
❑ 3438	33¢	California Statehood	4.00	1.25	.40
❑ 3439	33¢	Fanfin Anglefish	—	2.00	.40
❑ 3440	33¢	Sea Cucumber	—	2.00	.40
❑ 3441	33¢	Fangtooth	—	1.25	.40
❑ 3442	33¢	Amphipod	—	2.00	.40
❑ 3443	33¢	Medusa	—	1.25	.40
		Strip of 5 (3438–3443)	10.00 (10)	5.00	—

3444　　　　　　　**3445**　　　　　　**3446**

Scott No.			Plate Block	Unused	Used
❑ 3444	33¢	Thomas Wolfe	4.25	1.25	.55
❑ 3445	33¢	White House	4.25	1.25	.55
❑ 3446	33¢	Edward G. Robinson	4.25	1.25	.55

3447

Scott No.		PNC Strip (5)	Unused	Used
Coil Stamp.				
❑ 3447 (10¢)	New York Public Library Lion	4.00	.70	.50

3448
(3449–3450)

3451

Scott No.		Plate Block	Unused	Used
2000.				
❏ 3448 (34¢)	Flag over Farm, water-activated gum	4.00	1.25	.55
❏ 3449 (34¢)	Flag over Farm (~3448), self-adhesive, die cut 11½	5.00	2.00	.55
❏ 3450 (34¢)	Flag over Farm (~3448), self-adhesive, die cut 8	—	1.25	.34
	Booklet pane of 8	—	1.25	.34
❏ 3451 (34¢)	Statue of Liberty, self-adhesive	—	1.25	.34
	Booklet pane of 20	—	4.00	—

3452
(3453)

Scott No.		PNC Strip (5)	Unused	Used
Coil Stamps.				
❏ 3452 (34¢)	Statue of Liberty, water-activated gum	10.00	1.25	.34
❏ 3453 (34¢)	Statue of Liberty, self-adhesive	10.00	1.25	.34

3454–3457
(3458–3461)

3466
(3476–3477)

Scott No.		Plate Block	Unused	Used
2000.				
❏ 3454 (34¢)	Flower – Purple	—	1.25	.40
❏ 3455 (34¢)	Flower – Tan	—	2.20	.40
❏ 3456 (34¢)	Flower – Green	—	2.20	.40
❏ 3457 (34¢)	Flower – Red	—	1.25	.40
	Booklet pane of 20 (3454–3457)	—	16.00	—
❏ 3458 (34¢)	Flower – Purple (~3454)	—	1.25	.34
❏ 3459 (34¢)	Flower – Tan (~3455)	—	1.25	.34
❏ 3460 (34¢)	Flower – Green (~3456)	—	1.25	.34
❏ 3461 (34¢)	Flower – Red (~3457)	—	1.25	.34
	Booklet pane of 6 (3458–3461)	—	4.00	—

Scott No.		PNC Strip (5)	Unused	Used
Coil Stamps.				
❏ 3462 (34¢)	Flower – Green (~3456)	—	1.25	.34
❏ 3463 (34¢)	Flower – Red (~3457)	—	2.00	.34
❏ 3464 (34¢)	Flower – Tan (~3455)	—	2.00	.34
❏ 3465 (34¢)	Flower – Purple (~3454)	—	1.25	.34
	Strip of 4 (3462–3465)	4.00	2.00	.34
❏ 3466 34¢	Statue of Liberty, self-adhesive, rounded corners	5.00	1.25	.34

See also No. 3477.

3467
(3468, 3475,
3484, 3484A)

3468A
(3475A)

3469
(3470, 3495)

3471

3472

3473

Scott No.			Plate Block	Unused	Used
2001.					
❏ 3467	21¢	Buffalo, water activated gum	5.00	1.20	.34
❏ 3468	21¢	Buffalo, self-adhesive	4.25	1.00	.40
❏ 3468A	23¢	George Washington, self-adhesive	4.25	1.00	.34
❏ 3469	34¢	Flag over Farm, water-activated gum	4.25	1.00	.34
❏ 3470	34¢	Flag over Farm (~3470), self-adhesive, die cut 11½	4.25	1.50	.34
❏ 3471	55¢	Art Deco Eagle	7.00	2.50	.34
❏ 3471A	57¢	Art Deco Eagle (~3471)	7.00	2.50	.34
❏ 3472	$3.50	Capitol Dome	35.00	7.50	4.00
❏ 3473	$12.25	Washington Monument	125.00	25.00	10.00

3487–3490

Scott No.			PNC Strip (5)	Unused	Used

Coil Stamps.

			PNC Strip (5)	Unused	Used
❑ 3475	21¢	Buffalo (~3467), self-adhesive	6.00	1.00	.34
❑ 3475A	23¢	George Washington (~3468A), self-adhesive	4.00	1.00	.34
❑ 3476	34¢	Statue of Liberty (~3466), water-activated gum	8.00	1.25	.34
❑ 3477	34¢	Liberty (~3466), self-adhesive, square corners	7.00	1.25	.34
❑ 3478	34¢	Flower – Green	—	1.25	.34
❑ 3479	34¢	Flower – Red	—	1.25	.34
❑ 3480	34¢	Flower – Tan	—	1.25	.34
❑ 3481	34¢	Flower – Purple	—	1.25	.34
		Strip of 4 (3478–3481)	7.00	4.00	—

3482
(3483)

Scott No.			Plate Block	Unused	Used

2001.

			Plate Block	Unused	Used
❑ 3482	20¢	George Washington, self-adhesive, die cut 11½	—	1.00	.34
		Booklet pane of 10	—	6.00	.34
❑ 3483	20¢	Washington (~3482), self-adhesive, die cut 10½ x 11½	—	1.00	.34
		Booklet pane of 10	—	12.00	—

3485   **3491**   **3492**
             (3493)   (3494)

Scott No.			Plate Block	Unused	Used
❑ 3484	21¢	Buffalo (~3467), self-adhesive, die cut 11½	—	1.00	.34
		Booklet pane of 10	—	6.00	.34
❑ 3484A	21¢	Buffalo (~3467), self-adhesive, die cut 10½ x 11½	—	2.00	.34
		Booklet pane of 10	—	12.00	.34
❑ 3485	34¢	Statue of Liberty, self-adhesive, die cut 11	—	2.00	.34
		Booklet pane of 10	—	8.00	—
		Booklet pane of 20	—	16.00	—
❑ 3487	34¢	Flower – Purple (~3481)	—	1.25	.40
❑ 3488	34¢	Flower – Tan (~3480)	—	1.25	.40
❑ 3489	34¢	Flower – Green (~3478)	—	1.25	.40
❑ 3490	34¢	Flower – Red (~3479)	—	1.25	.40
		Booklet pane of 20 (3487–3480)	—	20.00	—
❑ 3491	34¢	Apple, self-adhesive, die cut 11½	—	1.25	.34
❑ 3492	34¢	Orange, self-adhesive, die cut 11½	—	1.25	.34
		Booklet pane of 20 (3491–3492)	—	20.00	.34
❑ 3493	34¢	Apple (~3491), self-adhesive, die cut 10½ x 11½	—	1.25	.34
❑ 3494	34¢	Orange (~3492)), self-adhesive, die cut 10½ x 11½	—	1.25	.34
		Booklet pane of 20 (3493–3494)	—	4.00	.34
❑ 3495	34¢	Flag over Farm (~3469), self-adhesive, die cut 8	—	1.25	.34
		Booklet pane of 18	—	12.00	—

3496   **3497**   **3499**
            (3498)

3500

3501

Scott No.			Plate Block	Unused	Used
❏ 3496 (34¢)		Love – Rose	—	1.25	.34
		Booklet pane of 20	—	16.00	.34
❏ 3497	34¢	Love – Rose	—	1.25	.34
		Booklet pane of 20	—	15.00	.34
❏ 3498	34¢	Love – Rose	—	1.25	.34
		Booklet pane of 20	—	7.00	.34

NOTE: No. 3497 measures 19½ x 26½ mm; No. 3498 measures 18 x 21 mm.

❏ 3499	55¢	Love – Rose	6.00	2.00	.65

NOTE: No. 3551 for 57c stamp of similar design.

❏ 3500	34¢	Year of the Snake	5.00	1.25	.40
❏ 3501	34¢	Roy Wilkins	4.00	1.25	.40

3502

3503

3504

Scott No.			Plate Block	Unused	Used
❑ 3502	34¢	Illustrators, pane of 20	—	16.00	—
❑ 3502a–t		Any single stamp	—	1.25	.34
❑ 3503	34¢	Diabetes Awareness	5.00	1.25	.34
❑ 3504	34¢	Nobel Prize 1901–2001	5.00	1.25	.34

3505

Scott No.			Plate Block	Unused	Used
❏ 3505	34¢	Pan American Inverts, souvenir sheet	—	10.00	7.00
❏ 3505a	1¢	Ship Inverted	—	.80	.60
❏ 3505b	2¢	Train Inverted	—	.80	.60
❏ 3505c	4¢	Automobile Inverted	—	.80	.60
❏ 3505d	80¢	Exposition Seal	—	4.00	2.00

NOTE: Nos. 3505a–3505c can be distinguished from the original errors by the date 2001 at lower left.

3506

3507

3508

3509

Scott No.			Plate Block	Unused	Used
❏ 3506	34¢	Great Plains Prairie, pane of 10	—	8.00	—
❏ 3506a–j		Any single stamp	—	1.25	.34
❏ 3507	34¢	Snoopy	5.00	2.00	.34
❏ 3508	34¢	Honoring Veterans	4.25	2.00	.34
❏ 3509	34¢	Frida Kahlo	4.25	1.25	.34

3510–3519

Scott No.			Plate Block	Unused	Used
❏ 3510	34¢	Ebbetts Field	—	1.25	.40
❏ 3511	34¢	Tiger Stadium	—	1.25	.40
❏ 3512	34¢	Crosley Field	—	1.25	.40
❏ 3513	34¢	Yankee Stadium	—	1.25	.40
❏ 3514	34¢	Polo Grounds	—	1.25	.40
❏ 3515	34¢	Forbes Field	—	1.25	.40
❏ 3516	34¢	Fenway Park	—	1.25	.40
❏ 3517	34¢	Comisky Park	—	1.25	.40
❏ 3518	34¢	Shibe Park	—	1.25	.40
❏ 3519	34¢	Wrigley Field	—	1.25	.40
		Block of 10 (3510–3519)	12.00 (10)	6.00	—

3520

3521

3522

Scott No.	PNC Strip (5)	Unused	Used
Coil Stamp.			
❑ 3520 (10¢) Atlas Statue, self-adhesive	4.25	.65	.40

Scott No.	Plate Block	Unused	Used
2001.			
❑ 3521 34¢ Leonard Bernstein	4.25	1.00	.34

Scott No.	PNC Strip (5)	Unused	Used
Coil Stamp.			
❑ 3522 (15¢) Woody Wagon, self-adhesive	4.25	1.00	.34

3523

Scott No.	Plate Block	Unused	Used
2001.			
❑ 3523 34¢ Lucille Ball	5.00	1.50	.40

AMISH QUILT 34 USA AMISH QUILT 34 USA AMISH QUILT 34 USA AMISH QUILT 34 USA

3524–3527

Venus Flytrap Yellow Trumpet Cobra Lily English Sundew Venus Flytrap

3528–3531

Scott No.			Plate Block	Unused	Used
❑ 3524	34¢	Amish quilt – Diamond in Square	—	1.00	.34
❑ 3525	34¢	Amish quilt – Starburst	—	1.00	.34
❑ 3526	34¢	Amish quilt – Diamond Pattern	—	1.00	.34
❑ 3427	34¢	Amish quilt – Double Ninepatch Pattern	—	1.00	.34
		Block or strip of 4 (3424–3427)	5.00	4.00	.34
❑ 3528	34¢	Venus Flytrap	—	1.50	.34
❑ 3529	34¢	Yellow Trumpet	—	1.50	.34
❑ 3530	34¢	Cobra Lily	—	1.50	.34
❑ 3531	34¢	English Sundew	—	1.50	.34
		Block or strip of 4 (3528–3531)	5.00	4.00	—

3532   **3533**

3534
(3535)

Scott No.			Plate Block	Unused	Used
❑ 3532	34¢	Eid Mubarak	4.25	1.50	.40
❑ 3533	34¢	Enrico Fermi	4.25	2.20	.40
❑ 3534	34¢	Porky Pig	—	2.20	.40
		Pane of 10	—	8.00	.40
❑ 3535	34¢	Porky Pig	—	1.50	.45
		Pane of 10, right stamp w/o die cut	—	10.00	—

3536

3537–3540
(3541–3544)

Scott No.			Plate Block	Unused	Used
❑ 3536	34¢	Christmas – Madonna & Child	—	1.50	.34
		Booklet pane of 20	—	15.00	.34
❑ 3537	34¢	Santa & Rocking Horse, black inscription	—	1.00	.34
❑ 3538	34¢	Santa & Tree on Shoulder, black inscription	—	1.00	.34
❑ 3539	34¢	Santa Holding Tree, black inscription	—	1.00	.34
❑ 3540	34¢	Santa Garland on Cap, black inscription	—	1.00	.34
		Block of 4 (3537–3540)	5.00	4.00	—
		Booklet pane of 5 (5 of 3540)	—	15.00	—

NOTE: Year date at lower right is smaller on booklet stamps than on those from pane of 20.

❑ 3541	34¢	Santa & Rocking Horse, red & green inscription	—	1.00	.34
❑ 3542	34¢	Santa & Tree on Shoulder, red & green inscription	—	1.00	.34
❑ 3543	34¢	Santa Holding Tree, red & green inscription	—	1.00	.34
❑ 3544	34¢	Santa Garland on Cap, red & green inscription	—	1.00	.34
		Booklet pane of 10 (3541–3544)	—	4.00	—

3545

3546

3547

3548

3549
(3550–3550A)

Scott No.			Plate Block	Unused	Used
❑ 3545	34¢	James Monroe	5.00	1.25	.40
❑ 3546	34¢	We Give Thanks	5.00	1.25	.40
❑ 3547	34¢	Hanukkah (~ 3118)	5.00	1.25	.40
❑ 3548	34¢	Kwanzaa (~3175)	5.00	1.25	.40
❑ 3549	34¢	United We Stand	—	1.25	.40
		Booklet Pane of 20	—	15.00	—

Scott No.			PNC Strip (5)	Unused	Used
Coils Stamps.					
❑ 3550	34¢	United We Stand (~3549), self-adhesive, square corners	8.00	1.50	.34
❑ 3550A	34¢	United We Stand (~3549), self-adhesive, rounded corners	10.00	1.50	.34

Scott No.			Plate Block	Unused	Used
2001.					
❑ 3551	57¢	Love – Rose (~3499)	6.00	2.00	.80

3552–3555

3556

3557

3558

3559

3560

Scott No.			Plate Block	Unused	Used
❏ 3552	34¢	Olympics – Ski Jumping	—	1.00	.34
❏ 3553	34¢	Olympics – Snowboarding	—	1.00	.34
❏ 3554	34¢	Olympics – Ice Hockey	—	1.00	.34
❏ 3555	34¢	Olympics – Figure Skating	—	1.00	.34
		Block or strip of 4 (3551–3555)	5.00	1.25	—
❏ 3556	34¢	Mentoring a Child	4.25	1.25	.40
❏ 3557	34¢	Langston Hughes	4.25	1.25	.40
❏ 3558	34¢	Happy Birthday	4.25	1.25	.40
❏ 3559	34¢	Year of the Horse	4.25	1.25	.40
❏ 3560	34¢	West Point	4.25	1.25	.40

3561–3610

Scott No.			Plate Block	Unused	Used
❑ 3561–					
3610	34¢	Greetings from America	—	40.00	—
		Any single stamp	—	1.50	.40

3611

3612

3c USA

3613
(3614)

Scott No.			Plate Block	Unused	Used
❏ 3611	34¢	Pine Forest, pane of 10	—	8.00	—
❏ 3611a–j		Any single stamp	—	1.50	.34

Scott No.			PNC Strip (5)	Unused	Used
Coil Stamp.					
❏ 3612	(5¢)	American Toleware	4.00	.40	.34
2002.					
❏ 3613	3¢	Red, white & blue Star	5.00	.40	.34
❏ 3614	3¢	Red, white & blue Star (~3613)	4.00	.40	.34

NOTE: On No. 3613 the date appears at lower left; on No. 3614 it appears at lower right.

3620
(3621–3625)

3626–3629

Scott No.		Plate Block	Unused	Used
❏ 3620 (37¢)	Flag, water activated	8.00	1.25	.34
❏ 3621 (37¢)	Flag (~3620), self-adhesive	4.00	1.25	.34

Scott No.		PNC Strip (5)	Unused	Used
❏ 3622 (37¢)	Flag (~3620), self-adhesive	8.00	1.25	.34

Scott No.		Plate Block	Unused	Used
❏ 3623 (37¢)	Flag (~3620), die cut 11.25	—	1.25	.34
	Booklet pane of 20	—	15.00	.34
❏ 3624 (37¢)	Flag (~3620), die cut 10½ x 10¾	—	1.25	.34
	Booklet pane of 4	—	4.00	.34
	Booklet pane of 20	—	16.00	.34
❏ 3625 (37¢)	Flag (~3620), die cut 8	—	1.25	.34
	Booklet pane of 18	—	14.00	.34
❏ 3626 (37¢)	Mail Wagon	—	1.25	.34
❏ 3627 (37¢)	Locomotive	—	1.25	.34
❏ 3628 (37¢)	Automobile	—	1.25	.34
❏ 3629 (37¢)	Fire Engine	—	1.25	.34
	Booklet pane of 20 (3626-3629)	—	15.00	—

3630
(3631–3636)

Scott No.			Plate Block	Unused	Used
❑ 3630	37¢	Flag	5.00	1.25	.34

Scott No.			PNC Strip (5)	Unused	Used
❑ 3631	37¢	Flag (~3630), water activated	7.00	1.25	.34
❑ 3632	37¢	Flag (~3630), self-adhesive, die cut 10	8.00	1.25	.34
❑ 3633	37¢	Flag (~3630), self-adhesive, die cut 8	7.00	2.50	.34

Scott No.			Plate Block	Unused	Used
❑ 3635	37¢	Flag (~3630), die cut 11.25	—	2.50	.34
		Booklet pane of 20	—	15.00	.34
❑ 3636	37¢	Flag (~3630), die cut 10½ x 10¾	—	2.50	.34
		Booklet pane of 20	—	14.00	—

3638–3641

Scott No.			PNC Strip (5)	Unused	Used
Coil Stamp.					
❑ 3638	37¢	Locomotive	—	1.25	.34
❑ 3639	37¢	Mail Wagon	—	1.25	.34
❑ 3640	37¢	Fire Engine	—	1.25	.34
❑ 3641	37¢	Automobile	—	1.25	.34
		Strip of 4 (3638–3642)	15.00	1.25	—

Scott No.			Plate Block	Unused	Used
❑ 3642	37¢	Mail Wagon (~3639)	—	1.25	.34
❑ 3643	37¢	Locomotive (~3638)	—	1.25	.34
❑ 3644	37¢	Automobile (~3641)	—	1.25	.34
❑ 3644	37¢	Fire Engine (~3640)	—	1.25	.34
		Booklet pane of 4 (3642-3644)	—	5.00	—
		Booklet pane of 20 (3642-3644)	—	15.00	—

3646

3647

3648

❑ 3646	60¢	Eagle	6.00	2.00	.85
❑ 3647	$3.85	Jefferson Memorial	35.00	8.00	4.00
❑ 3648	$13.65	Capitol Dome	100.00	35.00	10.00

3649

3650

3651

Scott No.			Plate Block	Unused	Used
❏ 3649	37¢	Photography, pane of 20	—	14.00	—
❏ 3649a–t		Any single stamp	—	2.50	.34
❏ 3650	37¢	John James Audubon	5.00	2.50	.34
❏ 3651	37¢	Harry Houdini	5.00	2.50	.34

3652

3653

3654

3655

3656

Scott No.			Plate Block	Unused	Used
❑ 3652	37¢	Andy Warhol	4.25	1.25	.55
❑ 3653-56	37¢	Teddy Bears	4.25	1.25	.55

3657

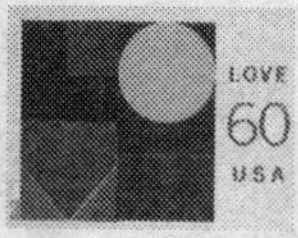

3658

3659

Scott No.			Plate Block	Unused	Used
❑ 3657	37¢	Love Pane of 20	15.00	1.25	.45
❑ 3658	60¢	Love SA	6.00	2.00	.75
❑ 3659	37¢	Ogden Nash SA	5.00	1.25	.75

3660

3661   **3662**   **3663**   **3664**

Scott No.			Plate Block	Unused	Used
❑ 3660	37¢	Duke Kahanamoku	12.00	4.00	1.25
❑ 3661-64	37¢	American Bats	4.00	2.00	1.25

3665   **3666**   **3667**   **3668**

Scott No.			Plate Block	Unused	Used
❑ 3665	37¢	Nellie Bly	—	6.25	4.50
❑ 3666	37¢	Ida M. Tarbell	—	6.25	4.50
❑ 3667	37¢	Ethel L. Payne	—	6.25	4.50
❑ 3668	37¢	Marguerite Higgins	—	6.25	4.50
		(block of 4)	7.00	—	—

3669

3670-71

Scott No.			Plate Block	Unused	Used
❏ 3669	37¢	Irving Berlin	4.00	1.50	.50
❏ 3670	37¢	Neuter and Spay	6.00	4.00	.75
❏ 3671	37¢	Neuter and Spay	6.00	4.00	.75

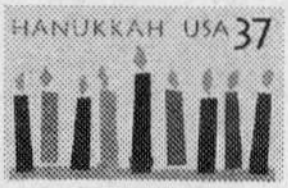

3672

3673

3674

3675

Scott No.			Plate Block	Unused	Used
❏ 3672	37¢	Hanukkah SA	4.25	1.25	.50
❏ 3673	37¢	Kwanzaa SA	4.25	1.25	.50
❏ 3674	37¢	Islamic Festival	4.25	1.25	.50
❏ 3675	37¢	Madonna	4.25	1.25	.50
		(pane of 20)	15.00	—	—

3676

3677

3678

3679

3680

3681

3682

3683

Scott No.			Plate Block	Unused	Used
❏ 3676-79	37¢	Snowman	4.00	3.50	—
❏ 3680-83	37¢	Snowman (strip of 5)	8.00	5.00	—

3684

3685

3686

3687

3688

3689

3690

3691

Scott No.			Plate Block	Unused	Used
❏ 3684-87	37¢	Snowman	5.00	4.50	—
❏ 3688-91	37¢	Snowman	5.00	—	—

3692

3693

3694

3695

Scott No.			Plate Block	Unused	Used
❏ 3692	37¢	Cary Grant	5.25	1.25	.40
❏ 3693	5¢	Sea Coast (strip of 5)	5.25	.50	.40
❏ 3694	37¢	Hawaiian Missionary	—	4.00	2.00
❏ 3695	37¢	Happy Birthday	5.25	1.25	.40

3696-3745

3746

3747

3748

3749

Scott No.			Plate Block	Unused	Used
❏ 3696-3745	37¢	Greetings From America (sheet of 50 singles)	35.00	—	—
❏ 3746	37¢	Thurgood Marshall SA	4.25	1.25	.40
❏ 3747	37¢	Year of the Ram SA	4.25	1.25	.40
❏ 3748	37¢	Zora Neale Hurston SA	4.25	1.25	.40
❏ 3749	2¢	Navajo jewelry	4.25	1.25	.40

3751

3757

3759

3766

3769

3770

Scott No.			Plate Block	Unused	Used
❏ 3751	10¢	U.S. Clock	1.50	.40	.34
❏ 3757	1¢	Tiffany Lamp		.40	.34
❏ 3759	3¢	Silver Coffeepot		.40	.34
❏ 3766	$1	Wisdom	10.00	2.00	1.00
❏ 3769	10¢	New York Public Library	—	.40	.34
❏ 3770	10¢	Atlas	—	.40	.34

3771

3772

Scott No.			Plate Block	Unused	Used
❏ 3771	80¢	Special Olympics	—	2.00	1.00
❏ 3772	37¢	American Filmmaking		5.00	4.25
		(sheets of 10)	8.00	—	—

3773

3774

3775

3776–80

Scott No.			Plate Block	Unused	Used
❑ 3773	37¢	Ohio Statehood	4.00	1.25	.34
❑ 3774	37¢	Pelican Island	4.00	1.25	.34
❑ 3775	50¢	Seacoast	—	.40	.34
		(strip of 5)	2.00	—	—
❑ 3776–80	37¢	Old Glory	—	.40	.34
		(strip of 5)	4.00	—	—

3781

3782

Scott No.			Plate Block	Unused	Used
❑ 3781	37¢	Cesar Chavez SA	4.00	1.00	.40
❑ 3782	37¢	Louisiana Purchase SA	4.00	1.00	.40

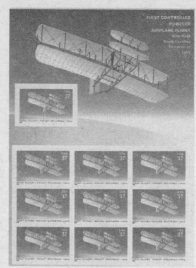

3783

3784

3784A

3785

Scott No.			Plate Block	Unused	Used
❑ 3783	37¢	First Flight	8.00	.85	.40
❑ 3784	37¢	Purple Heart	4.00	1.25	.40
❑ 3785	37¢	Sea Coast	4.00	1.25	.40

3786

3787–91

Scott No.			Plate Block	Unused	Used
❑ 3786	37¢	Audrey Hepburn	5.00	1.25	.55
❑ 3787–91	37¢	Cape Henry Lighthouse	10.00	1.25	.55

3792-96

3797–3801

Scott No.			Plate Block	Unused	Used
❏ 3792–96	25¢	Presorted First Class	10.00	7.00	—
❏ 3797–3801	25¢	Presorted (strip of 10)	—	8.00	—

3802

3803

3804

3805

3806

3807

Scott No.			Plate Block	Unused	Used
❏ 3802	37¢	Arctic Tundra (strip of 10)	—	8.00	—
❏ 3803	37¢	Korean War	5.00	1.00	.40
❏ 3804–07	37¢	Mary Cassatt	4.00	1.00	.40

3808–11

3812

3813

3814–18

Scott No.			Plate Block	Unused	Used
❏ 3808–11	37¢	Early Football Heroes	8.00	4.00	—
❏ 3812	37¢	Roy Acuff	7.00	4.00	2.00
❏ 3813	37¢	District of Columbia	8.00	1.25	.40
❏ 3814–18	37¢	Reptile (strip of 5)	8.00	1.25	.40

3819

3820

3821

3822

3823

3824

3821–24

3825

3826

3827

3828

Scott No.			Plate Block	Unused	Used
❏ 3819	37¢	Washington	7.00	1.00	.40
❏ 3820	37¢	J. Gossaett Christmas	7.00	1.00	.40
❏ 3821–24	37¢	Christmas (strip of 4)	—	8.00	.40
❏ 3821	37¢	Christmas	—	1.00	.40
❏ 3822	37¢	Christmas	—	1.00	.40
❏ 3823	37¢	Christmas	—	1.00	.40
❏ 3824	37¢	Christmas	—	1.00	.40
❏ 3825	37¢	ChristmasSA	—	1.00	.40
❏ 3826	37¢	ChristmasSA	—	1.00	.40
❏ 3827	37¢	ChristmasSA	—	1.00	.40
❏ 3828	37¢	ChristmasSA	—	1.00	.40

3829

3830

3831

3832

3833

3834

Scott No.			Plate Block	Unused	Used
❑ 3829	37¢	Egret	8.00	1.00	.40
❑ 3830	37¢	American Flag	8.00	1.00	.40
❑ 3831	37¢	Pacific Coral Reefs	—	1.00	.40
❑ 3832	37¢	Year of the Monkey	4.25	1.00	.40
❑ 3833	37¢	Candy Hearts Love	—	1.00	.40
❑ 3834	37¢	Paul Robeson	4.25	1.00	.40

3835 (sheet)

3835

3836

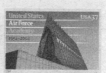

3838

3839

Scott No.			Plate Block	Unused	Used
❏ 3835	37¢	Dr. Seuss	4.25	1.00	.40
❏ 3836	37¢	Garden Blossoms	4.25	1.00	.40
❏ 3838	37¢	U. S. Air Force Academy	4.25	1.00	.40
❏ 3839	37¢	Henry Mancini	4.25	1.00	.40

3840–3843

3855

3856

Scott No.			Plate Block	Unused	Used
❑ 3840	37¢	Martha Graham	—	.75	.40
❑ 3841	37¢	Alvin Ailey	—	.75	.40
❑ 3842	37¢	Agnes de Mille	—	.75	.40
❑ 3843	37¢	George Balanchine	—	.75	.40
❑ 3855	37¢	Lewis	—	.75	.40
❑ 3856	37¢	Clark	—	.75	.40

3857–3861

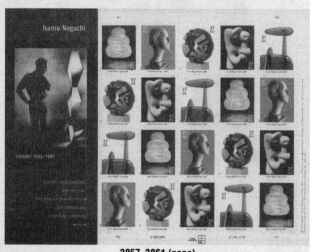

3857–3861 (pane)

Scott No.			Plate Block	Unused	Used
❑ 3857	37¢	Isamu Noguchi-Akari	—	.70	.38
❑ 3858	37¢	Isamu Noguchi-Margaret La Farge Osborn	—	.70	.38
❑ 3859	37¢	Isamu Noguchi-Black Sun	—	.70	.38
❑ 3860	37¢	Isamu Noguchi-Mother & Child	—	.70	.38
❑ 3861	37¢	Isamu Noguchi-Figure	—	.70	.38

3862   **3863**   **3864**

3865

Scott No.			Plate Block	Unused	Used
❏ 3862	37¢	World War II Memorial	—	.65	.38
❏ 3863	37¢	Summer Olympic Games	—	.65	.38
❏ 3864	5¢	Sea Coast	—	.65	.38
❏ 3865	37¢	Art of Disney-Goofy, Mickey, Donald	—	.65	.38

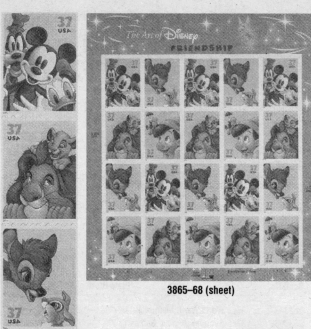

3865–68 (sheet)

3865-3868

3869

3870

Scott No.			Plate Block	Unused	Used
❏ 3866	37¢	Art of Disney-Bambi, Thumper	—	.65	.38
❏ 3867	37¢	Art of Disney-Mufasa, Simba	—	.65	.38
❏ 3868	37¢	Art of Disney-Jiminy, Pinocchio	—	.65	.38
❏ 3869	37¢	USS Constellation	—	.65	.38
❏ 3870	37¢	Buckminster Fuller	—	.65	.38

3871

3872

3873 a–j

3874

3875

Scott No.			Plate Block	Unused	Used
❏ 3871	37¢	James Baldwin	—	.65	.38
❏ 3872	37¢	Martin Johnson Heade	—	.65	.38
❏ 3873	37¢	American Indian Art	—	.65	.38
❏ 3874	37¢	Sea Coast	—	.55	.38
❏ 3875	37¢	Sea Coast	—	.55	.38

3876

3876 (sheet)

3877

3878

Scott No.			Plate Block	Unused	Used
❑ 3876	37¢	John Wayne	—	.55	.28
❑ 3877	37¢	Sickle Cell	—	.55	.28
❑ 3878	37¢	Cloudscapes	—	.55	.28

3879

3880

3881

3882

Scott No.			Plate Block	Unused	Used
❑ 3879	37¢	Madonna & Child	—	.55	.28
❑ 3880	37¢	Hanukkah	—	.55	.28
❑ 3881	37¢	Kwanzaa	—	.55	.28
❑ 3882	37¢	Moss Hart	—	.55	.28

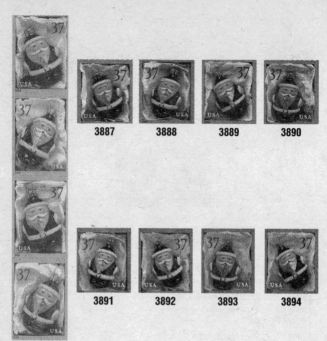

3887   3888   3889   3890

3891   3892   3893   3894

3883–3886

Scott No.			Plate Block	Unused	Used
❏ 3883–94	37¢	Holiday Ornaments	—	.55	.28

3895

3896

3897

3898

Scott No.			Plate Block	Unused	Used
❑ 3895	37¢	Lunar New Year	—	.55	.28
❑ 3896	37¢	Marian Anderson	—	.55	.28
❑ 3897	37¢	Ronald Reagan	—	.55	.28
❑ 3898	37¢	Love Bouquet	—	.55	.28

3899

3900

3901

3902

3903

3904

3905

Scott No.			Plate Block	Unused	Used
❑ 3899	37¢	Northeast Deciduous Forest	—	.55	.28
❑ 3900–03	37¢	Spring Flowers	—	.55	.28
❑ 3904	37¢	Robert Penn Warren	—	.55	.28
❑ 3905	37¢	Yip Harburg	—	.55	.28

3906–3909

3910

3911

Scott No.			Plate Block	Unused	Used
❏ 3906–09	37¢	American Scientists	—	.55	.28
❏ 3910	37¢	American Architecture	—	.55	.28
❏ 3911	37¢	Henry Fonda	—	.55	.28

3912–3915

3916–3925

Scott No.			Plate Block	Unused	Used
❏ 3912–15	37¢	Disney	—	.55	.28
❏ 3916–25	37¢	Aviation	—	.55	.28

3926   **3927**   **3928**   **3929**

3930   **3931**   **3932**

3933   **3934**   **3935**

Scott No.			Plate Block	Unused	Used
❑ 3926–29	37¢	Rio Blankets	—	.55	.28
❑ 3930	37¢	Presidential Libraries	—	.55	.28
❑ 3931–35	37¢	Sporty Cars	—	.55	.28

3936

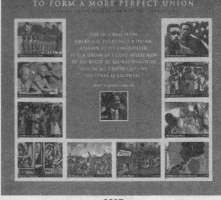

3937

3938

3939   **3940**   **3941**   **3942**

Scott No.			Plate Block	Unused	Used
❑ 3936	37¢	Arthur Ashe	—	.55	.28
❑ 3937	37¢	Civil Rights	—	.55	.28
❑ 3938	37¢	Child Health	—	.55	.28
❑ 3939–42	37¢	Dance	—	.55	.28

3943

3944

Scott No.			Plate Block	Unused	Used
❏ 3943	37¢	Greta Garbo	—	.55	.28
❏ 3944	37¢	Muppets	—	.55	.28

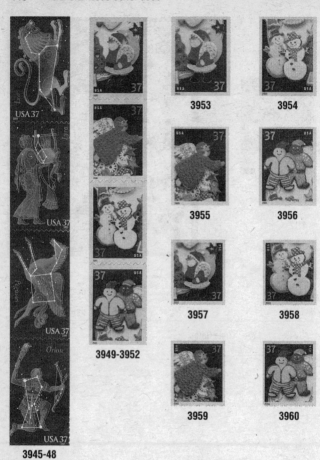

3953

3954

3955

3956

3957

3958

3959

3960

3949-3952

3945-48

Scott No.			Plate Block	Unused	Used
❑ 3945–48	37¢	Constellations	—	.55	.28
❑ 3949–60	37¢	Holiday Cookies	—	.55	.28

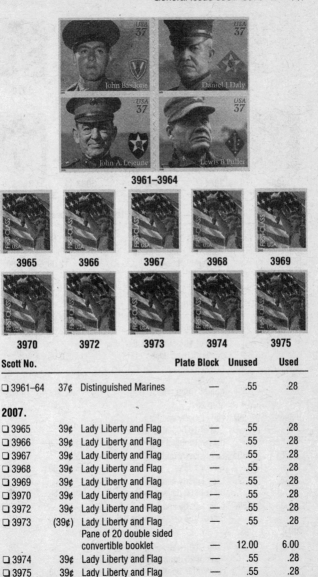

3961–3964

3965   3966   3967   3968   3969

3970   3972   3973   3974   3975

Scott No.			Plate Block	Unused	Used
❑ 3961–64	37¢	Distinguished Marines	—	.55	.28
2007.					
❑ 3965	39¢	Lady Liberty and Flag	—	.55	.28
❑ 3966	39¢	Lady Liberty and Flag	—	.55	.28
❑ 3967	39¢	Lady Liberty and Flag	—	.55	.28
❑ 3968	39¢	Lady Liberty and Flag	—	.55	.28
❑ 3969	39¢	Lady Liberty and Flag	—	.55	.28
❑ 3970	39¢	Lady Liberty and Flag	—	.55	.28
❑ 3972	39¢	Lady Liberty and Flag	—	.55	.28
❑ 3973	(39¢)	Lady Liberty and Flag	—	.55	.28
		Pane of 20 double sided convertible booklet	—	12.00	6.00
❑ 3974	39¢	Lady Liberty and Flag	—	.55	.28
❑ 3975	39¢	Lady Liberty and Flag	—	.55	.28

3976

3978   **3979**

3980   **3981**   **3982**   **3983**   **3985**

Scott No.			Plate Block	Unused	Used
❑ 3976	(39¢)	Love True Blue	—	.60	.28
		Pane of 20 double sided convertible booklet	—	12.00	5.00
Coil Stamp.					
❑ 3978	39¢	Lady Liberty and Flag	—	.60	.28
		Pane of 20 double sided convertible booklet	—	12.00	5.25
		Pane of 20 double cut	—	12.00	5.25
		Pane of 10 double sided convertible booklet	—	6.00	3.25
❑ 3979	39¢	Lady Liberty and Flag water activated			
		Coil of 100/3,000/10,000/ strip 25	—	.60	.28
❑ 3980	39¢	Lady Liberty and Flag			
		Coil of 10,000/strip of 25, die cut rounded corners	—	.60	.28
❑ 3981	39¢	Lady Liberty and Flag			
		Coil of 100	—	.60	.28
❑ 3982	39¢	Lady Liberty and Flag			
		Coil of 100 die cut gauge 10	—	.60	.28
❑ 3983	39¢	Lady Liberty and Flag			
		Coil of 100 die cut gauge 8.5	—	.60	.28
2007.					
❑ 3985	39¢	Lady Liberty and Flag	—	.60	.28
		Pane of 20 double sided convertible booklet	—	12.00	5.00

3987–3994

3995

3996

3997

Scott No.			Plate Block	Unused	Used
❏ 3987–94	39¢	Favorite Children's Book Animals			
		Pane of 16	—	8.00	4.00
		Any single stamp	—	.60	.28
❏ 3995	39¢	2006 Olympic Games			
		Pane of 20	—	10.00	4.00
		Any single stamp	—	.60	.28
❏ 3996	39¢	Black Heritage-Hattie McDaniel			
		Pane of 20	—	10.00	4.00
		Any single stamp	—	.60	.28
❏ 3997	39¢	Lunar New Year			
		Pane of 12	—	6.00	2.60
		Any single stamp	—	.60	.28

3998

3999

4003

Scott No.			Plate Block	Unused	Used
❑ 3998	39¢	Our Wedding Purple Dove	—	.55	.28
		Pane of 20 convertible booklet	—	11.00	5.00
❑ 3999	63¢	Our Wedding Green Dove	—	.75	.40
		Pane of 40 convertible booklet			
		20/39¢ & 20/63¢	—	25.00	20.00
❑ 4000	24¢	Common Buckeye	—	.50	.28
		Pane of 100, water activated,			
		perforated	—	45.00	22.00
❑ 4001	24¢	Common Buckeye	—	.50	.28
		Pane of 20 self adhesive	—	10.00	4.00
❑ 4001a		Pane of 10 self adhesive	—	4.00	2.00
		Booklet of 10 self adhesive	—	42.00	22.00

Coil.

❑ 4002	24¢	Common Buckeye Coil	—	.50	.28
		Coil of 100 self adhesive	—	42.00	22.00
❑ 4003	39¢	Crops of America–Pepper	—	.60	.28
		Coil of 100	—	52.00	22.00

4004   **4005**   **4006**   **4007**   **4008**

4009   **4010**   **4011**   **4012**   **4013**

4014   **4015**   **4016**   **4017**

Scott No.			Plate Block	Unused	Used
2007.					
❏ 4004	39¢	Crops of America–Beans	—	.60	.28
❏ 4005	39¢	Crops of America–Sun Flower	—	.60	.28
❏ 4006	39¢	Crops of America–Squash	—	.60	.28
❏ 4007	39¢	Crops of America–Corn	—	.60	.28
❏ 4008	39¢	Crops of America–Corn	—	.60	.28
❏ 4009	39¢	Crops of America–Squash	—	.60	.28
❏ 4010	39¢	Crops of America–Sun Flower	—	.60	.28
❏ 4011	39¢	Crops of America–Beans	—	.60	.28
❏ 4012	39¢	Crops of America–Pepper	—	.60	.25
		Pane of 20 double sided	—	10.00	4.00
❏ 4013	39¢	Crops of America–Pepper	—	.60	.28
		Booklet of 20	—	10.00	4.00
❏ 4014	39¢	Crops of America–Corn	—	.60	.28
❏ 4015	39¢	Crops of America–Squash	—	.60	.28
❏ 4016	39¢	Crops of America–Sun Flower	—	.60	.28
❏ 4017	39¢	Crops of America–Beans	—	.60	.28

4018

4019

4020

4021–4024

4025–4028

Scott No.			Plate Block	Unused	Used
❏ 4018	4.05	X Plane Priority Mail	35.00	10.00	7.00
		Pane of 20	—	16.00	12.00
❏ 4019	14.40	X Plane Express Mail	60.00	20.00	12.00
		Pane of 20	—	400.00	200.00
❏ 4020	39¢	Sugar Ray Robinson	—	.60	.28
		Pane of 20	—	10.00	4.00
❏ 4021–24	39¢	Benjamin Franklin			
		Pane of 4	—	10.00	4.00
		Any single stamp	—	.60	.28
❏ 4025–28	39¢	Art of Disney			
		Pane of 20	—	10.00	4.00
		Any single stamp	—	.60	.28

4029

4030

4031

4032

4033–4072

Scott No.			Plate Block	Unused	Used
❏ 4029	39¢	Love True Blue	—	.60	.28
		Pane of 20 double sided convertible booklet	—	10.00	5.00
❏ 4030	39¢	Katherine Anne Porter–Literary Arts Services	—	.60	.28
		Pane of 20	—	10.00	4.00
❏ 4031	39¢	Amber Alert	—	.60	.28
		Pane of 20	—	10.00	4.00
❏ 4032	39¢	Purple Heart	—	.60	.28
		Pane of 20	—	10.00	4.00
❏ 4033–72	39¢	Wonders of America			
		Pane of 40	—	20.00	8.00
		Any single stamp	—	.60	.28

4073

4074

4075

4076a–f

Scott No.			Plate Block	Unused	Used
❑ 4073	39¢	1606 Voyage of Samuel Champlain			
		Pane of 20 self adhesive	—	10.00	5.00
❑ 4074	39¢	1606 Voyage of Samuel Champlain			
		Souvenir sheet of 4 water activated	—	2.00	1.20
❑ 4074a		Any single stamp	—	1.00	.40
❑ 4075a	$1	Washington 2006 World Philatelic Exhibition	—	2.00	.75
❑ 4075b	$2	Washington 2006 World Philatelic Exhibition	—	4.00	2.50
❑ 4075c	$5	Washington 2006 World Philatelic Exhibition	—	8.00	5.00
		Souvenir sheet of 3 ($1 $2 $5) water activated	—	10.00	7.00
❑ 4076a–f	39¢	Distinguished American Diplomats			
		Pane of 6	—	4.00	1.50
		Any single stamp	—	.60	.28

4077

4078

4079

4080–4084

Scott No.			Plate Block	Unused	Used
❏ 4077	39¢	Judy Garland–Legends of Hollywood	—	.60	.28
		Pane of 20	—	10.00	4.25
❏ 4078	39¢	Ronald Reagan	—	.60	.25
		Pane of 20	—	10.00	4.25
❏ 4079	39¢	Happy Birthday–Holiday Celebrations	—	.60	.28
		Pane of 20	—	10.00	4.00
❏ 4081–84	39¢	Baseball Sluggers			
		Pane of 4	—	2.00	1.00
		Any single stamp	—	.60	.28

4084a–t

4085–4088

Scott No.			Plate Block	Unused	Used
❏ 4084a–t	39¢	DC Comics Super Heroes			
		Pane of 20	—	12.00	5.00
		Any single stamp	—	.60	.28
❏ 4085–88	39¢	American Motorcycles			
		Souvenir sheet of 4	—	2.00	1.00
		Any single stamp	—	.60	.28

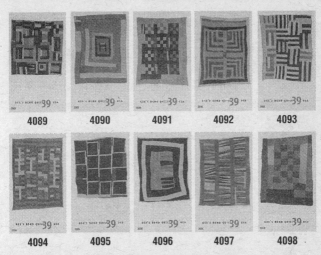

| 4089 | 4090 | 4091 | 4092 | 4093 |

| 4094 | 4095 | 4096 | 4097 | 4098 |

4099

4100

Scott No.			Plate Block	Unused	Used
❑ 4089–98	39¢	Quilts of Gee's Bend			
		Pane of 20 double sided	—	10.00	5.00
		Any single stamp	—	.60	.28
❑ 4099	39¢	Southern Florida Wetlands	—	.60	.28
		Pane of 10	—	5.00	2.00
❑ 4100	39¢	Christmas Madonna	—	.60	.28
		Pane of 20 double sided	—	10.00	5.00

4105 **4106** **4107** **4108**

4109 **4110** **4111** **4112**

4101-4104

4113 **4114** **4115** **4116**

Scott No.			Plate Block	Unused	Used
❑ 4101–16	39¢	Snow flakes	—	.60	.28

4117

4118

4119

Scott No.			Plate Block	Unused	Used
❑ 4117	39¢	Eid	—	.60	.28
		Pane of 20	—	11.00	4.00
❑ 4118	39¢	Hanukkah	—	.60	.28
		Pane of 20	—	11.00	4.00
❑ 4119	39¢	Kwanzaa	—	.60	.28
		Pane of 20	—	11.00	4.00

4120

4121

4122

Scott No.			Plate Block	Unused	Used
2008.					
❑ 4120	39¢	Ella Fitzgerald, Black Heritage Series	—	2.00	.30
❑ 4121	39¢	Oklahoma Statehood	—	2.00	.30
❑ 4122	39¢	Love Hershey Kiss	—	2.00	.30

4123a

4123a

4124 **4125** **4126** **4127** **4128**

4129

4130

Scott No.			Plate Block	Unused	Used
❑ 4123a	84¢	International Polar Year, Aurora Borealis & Aurora Australis,	—	1.75	1.25
		Souvenir sheet 2 stamps	—	4.00	3.50
❑ 4124	39¢	Henry Wadsworth Longfellow	—	1.75	.30
❑ 4125	41¢	Forever–Liberty Bell large	—	1.00	.30
❑ 4126	41¢	Forever–Liberty Bell small	—	1.00	.30
❑ 4127	41¢	Forever–Liberty Bell medium	—	1.00	.30
❑ 4128	41¢	Forever–Liberty Bell large, booklet	—	1.00	.30
❑ 4129	41¢	American Flag, perforated	—	1.00	.70
❑ 4130	41¢	American Flag, die cut 11.25x10.75	—	1.00	.70

4131 **4132** **4133** **4134** **4135**

4136

4137 **4138** **4139**

Scott No.			Plate Block	Unused	Used
Coil Stamp.					
❏ 4131	41¢	American Flag, coil	—	1.00	.70
❏ 4132	41¢	American Flag, coil die cut 9.5	—	1.00	.70
❏ 4133	41¢	American Flag, coil die cut 11	—	1.00	.70
❏ 4134	41¢	American Flag, coil die cut 8.4	—	1.00	.70
❏ 4135	41¢	American Flag, coil die cut 11	—	1.00	.70
❏ 4136	41¢	Settlement of Jamestown	—	1.00	.70
❏ 4137	26¢	Florida Panther, water activated stamp	—	.60	.50
❏ 4138	17¢	Big Horn Sheep	—	.50	.35
❏ 4139	26¢	Florida Panther	—	.60	.50

4140

4141

4142

Scott No.			PNC Strip	Unused	Used

Coil Stamps

Scott No.			PNC Strip	Unused	Used
❑ 4140	17¢	Big Horn Sheep, coil of 100	—	.40	.35
❑ 4141	26¢	Florida Panther, coil of 100	—	.65	.60
❑ 4142	26¢	Florida Panther	—	.80	.60

4143

Scott No.			Plate Block	Unused	Used
❑ 4143	41¢	Star Wars–Darth Vader	—	1.00	.70

4144   **4145**

Scott No.			Plate Block	Unused	Used
❏ 4144	$4.60	Air Force One, Priority Mail	—	9.00	7.25
❏ 4145	$16.25	Marine One, Express Mail	—	35.00	25.00

4146–50

4151   **4152**

Scott No.			Plate Block	Unused	Used
❏ 4146	41¢	Pacific Lighthouses, Diamond Head	—	1.25	.60
❏ 4147	41¢	Pacific Lighthouses, Five Finger	—	1.25	.60
❏ 4148	41¢	Pacific Lighthouses, Grays Harbor	—	1.25	.60
❏ 4149	41¢	Pacific Lighthouses, Umpqua River	—	1.25	.60
❏ 4150	41¢	Pacific Lighthouses, St. George Reef	—	1.25	.60
		5 stamp set	—	4.75	1.25
❏ 4151	41¢	Love Series–Purple Heart, water activated stamp	—	1.00	.75
❏ 4152	58¢	Love Series–Silver Heart, for 2 ounce rate	—	1.40	1.00

4153

4154

4155

4156

Scott No.			Plate Block	Unused	Used
❏ 4153	41¢	Pollination, Bumble Bees	—	1.00	.70
❏ 4154	41¢	Pollination, Calliope Hummingbird	—	1.00	.70
❏ 4155	41¢	Pollination, Lesser Long-nosed Bat	—	1.00	.70
❏ 4156	41¢	Pollination, Southern Dogfaced Butterfly	—	1.00	.70
		set of 4 stamps	—	4.25	2.00

4157

4158

Scott No.			PNC Strip	Unused	Used

Coil Stamps

Scott No.			PNC Strip	Unused	Used
❏ 4157	10¢	Patriotic Banner, non denominated definitive stamp coil of 3000, rounded corners	—	.35	.28
❏ 4158	10¢	Patriotic Banner, non denominated definitive stamp coil of 3000, regular corners	—	.35	.28

4159

Scott No.			Plate Block	Unused	Used
❏ 4159	41¢	Marvel Comics, 20 stamps, Spider Man, The Hulk, Sub Mariner, The Thing, Captain America, Silver Surfer, Spider Woman, Iron Man, Elektra, Wolverine, Amazing Spider Man cover, Incredible Hulk cover, Sub Mariner cover, Fantastic Four cover, Captain America cover, Silver Surfer cover, Spider Woman cover, Iron Man cover, Elektra cover, X Men cover			
		Pane of 20	—	20.00	16.00

4160–4163

4164

LOUIS COMFORT TIFFANY

4165

Scott No.			Plate Block	Unused	Used
❏ 4160	41¢	Vintage Mahogany Speedboats, Hitchinson	—	1.00	.70
❏ 4161	41¢	Vintage Mahogany Speedboats, Chris Craft	—	1.00	.70
❏ 4162	41¢	Vintage Mahogany Speedboats, Hacker Craft	—	1.00	.70
❏ 4163	41¢	Vintage Mahogany Speedboats, Gar Wood	—	1.00	.70
		set of 4 stamps	—	4.00	2.75
❏ 4164	41¢	Purple Heart	—	1.00	.70
❏ 4165	41¢	Louis Comfort Tiffany, single	—	1.00	.70

Scott No.			PNC Strip	Unused	Used
Coil Stamps					
❏ 4166	41¢	Flower Blossom—Iris, coil of 10	—	1.10	.70
❏ 4167	41¢	Flower Blossom—Dahlia, coil of 10	—	1.10	.70
❏ 4168	41¢	Flower Blossom—Vulcan Magnolia, coil of 10	—	1.10	.70
❏ 4169	41¢	Flower Blossom—Red Gerber Daisy, coil of 10	—	1.10	.70
❏ 4170	41¢	Flower Blossom—Purple Coneflower, coil of 10	—	1.10	.70
❏ 4171	41¢	Flower Blossom—Tulip, coil of 10	—	1.10	.70
❏ 4172	41¢	Flower Blossom—Water Lily coil of 10	—	1.10	.70
❏ 4173	41¢	Flower Blossom—Poppy, coil of 10	—	1.10	.70
❏ 4174	41¢	Flower Blossom—Spider Chrysanthemum coil of 10	—	1.10	.70
❏ 4175	41¢	Flower Blossom—Orange Gerber Daisy coil of 10	—	1.10	.70

4176 **4177** **4178** **4179** **4180**

4181 **4182** **4183** **4184** **4185**

Scott No.			Plate Block	Unused	Used
❏ 4176	41¢	Flower Blossom–Spider Chrysanthemum	—	1.25	.60
❏ 4177	41¢	Flower Blossom–Orange Gerber Daisy	—	1.25	.60
❏ 4178	41¢	Flower Blossom–Iris	—	1.25	.60
❏ 4179	41¢	Flower Blossom–Dahlia	—	1.25	.60
❏ 4180	41¢	Flower Blossom–Vulcan Magnolia	—	1.25	.60
❏ 4181	41¢	Flower Blossom–Red Gerber Daisy	—	1.25	.60
❏ 4182	41¢	Flower Blossom–Water Lily	—	1.25	.60
❏ 4183	41¢	Flower Blossom–Poppy	—	1.25	.60
❏ 4184	41¢	Flower Blossom–Purple Coneflower	—	1.25	.60
❏ 4185	41¢	Flower Blossom–Tulip	—	1.25	.60

4186

4187

4188

4189

Scott No.			PNC Strip	Unused	Used

Coil Stamps

❑ 4186	41¢	American Flag, 9.5 die cut, coil of 100	—	1.10	.30
❑ 4187	41¢	American Flag, 11 die cut, coil of 100	—	1.10	.30
❑ 4188	41¢	American Flag, coil of 100	—	1.10	.30
❑ 4189	41¢	American Flag, coil of 3,000/10,000	—	1.10	.28

4190

4191

Booklet			Plate Block	Unused	Used

| ❑ 4190 | 41¢ | American Flag, gray pole, booklet of 10 | — | 1.10 | .28 |
| ❑ 4191 | 41¢ | American Flag, black pole, booklet of 20 | — | 1.10 | .28 |

4192

4194

4194

4195

4196

4192–4195

Scott No.			Plate Block	Unused	Used
❏ 4192	41¢	The Art of Disney Magic– Mickey Mouse	—	1.10	.70
❏ 4193	41¢	The Art of Disney Magic– Tinker Bell & Peter Pan	—	1.10	.70
❏ 4194	41¢	The Art of Disney Magic– Dumbo & Timothy Mouse	—	1.10	.70
❏ 4195	41¢	The Art of Disney Magic– Aladdin & Genie	—	1.10	.70
		set of 4 stamps	—	4.00	2.50
❏ 4196	41¢	Celebrate	—	1.10	.70

4197

Scott No.			Plate Block	Unused	Used
❏ 4197	41¢	Legends of Hollywood-James Stewart	—	1.10	.70

4198

Scott No.			Plate Block	Unused	Used
❏ 4198	41¢	Nature of America Series–Alpine Tundra, elk, golden eagle, yellow bellied marmot, America pika, bighorn sheep, Magdalena alpine butterfly, white-tailed ptarmigan, Rocky Mountain parnassian butterfly, Melissa artic butterfly, brown capped rosy finch	—	1.10	.75
		Pane of 10	—	10.00	8.00

4199

Scott No.			Plate Block	Unused	Used
❏ 4199	41¢	Gerald R. Ford	—	1.50	.80

4200   **4201**   **4202**

4203   **4204**

4205   **4206**

Scott No.			Plate Block	Unused	Used
❏ 4200	41¢	Jury Duty–Serve with Pride	—	1.10	.70
❏ 4201	41¢	Mendez v Westminster School District	—	1.10	.70
❏ 4202	41¢	Holiday Celebrations–Eid	—	1.10	.70
❏ 4203	41¢	Polar Lights–Aurora Borealis	—	1.10	.80
❏ 4204	41¢	Polar Lights–Aurora Australis	—	1.10	.80
		2 stamp set	—	2.00	1.75
❏ 4205	41¢	Star Wars–Yoda	—	1.10	.75
❏ 4206	41¢	Madonna & Child by Luini	—	1.10	.75

4207–4210

4211

4212

4213

4214

Scott No.			Plate Block	Unused	Used
❏ 4207	41¢	Christmas Knits–deer	—	1.10	.70
❏ 4208	41¢	Christmas Knits–Christmas tree	—	1.10	.70
❏ 4209	41¢	Christmas Knits–snowman	—	1.10	.70
❏ 4210	41¢	Christmas Knits–bear	—	1.10	.70
		Strip of 4 stamps	—	4.00	2.00
		vending booklet of 20	—	4.00	2.00

Booklet			Plate Block	Unused	Used
❏ 4211	41¢	Christmas Knits–deer	—	1.00	.70
		vending booklet of 20	—	4.00	2.00
❏ 4212	41¢	Christmas Knits–Christmas tree	—	1.00	.70
		vending booklet of 20	—	4.00	2.00
❏ 4213	41¢	Christmas Knits–snowman	—	1.00	.70
		vending booklet of 20	—	4.00	2.00
❏ 4214	41¢	Christmas Knits–bear	—	1.00	.70
		vending booklet of 20	—	4.00	2.00

4215   **4216**   **4217**  **4218**

 4219

 4220

 **4221**

 4222

4223

Booklet			Plate Block	Unused	Used
❏ 4215	41¢	Christmas Knits–deer	—	1.00	.70
		atm convert. booklet of 20	—	4.00	2.00
❏ 4216	41¢	Christmas Knits–Christmas tree	—	1.00	.70
		atm convert. booklet of 20	—	4.00	2.00
❏ 4217	41¢	Christmas Knits–snowman	—	1.00	.70
		atm convert. booklet of 20	—	4.00	2.00
❏ 4218	41¢	Christmas Knits–bear	—	1.00	.70
		atm convert. booklet of 20	—	4.00	2.00

Scott No.			Plate Block	Unused	Used
❏ 4219	41¢	Holiday Celebrations–Hanukkah	—	1.00	.70
❏ 4220	41¢	Holiday Celebrations–Kwanzaa	—	1.00	.70
2009.					
❏ 4221	41¢	New Year	—	1.00	.65
❏ 4222	41¢	Charles Chestnutt	—	1.00	.65
❏ 4223	41¢	Marjorie Rawlings	—	1.00	.65

4224–27

4228–31

4231   **4232–35**

4236–39

Scott No.			Plate Block	Unused	Used
❑ 4224	41¢	Gerti Cori	—	1.00	.65
❑ 4225	41¢	Linus Pauling	—	1.00	.65
❑ 4226	41¢	Edwin Hubble	—	1.00	.65
❑ 4227	41¢	John Bardeen	—	1.00	.65
❑ 4228	42¢	Flag Dusk	—	1.00	.65
❑ 4229	42¢	Flag Night	—	1.00	.65
❑ 4230	42¢	Flag Dawn	—	1.00	.65
❑ 4231	42¢	Flag Midday	—	1.00	.65
Coil Stamp.					
❑ 4232-35	42¢	Flag Coil 9.5	—	4.00	2.00
❑ 4236-39	42¢	Flag Coil 11	—	4.00	2.00

4240–43

4244–47

4253–57   **4248–52**

Scott No.			Plate Block	Unused	Used
❑ 4240-43	42¢	Flag Coil 8.5	—	4.00	2.00
❑ 4244-47	42¢	Flag Coil R11	—	4.00	2.00
❑ 4248	42¢	Martha Gelhom	—	1.00	.65
❑ 4249	42¢	John Hersey	—	1.00	.65
❑ 4250	42¢	George Polk	—	1.00	.65
❑ 4251	42¢	Ruben Salazar	—	1.00	.65
❑ 4252	42¢	Eric Sevareid	—	1.00	.65
❑ 4253	27¢	Pomegranate	—	1.00	.45
❑ 4254	27¢	Star Fruit	—	1.00	.45
❑ 4255	27¢	Kiwi	—	1.00	.45
❑ 4256	27¢	Papaya	—	1.00	.45
❑ 4257	27¢	Guava	—	1.00	.45

4258–62

4263   4264   4265   4266   4267

4268   4269   4270

Scott No.			Plate Block	Unused	Used
Coil Stamp.					
❑ 4258	27¢	Papaya Coil	—	.65	.45
❑ 4259	27¢	Guava Coil	—	.65	.45
❑ 4260	27¢	Pomegranate Coil	—	.65	.45
❑ 4261	27¢	Star Fruit Coil	—	.65	.45
❑ 4262	27¢	Kiwi Coil	—	.65	.45
❑ 4263	42¢	Purple Heart wa	—	1.00	.65
❑ 4264	42¢	Purple Heart sa	—	1.00	.65
❑ 4265	42¢	Sinatra	—	1.00	.65
❑ 4266	42¢	Minnesota Statehood	—	1.00	.65
❑ 4267	62¢	Dragonfly	—	1.25	.75
❑ 4268	$4.80	Mt. Rushmore	—	10.00	7.00
❑ 4269	$16.50	Hoover Dam	—	35.00	25.00
❑ 4270	42¢	Love Heart	—	1.00	.65

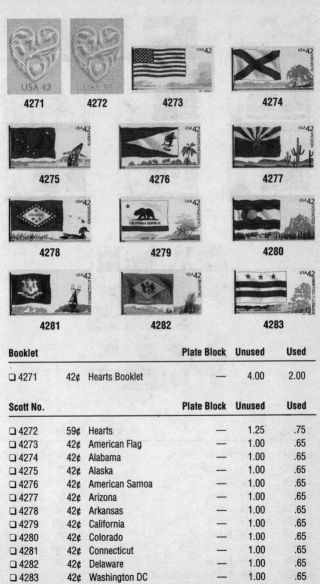

Booklet			Plate Block	Unused	Used
❏ 4271	42¢	Hearts Booklet	—	4.00	2.00

Scott No.			Plate Block	Unused	Used
❏ 4272	59¢	Hearts	—	1.25	.75
❏ 4273	42¢	American Flag	—	1.00	.65
❏ 4274	42¢	Alabama	—	1.00	.65
❏ 4275	42¢	Alaska	—	1.00	.65
❏ 4276	42¢	American Samoa	—	1.00	.65
❏ 4277	42¢	Arizona	—	1.00	.65
❏ 4278	42¢	Arkansas	—	1.00	.65
❏ 4279	42¢	California	—	1.00	.65
❏ 4280	42¢	Colorado	—	1.00	.65
❏ 4281	42¢	Connecticut	—	1.00	.65
❏ 4282	42¢	Delaware	—	1.00	.65
❏ 4283	42¢	Washington DC	—	1.00	.65

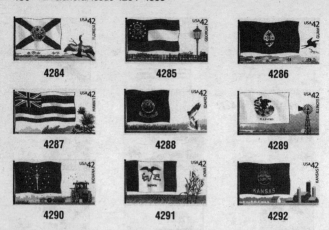

4284 4285 4286

4287 4288 4289

4290 4291 4292

4333

Scott No.			Plate Block	Unused	Used
❏ 4284	42¢	Florida	—	1.00	.65
❏ 4285	42¢	Georgia	—	1.00	.65
❏ 4286	42¢	Guam	—	1.00	.65
❏ 4287	42¢	Hawaii	—	1.00	.65
❏ 4288	42¢	Idaho	—	1.00	.65
❏ 4289	42¢	Illinois	—	1.00	.65
❏ 4290	42¢	Indiana	—	1.00	.65
❏ 4291	42¢	Iowa	—	1.00	.65
❏ 4202	42¢	Kansas	—	1.00	.65
❏ 4333	42¢	Charles & Ray Eames	—	15.00	10.00

4334

4335

4336–40

4336–40

4338

4341

Scott No.			Plate Block	Unused	Used
❑ 4334	42¢	Olympics	—	1.00	.65
❑ 4335	42¢	Celebrate	—	1.00	.65
❑ 4336	42¢	Black Cinema	—	1.00	.65
❑ 4337	42¢	Black Cinema—Gods	—	1.00	.65
❑ 4338	42¢	Black Cinema—Tam Tam	—	1.00	.65
❑ 4339	42¢	Black Cinema—Caldonia	—	1.00	.65
❑ 4340	42¢	Black Cinema—Hallelujah	—	1.00	.65
❑ 4341	42¢	Ballgame	—	1.00	.65

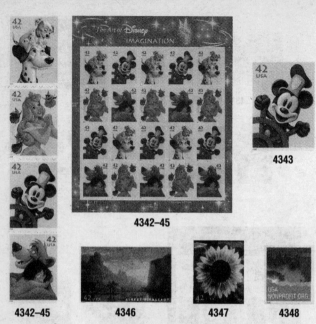

4343

4342–45

4342–45   **4346**   **4347**   **4348**

4349

Scott No.			Plate Block	Unused	Used
❏ 4342	42¢	Disney Pongo	—	1.00	.65
❏ 4343	42¢	Steamboat Willie	—	1.00	.65
❏ 4344	42¢	Princesses	—	1.00	.65
❏ 4345	42¢	Mowgli and Baloo	—	1.00	.65
❏ 4346	42¢	Albert Bierstadt	—	1.00	.65
❏ 4347	42¢	Sunflower	—	1.00	.65
❏ 4348	5¢	Sun Coast	—	.40	.20
❏ 4349	42¢	Latin Jazz	—	1.00	.65

4350

4351

4350

4352

4353–57

Scott No.			Plate Block	Unused	Used
❏ 4350	42¢	Bette Davis	—	1.00	.65
❏ 4351	42¢	EID	—	1.00	.65
❏ 4352	42¢	Great Lakes Dunes	—	10.00	—
❏ 4353	42¢	Tail Fins and Chrome	—	1.00	.65
❏ 4354	42¢	Tail Fins and Chrome	—	1.00	.65
❏ 4355	42¢	Tail Fins and Chrome	—	1.00	.65
❏ 4356	42¢	Tail Fins and Chrome	—	1.00	.65
❏ 4357	42¢	Tail Fins and Chrome	—	1.00	.65

4358	4359	4360	4361	4362
4363	4364	4365	4366	4367
4368	4369	4370	4371	

Scott No.			Plate Block	Unused	Used
❏ 4358	42¢	Alzheimer's Awareness	—	1.00	.65
❏ 4359	42¢	Madonna and Child	—	1.00	.65

Booklet			Plate Block	Unused	Used
❏ 4360	42¢	Christmas Drummer blkt	—	1.00	.65
❏ 4361	42¢	Christmas Santa blkt	—	1.00	.65
❏ 4362	42¢	Christmas King blkt	—	1.00	.65
❏ 4363	42¢	Christmas Soldier blkt	—	1.00	.65

Scott No.			Plate Block	Unused	Used
❏ 4364	42¢	Christmas Drummer vend	—	1.00	.65
❏ 4365	42¢	Christmas Santa vend	—	1.00	.65
❏ 4366	42¢	Christmas King vend	—	1.00	.65
❏ 4367	42¢	Christmas Soldier vend	—	1.00	.65
❏ 4368	42¢	Christmas Drummer atm	—	1.00	.65
❏ 4369	42¢	Christmas Santa atm	—	1.00	.65
❏ 4370	42¢	Christmas King atm	—	1.00	.65
❏ 4371	42¢	Christmas Soldier atm	—	1.00	.65

4372

4373

Scott No.			Plate Block	Unused	Used
❑ 4372	42¢	Hanukkah	—	1.00	.65
❑ 4373	42¢	Kwanzaa	—	1.00	.65

4374

4375

4376

4377

4378

4379

4380–83

Scott No.			Plate Block	Unused	Used
2010.					
❑ 4374	42¢	Alaska Statehood		.95	.60
❑ 4375	42¢	Chinese New Year—Ox		.95	.60
❑ 4376	42¢	Oregon Statehood		.95	.60
❑ 4377	42¢	Edgar Allan Poe		.95	.60
❑ 4378	$4.95	Redwood Forest Priority Mail		12.00	10.00
❑ 4379	$17.50	Old Faithful Express Mail		38.00	30.00
❑ 4380	42¢	Abraham Lincoln— Rail Splitter		.95	.60
❑ 4381	42¢	Abraham Lincoln—Lawyer		.95	.60
❑ 4382	42¢	Abraham Lincoln—Politician		.95	.60
❑ 4383	42¢	Abraham Lincoln—President		.95	.60

4384

Scott No.			Plate Block	Unused	Used
❑ 4384	42¢	Civil Rights Pioneers pane		6.00	5.00

4385

Scott No.			PNC Strip	Unused	Used

Coil Stamp.

❑ 4385	10¢	Patriotic Banner coil		.30	.20

4386   **4387**   **4388**   **4389**   **4390**

Scott No.			Plate Block	Unused	Used
❑ 4386	61¢	Richard Wright		2.00	1.50
❑ 4387	28¢	Polar Bear		1.00	.75
❑ 4388	64¢	Dolphin		1.50	1.25
❑ 4389	28¢	Polar Bear		1.00	.75
❑ 4390	44¢	Purple Heart		1.00	.35

| 4391 | 4392 | 4393 | 4394 | 4395 | 4396 |

Scott No.			PNC Strip	Unused	Used

Coil Stamp.

❏ 4391	44¢	Flag coil		1.00	.25
❏ 4392	44¢	Flag coil—11 perf		1.00	.50
❏ 4393	44¢	Flag coil—9 1/2 perf		1.00	.50
❏ 4394	44¢	Flag coil—8 1/2 perf		1.00	.50
❏ 4395	44¢	Flag coil—11 perf		1.00	.50
❏ 4396	44¢	Flag coil—11 1/4 perf—10 3/4		1.00	.50

4397

4399–4403

4398

4404–05

Scott No.			Plate Block	Unused	Used
❏ 4397	44¢	Wedding Rings		1.00	.50
❏ 4398	61¢	Wedding Cake		1.50	1.25
❏ 4399	44¢	Homer Simpson		1.00	.60
❏ 4400	44¢	Marge Simpson		1.00	.60
❏ 4401	44¢	Bart Simpson		1.00	.60
❏ 4402	44¢	Lisa Simpson		1.00	.60
❏ 4403	44¢	Maggie Simpson		1.00	.60
❏ 4404	44¢	Love—King of Heats		1.00	.60
❏ 4405	44¢	Love—Queen of Hearts		1.00	.60

4406   4407   4408

4409–13

4414

Scott No.			Plate Block	Unused	Used
❑ 4406	44¢	Bob Hope		1.00	.60
❑ 4407	44¢	Celebrate!		1.00	.60
❑ 4408	44¢	Anna Julia Cooper		1.00	.60
❑ 4409	44¢	Matagorda Island—Texas		1.00	.60
❑ 4410	44¢	Sabine Pass, Louisiana		1.00	.60
❑ 4411	44¢	Biloxi, Mississippi		1.00	.60
❑ 4412	44¢	Sand Island, Alabama		1.00	.60
❑ 4413	44¢	Fort Jefferson, Florida		1.00	.60
❑ 4414	44¢	Early TV Memories		1.00	.60

4415

4416

4417–20

4421

4422

Scott No.			Plate Block	Unused	Used
❏ 4415	44¢	Hawaii Statehood		1.00	.60
❏ 4416	44¢	EID		1.00	.60
❏ 4417	44¢	Thanksgiving Day Parade—Crowd		1.00	.60
❏ 4418	44¢	Thanksgiving Day Parade—Drum Major		1.00	.60
❏ 4419	44¢	Thanksgiving Day Parade—Musicians		1.00	.60
❏ 4420	44¢	Thanksgiving Day Parade—Turkey Ball		1.00	.60
❏ 4421	44¢	Gary Cooper		1.00	.60
❏ 4422	44¢	Supreme Court Justices		1.00	.60

4423

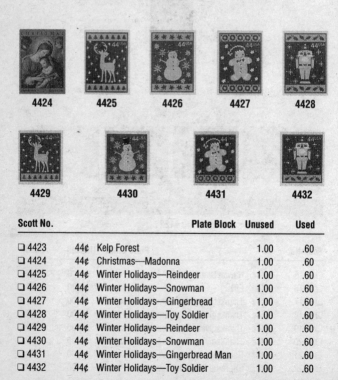

4424   **4425**   **4426**   **4427**   **4428**

4429   **4430**   **4431**   **4432**

Scott No.			Plate Block	Unused	Used
❏ 4423	44¢	Kelp Forest		1.00	.60
❏ 4424	44¢	Christmas—Madonna		1.00	.60
❏ 4425	44¢	Winter Holidays—Reindeer		1.00	.60
❏ 4426	44¢	Winter Holidays—Snowman		1.00	.60
❏ 4427	44¢	Winter Holidays—Gingerbread		1.00	.60
❏ 4428	44¢	Winter Holidays—Toy Soldier		1.00	.60
❏ 4429	44¢	Winter Holidays—Reindeer		1.00	.60
❏ 4430	44¢	Winter Holidays—Snowman		1.00	.60
❏ 4431	44¢	Winter Holidays—Gingerbread Man		1.00	.60
❏ 4432	44¢	Winter Holidays—Toy Soldier		1.00	.60

4433

4434

Scott No.			Plate Block	Unused	Used
❑ 4433	44¢	Hanukkah		1.00	.60
❑ 4434	44¢	Kwanzaa		1.00	.60

SEMIPOSTAL STAMPS

NOTE: The listings include the initial postage value and surtax. The postage value changes to match first class postage as rates increase. In most cases, the surtax decreases by a corresponding amount. When the surtax falls below a certain amount, the Postal Service raises the price of a stamp, such as was the case for the Breast Cancer stamp, which rose from 40¢ to 45¢.

B1

Scott No.			Plate Block	Unused	Used
1998.					
❑ B1	(32¢+8¢)	Breast Cancer	20.00	1.55	.38

B2

Scott No.			Plate Block	Unused	Used
2002.					
❑ B2	(34¢+11¢)	Heroes of 2001	5.00	1.75	.40

AIRMAIL STAMPS

C1
(C2–C3)

Scott No.			Plate Block	Unused	Used
1918. (NH Add 60%)					
❏ C1	6¢	Orange	1500.00 (6)	75.00	40.00
❏ C2	16¢	Green (~C1)	2200.00 (6)	100.00	50.00
❏ C3	24¢	Carmine & Blue (~C1)	2500.00 (12)	100.00	50.00

C4   **C5**   **C6**

			Plate Block	Unused	Used
1923. (NH Add 60%)					
❏ C4	8¢	Dark Green	550.00 (6)	25.00	15.00
❏ C5	16¢	Dark Blue	3500.00 (6)	80.00	45.00
❏ C6	24¢	Carmine	4000.00 (6)	120.00	45.00

C7
(C8–C9)

			Plate Block	Unused	Used
1926–1927. (NH Add 60%)					
❏ C7	10¢	Biplanes & Map	100.00 (6)	6.00	2.00
❏ C8	15¢	Biplanes & Map (~C7)	100.00 (6)	6.00	5.00
❏ C9	20¢	Biplanes & Map (~C7)	200.00 (6)	12.00	5.00

C10

Scott No.			Plate Block	Unused	Used
1927. (NH Add 60%)					
❑ C10	10¢	Lindbergh	300.00 (6)	12.00	7.00
		Booklet Pane of 3	150.00	75.00	7.00

C11

1928. (NH Add 50%)					
❑ C11	5¢	Beacon	325.00 (8)	7.00	4.00

C12
(C16)

1930. Flat Plate Press. (NH Add 60%)					
❑ C12	5¢	Winged Globe, perf 11	235.00 (6)	15.00	4.00

C13

C14

C15

Scott No.			Plate Block	Unused	Used
1930. (NH Add 50%)					
❑ C13	65¢	Graf Zeppelin	4000.00 (6)	325.00	325.00
❑ C14	$1.30	Graf Zeppelin	10000.00 (6)	625.00	450.00
❑ C15	$2.60	Graf Zeppelin	14000.00 (6)	850.00	700.00

C17

1931–1932. Rotary Press. (NH Add 60%)

❑ C16	5¢	Winged Globe (~C12), perf 10½ x 11	160.00	8.00	3.00
❑ C17	8¢	Winged Globe, perf 10½ x 11	60.00	6.00	3.00

C18

1933. (NH Add 50%)

❑ C18	50¢	Zeppelin	1550.00 (6)	125.00	80.00

C19

Scott No.			Plate Block	Unused	Used

1934. (NH Add 30%)

| ❏ C19 | 6¢ | Winged Globe | 60.00 | 6.00 | .40 |

NOTE: Prices for stamps from 1935 forward are for never-hinged (NH) examples.

C20  **C21**  **C22**

1935–1937.

❏ C20	25¢	Pan-Am Clipper	40.00 (6)	6.00	4.00
❏ C21	20¢	Pan-Am Clipper	150.00 (6)	10.00	6.00
❏ C22	50¢	Clipper	175.00 (6)	10.00	6.00

C23  **C24**

1938.

| ❏ C23 | 6¢ | Eagle & Shield | 25.00 | 1.75 | .50 |

1939.

| ❏ C24 | 30¢ | Transatlantic Airmail | 260.00 (6) | 12.00 | 4.00 |

C25
(C26–C31)

Scott No.			Plate Block	Unused	Used
1941–1944. Transport Plane Series.					
❏ C25	6¢	Carmine	5.00	.40	.25
❏ C26	8¢	Olive Green (~C25)	5.00	.70	.45
❏ C27	10¢	Violet (~C25)	12.00	2.00	.45
❏ C28	15¢	Brown Carmine (~C25)	14.00	4.00	.55
❏ C29	20¢	Bright Green (~C25)	12.00	4.00	.55
❏ C30	30¢	Blue (~C25)	14.00	4.00	.75
❏ C31	50¢	Orange (~C25)	80.00	14.00	4.00

C32   **C33**   **C34**
                 (C37)

C35   **C36**

1946–1947.					
❏ C32	5¢	DC-4 Skymaster, large	2.25	.40	.34
❏ C33	5¢	DC-4 Skymaster, small	2.25	.40	.34
❏ C34	10¢	Pan American Union Building	2.25	.45	.34
❏ C35	15¢	New York Skyline	2.25	.60	.34
❏ C36	25¢	Golden Gate	4.50	1.00	.34

Scott No.			Line Pair	Unused	Used

1948. Coil Stamp.

| ❑ C37 | 5¢ | DC-4 Skymaster (~C33) | 10.00 | 2.00 | 1.75 |

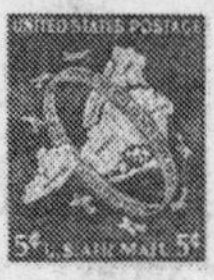

C38

Scott No.			Plate Block	Unused	Used

1948.

| ❑ C38 | 5¢ | New York City | 5.00 | .50 | .40 |

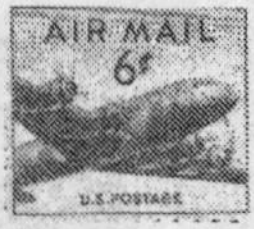

C39
(C41)

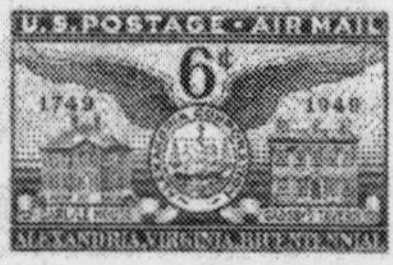

C40

1949.

| ❑ C39 | 6¢ | DC-4 Skymaster | 1.50 | .50 | .35 |
| ❑ C40 | 6¢ | Alexandria | 1.50 | .50 | .35 |

Scott No.			Line Pair	Unused	Used

1949. Coil Stamp.

| ❑ C41 | 6¢ | DC-4 Skymaster (~C39) | 14.00 | 4.25 | .35 |

C42

C43

C44

C45

Scott No.			Plate Block	Unused	Used
1949.					
❏ C42	10¢	UPU Centennial	2.65	.45	.40
❏ C43	15¢	UPU Centennial	2.65	.50	.45
❏ C44	25¢	UPU Centennial	6.00	.75	.60
❏ C45	6¢	Wright Brothers	2.65	.60	.35

C46

C47

C48
(C50)

			Plate Block	Unused	Used
1952.					
❏ C46	80¢	Diamond Head	30.00	8.00	2.50
1953.					
❏ C47	6¢	Wright Brothers	2.75	.40	.35
1954.					
❏ C48	4¢	Eagle in Flight	2.75	.40	.35

C49

C51
(C52, C60–C61)

1957.

☐ C49	6¢	50th Anniversary – Air Force	2.25	.40	.34

1958.

☐ C50	5¢	Eagle in Flight (~C48)	2.25	.40	.34
☐ C51	7¢	Jetliner Silhouette, blue	2.25	.40	.34

Scott No.			Line Pair	Unused	Used

1958. Coil Stamp.

☐ C52	7¢	Jetliner Silhouette (~C51), blue	18.00	4.00	.40

C53

C54

C55

Scott No.			Plate Block	Unused	Used

1959.

☐ C53	7¢	Alaska Statehood	1.75	.50	.34
☐ C54	7¢	Balloon Jupiter	2.00	.50	.34
☐ C55	7¢	Hawaii Statehood	1.75	.50	.34

C56

Scott No.			Plate Block	Unused	Used
❑ C56	10¢	Pan American Games	2.00	.80	.60

C57　　　　　**C58**

C59

1959–1961.

❑ C57	10¢	Liberty Bell	8.00	2.00	1.00
❑ C58	15¢	Statue of Liberty	2.00	1.75	.35
❑ C59	25¢	Abraham Lincoln	4.25	1.75	.34

1960.

❑ C60	7¢	Jetliner Silhouette (~C51), carmine	1.00	.45	.34

Scott No.			Line Pair	Unused	Used

Coil Stamp.

❑ C61	7¢	Jetliner Silhouette (~C51), carmine	38.00	5.00	.65

| | C62 | | C63 | | C64 |
| | | | | | (C65) |

Scott No.			Plate Block	Unused	Used
1961.					
☐ C62	13¢	Liberty Bell	2.25	.75	.34
☐ C63	15¢	Statue of Liberty	2.25	.75	.34

NOTE: No. C58 contains a border extension around the Statue of Liberty; No. C63 does not.

Scott No.			Plate Block	Unused	Used
1962.					
☐ C64	8¢	Jetliner over Capitol	2.00	.50	.34

Scott No.			Line Pair	Unused	Used
Coil Stamp.					
☐ C65	8¢	Jetliner over Capitol (~C64)	7.00	.75	.34

| | C66 | C67 | C68 |

Scott No.			Plate Block	Unused	Used
1963.					
☐ C66	15¢	Montgomery Blair	6.00	4.00	1.00
☐ C67	6¢	Eagle Perched on Rock	2.60	.50	.34
☐ C68	8¢	Amelia Earhart	2.60	.45	.34

C69

Scott No.			Plate Block	Unused	Used
1964.					
❏ C69	8¢	Robert Goddard	2.00	.70	.40

C70 **C71** **C72**
(C73)

Scott No.			Plate Block	Unused	Used
1967.					
❏ C70	8¢	Alaska Purchase	2.60	.75	.35
❏ C71	20¢	Columbia Jays	4.00	1.00	.35
❏ C72	10¢	Runway of Stars	2.75	.75	.35

Scott No.			Line Pair	Unused	Used
1968. Coil Stamp.					
❏ C73	10¢	Runway of Stars (~C72)	2.50	.75	.35

C74

C75

Scott No.			Plate Block	Unused	Used
1968.					
❑ C74	10¢	50th Anniversary of Airmail	4.25	.70	.40
❑ C75	20¢	USA & Jet	4.25	.70	.40

C76

1969.					
❑ C76	10¢	First Man on the Moon	2.00	.70	.40

C77	**C78** (C82)	**C79** (C83)	**C80**

Scott No.			Plate Block	Unused	Used
1971–1973.					
❑ C77	9¢	Delta Wing	2.50	.55	.35
❑ C78	11¢	Jetliner	2.50	.55	.35
❑ C79	13¢	Winged Letter	2.50	.55	.35
❑ C80	17¢	Statue of Liberty	2.50	.60	.40

C81

Scott No.			Plate Block	Unused	Used
❑ C81	21¢	USA & Jet	3.00	.85	.34

Scott No.			Line Pair	Unused	Used
Coil Stamps.					
❑ C82	11¢	Jetliner (~C78)	1.25	.80	.34
❑ C83	13¢	Winged Letter (~C79)	2.00	.80	.34

C84	C85	C86

Scott No.			Plate Block	Unused	Used
1972.					
❑ C84	11¢	City of Refugee	2.75	.55	.40
❑ C85	11¢	Olympics - Skiers	4.00	.55	.25
1973.					
❑ C86	11¢	Progress in Electronics	2.60	.55	.40

C87

C88

C89

C90

Scott No.			Plate Block	Unused	Used
1974.					
❏ C87	18¢	Statue of Liberty	3.00	1.25	.60
❏ C88	26¢	Mount Rushmore	4.25	1.25	.35
1976.					
❏ C89	25¢	Jetliner & Globes	4.25	1.25	.35
❏ C90	31¢	Jetliner - Stars & Stripes	4.25	1.25	.35

C91–92

1979.					
❏ C91	31¢	Wright Bros., large portraits	—	1.25	1.10
❏ C92	31¢	Wright Bros., small portraits	—	1.25	1.10
		Pair (C91–C92)	6.00	2.00	1.10

| C93–94 | C95–96 | C97 |

Scott No.			Plate Block	Unused	Used
❑ C93	21¢	Octave Chanute, large portrait	—	1.25	.80
❑ C94	21¢	Octave Chanute, small portrait	—	1.25	.40
		Pair (C93–C93)	6.00	2.50	1.00
1980.					
❑ C95	25¢	Wiley Post, large portrait	—	5.00	2.25
❑ C96	25¢	Wiley Post, small portrait	—	5.00	2.25
		Pair (C95–C96)	5.00	3.00	2.25
❑ C97	31¢	Olympics - High Jumper	12.00	1.50	.75

| C98 | C99 | C100 |
| (C98A) | | |

1981.					
❑ C98	40¢	Philip Mazzei, perf 11	16.00	2.00	.40
❑ C98A	40¢	Philip Mazzei, perf 10½ x 11½	12.00	6.00	2.00
❑ C99	28¢	Blanche Stuart Scott	12.00	1.25	.40
❑ C100	35¢	Glenn Curtiss	14.00	1.25	.40

C101–104

C105–108

Scott No.			Plate Block	Unused	Used
1983.					
❑ C101	28¢	Olympics - Gymnastics	—	1.75	.55
❑ C102	28¢	Olympics - Hurdles	—	1.75	.55
❑ C103	28¢	Olympics - Basketball	—	1.75	.55
❑ C104	28¢	Olympics - Soccer	—	1.75	.55
		Block of 4 (C101–C104)	6.00	5.50	4.00
❑ C105	40¢	Olympics - Shot Put	—	1.65	.55
❑ C106	40¢	Olympics - Gymnast on Rings	—	1.65	.55
❑ C107	40¢	Olympics - Swimming	—	1.65	.55
❑ C108	40¢	Olympics - Weight Lifting	—	1.65	.55
		Block of 4 (C105–C108)	8.00	6.00	4.00

C109–112

Scott No.			Plate Block	Unused	Used
❑ C109	35¢	Olympics - Fencing	—	1.50	.50
❑ C110	35¢	Olympics - Cycling	—	1.50	.50
❑ C111	35¢	Olympics - Volleyball	—	1.50	.50
❑ C112	35¢	Olympics - Pole Vault	—	1.50	.50
		Block of 4 (C109–C112)	7.00	6.00	4.00

C113

C114

C115

C116

1985.

❑ C113	33¢	Alfred V. Verville	5.00	1.50	.50
❑ C114	39¢	Lawrence & Elmer Sperry	5.00	1.50	.50
❑ C115	44¢	Transatlantic Airmail Clipper	7.00	1.50	.50
❑ C116	44¢	Junipero Serra	10.00	2.00	.60

C117   **C118**

C119

Scott No.			Plate Block	Unused	Used
1988.					
❑ C117	44¢	New Sweden	10.00	2.50	.75
❑ C118	45¢	Samuel Langley	8.00	2.50	.75
❑ C119	36¢	Igor Sikorsky	8.00	2.00	.75

C120   **C121**

1989.					
❑ C120	45¢	French Revolution	6.00	2.50	1.00
❑ C121	45¢	Carved Figure	7.00	2.50	1.00

C122–125

20ᵗʰ Universal Postal Congress

A glimpse at several
potential mail delivery
methods of the future
is the theme of these four
stamps issued by the U.S.
in commemoration of the
convening of the 20th
Universal Postal Congress
in Washington, D.C. from
November 13 through
December 14, 1989. The
United States, as host
nation to the Congress
for the first time in ninety-
two years, welcomed more
than 1,000 delegates
from most of the member
nations of the Universal
Postal Union to the major
international event.
©USPS 1988

C126

Scott No.			Plate Block	Unused	Used
❑ C122	45¢	Shuttle in Flight	—	2.50	.60
❑ C123	45¢	Hovercraft	—	2.50	.60
❑ C124	45¢	Moon Rover	—	2.50	.60
❑ C125	45¢	Shuttle Docking	—	2.50	.60
		Block of 4 (C122–C125)	10.00	7.00	5.00
❑ C126	$1.80	Souvenir sheet (~C122–C125)	—	7.00	5.00
❑ C126a-d		Any single stamp, imperforate	—	2.50	.70

C127

Scott No.			Plate Block	Unused	Used
1990.					
❏ C127	45¢	Tropical Beach	8.00	2.50	.75

C128

C129
(C132)

C130

C131

1991.					
❏ C128	50¢	Harriet Quimby	8.00	2.00	.75
❏ C129	40¢	William Piper	6.00	1.50	.75
❏ C130	50¢	Antarctic Treaty	8.00	1.50	.80
❏ C131	50¢	Crossing from Asia	8.00	2.00	.65
❏ C132	40¢	William Piper (~C129)	32.00	2.50	.80

NOTE: On No. C132, the top of Piper's hair touches the top of the stamp; on No. C129, it does not.

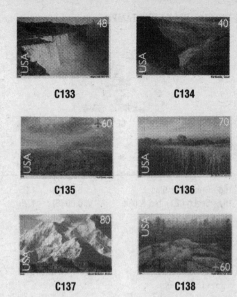

C133

C134

C135

C136

C137

C138

Scott No.			Plate Block	Unused	Used
1993.					
☐ C133	48¢	Niagara Falls	6.00	1.50	.50
☐ C134	40¢	Rio Grande	5.00	2.00	.75
☐ C135	60¢	Grand Canyon	7.00	1.50	.50
☐ C136	70¢	Nine Mile Prairie	8.00	2.25	.75
☐ C137	80¢	Mount McKinley	9.00	2.00	.75
☐ C138	60¢	Acadia National Park	6.00	2.25	.75

AIRMAIL SPECIAL DELIVERY STAMPS

CE1
(CE2)

Scott No.			Plate Block	Unused	Used
❑ CE1	16¢	Great Seal, blue	18.00 (6)	1.25	.80
❑ CE2	16¢	Seal (~CE1), red & blue	10.00 (6)	1.25	.70

SPECIAL DELIVERY STAMPS

	E1	E2 (E3)	E4 (E5)

E6
(E08–E11)

Scott No.			Plate Block	Unused	Used
1885. (NH Add 100%)					
☐ E1	10¢	Blue, inscribed "At Any Special Delivery Office"	—	225.00	36.00
1888. (NH Add 100%)					
☐ E2	10¢	Blue, inscribed "At Any Post Office"	—	175.00	18.00
1893. (NH Add 100%)					
☐ E3	10¢	Orange (~E2)	—	125.00	16.00
1894. (NH Add 100%)					
☐ E4	10¢	Blue, line below "Ten Cents"	—	400.00	28.00
1895. Double Line Watermark. (NH Add 100%)					
☐ E5	10¢	Blue (~E4)	—	135.00	7.00
1902. Double Line Watermark. (NH Add 100%)					
☐ E6	10¢	Bicycle Messenger	—	100.00	7.00

E7
(E08–E11)

E12
(E13, E15–E18)

E14
(E19)

Scott No.			Plate Block	Unused	Used
1908. (NH Add 80%)					
❏ E7	10¢	Mercury's Helmet	—	50.00	35.00
1911. Perforated 12, Single Line Watermark. (NH Add 80%)					
❏ E8	10¢	Bicycle Messenger (~E6)	—	85.00	10.00
1914. Perforated 10, Single Line Watermark. (NH Add 80%)					
❏ E9	10¢	Bicycle Messenger (~E6)	—	150.00	10.00
1916. Perforated 10, Unwatermarked. (NH Add 80%)					
❏ E10	10¢	Pale Ultramarine (~E6)	—	220.00	25.00
1917. Perforated 11, Unwatermarked. (NH Add 80%)					
❏ E11	10¢	Ultramarine (~E6)	155.00 (6)	18.00	5.00
1922–1925. Perforated 11. (NH Add 80%)					
❏ E12	10¢	Motorcycle Messenger	300.00 (6)	30.00	1.00
❏ E13	10¢	Deep Orange (~E12)	240.00 (6)	25.00	5.00
❏ E14	20¢	Special Delivery Truck	40.00 (6)	6.00	5.00
1927–1951. Perforated 11 x 10½. (NH Add 50%)					
❏ E15	10¢	Gray Violet (~E12)	6.00	1.20	.50
❏ E16	15¢	Orange (~E12)	6.00	1.20	.50
❏ E17	13¢	Blue (~E12)	5.00	1.20	.50
❏ E18	17¢	Yellow (~E12)	20.00	6.00	4.00
❏ E19	20¢	Black (~E14)	8.50	2.00	.50

NOTE: Prices for stamps from 1935 forward are for never-hinged (NH) examples.

	E20	**E22**
	(E21)	(E23)

Scott No.			Plate Block	Unused	Used
1954-1971.					
❏ E20	20¢	Letter & Hand, blue	4.25	.75	.40
❏ E21	30¢	Letter & Hand (~E20), maroon	4.25	1.50	.40
❏ E22	45¢	Stylized Arrows	7.00	2.50	.40
❏ E23	60¢	Stylized Arrows (~E22)	7.00	2.50	.35

REGISTERED MAIL STAMP

F1

Scott No.			Plate Block	Unused	Used
1911.					
❏ F1	10¢	Eagle	30.00 (6)	14.00	8.25

CERTIFIED MAIL STAMP

FA1

Scott No.			Plate Block	Unused	Used
1955.					
❏ FA1	10¢	Letter Carrier	8.00	1.50	1.00

POSTAGE DUE STAMPS

NOTE: Prices for unused stamps issued before 1890 are for examples without original gum. Examples with original gum command a premium, which can amount to as much as 50 percent or more. Beware regummed examples. Prices are for sound stamps. Those with faults or defects sell for much less.

J1
(J2–J28)

Scott No.			Unused	Used
1879.				
❑ J1	1¢	Brown	40.00	8.00
❑ J2	2¢	Brown (~J1)	200.00	8.00
❑ J3	3¢	Brown (~J1)	40.00	8.00
❑ J4	5¢	Brown (~J1)	325.00	25.00
❑ J5	10¢	Brown (~J1)	420.00	18.00
❑ J6	30¢	Brown (~J1)	250.00	28.00
❑ J7	50¢	Brown (~J1)	375.00	32.00
1884–1889.				
❑ J15	1¢	Red Brown (~J1)	50.00	6.00
❑ J16	2¢	Red Brown (~J1)	50.00	6.00
❑ J17	3¢	Red Brown (~J1)	500.00	100.00
❑ J18	5¢	Red Brown (~J1)	325.00	20.00
❑ J19	10¢	Red Brown (~J1)	310.00	20.00
❑ J20	30¢	Red Brown (~J1)	140.00	35.00
❑ J21	50¢	Red Brown (~J1)	850.00	100.00
1891–1893.				
❑ J22	1¢	Bright Claret (~J1)	25.00	4.00
❑ J23	2¢	Bright Claret (~J1)	25.00	4.00
❑ J24	3¢	Bright Claret (~J1)	50.00	4.00
❑ J25	5¢	Bright Claret (~J1)	80.00	6.00
❑ J26	10¢	Bright Claret (~J1)	100.00	18.00
❑ J27	30¢	Bright Claret (~J1)	300.00	100.00
❑ J28	50¢	Bright Claret (~J1)	300.00	125.00

J29
(J30–J68)

Scott No.			Unused	Used

1894. (NH Add 60%)

☐ J29	1¢	Vermilion	1500.00	385.00
☐ J30	2¢	Vermilion (~J29)	600.00	200.00
☐ J31	1¢	Claret (~J29)	80.00	8.00
☐ J32	2¢	Claret (~J29)	80.00	6.00
☐ J33	3¢	Claret (~J29)	175.00	38.00
☐ J34	5¢	Claret (~J29)	250.00	38.00
☐ J35	10¢	Claret (~J29)	235.00	25.00
☐ J36	30¢	Claret (~J29)	300.00	125.00
☐ J37	50¢	Claret (~J29)	1200.00	325.00

1895. Perforated 12, Double Line Watermark. (NH Add 60%)

☐ J38	1¢	Claret (~J29)	16.00	4.00
☐ J39	2¢	Claret (~J29)	16.00	4.00
☐ J40	3¢	Claret (~J29)	50.00	4.00
☐ J41	5¢	Claret (~J29)	45.00	4.00
☐ J42	10¢	Claret (~J29)	75.00	5.00
☐ J43	30¢	Claret (~J29)	450.00	55.00
☐ J44	50¢	Claret (~J29)	350.00	40.00

1910–1912. Perforated 12, Single Line Watermark. (NH Add 60%)

☐ J45	1¢	Claret (~J29)	40.00	5.00
☐ J46	2¢	Claret (~J29)	40.00	5.00
☐ J47	3¢	Claret (~J29)	475.00	25.00
☐ J48	5¢	Claret (~J29)	80.00	10.00
☐ J49	10¢	Claret (~J29)	125.00	16.00
☐ J50	50¢	Claret (~J29)	800.00	115.00

Scott No.			Unused	Used

1914–1916. Perforated 10, Single Line Watermark. (NH Add 50%)

			Unused	Used
❑ J52	1¢	Carmine (~J29)	52.00	12.00
❑ J53	2¢	Carmine (~J29)	52.00	5.00
❑ J54	3¢	Carmine (~J29)	750.00	50.00
❑ J55	5¢	Carmine (~J29)	35.00	5.00
❑ J56	10¢	Carmine (~J29)	75.00	5.00
❑ J57	30¢	Carmine (~J29)	200.00	20.00
❑ J58	50¢	Carmine (~J29)	7000.00	825.00

1916. Perforated 10, Unwatermarked. (NH Add 80%)

			Unused	Used
❑ J59	1¢	Rose (~J29)	2000.00	275.00
❑ J60	2¢	Rose (~J29)	150.00	35.00

Scott No.			Plate Block	Unused	Used

1917–1926. Perforated 11, Unwatermarked. (NH Add 60%)

			Plate Block	Unused	Used
❑ J61	1¢	Carmine Rose (~J29)	40.00 (6)	2.20	.50
❑ J62	2¢	Carmine Rose (~J29)	40.00 (6)	2.20	.50
❑ J63	3¢	Carmine Rose (~J29)	125.00 (6)	15.00	.45
❑ J64	5¢	Carmine Rose (~J29)	125.00 (6)	15.00	.45
❑ J65	10¢	Carmine Rose (~J29)	125.00 (6)	15.00	.45
❑ J66	30¢	Carmine Rose (~J29)	400.00 (6)	75.00	.80
❑ J67	50¢	Carmine Rose (~J29)	675.00 (6)	100.00	.50
❑ J68	½¢	Dull Red (~J29)	25.00 (6)	5.00	.50

J69
(J70–J76, J79–J86)

1930–1931. Perforated 11. (NH Add 60%)

			Plate Block	Unused	Used
❑ J69	½¢	Carmine	55.00 (6)	6.00	2.00
❑ J70	1¢	Carmine (~J69)	55.00 (6)	6.00	1.00
❑ J71	2¢	Carmine (~J69)	50.00 (6)	6.00	1.00
❑ J72	3¢	Carmine (~J69)	240.00 (6)	25.00	4.00
❑ J73	5¢	Carmine (~J69)	240.00 (6)	22.00	2.00

J77
(J78, J87)

Scott No.			Plate Block	Unused	Used
❏ J74	10¢	Carmine (~J69)	500.00 (6)	45.00	1.50
❏ J75	30¢	Carmine (~J69)	1250.00 (6)	135.00	2.00
❏ J76	50¢	Carmine (~J69)	1250.00 (6)	135.00	1.50
❏ J77	$1	Carmine	225.00 (6)	25.00	1.50
❏ J78	$5	Carmine (~J77)	320.00 (6)	30.00	1.50

1931–1956. Perforated 10½ x 11 or 11 x 10½. (NH Add 45%)

❏ J79	½¢	Carmine (~J69)	26.00	2.00	.40
❏ J80	1¢	Carmine (~J69)	6.00	1.50	.35
❏ J81	2¢	Carmine (~J69)	6.00	1.50	.35
❏ J82	3¢	Carmine (~J69)	6.00	1.50	.40
❏ J83	5¢	Carmine (~J69)	6.00	.75	.40
❏ J84	10¢	Carmine (~J69)	14.00	2.00	.40
❏ J85	30¢	Carmine (~J69)	75.00	8.00	.45
❏ J86	50¢	Carmine (~J69)	80.00	20.00	.45
❏ J87	$1	Red (~J77)	240.00	50.00	.45

NOTE: Prices for stamps from this point forward are for never-hinged (NH) examples.

J89
(J88, J90–J104)

Scott No.			Plate Block	Unused	Used
1959.					
❏ J88	½¢	Red & Black (~J89)	200.00	2.25	1.50
❏ J89	1¢	Red & Black	2.25	.60	.40

Scott No.			Plate Block	Unused	Used
❑ J90	2¢	Red & Black (~J89)	1.25	.40	.35
❑ J91	3¢	Red & Black (~J89)	1.25	.40	.35
❑ J92	4¢	Red & Black (~J89)	1.25	.40	.35
❑ J93	5¢	Red & Black (~J89)	1.25	.40	.35
❑ J94	6¢	Red & Black (~J89)	.2.25	.40	.35
❑ J95	7¢	Red & Black (~J89)	2.25	.40	.35
❑ J96	8¢	Red & Black (~J89)	2.25	.40	.35
❑ J97	10¢	Red & Black (~J89)	2.25	.40	.35
❑ J98	30¢	Red & Black (~J89)	5.00	2.00	.35
❑ J99	50¢	Red & Black (~J89)	7.00	2.00	.35
❑ J100	$1	Red & Black (~J89)	12.00	4.00	.35
❑ J101	$5	Red & Black (~J89)	60.00	12.00	.45

1978.

❑ J102	11¢	Red & Black (~J89) ·	5.25	.85	.75
❑ J103	13¢	Red & Black (~J89)	5.25	.85	.75

1985.

❑ J104	17¢	Red & Black (~J89)	40.00	.85	.75

U.S. OFFICES IN CHINA

K1 Surcharge Style 1   **K1 Surcharge Style 2**

Scott No.			Plate Block	Unused	Used

1919. New values surcharged (Style 1) on Washington-Franklin Series Stamps. (NH Add 75%)

			Plate Block	Unused	Used
❑ K1	2¢	On 1¢ green	125.00 (6)	50.00	35.00
❑ K2	4¢	On 2¢ rose	125.00 (6)	50.00	35.00
❑ K3	6¢	On 3¢ violet	160.00 (6)	60.00	35.00
❑ K4	8¢	On 4¢ brown	160.00 (6)	60.00	35.00
❑ K5	10¢	On 5¢ blue	160.00 (6)	60.00	35.00
❑ K6	12¢	On 6¢ orange	200.00 (6)	80.00	60.00
❑ K7	14¢	On 7¢ black	335.00 (6)	110.00	75.00
❑ K8	16¢	On 8¢ olive bistre	225.00 (6)	65.00	60.00
❑ K8a	16¢	On 8¢ olive green	225.00 (6)	60.00	60.00
❑ K9	18¢	On 9¢ orange red	225.00 (6)	80.00	60.00
❑ K10	20¢	On 10¢ yellow orange	225.00 (6)	80.00	60.00
❑ K11	24¢	On 12¢ brown carmine	185.00 (6)	80.00	60.00
❑ K11a	24¢	On 12¢ claret brown	325.00 (6)	100.00	75.00
❑ K12	30¢	On 15¢ gray	325.00 (6)	100.00	75.00
❑ K13	40¢	On 20¢ ultramarine	500.00 (6)	150.00	125.00
❑ K14	60¢	On 30¢ orange red	500.00 (6)	140.00	125.00
❑ K15	$1	On 50¢ violet	850.00 (6)	425.00	60.00
❑ K16	$2	On $1 violet brown	750.00 (6)	425.00	325.00

1922. New Values Surcharged (Style 2) on Washington-Franklin Series Stamps. (NH Add 75%)

			Plate Block	Unused	Used
❑ K17	2¢	On 1¢ green	235.00 (6)	125.00	95.00
❑ K18	4¢	On 2¢ carmine	235.00 (6)	125.00	95.00

OFFICIAL STAMPS

NOTE: Prices for unused stamps issued before 1890 are for examples without original gum. Examples with original gum command a premium, which can amount to as much as 50 percent or more. Beware regummed examples. Prices are for sound stamps. Those with faults or defects sell for much less.

Official stamps of the nineteenth century (O1–O120) for the various departments utilize the same portraits with each group inscribed for its department. The Post Office Department stamps (O47–O56) are the exception and utilize a different design.

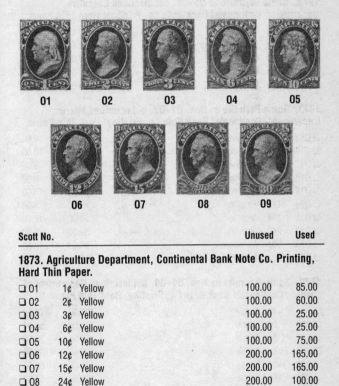

Scott No.			Unused	Used

1873. Agriculture Department, Continental Bank Note Co. Printing, Hard Thin Paper.

Scott No.			Unused	Used
☐ O1	1¢	Yellow	100.00	85.00
☐ O2	2¢	Yellow	100.00	60.00
☐ O3	3¢	Yellow	100.00	25.00
☐ O4	6¢	Yellow	100.00	25.00
☐ O5	10¢	Yellow	100.00	75.00
☐ O6	12¢	Yellow	200.00	165.00
☐ O7	15¢	Yellow	200.00	165.00
☐ O8	24¢	Yellow	200.00	100.00
☐ O9	30¢	Yellow	200.00	160.00

| O10 | O15 | O24 | O25 |

Scott No.			Unused	Used

1873. Same Portraits as O1–O5, but inscribed Executive Department, Continental Bank Note Co. Printing, Hard Thin Paper.

			Unused	Used
☐ O10	1¢	Carmine	400.00	235.00
☐ O11	2¢	Carmine	360.00	200.00
☐ O12	3¢	Carmine	360.00	200.00
☐ O13	6¢	Carmine	500.00	350.00
☐ O14	10¢	Carmine	600.00	425.00

1873. Same Portraits as Nos. O1–O7, but inscribed Interior Department, Continental Bank Note Co. Printing, Hard Thin Paper.

			Unused	Used
☐ O15	1¢	Vermilion (~O1)	35.00	8.00
☐ O16	2¢	Vermilion (~O2)	35.00	10.00
☐ O17	3¢	Vermilion (~O3)	40.00	8.00
☐ O18	6¢	Vermilion (~O4)	40.00	8.00
☐ O19	10¢	Vermilion	30.00	10.00
☐ O20	12¢	Vermilion	45.00	8.00
☐ O21	15¢	Vermilion	60.00	12.00
☐ O22	24¢	Vermilion	50.00	10.00
☐ O23	30¢	Vermilion	65.00	12.00
☐ O24	90¢	Vermilion	150.00	38.00

1873. Same Portraits as Nos. O1–O9, but inscribed Department of Justice, Continental Bank Note Co. Printing, Hard Thin Paper.

			Unused	Used
☐ O25	1¢	Purple	125.00	70.00
☐ O26	2¢	Purple	175.00	55.00
☐ O27	3¢	Purple	150.00	35.00
☐ O28	6¢	Purple	150.00	32.00
☐ O29	10¢	Purple	175.00	60.00
☐ O30	12¢	Purple	140.00	50.00
☐ O31	15¢	Purple	200.00	150.00
☐ O32	24¢	Purple	600.00	225.00
☐ O33	30¢	Purple	500.00	200.00
☐ O34	90¢	Purple	750.00	350.00

O35   O47

Scott No.			Unused	Used

1873. Same Portraits as Nos. O1–O9, but inscribed Navy Department, Continental Bank Note Co. Printing, Hard Thin Paper.

☐ O35	1¢	Ultramarine	65.00	35.00
☐ O36	2¢	Ultramarine	65.00	20.00
☐ O37	3¢	Ultramarine	65.00	15.00
☐ O38	6¢	Ultramarine	65.00	15.00
☐ O39	7¢	Ultramarine	275.00	175.00
☐ O40	10¢	Ultramarine	65.00	35.00
☐ O41	12¢	Ultramarine	80.00	40.00
☐ O42	15¢	Ultramarine	125.00	45.00
☐ O43	24¢	Ultramarine	175.00	70.00
☐ O44	30¢	Ultramarine	140.00	25.00
☐ O45	90¢	Ultramarine	450.00	175.00

1873. Post Office Department, Continental Bank Note Co. Printing, Hard Thin Paper.

☐ O47	1¢	Black	16.00	8.00
☐ O48	2¢	Black (~O47)	16.00	6.00
☐ O49	3¢	Black (~O47)	7.00	4.00
☐ O50	6¢	Black (~O47)	15.00	5.00
☐ O51	10¢	Black (~O47)	55.00	25.00
☐ O52	12¢	Black (~O47)	35.00	8.00
☐ O53	15¢	Black (~O47)	35.00	16.00
☐ O54	24¢	Black (~O47)	65.00	16.00
☐ O55	30¢	Black (~O47)	65.00	16.00
☐ O56	90¢	Black (~O47)	65.00	16.00

O57

O68
(O69–O71)

O72

Scott No.			Unused	Used

1873. Same Portraits as Nos. O1–O9, but inscribed State Department, Continental Bank Note Co. Printing, Hard Thin Paper.

			Unused	Used
❏ O57	1¢	Green	85.00	45.00
❏ O58	2¢	Green	150.00	65.00
❏ O59	3¢	Green	75.00	25.00
❏ O60	6¢	Green	60.00	25.00
❏ O61	7¢	Green	140.00	60.00
❏ O62	10¢	Green	140.00	60.00
❏ O63	12¢	Green	150.00	70.00
❏ O64	15¢	Green	150.00	50.00
❏ O65	24¢	Green	325.00	160.00
❏ O66	30¢	Green	325.00	140.00
❏ O67	90¢	Green	575.00	165.00
❏ O68	$2	Green	650.00	—
❏ O69	$5	Green & Black (~O68)	4500.00	2200.00
❏ O70	$10	Green & Black (~O68)	2500.00	1500.00
❏ O71	$20	Green & Black (~O68)	2400.00	1400.00

1873. Same Portraits as Nos. O1–O9, but inscribed Treasury Department, Continental Bank Note Co. Printing, Hard Thin Paper.

			Unused	Used
❏ O72	1¢	Brown	30.00	8.00
❏ O73	2¢	Brown	40.00	8.00
❏ O74	3¢	Brown	40.00	10.00
❏ O75	6¢	Brown	40.00	6.00
❏ O76	7¢	Brown	110.00	16.00
❏ O77	10¢	Brown	110.00	16.00
❏ O78	12¢	Brown	110.00	16.00
❏ O79	15¢	Brown	50.00	10.00
❏ O80	24¢	Brown	335.00	50.00

Scott No.			Unused	Used
❑ 081	30¢	Brown	100.00	10.00
❑ 082	90¢	Brown	100.00	10.00

083

1873. Same Portraits as Nos. O1–O9, but inscribed War Department, Continental Bank Note Co. Printing, Hard Thin Paper.

❑ 083	1¢	Rose	150.00	16.00
❑ 084	2¢	Rose	150.00	16.00
❑ 085	3¢	Rose	150.00	10.00
❑ 086	6¢	Rose	250.00	10.00
❑ 087	7¢	Rose	100.00	50.00
❑ 088	10¢	Rose	45.00	15.00
❑ 089	12¢	Rose	125.00	8.00
❑ 090	15¢	Rose	45.00	18.00
❑ 091	24¢	Rose	45.00	18.00
❑ 092	30¢	Rose	45.00	8.00
❑ 093	90¢	Rose	60.00	25.00

1879. Agriculture Department, American Bank Note Co. Printing, Soft Porous Paper.

❑ 094	1¢	Yellow (~O1)	3000.00	—
❑ 095	3¢	Yellow (~O3)	2000.00	60.00

1879. Same Portraits as Nos. O1–O8, but inscribed Interior Department, American Bank Note Co. Printing, Soft Porous Paper.

❑ 096	1¢	Vermilion	180.00	1200.00
❑ 097	2¢	Vermilion	10.00	6.00
❑ 098	3¢	Vermilion	400.00	6.00
❑ 099	6¢	Vermilion	600.00	6.00
❑ 0100	10¢	Vermilion	80.00	55.00
❑ 0101	12¢	Vermilion	125.00	80.00
❑ 0102	15¢	Vermilion	200.00	175.00
❑ 0103	24¢	Vermilion	2000.00	—

Scott No.			Unused	Used

1879. Same Portraits as Nos. O3 & O4, but inscribed Department of Justice, American Bank Note Co. Printing, Soft Porous Paper.

❑ O106	3¢	Purple	100.00	75.00
❑ O107	6¢	Purple	200.00	100.00

1879. Post Office Department, American Bank Note Co. Printing, Soft Porous Paper.

❑ O108	3¢	Black (~O47)	18.00	10.00

1879. Same Portraits as Nos. O3–O9, but inscribed Treasury Department, American Bank Note Co. Printing, Soft Porous Paper.

❑ O109	3¢	Brown	40.00	6.00
❑ O110	6¢	Brown	75.00	25.00
❑ O111	10¢	Brown	120.00	42.00
❑ O112	30¢	Brown	800.00	225.00
❑ O113	90¢	Brown	1000.00	225.00

1879. Same Portratis as Nos. O1–O9, but inscribed War Department, American Bank Note Co. Printing, Soft Porous Paper.

❑ O114	1¢	Rose	9.00	6.00
❑ O115	2¢	Rose	9.00	6.00
❑ O116	3¢	Rose	9.00	6.00
❑ O117	6¢	Rose	9.00	6.00
❑ O118	10¢	Rose	40.00	20.00
❑ O119	12¢	Rose	25.00	15.00
❑ O120	30¢	Rose	75.00	50.00

O121
(O122–O126)

O127
(O128–O152)

Scott No.			Unused	Used
1910–1911. Postal Savings Stamps. Double Line Watermark.				
❑ O121	2¢	Black	15.00	5.00
❑ O122	50¢	Dark Green (~121)	125.00	40.00
❑ O123	$1	Ultramarine (~121)	135.00	10.00
Postal Savings Stamps. Single Line Watermark.				
❑ O124	1¢	Dark Violet (~121)	12.00	5.00
❑ O125	2¢	Black (~121)	40.00	8.00
❑ O126	10¢	Carmine (~121)	25.00	5.00

Scott No.			Plate Block	Unused	Used
1983–1985. Engraved.					
❑ O127	1¢	Great Seal	1.50	.60	.40
❑ O128	4¢	Great Seal (~O127)	1.50	.60	.40
❑ O129	13¢	Great Seal (~O127)	4.00	.80	.75
❑ O130	17¢	Great Seal (~O127)	4.00	.80	.75
❑ O132	$1	Great Seal (~O127)	12.00	4.00	2.00
❑ O133	$5	Great Seal (~O127)	50.00	14.00	7.00

Scott No.			PNC Strip (5)	Unused	Used
Coil Stamps.					
❑ O135	20¢	Great Seal (~O127)	18.00	8.00	4.00
❑ O136	22¢	Great Seal (~O127)	16.00	8.00	4.00

Scott No.			Plate Block	Unused	Used
1985.					
❑ O138 (14¢)		"D" & Great Seal (~O127)	45.00	8.00	6.00

Scott No.		PNC Strip (5)	Unused	Used
Coil Stamps.				
❏ O138A 15¢	Great Seal (~O127)	—	1.75	.75
❏ O138B 20¢	Great Seal (~O127)	—	1.75	.75
❏ O139 (22¢)	"D" & Great Seal (~O127)	50.00	6.00	4.00
❏ O140 (25¢)	"E" & Great Seal (~O127)	—	2.75	1.75
❏ O141 25¢	Great Seal (~O127)	—	2.75	1.75

Scott No.		Plate Block	Unused	Used
1989. Lithographed.				
❏ O143 1¢	Great Seal (~O127)	—	.60	.40

Scott No.		PNC Strip (5)	Unused	Used
Coil Stamps.				
❏ O144 29¢	Great Seal (~O127)	—	2.00	1.50
❏ O145 29¢	Great Seal (~O127)	—	1.25	.75

Scott No.		Plate Block	Unused	Used
1991. Lithographed.				
❏ O146 4¢	Great Seal (~O127)	—	.80	.30
❏ O146A 10¢	Great Seal (~O127)	—	2.00	.80
❏ O147 19¢	Great Seal (~O127)	—	1.50	.80
❏ O148 23¢	Great Seal (~O127)	—	1.50	.80
❏ O151 $1	Great Seal (~O127)	—	3.50	2.00

O153
(O154–O157)

Scott No.	PNC Strip (5)	Unused	Used
Coil Stamps.			
❑ O152 (32¢) "G" & Great Seal (~O127)	—	1.75	1.50
❑ O153 32¢ Great Seal	—	2.25	.85

NOTE: No. O153 contains a line of micro-type below the Great Seal.

Scott No.	Plate Block	Unused	Used
1995-2001.			
❑ O154 1¢ Great Seal (~O153)	—	.55	.40
❑ O155 20¢ Great Seal (~O153)	—	1.50	.60
❑ O156 23¢ Great Seal (~O153)	—	1.50	.75

NOTE: Nos. O154–O156 contain a line of micro-type below the Great Seal.

Scott No.	PNC Strip (5)	Unused	Used
1999-2002. Coil Stamps.			
❑ O157 33¢ Great Seal (~O153)	—	1.00	.85
❑ O158 34¢ Great Seal (~O127)	—	1.25	.85

NOTE: No. O157 contains a line of micro-type below the Great Seal.

PARCEL POST STAMPS

Q1

Q2

Q3

Q4

Q5

Q6

Q7

Q8

Q9

Q10

Q11

Q12

Scott No.			Plate Block	Unused	Used
1912–1913.		(NH Add 85%)			
☐ Q1	1¢	P.O. Clerk	125.00 (6)	6.00	4.00
☐ Q2	2¢	City Carrier	125.00 (6)	6.00	4.00
☐ Q3	3¢	Railway Clerk	170.00 (6)	12.00	5.00
☐ Q4	4¢	Rural Carrier	650.00 (6)	40.00	4.00
☐ Q5	5¢	Mail Train	700.00 (6)	40.00	4.00
☐ Q6	10¢	Steamship	725.00 (6)	45.00	4.00
☐ Q7	15¢	Mail Truck	350.00 (6)	75.00	12.00
☐ Q8	20¢	Airplane	500.00 (6)	100.00	25.00
☐ Q9	25¢	Manufacturing	440.00 (6)	80.00	8.00
☐ Q10	50¢	Dairying	1750.00 (6)	225.00	45.00
☐ Q11	75¢	Harvesting	725.00 (6)	120.00	45.00
☐ Q12	$1	Fruit Growing	1200.00 (6)	275.00	28.00

PARCEL POST POSTAGE DUE STAMPS

JQ1
(JQ2–JQ5)

Scott No.			Plate Block	Unused	Used
1912.	(NH Add 80%)				
❏ JQ1	1¢	Dark Green	400.00 (6)	15.00	8.00
❏ JQ2	2¢	Dark Green (~JQ1)	475.00 (6)	80.00	12.00
❏ JQ3	5¢	Dark Green (~JQ1)	475.00 (6)	20.00	8.00
❏ JQ4	10¢	Dark Green (~JQ1)	1100.00 (6)	150.00	50.00
❏ JQ5	25¢	Dark Green (~JQ1)	725.00 (6)	150.00	8.00

SPECIAL HANDLING STAMPS

QE1
(QE2–QE5)

Scott No.			Plate Block	Unused	Used
1925–1929.	(NH Add 66%)				
❏ QE1	10¢	Yellow Green	45.00 (6)	6.00	2.00
❏ QE2	15¢	Yellow Green (~QE1)	45.00 (6)	6.00	2.00
❏ QE3	20¢	Yellow Green (~QE1)	60.00 (6)	5.00	2.00
❏ QE4	25¢	Yellow Green (~QE1)	225.00 (6)	35.00	12.00
❏ QE4A	25¢	Deep Green (~QE1)	275.00 (6)	35.00	12.00

FEDERAL DUCK STAMPS

Courtesy of Bob and Rita Dumaine at the Sam Houston Duck Company
P. O. Box 820087, Houston, TX 77282
(Specialized duck catalog $5.00, refundable with purchase; or available
as a free download at Shduck.com)

JUST WHAT ARE DUCK STAMPS?

The federal duck stamp was created through a wetlands conservation
program. President Herbert Hoover signed the Migratory Bird Conservation Act in 1929 to authorize the acquisition and preservation of wetlands as waterfowl habitat.

The law, however, did not provide a permanent source of funds to buy
and preserve wetlands. On March 16, 1934, Congress passed, and
President Franklin Roosevelt signed, the Migratory Bird Hunting Stamp
Act. Popularly known as the Duck Stamp Act, the bill's whole purpose
was to generate revenue designated for one specific use: acquiring wetlands for what is now known as the National Refuge System.

It has been proven that sales of duck stamps increase when the public has been informed of how the revenue generated through stamp
sales is used.

Jay N. "Ding" Darling, a conservationist and Pulitzer Prize–winning polit-
ical cartoonist, was appointed the head of the Duck Stamp Program. Darling's pencil sketch of mallards alighting was used on the first duck stamp.
The same design was reproduced on Scott 2092, a commemorative marking the 50th anniversary of the Migratory Bird Hunting Stamp Act.

In reality, a "duck stamp" is a permit to hunt, basically a receipt for payment of fees collected. Funds generated are used for the preservation
and conservation of wetlands.

The term "duck stamp" is a shortened term for the message "Migratory Bird Hunting and Conservation Stamp," which appears on the federal duck stamp.

In fact, use of the word "duck" is inaccurate, since many migratory
waterfowl, including geese, swans, brants, and more, are intended to
benefit from the sale of duck stamps.

WHO ISSUES DUCK STAMPS?

Federal duck stamps are now issued by the U.S. Fish and Wildlife Service, Department of the Interior United States Government, and have been issued by all states. Currently, 37 states issue duck stamps.

Many foreign countries, including Canada and its provinces, Sweden, Australia, Russia, Iceland, the United Kingdom, Costa Rica, Hungary, Venezuela, Italy, Argentina, Belgium, Mexico, Ireland, Spain, Denmark, Israel, Croatia, and New Zealand have issued duck stamps.

The issuing authorities within the various governments that release duck stamps are usually conservation and wildlife departments. These programs must be created by some form of legislation for the resulting stamps to be accepted as a valid governmental issue.

Labels featuring ducks are also issued by various special interest groups, such as Ducks Unlimited, the National Fish and Wildlife Foundation, the National Duck Stamp Collectors Society, and the National Wildlife Federation. Their issues are referred to as "society stamps." These items technically are not duck stamps, because the fee structure and disposition of funds are not legislated. However, society stamps are very collectible and often appreciate in value. Funds raised by these organizations are also used for waterfowl and conservation efforts.

Valid organizations and societies of this type perform a major service to conservation by their donations and efforts, and they merit public support.

WHEN ARE DUCK STAMPS ISSUED?

Duck stamps are issued once a year. In most states, hunters are required to purchase both a federal and state stamp before hunting waterfowl.

Waterfowl hunting seasons vary, but most begin in September or October, so naturally, stamps are needed prior to opening day of the hunting season.

Currently, the federal stamp and more than half of the state stamps are issued in July. Some are issued on the first day of the new year, and a few at the last minute in September or early October.

THE COST OF DUCK STAMPS

The annual federal duck stamp had a face value of $1 in 1934, jumped to $2 in 1949, and to $3 in 1959. In 1972 the price increased to $5, then up to $7.50 in 1979, $10 in 1987, $12.50 in 1989, and to $15 beginning in 1991.

For every $15 stamp sold, the federal government retains $14.70 for wetlands acquisition and conservation, so very little gets lost in the system for overhead.

Most state conservation stamps have a face value of $5. Alaska and Massachusetts are the lowest price at $5.00 and Louisiana's non-resident is the highest at $25.00.

Funds generated from state stamps are designated for wetlands restoration and preservation, much like the federal funds, but with a more localized purpose.

Most state agencies sell their stamps at face value. However, some also charge a premium to collectors buying single stamps, to help cover overhead costs. Some states also produce special limited editions for collectors.

FORMAT OF STAMPS

The federal stamp is presently issued in panes of 20 stamps. Originally, the stamps were issued in panes of 28, but because of a change in the printing method (and to make stamps easier to count) the 30-stamp format was adopted in 1959. Then switched to 20 in 2000.

Beginning in 1998, the department of the Interior also issued a single-sheet, self-adhesive Federal stamp to be used in ATM machines and to ease handling in sporting good stores.

Most states and foreign governments follow the federal format. Many states issue a ten-stamp pane for ease of handling and mailing to field offices.

TYPES OF STAMPS

Currently, 37 states issue stamps, of which 11 issue one for collectors and another for hunter use.

Collector stamps are usually in panes of 10 or 30 without tabs. Hunter-type stamps are usually issued in panes of five or 10, many with tabs attached. Hunters use the tabs to list their name, address, age, and other data. Some states use only serial numbers to designate their hunter-type stamp.

State stamps are therefore referred to as either collector stamps or hunter-type stamps. Most dealers will distinguish between these types on their price lists. Separate albums exist for both types and are available from most dealers.

Plate blocks, better described as control number blocks, are designations given to a block of stamps, usually four, with a plate or control number present on the selvage. Such a block is usually located in one or all four corners of a pane. Federal stamps prior to 1959 plus the 1964 issue are collected in blocks of six and must have selvage on two sides.

Governors' Editions have been issued by several state agencies as a means of raising additional income. These stamps are printed in small quantities, most fewer than 1,000. They have a face value of approximately $50, and are imprinted with the name of the state governor.

Governors also hand-sign a limited number of stamps. These are usually available at a premium, generally twice the price of normal singles. Hand-signed or autographed stamps are issued in very small quantities and are scarce to rare.

Governors' Editions are valid for hunting by all issuing states thus far. Obviously none would be used for that purpose, however, as it would destroy the mint condition and lower the value of the stamp.

Artist-Signed Stamps are mint examples of duck stamps autographed by the artist responsible for the artwork on the stamp. Such stamps are rapidly gaining popularity with collectors, and most can be purchased for a small premium over mint examples.

Early federal stamps are particularly valuable and difficult to acquire. Signed stamps by artists now deceased also command a substantial premium.

Printed Text Stamps are another popular collectible. Generally, these preceded the later pictorial issues. The term is applied to stamps required for duck hunting that contain only writing but no waterfowl illustration.

Certain American Indian reservations and tribes also issue waterfowl hunting stamps. The stamps of these sovereign Indian nations allow holders to hunt on that reservation when a federal stamp also is purchased. Reservation stamps are becoming increasingly popular with collectors as more people discover their existence.

ERRORS

With the printing of such a large number of stamps year after year by many different states and printing agencies, errors do occur, but are seldom found. A few federal stamps are known to exist with major errors, but only a few, namely on the 1934, 1946, 1955, 1957, 1959, 1962, 1982, 1985, 1986, 1990, 1991, 1993, and 2003 issues. In addition, the Federal duck stamp mini-sheets exist missing the artist's signature, which qualifies as a major error.

Stamps without perforations, with missing or incorrect color, missing or inverted writing on the reverse are all major errors. Smaller flaws, such as color shifts, misplaced perforations, hickeys (or donuts), and other such anomalies are termed freaks, rather than errors. These, too, are collectible and have value, but they do not command the same attention as major errors. Major errors are extremely rare and exist in small numbers. All errors and freaks on duck stamps are very desirable and add a great deal of interest and value to a collection.

HOW TO COLLECT DUCK STAMPS

The first basic rule is to remember that stamp collecting is very personal. You can make your own rules.

Most collectors prefer to collect mint condition duck stamps. Others prefer collecting stamps on licenses, autographed stamps, plate blocks, stamps signed by hunters, art prints, souvenir cards, first day covers, or a combination. The bottom line, however, is to collect what interests you.

Quality is a very important factor in a stamp collection. This applies not only to duck stamps, but all types. Preserving the mint condition of a stamp is crucial for determining value. A perfectly centered stamp will usually sell for a substantial premium over a stamp with normal centering. Very fine is the norm in stamp collecting, and is the condition priced by Scott.

Care should be taken not to damage a stamp, including the gum. The mint state of a stamp includes the freshness and original gum, so stamp mounts should be utilized when placing a stamp in your album. When a stamp has never been hinged, the abbreviation "NH" is used by dealers.

COLLECTORS ORGANIZATION

The National Duck Stamp Collectors Society exists for the benefit of those who collect duck stamps. Dues are $20 a year and are tax exempt. The NDSCS issues a quarterly newsletter. Send your $20 directly to the NDSCS, Membership Chairman, P.O. Box 43, Harleysville, PA 19438.

Bob Dumaine is a recognized expert in duck stamps, founder of the National Duck Stamp Collectors Society, publisher of *The Duck Report,* a past judge in the Federal Duck Stamp Contest and several Federal junior duck stamp contests, and serves on the expertizing committee of Professional Stamp Experts and co-authored an award-winning 208 page book, *The Duck Stamp Story.* In 2008 Mr. Dumaine was inducted in to the Philatelic Writer's Hall of Fame. Rita Dumaine has also served as a judge in the Federal junior duck contests. She recently was the editor of "Duck Trades," the newsletter of the National Duck Stamp Collectors Society. Dumaine is the owner of Sam Houston Duck Co., a firm that specializes in duck stamps and related material.

Request your copy of their award-winning Duck Stamp Catalog—80 color illustrated pages jam-packed with information on federal and state duck stamps, artist-signed stamps, prints, conservation issues and much more. Catalog $5.00, refundable with first order.

Sam Houston Duck Company, P.O. Box 820087, Houston, TX 77282; 1-800-231-5926; Fax 1-281-496-1445. Visit our Web site at www. shduck.com.

FEDERAL DUCK STAMP DUCKLINGS

The Federal Junior Duck Stamp Program, a nonprofit organization to promote interest among young people, unveiled the design of its first federal junior duck stamp in 1993. The program also includes a conservation education curriculum that helps students of all ages. It focuses on wildlife conservation and management, wildlife art, and philately.

The resulting stamp, unlike the federal issue, is not valid as a revenue, but emulates the federal program in terms of art selection and the creation of stamps, prints, and other items for sale. All proceeds from the junior duck stamp go to the United States Fish and Wildlife Foundation to further its efforts.

DUCK STAMP AGENCIES

Courtesy of Sam Houston Duck Co.
(approximate issue month follows state name)

Alabama, (8) Accounting Section, Duck Stamp, Dept. of Conservation & Natural Resources, 64 N. Union, Montgomery, AL 36130, (334)242-3829.

Alaska, (7) State of Alaska, Dept. of Fish & Game, Licensing Section, P.O. Box 25525, Juneau, AK 99802-5525, (907)465-2376.

Arizona, (7) Game & Fish Dept., 5000 W. Carefree Hwy., Phoenix, AZ 85086, (602)789-3212.

Arkansas, (7) Game & Fish Commission, Collector Stamps, 2 Natural Resources Dr., Little Rock, AR 72205, (501)223-6300.

California, (9) Dept. of Fish & Game, License Section, 1740 N. Market Blvd., Sacramento, CA 95834, (916)928-5805.

Colorado, (7) Colorado Wildlife Heritage Foundation, P.O. Box 211512, Denver, CO 80022, (303)291-7212

Connecticut, (8) Wildlife Division, Dept. of Environmental Protection, 79 Elm St., Hartford, CT 06106, (860)424-3011.

Delaware, (7) Divison of Fish & Wildlife, 89 Kings Hwy., Dover, DE 19901, (302)739-9911.

Florida, (-) Game & Fish Comm, Finance, Sect., 620 S. Meridian St., Tallahassee, FL 32399-1600, (850)488-5878. (Last stamp issued 2003.)

Georgia, (-) Dept. of Natural Resources, 2189 North Lake Pkwy. Bldg. 10 Ste. 108, Tucker, GA 30084, (770)414-3333. (Last stamp issued 1999.)

Hawaii, (9) Division of Forestry & Wildlife, 1151 Punch Bowl St., Room 325, Honolulu, HI 96813, (808)587-0166.

Idaho, (-) Collector Stamps, Idaho Dept. of Fish & Game, Box 25, Boise, ID 83707, (208)334-3717. (Last stamp issued 1998.)

Illinois, (12) Illinois Dept. of Natural Resources, License Section, P.O. Box 19459, Springfield, IL 62794-9459, (217)782-2191.

Indiana, (12) Indiana Division of Fish & Wildlife, License Section (Stamp). 402 W. Washington Rm. W273, Indianapolis, IN 46204-2267, (317)232-4080.

Iowa, (12) Dept. of Natural Resources, License Section, Wallace State Office Building, Des Moines, IA 50319, (515)281-5918.

Kansas, (-) Fish & Game, Pratt Headquarters, 512 SE 25th Ave., Pratt, KS 67124, (316)672-0735. (Last stamp issued 2004)

Kentucky, (12) Dept. of Fish & Wildlife Resources, 1 Sportsman Lane, Frankfort, KY 40601, (502)564-3400. Online orders only, http://fw.ky.gov.

Louisiana, (6) Dept. of Wildlife & Fisheries, P.O. Box 98000, ATTN: Licensing Section, Baton Rouge, LA 70898-9000, (225)765-2500.

Maine, (8) Dept. of Inland Fisheries & Wildlife, 284 State St., State House Station 41, Augusta, ME 04333, (207)287-8000.

Maryland, (8) Dept. of Natural Resources, Licensing & Registration Services, Box 1869, Annapolis, MD 21404, (410)260-3220.

Massachusetts, (12) Division of Fisheries & Game, License Section, 251 Causeway St., Suite 400, Boston, MA 02114-2104, (617)626-1577.

Michigan, (5) Duck Hunters Assn., P.O. Box 20, Midland, MI 48640, (989)631-5079.

Minnesota, (3) Dept. of Natural Resources, License Bureau, 500 Lafayette Rd., St. Paul, MN 55155-4026, (651)297-1230.

Mississippi, (7) Dept. of Wildlife, Fish & Parks, Waterfowl Stamp Coordinator, Box 451, Jackson, MS 39205-0451, (601)432-2263.

Missouri, (-) Dept. of Conservation, Fiscal Section, Box 180, Jefferson, MO 65105, (573)751-4115. (Last stamp issued in 1996.)

Montana, (-) Dept. of Fish, Wildlife & Parks, P.O. Box 200701, Helena, MT 59620-0701, (406)444-2612 (Last stamp issued 2003.)

Nebraska, (8) Game & Parks Commission, License Section, P.O. Box 30370, Lincoln, NE 68503, (402)471-0641.

Nevada, (6) Div. of Wildlife, ATTN: License Office, Stamp Sales, 4600 Kietzke Ln., Suite D-135, Reno, NV 89502, (775)688-1513.

New Hampshire, (-) Fish & Game Dept., License Section, 2 Hazen Dr., Concord, NH 03301, (603)271-6832. (Last stamp issued 2007.)

New Jersey, (-) Division of Fish & Wildlife, Waterfowl Stamp, P.O. Box 400, Trenton, NJ 08625-0400, (609)292-2965. (Last stamp issued 2008.)

New Mexico, (-) Dept. of Game & Fish, State Capitol, Villagra Bldg., Santa Fe, NM 87503, (505)827-7920. (Last stamp issued in 1994.)

New York, (-) Dept. of Conservation, Division Headquarters, 625 Broadway, Albany, NY 12233-4750, (518)457-4480. (Last stamp issued in 2002.)

North Carolina, (7) Wildlife Resources Commission, Direct Sales Unit, 1710 Mail Service Ctr., Raleigh, NC 27699, (919)707-0288.

North Dakota, (7) Game & Fish Dept., Collector Stamps 100 N. Bismark Expressway, Bismark, ND 58501, (701)328-6334.

Ohio, (8) Division of Wildlife, License Section, 2045 Morse Rd., Bldg "G", Columbus, OH 43229-6693, (614)265-7036.

Oklahoma, (8) Dept. of Wildlife Conservation, P.O. Box 53465, Oklahoma City, OK 73152, (405)522-3649.

Oregon, (12) Dept. of Fish & Wildlife, ATTN: Licensing Services, 3406 Cherry Ave. NE, Salem, Oregon 97303, (503)947-6324.

Pennsylvania, (3) Game Commission, License Section, 2001 Elmerton Ave., Harrisburg, PA 17110-9797, (888)888-3459.

Rhode Island, (9) Rhode Island Fish & Wildlife, Division of Fish & Wildlife, 4808 Tower Hill Rd., Wakefield, RI 02879-2207, (401)789-3094.

South Carolina, (7) Dept. of Natural Resources, License Section, P.O. Box 167, Columbia, SC 29202, (803)734-3833.

South Dakota, (-) Game, Fish & Parks, License Division, 412 W. Missouri, Pierre, SD 57501, (605)773-5527. (Last stamp issued 2007.)

Tennessee, (7) Wildlife Resources Agency, ATTN.: Wildlife Stamps, Box 40747, Nashville, TN 37204, (615)781-6585.

Texas, (8) Parks & Wildlife Dept., License Office, 4200 Smith School Rd., Austin, TX 78744, (512)389-8250.

Utah, (-) Division of Wildlife Resources, 1596 W. North Temple, Salt Lake City, UT 84116-3195, (801)538-4841. (Last stamp issued in 1997.)

Vermont, (9) Dept. of Fish & Wildlife, Stamp Order, 103 S. Main St., 10 South, Waterbury, VT 05671-0501, (802)878-1564.

Virginia, (10) c/o VA. Ducks Unlimited, 6103 Miles Ln., Warrenton, VA 20187, (202)720-1764.

Washington, (7) Dept. of Wildlife, 600 Capitol Way North, Olympia, WA 98501-1091, (360)902-2200.

West Virginia, (-) Dept. of Natural Resources, Waterfowl Stamp Program, Box 67, Elkins, WV 26241, (304)637-0245. (Last stamp issued in 1996.)

Wisconsin, (8) Dept. of Natural Resources, Box 7924, Madison, WI 53707, (608)264-6137.

Wyoming, (1) Game & Fish Dept., ATTN: Alternative Enterprises, 5440 Bishop Blvd., Cheyenne, WY 82006, (307)777-4570.

FEDERAL & INTERNATIONAL AGENCIES

U.S. Dept. of Wildlife, (7) Duck Stamp Office, 4401 North Fairfax Drive, 4th Floor, Arlington, VA 22203, (703)358-2000.

Argentina, (-) National Art Publishing Corp., 11000 Metro Pkwy. Ste #32, Ft. Myers, FL 33912-1293, (941)939-7518. (Last stamp issued 1996.)

Australia, (-) Jan Sec Fine Stamps, 4/358 Pacific Hwy., Linfield NSW 2070, Australia - P.O. Box 214. (Last stamp issued 1996.)

Canada, (8) Wildlife Habitat Canada, 9 Hinton Ave. North Ste. #200, Ottawa, Ontario, Canada K1Y 4P1.

Quebec, Rosseau Timbres 585, Rue Sainte Catherine Ouest Rez-de-Chausse'e Montréal, QC HB3 3Y5 Canada (514)284-8686

Croatia, (-) Duck Stamp Fulfillment Center, P.O. Box 17, Sullivan, IL 61951, (217)797-6770. (Last stamp issued 1997.)

Denmark, (-) Duck Stamp Fulfillment Center, 1015 West Jackson, Sullivan, IL 61951, (217)728-8321. (Last stamp issued 1997.)

Ireland, (-) Duck Stamp Fulfillment Center, 1015 West Jackson, Sullivan, IL 61951, (217)728-8321. (Last stamp issued 1998.)

Israel, (-) Mystic Stamp Co, NY. (Last stamp issued 1998.)

Italy, (-) Duck Stamp Fulfillment Center, 1015 West Jackson, Sullivan, IL 61951, (217)728-8321. (Last stamp issued 1998.)

Mexico, (-) Duck Stamp Fulfillment Center, 1015 West Jackson, Sullivan, IL 61951, (217)728-8321. (Last stamp issued 1997.)

New Zealand, (9) Duck Stamp Fulfillment Center, 1015 West Jackson, Sullivan, IL 61951, (217)728-8321. (Last stamp issued 1997.)

Russia, Mystic Stamp Co., NY (Last stamp issued 2006)

Spain, (-) National Art Publishing Corp., 11000 Metro Pkwy. Ste. #32, Ft. Myers, FL 33912-1293, (941)939-7518. (Last stamp issued 1996.)

Sweden, (-) Duck Stamp Fulfillment Center, 1015 West Jackson, Sullivan, IL 61951, (217)728-8321. (Last stamp issued 1997.)

United Kingdom, Wildlife Habitat Trust, c/o BASC, Marford Mill, Rossett, Wrexham, LL12 0 HC United Kingdom 44-573-014, Fax 44-573-013.

Venezuela, (-) National Art Publishing Corp., 11000 Metro Pkwy. Ste. #32, Ft. Myers, FL 33912-129, (941)939-7518. (Last stamp issued 1996.)

FEDERAL MIGRATORY BIRD HUNTING STAMPS

NOTE: The year of issue appears in parentheses. Stamps are inscribed with an expiration date, which is one year later than the issue date; for example, the 1934 stamp reads, "Void After June 30, 1935." Stamps are canceled (used) by the application of the hunter's signature.

PRICING NOTE: Prices are for very fine (VF) never-hinged (NH) examples.

RW1

Scott No.			Plate Block	Unused	Used
❏ RW1	$1	Mallards (1934), blue	17500.00 (6)	1050.00	175.00
❏ RW2	$1	Canvasbacks (1935), rose lake	13500.00 (6)	1000.00	175.00
❏ RW3	$1	Canada Geese (1936), brown black	4250.00 (6)	400.00	100.00
❏ RW4	$1	Scaups (1937), light green	3500.00 (6)	375.00	65.00
❏ RW5	$1	Pintails (1938), light violet	4000.00 (6)	550.00	85.00
❏ RW6	$1	Green-Winged Teal (1939), chocolate	3750.00 (6)	300.00	65.00
❏ RW7	$1	Black Ducks (1940), sepia	2450.00 (6)	300.00	65.00
❏ RW8	$1	Ruddy Ducks (1941), brown carmine	2650.00 (6)	300.00	65.00
❏ RW9	$1	Widgeon (1942), violet brown	2650.00 (6)	300.00	65.00
❏ RW10	$1	Wood Ducks (1943), deep rose	775.00 (6)	160.00	65.00
❏ RW11	$1	White Fronted Geese (1944), red orange	825.00 (6)	140.00	40.00
❏ RW12	$1	Shovelers (1945), black	525.00 (6)	95.00	30.00

Scott No.			Plate Block	Unused	Used
❏ RW13	$1	Redheads (1946), red brown	365.00 (6)	65.00	15.00
❏ RW14	$1	Snow Geese (1947), black	365.00 (6)	65.00	15.00
❏ RW15	$1	Buffleheads (1948), bright blue	365.00 (6)	65.00	15.00
❏ RW16	$2	Goldeneyes (1949), bright green	525.00 (6)	95.00	20.00
❏ RW17	$2	Trumpeter Swans (1950), violet	650.00 (6)	115.00	14.00
❏ RW18	$2	Gadwalls (1951), gray black	650.00 (6)	115.00	14.00
❏ RW19	$2	Harlequins (1952), ultramarine	650.00 (6)	115.00	14.00
❏ RW20	$2	Blue-winged Teal (1953), dark rose brown	700.00 (6)	115.00	14.00
❏ RW21	$2	Ring-necked Ducks (1954), black	650.00 (6)	115.00	14.00
❏ RW22	$2	Blue Geese (1955), dark blue	650.00 (6)	115.00	14.00
❏ RW23	$2	Mergansers (1956), black	650.00 (6)	115.00	14.00
❏ RW24	$2	American Eider (1957), emerald	650.00 (6)	115.00	14.00
❏ RW25	$2	Canada Geese (1958), black	650.00 (6)	115.00	14.00
❏ RW26	$3	Labrador (1959) multicolored	675.00	125.00	14.00
❏ RW27	$3	Redheads (1960), multicolored	600.00	115.00	15.00
❏ RW28	$3	Mallards (1961), multicolored	675.00	115.00	15.00
❏ RW29	$3	Pintails (1962), multicolored	700.00	135.00	15.00
❏ RW30	$3	American Brant (1963), multicolored	700.00	125.00	20.00
❏ RW31	$3	Nene Geese (1964), multicolored	2450.00	125.00	20.00

RW32

Scott No.			Plate Block	Unused	Used
❏ RW32	$3	Canvasbacks (1965), multicolored	675.00	125.00	16.00
❏ RW33	$3	Whistling Swans (1966), multicolored	675.00	125.00	16.00
❏ RW34	$3	Oldsquaws (1967), multicolored	725.00	140.00	16.00
❏ RW35	$3	Mergansers (1968), multicolored	375.00	85.00	14.00
❏ RW36	$3	White-winged Scoters (1969), multicolored	375.00	85.00	14.00
❏ RW37	$3	Ross' Geese (1970), multicolored	375.00	85.00	14.00
❏ RW38	$3	Cinnamon Teal (1971), multicolored	230.00	50.00	10.00
❏ RW39	$5	Emperor Geese (1972), multicolored	120.00	25.00	10.00
❏ RW40	$5	Steller's Eiders (1973), multicolored	120.00	24.00	10.00
❏ RW41	$5	Wood Ducks (1974), multicolored	95.00	20.00	10.00
❏ RW42	$5	Decoy/Canvasbacks (1975), multicolored	95.00	20.00	10.00
❏ RW43	$5	Canada Geese (1976), emerald & black	95.00	20.00	10.00
❏ RW44	$5	Ross' Geese (1977), multicolored	95.00	20.00	10.00
❏ RW45	$5	Mergansers (1978), multicolored	95.00	20.00	10.00
❏ RW46	$7.50	Green-winged Teal (1979), multicolored	85.00	22.00	12.00

Scott No.			Plate Block	Unused	Used
❑ RW47	$7.50	Mallards (1980), multicolored	85.00	120.00	15.00
❑ RW48	$7.50	Ruddy Ducks (1981), multicolored	85.00	120.00	15.00
❑ RW49	$7.50	Canvasbacks (1982), multicolored	85.00	120.00	16.00
❑ RW50	$7.50	Pintails (1983), multicolored	85.00	120.00	16.00
❑ RW51	$7.50	Widgeons (1984), multicolored	85.00	120.00	16.00
❑ RW52	$7.50	Cinnamon Teal (1985), multicolored	85.00	120.00	16.00
❑ RW53	$7.50	Fulvous Whistling Duck (1986), multicolored	85.00	120.00	16.00
❑ RW54	$10	Redheads (1987), multicolored	95.00	28.00	16.00
❑ RW55	$10	Snow Goose (1988), multicolored	95.00	28.00	16.00
❑ RW56	$12.50	Lesser Scaup (1989), multicolored	125.00	30.00	16.00
❑ RW57	$12.50	Black-bellied Whistling Duck (1990), multicolored	125.00	30.00	16.00
❑ RW58	$15	King Eider (1991), multicolored	145.00	38.00	20.00
❑ RW59	$15	Spectacled Eiders (1992), multicolored	145.00	38.00	18.00
❑ RW60	$15	Canvasbacks (1993), multicolored	145.00	38.00	18.00
❑ RW61	$15	Red-breasted Mergansers (1994), multicolored	140.00	38.00	18.00
❑ RW62	$15	Mallards (1995), multicolored	140.00	38.00	18.00
❑ RW63	$15	Sun Scoter (1996), multicolored	140.00	38.00	18.00

RW64

Scott No.			Plate Block	Unused	Used
❑ RW64	$15	Canada Goose (1997), multicolored	145.00	32.00	22.00
❑ RW65	$15	Barrow Golden Eyes (1998), multicolored	195.00	45.00	22.00
❑ RW65		PSA Type (1998)	—	25.00	15.00
❑ RW66	$15	Greater Scaup (1999), multicolored	150.00	32.00	20.00
❑ RW66		PSA Type (1999)	—	25.00	15.00
❑ RW67	$15	Mottled duck (2000), multicolored	150.00	32.00	20.00
❑ RW67		PSA Type (2000)	—	25.00	15.00
❑ RW68	$15	Pintail (2001), multicolored	150.00	32.00	20.00
❑ RW68		PSA Type (2001)	—	25.00	15.00
❑ RW69	$15	Black Scoter (2002), multicolored	150.00	32.00	20.00
❑ RW69		PSA Type (2002)	—	25.00	15.00
❑ RW70	$15	Snow Goose (2003), multicolored	150.00	32.00	20.00
❑ RW70		PSA Type (2003)	—	25.00	15.00
❑ RW71	$15	Red Heads (2004), multicolored	150.00	32.00	20.00
❑ RW71		PSA Type (2004)	135.00	25.00	16.00
❑ RW71		PSA Type (2004)	—	25.00	16.00
❑ RW72		Hooded Mergansers (2005)	130.00	24.00	16.00
❑ RW72c		Type II w/frame line (2005)	130.00	24.00	16.00
❑ RW72		PSA Type (2005)	—	24.00	16.00

RW72b

Scott No.		Plate Block	Unused	Used
❏ RW72b	Pane of one (2005) s/s (a/s) (1,000 issued)		2250.00	
❏ RW73	Ross's Goose (2006)	130.00	24.00	15.00
❏ RW73	PSA Type (2006)	—	24.00	15.00

RW73b

Scott No.		Plate Block	Unused	Used
❏ RW73b	Pane of one (2006) s/s (a/s) (10,000 issued)	225.00		
❏ RW73b	Pane of one, 2 signatures	265.00		
❏ RW73c	Error—Missing signature		35.00	
❏ RW74	Ringed neck ducks (2007)	130.00	24.00	15.00
❏ RW74	PSA Type (2007)	—	24.00	15.00

RW74b

Scott No.		Plate Block	Unused	Used
❏ RW74b	Pane of one (2007) s/s (a/s) (10,000 issued)	225.00		
❏ RW74c	Missing signature		2500.00	
❏ RW75	Northern Pintails (2008)	130.00	24.00	15.00
❏ RW75	PSA Type (2008)	—	24.00	15.00

RW75b

Scott No.		Plate Block	Unused	Used
❏ RW75b	Pane of one (2008) s/s (a/s) (10,000 issued)	65.00		
❏ RW75c	Missing signature		825.00	
❏ RW75	Souvenir Sheet of 2 (2008)	85.00		
❏ RW76	Long tailed duck (2009)	130.00	24.00	15.00
❏ RW76a	PSA type (2009)		24.00	15.00
❏ RW76b	Pane of one (2009) s/s (a/s) (10,000 issued)		65.00	

FEDERAL JUNIOR STAMPS

Scott No.		Single	Block of 4
❑ JDS1	Redhead 1993	65.00	295.00
❑ JDS2	Hooded Merganser 1994	150.00	725.00
❑ JDS3	Pintail 1995	350.00	1700.00
❑ JDS4	Canvasback 1996	450.00	—
❑ JDS5	Canada Goose 1997	395.00	1950.00
❑ JDS6	Black Duck 1998	395.00	—
❑ JDS7	Wood Duck 1999	400.00	—
❑ JDS8	Pintail 2000	295.00	1195.00
❑ JDS9	Trumpter Swan 2001	75.00	310.00
❑ JDS10	Mallard 2002	40.00	165.00
❑ JDS11	Green-winged Teal 2003	20.00	90.00
❑ JDS12	Fulvous Whistling 2004	20.00	90.00
❑ JDS13	Ringed-neck Duck 2005	15.00	65.00
❑ JDS14	Redhead 2006	15.00	65.00
❑ JDS15	Wigeon 2007	10.00	42.00
❑ JDS16	2008	10.00	42.00
❑ JDS17	2009	10.00	42.00

MINT SHEETS

❏ 643	2¢	Vermont	325.00	❏ 724	3¢	Penn	75.00
❏ 644	2¢	Burgoyne	325.00	❏ 725	3¢	Webster	100.00
❏ 645	2¢	Valley Forge	225.00	❏ 726	3¢	Oglethorpe	80.00
❏ 646	2¢	Molly Pitcher	225.00	❏ 727	3¢	Newburgh	45.00
❏ 647	2¢	Hawaii	850.00	❏ 728	1¢	Chicago	45.00
❏ 648	5¢	Hawaii	2200.00	❏ 729	3¢	Chicago	45.00
❏ 649	2¢	Aeronautics	160.00	❏ 732	3¢	N.R.A.	45.00
❏ 650	5¢	Aeronautics	435.00	❏ 733	3¢	Byrd	55.00
❏ 651	2¢	George R. Clark	150.00	❏ 734	5¢	Kosciuszko	150.00
❏ 653	½¢	Hale	50.00	❏ 736	3¢	Maryland	40.00
❏ 654	2¢	Edison-Flat	200.00	❏ 737	3¢	Mother's Day Rotary	20.00
❏ 655	2¢	Edison-Rotary	1400.00	❏ 738	3¢	Mother's Day Flat	25.00
❏ 657	2¢	Sullivan	250.00	❏ 739	3¢	Wisconsin	20.00
❏ 680	2¢	Fallen Timbers	250.00	❏ 740	1¢	Nat'l. Parks	20.00
❏ 681	2¢	Ohio Canal	140.00	❏ 741	2¢	Nat'l. Parks	20.00
❏ 682	2¢	Mass. Bay	125.00	❏ 742	3¢	Nat'l. Parks	20.00
❏ 683	2¢	Carolina-Charleston	185.00	❏ 743	4¢	Nat'l. Parks	40.00
❏ 684	1½¢	Harding	75.00	❏ 744	5¢	Nat'l. Parks	75.00
❏ 685	4¢	Taft	140.00	❏ 745	6¢	Nat'l. Parks	100.00
❏ 688	2¢	Braddock	200.00	❏ 746	7¢	Nat'l. Parks	80.00
❏ 689	2¢	Von Steuben	100.00	❏ 747	8¢	Nat'l. Parks	200.00
❏ 690	2¢	Pulaski	60.00	❏ 748	9¢	Nat'l. Parks	200.00
❏ 702	2¢	Red Cross	35.00	❏ 749	10¢	Nat'l. Parks	250.00
❏ 703	2¢	Yorktown	35.00	❏ 752	3¢	Newburg	400.00
❏ 704	½¢	Wash. Bicent'l	35.00	❏ 753	3¢	Byrd	600.00
❏ 705	1¢	Wash. Bicent'l	35.00	❏ 754	3¢	Mother's Day	220.00
❏ 706	1½¢	Wash. Bicent'l	75.00	❏ 755	3¢	Wisconsin	175.00
❏ 707	2¢	Wash. Bicent'l	32.00	❏ 756	1¢	Park	100.00
❏ 708	3¢	Wash. Bicent'l	100.00	❏ 757	2¢	Park	100.00
❏ 709	4¢	Wash. Bicent'l	55.00	❏ 758	3¢	Park	150.00
❏ 710	5¢	Wash. Bicent'l	275.00	❏ 759	4¢	Park	300.00
❏ 711	6¢	Wash. Bicent'l	500.00	❏ 760	5¢	Park	500.00
❏ 712	7¢	Wash. Bicent'l	100.00	❏ 761	6¢	Park	600.00
❏ 713	8¢	Wash. Bicent'l	500.00	❏ 762	7¢	Park	525.00
❏ 714	9¢	Wash. Bicent'l	500.00	❏ 763	8¢	Park	600.00
❏ 715	10¢	Wash. Bicent'l	1650.00	❏ 764	9¢	Park	800.00
❏ 716	2¢	Lake Placid	100.00	❏ 765	10¢	Park	1000.00
❏ 717	2¢	Arbor Day	50.00	❏ 766a	1¢	Chicago	500.00
❏ 718	2¢	Olympics	225.00	❏ 767a	3¢	Chicago	500.00
❏ 719	5¢	Olympics	350.00	❏ 768a	3¢	Byrd	600.00
❏ 720	3¢	Washington	55.00	❏ 769	1¢	Park	275.00

❑ 770	3¢	Park	700.00		❑ 862	5¢	Alcott	45.00
❑ 771	16¢	Air Spec. Deal	800.00		❑ 863	10¢	Clemens	200.00
❑ 772	3¢	Connecticut	20.00		❑ 864	1¢	Longfellow	35.00
❑ 773	3¢	San Diego	18.00		❑ 865	2¢	Whittier	30.00
❑ 774	3¢	Boulder Dam	18.00		❑ 866	3¢	Lowell	30.00
❑ 775	3¢	Michigan	20.00		❑ 867	5¢	Whitman	60.00
❑ 776	3¢	Texas	20.00		❑ 868	10¢	Riley	240.00
❑ 777	3¢	Rhode Island	35.00		❑ 869	1¢	Mann	20.00
❑ 782	3¢	Arkansas	20.00		❑ 870	2¢	Hopkins	20.00
❑ 783	3¢	Oregon	18.00		❑ 871	3¢	Elliot	20.00
❑ 784	3¢	Susan B. Anthony	25.00		❑ 872	5¢	Willard	60.00
❑ 785	1¢	Army	25.00		❑ 873	10¢	B.T. Washington	200.00
❑ 786	2¢	Army	15.00		❑ 874	1¢	Audubon	25.00
❑ 787	3¢	Army	25.00		❑ 875	2¢	Long	20.00
❑ 788	4¢	Army	50.00		❑ 876	3¢	Burbank	25.00
❑ 789	5¢	Army	50.00		❑ 877	5¢	Reed	50.00
❑ 790	1¢	Navy	12.00		❑ 878	10¢	Addams	150.00
❑ 791	2¢	Navy	15.00		❑ 879	1¢	Fosters	25.00
❑ 792	3¢	Navy	18.00		❑ 880	2¢	Sousa	20.00
❑ 793	4¢	Navy	45.00		❑ 881	3¢	Herbert	20.00
❑ 794	5¢	Navy	50.00		❑ 882	5¢	MacDowell	65.00
❑ 795	3¢	N.W. Territory	35.00		❑ 883	10¢	Nevin	350.00
❑ 796	5¢	Virginia Dare	35.00		❑ 884	1¢	Sturat	25.00
❑ 798	3¢	Constitution	35.00		❑ 885	2¢	Whistler	25.00
❑ 799	3¢	Hawaii	20.00		❑ 886	3¢	St. Gaudens	25.00
❑ 800	3¢	Alaska	25.00		❑ 887	5¢	French	50.00
❑ 801	3¢	Puerto Rico	25.00		❑ 888	10¢	Remington	200.00
❑ 802	3¢	Virgin Islands	25.00		❑ 889	1¢	Whitney	25.00
❑ 835	3¢	Ratification	30.00		❑ 890	2¢	Morse	25.00
❑ 836	3¢	Swede-Finn	18.00		❑ 891	3¢	McCormick	30.00
❑ 837	3¢	N.W. Territory	40.00		❑ 892	5¢	Howe	100.00
❑ 838	3¢	Iowa	25.00		❑ 893	10¢	Bell	1500.00
❑ 852	3¢	Golden Gate	18.00		❑ 894	3¢	Pony Express	35.00
❑ 853	3¢	N.Y. Fair	18.00		❑ 895	3¢	Pan America	35.00
❑ 854	3¢	Inauguration	50.00		❑ 896	3¢	Idaho	25.00
❑ 855	3¢	Baseball	150.00		❑ 897	3¢	Wyoming	25.00
❑ 856	3¢	Canal Zone	25.00		❑ 898	3¢	Coronado	22.00
❑ 857	3¢	Printing	25.00		❑ 899	1¢	Defense	26.00
❑ 858	3¢	Four States	25.00		❑ 900	2¢	Defense	26.00
❑ 859	1¢	Irving	25.00		❑ 901	3¢	Defense	26.00
❑ 860	2¢	Cooper	25.00		❑ 902	3¢	Emancipation	26.00
❑ 861	3¢	Emerson	15.00		❑ 903	3¢	Vermont	26.00

❏ 904	3¢	Kentucky	25.00	❏ 945	3¢	Edison	20.00
❏ 905	3¢	Win the War	25.00	❏ 946	3¢	Pulitzer	18.00
❏ 906	5¢	China	75.00	❏ 947	3¢	CIPEX	18.00
❏ 907	2¢	Allied Nations	20.00	❏ 949	3¢	Doctors	18.00
❏ 908	1¢	Four Freedoms	20.00	❏ 950	3¢	Utah	8.50
❏ 909	5¢	Poland	14.00	❏ 951	3¢	Constitution	10.00
❏ 910	5¢	Czechoslovakia	15.00	❏ 952	3¢	Everglades	14.00
❏ 911	5¢	Norway	14.00	❏ 953	3¢	Carver	16.00
❏ 912	5¢	Luxembourg	20.00	❏ 954	3¢	Gold Rush	15.00
❏ 913	5¢	Netherlands	20.00	❏ 955	3¢	Mississippi	15.00
❏ 914	5¢	Belgium	20.00	❏ 956	3¢	Chaplains	15.00
❏ 915	5¢	France	12.00	❏ 957	3¢	Wisconsin	15.00
❏ 916	5¢	Greece	40.00	❏ 958	5¢	Swedish Pioneer	15.00
❏ 917	5¢	Yugoslavia	30.00	❏ 959	3¢	Women	15.00
❏ 918	5¢	Albania	30.00	❏ 960	3¢	White	14.00
❏ 919	5¢	Austria	22.00	❏ 961	3¢	U.S. Canada	12.00
❏ 920	5¢	Denmark	25.00	❏ 962	3¢	Key	15.00
❏ 921	5¢	Korea	20.00	❏ 963	3¢	Youth	12.00
❏ 909–21		Set of 13	250.00	❏ 964	3¢	Oregon	12.00
❏ 922	3¢	Railroad	20.00	❏ 965	3¢	Stone	16.00
❏ 923	3¢	Steamship	25.00	❏ 966	3¢	Palomar	16.00
❏ 924	3¢	Telegraph	18.00	❏ 967	3¢	Barton	16.00
❏ 925	3¢	Corregidor	18.00	❏ 968	3¢	Poultry	16.00
❏ 926	3¢	Motion Pictures	18.00	❏ 969	3¢	Gold Star	8.00
❏ 927	3¢	Florida	18.00	❏ 970	3¢	Fort Kearny	10.00
❏ 928	5¢	United Nations	18.00	❏ 971	3¢	Firemen	15.00
❏ 929	3¢	Iwo Jima	20.00	❏ 972	3¢	Indian Centennial	15.00
❏ 930	1¢	Roosevelt	12.00	❏ 973	3¢	Rough Riders	15.00
❏ 931	2¢	Roosevelt	12.00	❏ 974	3¢	Juliette Low	15.00
❏ 932	3¢	Roosevelt	12.00	❏ 975	3¢	Will Rogers	16.00
❏ 933	5¢	Roosevelt	15.00	❏ 976	3¢	Fort Bliss	16.00
❏ 934	3¢	Army	18.00	❏ 977	3¢	Moina Michael	16.00
❏ 935	3¢	Navy	18.00	❏ 978	3¢	Gettysburg	15.00
❏ 936	3¢	Coast Guard	18.00	❏ 979	3¢	Turners	15.00
❏ 937	3¢	Alfred E. Smith	20.00	❏ 980	3¢	Harris	18.00
❏ 938	3¢	Texas	16.00	❏ 981	3¢	Minnesota	14.00
❏ 939	3¢	Merchant Marine	15.00	❏ 982	3¢	Washington & Lee	14.00
❏ 940	3¢	Discharge Emblem	20.00	❏ 983	3¢	Puerto Rico	12.00
❏ 941	3¢	Tennessee	18.00	❏ 984	3¢	Annapolis	15.00
❏ 942	3¢	Iowa	16.00	❏ 985	3¢	G.A.R.	15.00
❏ 943	3¢	Smithsonian	16.00	❏ 986	3¢	Poe	20.00
❏ 944	3¢	Kearny	10.00	❏ 987	3¢	Bankers	20.00

❏ 988	3¢	Gompers	18.00		❏ 1030	½¢	Franklin	14.00
❏ 989	3¢	Capitol Statue	18.00		❏ 1031	1¢	Washington	14.00
❏ 990	3¢	White House	18.00		❏ 1031A	1¼¢	Palace of Governors	14.00
❏ 991	3¢	Supreme Court	18.00		❏ 1032	1½¢	Mount Vernon	25.00
❏ 992	3¢	Capitol Building	12.00		❏ 1033	2¢	Jefferson	15.00
❏ 993	3¢	Casey Jones	15.00		❏ 1034	2½¢	Bunker Hill	20.00
❏ 994	3¢	Kansas City	18.00		❏ 1035	3¢	Liberty	15.00
❏ 995	3¢	Boy Scouts	18.00		❏ 1036	4¢	Lincoln	32.00
❏ 996	3¢	Indiana	18.00		❏ 1037	4½¢	Hermitage	32.00
❏ 997	3¢	California	12.00		❏ 1038	5¢	Monroe	32.00
❏ 998	3¢	Confederate	15.00		❏ 1039	6¢	Roosevelt	35.00
❏ 999	3¢	Nevada	15.00		❏ 1040	7¢	Wilson	32.00
❏ 1000	3¢	Cadillac at Detroit	15.00		❏ 1041	8¢	Liberty	35.00
❏ 1001	3¢	Colorado	15.00		❏ 1042	8¢	Liberty (re-engraved)	32.00
❏ 1002	3¢	Chemical	15.00		❏ 1042A	8¢	Pershing	35.00
❏ 1003	3¢	Battle of Brooklyn	14.00		❏ 1043	9¢	Alamo	50.00
❏ 1004	3¢	Betsy Ross	14.00		❏ 1044	10¢	Independence Hall	50.00
❏ 1005	3¢	4-H Clubs	18.00		❏ 1044A	11¢	Liberty	50.00
❏ 1006	3¢	B&O Railroad	15.00		❏ 1045	12¢	Harrison	60.00
❏ 1007	3¢	A.A.A.	15.00		❏ 1046	15¢	Jay	100.00
❏ 1008	3¢	NATO	15.00		❏ 1047	20¢	Monticello	80.00
❏ 1009	3¢	Grand Coulee Dam	14.00		❏ 1048	25¢	Revere	175.00
❏ 1010	3¢	Lafayette	18.00		❏ 1049	30¢	Lee	225.00
❏ 1011	3¢	Rushmore	14.00		❏ 1050	40¢	Marshall	325.00
❏ 1012	3¢	Engineers	14.00		❏ 1051	50¢	Stone	225.00
❏ 1013	3¢	Armed Forces Women	10.00		❏ 1052	$1	Henry	600.00
❏ 1014	3¢	Gutenberg	8.00		❏ 1053	$5	Hamilton	775.00
❏ 1015	3¢	Newspaper Boys	12.00		❏ 1060	3¢	Nebraska	14.00
❏ 1016	3¢	Red Cross	12.00		❏ 1061	3¢	Kansas	14.00
❏ 1017	3¢	National Guard	12.00		❏ 1062	3¢	George Eastman	16.00
❏ 1018	3¢	Ohio	25.00		❏ 1063	3¢	Lewis & Clark	16.00
❏ 1019	3¢	Washington	10.00		❏ 1064	3¢	Penn Academy	16.00
❏ 1020	3¢	Louisiana	16.00		❏ 1065	3¢	Colleges	16.00
❏ 1021	5¢	Opening of Japan	16.00		❏ 1066	8¢	Rotary	16.00
❏ 1022	3¢	Bar Association	15.00		❏ 1067	3¢	Reserves	14.00
❏ 1023	3¢	Sagamore Hill	15.00		❏ 1068	3¢	Vermont	16.00
❏ 1024	3¢	Future Farmers	15.00		❏ 1069	3¢	Great Lakes	16.00
❏ 1025	3¢	Trucking	15.00		❏ 1070	3¢	Atoms for Peace	16.00
❏ 1026	3¢	Patton	15.00		❏ 1071	3¢	Ft. Ticonderoga	16.00
❏ 1027	3¢	New York City	15.00		❏ 1072	3¢	Andrew Mellon	25.00
❏ 1028	3¢	Gadsden Purchase	15.00		❏ 1073	3¢	Benj. Franklin	15.00
❏ 1029	3¢	Columbia U.	15.00		❏ 1074	3¢	B. T. Washington	15.00

❑ 1076	3¢	FIPEX	14.00	❑ 1121	4¢	Webster	15.00
❑ 1077	3¢	Wild Turkey	14.00	❑ 1122	4¢	Forest Conserv.	10.00
❑ 1078	3¢	Antelope	8.00	❑ 1123	4¢	Ft. Duquesne	14.00
❑ 1079	3¢	King Salmon	12.00	❑ 1124	4¢	Oregon	10.00
❑ 1080	3¢	Pure Food & Drug	10.00	❑ 1125	4¢	San Martin	12.00
❑ 1081	3¢	Wheatland	12.00	❑ 1126	8¢	San Martin	16.00
❑ 1082	3¢	Labor Day	15.00	❑ 1127	4¢	NATO	16.00
❑ 1083	3¢	Nassau Hall	15.00	❑ 1128	4¢	Arctic Exploration	16.00
❑ 1084	3¢	Devils Tower	11.00	❑ 1129	8¢	World Peace	16.00
❑ 1085	3¢	Children	11.00	❑ 1130	4¢	Silver Centennial	16.00
❑ 1086	3¢	Hamilton	11.00	❑ 1131	4¢	Seaway	14.00
❑ 1087	3¢	Polio	11.00	❑ 1132	4¢	49-Star Flag	11.00
❑ 1088	3¢	Geodetic	11.00	❑ 1133	4¢	Soil Conserv.	11.00
❑ 1089	3¢	Architects	11.00	❑ 1134	4¢	Petroleum	14.00
❑ 1090	3¢	Steel Industry	11.00	❑ 1135	4¢	Dental Health	15.00
❑ 1091	3¢	Naval Review	11.00	❑ 1136	4¢	Reuter	15.00
❑ 1092	3¢	Oklahoma	11.00	❑ 1137	8¢	Reuter	16.00
❑ 1093	3¢	Teachers	11.00	❑ 1138	4¢	McDowell	18.00
❑ 1094	4¢	48-Star Flag	11.00	❑ 1139	4¢	Credo – Washington	16.00
❑ 1095	3¢	Shipbuilding	15.00	❑ 1140	4¢	Credo – Franklin	16.00
❑ 1096	8¢	Magsaysay	12.00	❑ 1141	4¢	Credo – Jefferson	16.00
❑ 1097	3¢	Lafayette	15.00	❑ 1142	4¢	Credo – Key	16.00
❑ 1098	3¢	Whooping Cranes	12.00	❑ 1143	4¢	Credo – Lincoln	16.00
❑ 1099	3¢	Religious Freedom	10.00	❑ 1144	4¢	Credo – Henry	16.00
❑ 1100	3¢	Horticulture	10.00	❑ 1145	4¢	Boy Scouts	16.00
❑ 1104	3¢	Brussels Exhib.	10.00	❑ 1146	4¢	Winter Olympics	8.00
❑ 1105	3¢	James Monroe	12.00	❑ 1147	4¢	Masaryk	12.00
❑ 1106	3¢	Minnesota	10.00	❑ 1148	8¢	Masaryk	15.00
❑ 1107	3¢	Geophysical Year	10.00	❑ 1149	4¢	Refugee Year	14.00
❑ 1108	3¢	Gunston Hall	10.00	❑ 1150	4¢	Water Conserv.	14.00
❑ 1109	3¢	Mackinac Bridge	10.00	❑ 1151	4¢	SEATO	14.00
❑ 1110	4¢	Bolivar	12.00	❑ 1152	4¢	Women	10.00
❑ 1111	8¢	Bolivar	15.00	❑ 1153	4¢	50-Star Flag	10.00
❑ 1112	4¢	Atlantic Cable	11.00	❑ 1154	4¢	Pony Express	14.00
❑ 1113	1¢	Lincoln	11.00	❑ 1155	4¢	Handicapped	10.00
❑ 1114	3¢	Lincoln	14.00	❑ 1156	4¢	Forestry	10.00
❑ 1115	4¢	Lincoln-Douglas	15.00	❑ 1157	4¢	Mexican Ind.	10.00
❑ 1116	4¢	Lincoln	14.00	❑ 1158	4¢	U.S.-Japan	10.00
❑ 1117	4¢	Kossuth	12.00	❑ 1159	4¢	Paderewski	12.00
❑ 1118	8¢	Kossuth	18.00	❑ 1160	8¢	Paderewski	20.00
❑ 1119	4¢	Free Press	10.00	❑ 1161	4¢	Robert Taft	20.00
❑ 1120	4¢	Overland Mail	14.00	❑ 1162	4¢	Wheels of Freedom	12.00

❏ 1163	4¢	Boys' Clubs	16.00	❏ 1205	4¢	Christmas Wreath	15.00
❏ 1164	4¢	Automated P.O.	18.00	❏ 1206	4¢	Education	12.00
❏ 1165	4¢	Mannerheim	15.00	❏ 1207	4¢	Winslow Homer	15.00
❏ 1166	8¢	Mannerheim	20.00	❏ 1208	5¢	U.S. Flag	16.00
❏ 1167	4¢	Campfire Girls	17.00	❏ 1209	1¢	Jackson	12.00
❏ 1168	4¢	Garibaldi	17.00	❏ 1213	5¢	Washington	20.00
❏ 1169	8¢	Garibaldi	17.00	❏ 1230	5¢	Carolina	20.00
❏ 1170	4¢	George	17.00	❏ 1231	5¢	Food for Peace	15.00
❏ 1171	4¢	Carnegie	22.00	❏ 1232	5¢	West Virginia	15.00
❏ 1172	4¢	Dulles	22.00	❏ 1233	5¢	Emancipation	15.00
❏ 1173	4¢	Echo I	22.00	❏ 1234	5¢	Alliance for Progress	15.00
❏ 1174	4¢	Gandhi	12.00	❏ 1235	5¢	Hull	15.00
❏ 1175	8¢	Gandhi	20.00	❏ 1236	5¢	E. Roosevelt	14.00
❏ 1176	4¢	Range Conserv.	12.00	❏ 1237	5¢	Sciences	12.00
❏ 1177	4¢	Greeley	20.00	❏ 1238	5¢	City Mail	12.00
❏ 1178	4¢	Ft. Sumter	25.00	❏ 1239	5¢	Red Cross	12.00
❏ 1179	4¢	Shiloh	18.00	❏ 1240	5¢	Christmas Tree	20.00
❏ 1180	5¢	Gettysburg	20.00	❏ 1241	5¢	Audubon	14.00
❏ 1181	5¢	Wilderness	18.00	❏ 1242	5¢	Sam Houston	12.00
❏ 1182	5¢	Appomattox	35.00	❏ 1243	5¢	Russell	16.00
❏ 1183	4¢	Kansas	14.00	❏ 1244	5¢	World's Fair	12.00
❏ 1184	4¢	Norris	15.00	❏ 1245	5¢	John Muir	12.00
❏ 1185	4¢	Naval Aviation	14.00	❏ 1246	5¢	J.F.K.	30.00
❏ 1186	4¢	Workmen's Comp.	14.00	❏ 1247	5¢	New Jersey	15.00
❏ 1187	4¢	Remington	14.00	❏ 1248	5¢	Nevada	12.00
❏ 1188	4¢	China	14.00	❏ 1249	5¢	Register & Vote	12.00
❏ 1189	4¢	Basketball	15.00	❏ 1250	5¢	Shakespeare	12.00
❏ 1190	4¢	Nursing	16.00	❏ 1251	5¢	Doctors Mayo	14.00
❏ 1191	4¢	New Mexico	12.00	❏ 1252	5¢	Music	11.00
❏ 1192	4¢	Arizona	12.00	❏ 1253	5¢	Homemakers	11.00
❏ 1193	4¢	Project Mercury	12.00	❏ 1254–57	5¢	Christmas	36.00
❏ 1194	4¢	Malaria	12.00	❏ 1258	5¢	Verrazano Bridge	15.00
❏ 1195	4¢	Hughes	12.00	❏ 1259	5¢	Modern Art	10.00
❏ 1196	4¢	Seattle Fair	12.00	❏ 1260	5¢	Amateur Radio	15.00
❏ 1197	4¢	Louisiana	16.00	❏ 1261	5¢	New Orleans	20.00
❏ 1198	4¢	Homestead	10.00	❏ 1262	5¢	Physical Fitness	12.00
❏ 1199	4¢	Girl Scouts	8.00	❏ 1263	5¢	Fight Cancer	12.00
❏ 1200	4¢	McMahon	14.00	❏ 1264	5¢	Churchill	15.00
❏ 1201	4¢	Apprenticeship	8.00	❏ 1265	5¢	Magna Carta	15.00
❏ 1202	4¢	Rayburn	12.00	❏ 1266	5¢	Cooperation Year	12.00
❏ 1203	4¢	Hammarskjold	8.00	❏ 1267	5¢	Salvation Army	12.00
❏ 1204	4¢	Hammarskjold invert	14.00	❏ 1268	5¢	Dante Alighieri	12.00

❑ 1269	5¢	Herbert Hoover	14.00
❑ 1270	5¢	Robert Fulton	14.00
❑ 1271	5¢	Florida	14.00
❑ 1272	5¢	Traffic Safety	10.00
❑ 1273	5¢	John S. Copley	14.00
❑ 1274	11¢	I.T.U.	30.00
❑ 1275	5¢	Stevenson	12.00
❑ 1276	5¢	Christmas	15.00
❑ 1278	1¢	Jefferson	9.00
❑ 1279	1¼¢	Gallatin	20.00
❑ 1280	2¢	Wright	12.00
❑ 1281	3¢	Parkman	12.00
❑ 1282	4¢	Lincoln	32.00
❑ 1283	5¢	Washington	20.00
❑ 1283B	5¢	Washington	15.00
❑ 1284	6¢	Roosevelt	32.00
❑ 1285	8¢	Einstein	35.00
❑ 1286	10¢	Jackson	42.00
❑ 1286A	12¢	Ford	35.00
❑ 1287	13¢	Kennedy	50.00
❑ 1288	15¢	Holmes (type I)	40.00
❑ 1288A	15¢	Holmes (type II)	100.00
❑ 1289	20¢	Marshall	100.00
❑ 1290	25¢	Douglass	100.00
❑ 1291	30¢	Dewey	140.00
❑ 1292	40¢	Paine	155.00
❑ 1293	50¢	Stone	155.00
❑ 1294	$1	O'Neill	300.00
❑ 1306	5¢	Migratory Bird	12.00
❑ 1307	5¢	Humane Treatment	12.00
❑ 1308	5¢	Indiana	15.00
❑ 1309	5¢	Clown	14.00
❑ 1310	5¢	SIPEX	14.00
❑ 1312	5¢	Bill of Rights	14.00
❑ 1313	5¢	Poland	14.00
❑ 1314	5¢	Park Service	14.00
❑ 1315	5¢	Marine Reserve	14.00
❑ 1316	5¢	Women's Clubs	14.00
❑ 1317	5¢	J. Appleseed	14.00
❑ 1318	5¢	Beautification	14.00
❑ 1319	5¢	Great River Road	15.00
❑ 1320	5¢	Servicemen	12.00

❑ 1321	5¢	Christmas	12.00
❑ 1322	5¢	Cassatt	12.00
❑ 1323	5¢	Grange	12.00
❑ 1324	5¢	Canada	8.00
❑ 1325	5¢	Erie Canal	16.00
❑ 1326	5¢	Peace	20.00
❑ 1327	5¢	Thoreau	20.00
❑ 1328	5¢	Nebraska	20.00
❑ 1329	5¢	Voice of America	10.00
❑ 1330	5¢	Davy Crockett	15.00
❑ 1331–32	5¢	Space Twins	35.00
❑ 1333	5¢	Urban Planning	12.00
❑ 1334	5¢	Finland	12.00
❑ 1335	5¢	Eakins	15.00
❑ 1336	5¢	Christmas	10.00
❑ 1337	5¢	Mississippi	20.00
❑ 1338	6¢	Flag	20.00
❑ 1338D	6¢	Flag	18.00
❑ 1338F	8¢	Flag	25.00
❑ 1339	6¢	Illinois	18.00
❑ 1340	6¢	Hemisfair '68	10.00
❑ 1341	$1	Airlift	145.00
❑ 1342	6¢	Youth	8.00
❑ 1343	6¢	Law & Order	12.00
❑ 1344	6¢	Register & Vote	12.00
❑ 1345–54	6¢	Flags	22.00
❑ 1355	6¢	Disney	50.00
❑ 1356	6¢	Marquette	18.00
❑ 1357	6¢	Daniel Boone	18.00
❑ 1358	6¢	Arkansas River	18.00
❑ 1359	6¢	Leif Erikson	18.00
❑ 1360	6¢	Cherokee Strip	18.00
❑ 1361	6¢	Trumball	18.00
❑ 1362	6¢	Waterfowl	15.00
❑ 1363	6¢	Christmas	12.00
❑ 1364	6¢	Chief Joseph	18.00
❑ 1365–68	6¢	Beautification	25.00
❑ 1369	6¢	American Legion	14.00
❑ 1370	6¢	Grandma Moses	14.00
❑ 1371	6¢	Apollo 8	15.00
❑ 1372	6¢	W. C. Handy	16.00
❑ 1373	6¢	California	14.00

❑ 1374	6¢	Powell	20.00
❑ 1375	6¢	Alabama	20.00
❑ 1376–79	6¢	Botanical	35.00
❑ 1380	6¢	Webster	15.00
❑ 1381	6¢	Baseball	45.00
❑ 1382	6¢	Football	30.00
❑ 1383	6¢	Eisenhower	10.00
❑ 1384	6¢	Christmas	14.00
❑ 1385	6¢	Hope	14.00
❑ 1386	6¢	Harnett	14.00
❑ 1387–90	6¢	Conservation	10.00
❑ 1391	6¢	Maine	14.00
❑ 1392	6¢	Bison	14.00
❑ 1393	6¢	Eisenhower	20.00
❑ 1393D	7¢	Franklin	25.00
❑ 1394	8¢	Eisenhower	24.00
❑ 1395	8¢	Eisenhower	24.00
❑ 1396	8¢	U.S.P.S. Logo	25.00
❑ 1397	14¢	LaGuardia	35.00
❑ 1398	16¢	Pyle	50.00
❑ 1399	18¢	Blackwell	75.00
❑ 1400	21¢	Giannini	75.00
❑ 1405	6¢	Masters	18.00
❑ 1406	6¢	Suffrage	18.00
❑ 1407	6¢	South Carolina	18.00
❑ 1408	6¢	Stone Mountain	15.00
❑ 1409	6¢	Fort Snelling	12.00
❑ 1410–13	6¢	Conservation	18.00
❑ 1414	6¢	Christmas	15.00
❑ 1414a	6¢	Precanceled	15.00
❑ 1415–18	6¢	Toys	25.00
❑ 1415a–18a	6¢	Toys precancel	35.00
❑ 1419	6¢	U.N.	15.00
❑ 1420	6¢	Pilgrims	15.00
❑ 1421–22	6¢	Veterans	15.00
❑ 1423	6¢	Wool	15.00
❑ 1424	6¢	MacArthur	16.00
❑ 1425	6¢	Give Blood	15.00
❑ 1426	8¢	Missouri	15.00
❑ 1427–30	8¢	Wildlife	15.00
❑ 1431	8¢	Antarctic	12.00
❑ 1432	8¢	Bicentennial	15.00
❑ 1433	8¢	John Sloan	12.00
❑ 1434–35	8¢	Space Achiev.	14.00
❑ 1436	8¢	Dickinson	16.00
❑ 1437	8¢	Puerto Rico	15.00
❑ 1438	8¢	Drug Abuse	15.00
❑ 1439	8¢	CARE	15.00
❑ 1440	8¢	Landmarks	15.00
❑ 1444	8¢	Christmas	15.00
❑ 1445	8¢	Partridge	15.00
❑ 1446	8¢	Lanier	20.00
❑ 1447	8¢	Peace Corps	14.00
❑ 1448–51	2¢	Cape Hatteras	14.00
❑ 1452	6¢	Wolf Trap	14.00
❑ 1453	8¢	Old Faithful	12.00
❑ 1454	15¢	Mt. McKinley	22.00
❑ 1455	8¢	Family Planning	15.00
❑ 1456–59	8¢	Craftsmen	15.00
❑ 1460	6¢	Cycling	10.00
❑ 1461	8¢	Bobsledding	14.00
❑ 1462	15¢	Running	22.00
❑ 1463	8¢	P.T.A.	16.00
❑ 1464	8¢	Wildlife	14.00
❑ 1468	8¢	Mail Order	15.00
❑ 1469	8¢	Osteopath	22.00
❑ 1470	8¢	Tom Sawyer	16.00
❑ 1471	8¢	Christmas	16.00
❑ 1472	8¢	Santa	14.00
❑ 1473	8¢	Pharmacy	22.00
❑ 1474	8¢	Stamp Collecting	16.00
❑ 1475	8¢	LOVE	14.00
❑ 1476	8¢	Printing Press	14.00
❑ 1477	8¢	Broadside	14.00
❑ 1478	8¢	Post Rider	12.00
❑ 1479	8¢	Drummer	15.00
❑ 1480–83	8¢	Tea Party	16.00
❑ 1484	8¢	Gershwin	14.00
❑ 1485	8¢	Jeffers	12.00
❑ 1486	6¢	Tanner	14.00
❑ 1487	8¢	Cather	12.00
❑ 1488	8¢	Copernicus	14.00
❑ 1489–98	8¢	Postal People	16.00
❑ 1499	8¢	Truman	16.00

❑ 1500	6¢	Electronics	16.00		❑ 1572–75	10¢	Transportation	16.00
❑ 1501	8¢	Electroncs	16.00		❑ 1576	10¢	Peace Thru Law	18.00
❑ 1502	15¢	Electronics	20.00		❑ 1577–78	10¢	Banking/Commerce	18.00
❑ 1503	8¢	L.B. J.	12.00		❑ 1579	10¢	Christmas	15.00
❑ 1504	8¢	Angus Cattle	15.00		❑ 1580	10¢	Prang	18.00
❑ 1505	10¢	Chautauqua	15.00		❑ 1580B	10¢	Prang	35.00
❑ 1506	10¢	Winter Wheat	20.00		❑ 1581	1¢	Inkwell	14.00
❑ 1507	8¢	Christmas	15.00		❑ 1582	2¢	Lectern	14.00
❑ 1508	8¢	Christmas Tree	15.00		❑ 1584	3¢	Ballot Box	14.00
❑ 1509	10¢	Crossed Flags	38.00		❑ 1585	4¢	Books	14.00
❑ 1510	10¢	Jeff. Memorial	38.00		❑ 1591	9¢	Capitol Dome	35.00
❑ 1511	10¢	ZIP Code	38.00		❑ 1592	10¢	Justice	35.00
❑ 1525	10¢	V.F.W.	15.00		❑ 1593	11¢	Printing Press	35.00
❑ 1526	10¢	Robert Frost	25.00		❑ 1594	12¢	Torch	35.00
❑ 1527	10¢	Expo '74	15.00		❑ 1596	13¢	Eagle	35.00
❑ 1528	10¢	Horse Racing	20.00		❑ 1597	15¢	U.S. Flag	55.00
❑ 1529	10¢	Skylab	15.00		❑ 1599	16¢	Liberty	55.00
❑ 1530–37	10¢	UPU	15.00		❑ 1603	24¢	North Church	65.00
❑ 1538–41	10¢	Minerals	15.00		❑ 1604	28¢	Ft. Nisqually	80.00
❑ 1542	10¢	Ft. Harrod	25.00		❑ 1605	29¢	Lighthouse	125.00
❑ 1543–46	10¢	Independence	25.00		❑ 1606	30¢	School House	125.00
❑ 1547	10¢	Energy	15.00		❑ 1608	50¢	Lamp	135.00
❑ 1548	10¢	Sleepy Hollow	15.00		❑ 1610	$1	Lamp	325.00
❑ 1549	10¢	Retarded Children	15.00		❑ 1611	$2	Lamp	525.00
❑ 1550	10¢	Christmas	15.00		❑ 1612	$5	Lantern	1250.00
❑ 1551	10¢	Currier & Ives	15.00		❑ 1622	13¢	Flag & Hall	50.00
❑ 1552	10¢	Weather Vane	16.00		❑ 1622C	13¢	Flag & Hall	175.00
❑ 1553	10¢	West	26.00		❑ 1629–31	13¢	Fife & Drum	35.00
❑ 1554	10¢	Dunbar	26.00		❑ 1632	13¢	Interphil	35.00
❑ 1555	10¢	Griffith	26.00		❑ 1633–82	13¢	State Flags	35.00
❑ 1556	10¢	Pioneer 10	18.00		❑ 1683	13¢	Telephone	25.00
❑ 1557	10¢	Mariner 10	16.00		❑ 1684	13¢	Aviation	25.00
❑ 1558	10¢	Bargaining	15.00		❑ 1685	13¢	Chemistry	30.00
❑ 1559	8¢	Ludington	15.00		❑ 1691–94	13¢	Signers	35.00
❑ 1560	10¢	Poor	15.00		❑ 1695–98	13¢	Olympics	32.00
❑ 1561	10¢	Salomon	16.00		❑ 1699	13¢	Maass	22.00
❑ 1562	18¢	Francisco	25.00		❑ 1700	13¢	Ochs	16.00
❑ 1563	10¢	Lexington-Concord	14.00		❑ 1701	13¢	Christmas	25.00
❑ 1564	10¢	Bunker Hill	16.00		❑ 1702	13¢	Winter Pastime	25.00
❑ 1565–68	10¢	Armed Forces	16.00		❑ 1703	13¢	Winter Pastime	25.00
❑ 1569–70	10¢	Apollo-Soyuz	15.00		❑ 1704	13¢	Princeton	25.00
❑ 1571	10¢	Women's Year	15.00		❑ 1705	13¢	Recording	25.00

❑ 1706–09	13¢	Pottery	15.00		❑ 1789	15¢	Jones, 11x12	25.00
❑ 1710	13¢	Spirit of St. Louis	25.00		❑ 1789A	15¢	Jones, 11	35.00
❑ 1711	13¢	Colorado	25.00		❑ 1789B	15¢	Jones, 12	—
❑ 1712–15	13¢	Butterflies	25.00		❑ 1790	10¢	Olympics	20.00
❑ 1716	13¢	Lafayette	25.00		❑ 1791–94	15¢	Olympics	32.00
❑ 1717–20	13¢	Craftsmen	25.00		❑ 1795–98	15¢	Olympics	32.00
❑ 1721	13¢	Peace Bridge	25.00		❑ 1799	15¢	Madonna	45.00
❑ 1722	13¢	Oriskany	22.00		❑ 1800	15¢	Santa	45.00
❑ 1723–24	13¢	Energy	22.00		❑ 1801	15¢	Rogers	25.00
❑ 1725	13¢	Alta	25.00		❑ 1802	15¢	Vietnam Vets	32.00
❑ 1726	13¢	Confederation	25.00		❑ 1803	15¢	W. C. Fields	20.00
❑ 1727	13¢	Talking Pictures	25.00		❑ 1804	15¢	Banneker	38.00
❑ 1728	13¢	Saratoga	20.00		❑ 1805–10	15¢	Letters	38.00
❑ 1729	13¢	Valley Forge	45.00		❑ 1818	(18¢)	"B" Stamp	50.00
❑ 1730	13¢	Mailbox	45.00		❑ 1821	15¢	Perkins	40.00
❑ 1731	13¢	Sandburg	25.00		❑ 1822	15¢	Madison	85.00
❑ 1732–33	13¢	Cook	30.00		❑ 1823	15¢	Bissell	32.00
❑ 1734	13¢	Indian	65.00		❑ 1824	15¢	Keller	30.00
❑ 1735	(15¢)	"A" Stamp	45.00		❑ 1825	15¢	V.A.	32.00
❑ 1744	13¢	Tubman	40.00		❑ 1826	15¢	Galvez	30.00
❑ 1745–48	13¢	Quilts	20.00		❑ 1827–30	15¢	Coral	25.00
❑ 1753	13¢	French Alliance	15.00		❑ 1831	15¢	Labor	25.00
❑ 1754	13¢	Pap Test	25.00		❑ 1832	15¢	Wharton	25.00
❑ 1755	13¢	Rodgers	38.00		❑ 1833	15¢	Learning	36.00
❑ 1756	15¢	Cohan	35.00		❑ 1834–37	15¢	Masks	36.00
❑ 1757	13¢	CAPEX	22.00		❑ 1838–41	15¢	Architecture	36.00
❑ 1758	15¢	Photography	22.00		❑ 1842	15¢	Madonna	22.00
❑ 1759	15¢	Viking	25.00		❑ 1843	15¢	Drum & Wreath	22.00
❑ 1760–63	15¢	Owls	25.00		❑ 1844	1¢	Dix	15.00
❑ 1764–67	15¢	Trees	20.00		❑ 1845	2¢	Stravinsky	12.00
❑ 1768	15¢	Madonna	45.00		❑ 1846	3¢	Clay	18.00
❑ 1769	15¢	Rocking Horse	45.00		❑ 1847	4¢	Schurz	18.00
❑ 1770	15¢	R. F. Kennedy	35.00		❑ 1848	5¢	Buck	18.00
❑ 1771	15¢	M.L. King.	35.00		❑ 1849	6¢	Lippmann	20.00
❑ 1772	15¢	Year of Child	35.00		❑ 1850	7¢	Baldwin	35.00
❑ 1773	15¢	Steinbeck	25.00		❑ 1851	8¢	Knox	35.00
❑ 1774	15¢	Einstein	35.00		❑ 1852	9¢	Thayer	35.00
❑ 1775–78	15¢	Toleware	35.00		❑ 1853	10¢	Russell	40.00
❑ 1779–82	15¢	Architecture	35.00		❑ 1854	11¢	Partridge	65.00
❑ 1783–86	15¢	Flowers	35.00		❑ 1855	13¢	Horse	65.00
❑ 1787	15¢	Seeing for Me	35.00		❑ 1856	14¢	Lewis	65.00
❑ 1788	15¢	Spec. Olympics	25.00		❑ 1857	17¢	Carson	65.00

❏ 1858	18¢	Mason	50.00	❏ 2003	20¢	Netherlands	35.00
❏ 1859	19¢	Sequoyah	70.00	❏ 2004	20¢	Library of Congress	32.00
❏ 1860	20¢	Bunche	70.00	❏ 2006–09	20¢	Energy	40.00
❏ 1861	20¢	Gallaudet	75.00	❏ 2010	20¢	Alger	40.00
❏ 1862	20¢	Truman	65.00	❏ 2011	20¢	Aging	35.00
❏ 1863	22¢	Audubon	80.00	❏ 2012	20¢	Barrymores	35.00
❏ 1864	30¢	Laubach	100.00	❏ 2013	20¢	Walker	35.00
❏ 1865	35¢	Drew	125.00	❏ 2014	20¢	Peace Garden	35.00
❏ 1866	37¢	Millikan	100.00	❏ 2015	20¢	Libraries	30.00
❏ 1867	39¢	Clark	125.00	❏ 2016	20¢	Robinson	100.00
❏ 1868	40¢	Gilbreth	125.00	❏ 2017	20¢	Touro	60.00
❏ 1869	50¢	Nimitz	125.00	❏ 2018	20¢	Wolf Trap	32.00
❏ 1874	15¢	Dirksen	25.00	❏ 2019	20¢	Architecture	35.00
❏ 1875	15¢	Young	25.00	❏ 2023	20¢	Francis of Assisi	30.00
❏ 1876–79	18¢	Flowers	35.00	❏ 2024	20¢	de Léon	42.00
❏ 1890	18¢	Flag-Grain	65.00	❏ 2025	13¢	Kitten & Puppy	32.00
❏ 1894	20¢	Flag-Court	100.00	❏ 2026	20¢	Madonna	35.00
❏ 1910	18¢	Red Cross	35.00	❏ 2027	20¢	Christmas	40.00
❏ 1911	18¢	Savings & Loan	25.00	❏ 2031	20¢	Science/Industry	32.00
❏ 1912–19	18¢	Space	35.00	❏ 2032–35	20¢	Ballooning	35.00
❏ 1920	18¢	Management	35.00	❏ 2036	20¢	Sweden	35.00
❏ 1921–24	18¢	Habitats	35.00	❏ 2037	20¢	C.C.C.	35.00
❏ 1925	18¢	Disabled	35.00	❏ 2038	20¢	Priestley	35.00
❏ 1926	18¢	Millay	35.00	❏ 2039	20¢	Volunteer	35.00
❏ 1927	18¢	Alcoholism	60.00	❏ 2040	20¢	German Immigr.	35.00
❏ 1928–31	18¢	Architecture	45.00	❏ 2041	20¢	Brooklyn Bridge	35.00
❏ 1932	18¢	Zaharias	45.00	❏ 2042	20¢	T.V.A.	35.00
❏ 1933	18¢	Jones	75.00	❏ 2043	20¢	Fitness	32.00
❏ 1934	18¢	Remington	30.00	❏ 2044	20¢	Joplin	32.00
❏ 1935	18¢	Hoban	35.00	❏ 2045	20¢	Medal of Honor	35.00
❏ 1936	20¢	Hoban	35.00	❏ 2046	20¢	Babe Ruth	125.00
❏ 1937–38	18¢	Yorktown Map	35.00	❏ 2047	20¢	Hawthorne	40.00
❏ 1939	(20¢)	Madonna	50.00	❏ 2048	13¢	Olympics	35.00
❏ 1940	(20¢)	Teddy Bear	30.00	❏ 2052	20¢	Treaty of Paris	25.00
❏ 1941	20¢	Hanson	35.00	❏ 2053	20¢	Civil Service	50.00
❏ 1942–45	20¢	Cactus	30.00	❏ 2054	20¢	The Met	38.00
❏ 1946	(20¢)	"C" Stamp	55.00	❏ 2055–58	20¢	Inventors	45.00
❏ 1950	20¢	F.D.R.	30.00	❏ 2059–62	20¢	Streetcars	45.00
❏ 1951	20¢	Love	40.00	❏ 2063	20¢	Madonna	30.00
❏ 1952	20¢	Washington	35.00	❏ 2064	20¢	Santa Claus	35.00
❏ 1953–02	20¢	State Birds	60.00	❏ 2065	20¢	Martin Luther	35.00
❏ 1953A–02A	20¢	State Birds	60.00	❏ 2066	20¢	Alaska	35.00

❑ 2067–70	20¢	Olympics	40.00	❑ 2152	22¢	Korea Veterans	50.00
❑ 2071	20¢	FDIC	35.00	❑ 2153	22¢	Social Security	40.00
❑ 2072	20¢	Love	35.00	❑ 2154	22¢	WW I Veterans	45.00
❑ 2073	20¢	Woodson	35.00	❑ 2155–58	22¢	Horses	125.00
❑ 2074	20¢	Conservation	35.00	❑ 2159	22¢	Education	75.00
❑ 2075	20¢	Credit Union	35.00	❑ 2160–63	22¢	Youth Year	65.00
❑ 2076–79	20¢	Orchids	35.00	❑ 2164	22¢	Hunger	50.00
❑ 2080	20¢	Hawaii	35.00	❑ 2165	22¢	Madonna	50.00
❑ 2081	20¢	Archives	34.00	❑ 2166	22¢	Poinsettia	50.00
❑ 2082–85	20¢	Olympics	50.00	❑ 2167	22¢	Arkansas	65.00
❑ 2086	20¢	Louisiana Expo	40.00	❑ 2168	1¢	Mitchell	16.00
❑ 2087	20¢	Health Research	40.00	❑ 2169	2¢	Lyon	16.00
❑ 2088	20¢	Fairbanks	40.00	❑ 2170	3¢	White	16.00
❑ 2089	20¢	Thorpe	40.00	❑ 2171	4¢	Flanagan	16.00
❑ 2090	20¢	McCormack	32.00	❑ 2172	5¢	Black	35.00
❑ 2091	20¢	Seaway	40.00	❑ 2173	5¢	Marin	25.00
❑ 2092	20¢	Wetlands	50.00	❑ 2175	10¢	Red Cloud	42.00
❑ 2093	20¢	Roanoke	35.00	❑ 2176	14¢	Howe	45.00
❑ 2094	20¢	Melville	55.00	❑ 2177	15¢	Cody	100.00
❑ 2095	20¢	Moses	55.00	❑ 2178	17¢	Lockwood	55.00
❑ 2096	20¢	Smokey	40.00	❑ 2179	20¢	Apgar	75.00
❑ 2097	20¢	Clemente	140.00	❑ 2180	21¢	Carlson	75.00
❑ 2098–01	20¢	Dogs	32.00	❑ 2181	23¢	Cassatt	75.00
❑ 2102	20¢	Anti-Crime	32.00	❑ 2182	25¢	London	75.00
❑ 2103	20¢	Hispanic	25.00	❑ 2183	28¢	Sitting Bull	125.00
❑ 2104	20¢	Family Unity	45.00	❑ 2184	29¢	Warren	125.00
❑ 2105	20¢	E. Roosevelt	35.00	❑ 2185	29¢	Jefferson	125.00
❑ 2106	20¢	Readers	35.00	❑ 2186	35¢	Chavez	125.00
❑ 2107	20¢	Madonna	32.00	❑ 2187	40¢	Chenault	125.00
❑ 2108	20¢	Santa Claus	32.00	❑ 2188	45¢	Cushing	150.00
❑ 2109	20¢	Vietnam Memorial	40.00	❑ 2189	52¢	Humphrey	175.00
❑ 2110	22¢	Kern	35.00	❑ 2190	56¢	Harvard	175.00
❑ 2111	(22¢)	"D" Stamp	140.00	❑ 2191	65¢	Arnold	175.00
❑ 2114	22¢	Flag	60.00	❑ 2192	75¢	Wilkie	220.00
❑ 2137	22¢	Bethune	50.00	❑ 2193	$1	Revel	350.00
❑ 2138–41	22¢	Decoys	125.00	❑ 2194	$1	Hopkins	85.00
❑ 2142	22¢	Special Olympics	32.00	❑ 2195	$2	Bryan	535.00
❑ 2143	22¢	Love	35.00	❑ 2196	$5	Harte	275.00
❑ 2144	22¢	Electrification	60.00	❑ 2202	22¢	Love	50.00
❑ 2145	22¢	AMERIPEX	36.00	❑ 2203	22¢	Truth	50.00
❑ 2146	22¢	Adams	36.00	❑ 2204	22¢	Texas	40.00
❑ 2147	22¢	Bartholdi	28.00	❑ 2210	22¢	Hospitals	40.00

❏ 2211	22¢	Ellington	40.00	❏ 2376	22¢	Rockne	45.00
❏ 2220–23	22¢	Explorers	60.00	❏ 2377	25¢	Ouimet	50.00
❏ 2224	22¢	Liberty	55.00	❏ 2378	25¢	Love	75.00
❏ 2235–38	22¢	Navajo Carpets	55.00	❏ 2379	45¢	Love	75.00
❏ 2239	22¢	Eliot	55.00	❏ 2380	25¢	Gymnast	55.00
❏ 2240–43	22¢	Carvings	55.00	❏ 2386–89	25¢	Explorers	60.00
❏ 2244	22¢	Madonna	65.00	❏ 2390–93	25¢	Carousel	75.00
❏ 2245	22¢	Village Scene	65.00	❏ 2394	$8.75	Express Mail	535.00
❏ 2246	22¢	Michigan	38.00	❏ 2399	25¢	Madonna	42.00
❏ 2247	22¢	Pan Am Games	38.00	❏ 2400	25¢	Winter Scene	42.00
❏ 2248	22¢	Love	60.00	❏ 2401	25¢	Montana	50.00
❏ 2249	22¢	du Sable	45.00	❏ 2402	25¢	Randolph	50.00
❏ 2250	22¢	Caruso	45.00	❏ 2403	25¢	North Dakota	45.00
❏ 2251	22¢	Girl Scouts	30.00	❏ 2404	25¢	Washington	42.00
❏ 2275	22¢	United Way	30.00	❏ 2410	25¢	Stamp Expo '89	42.00
❏ 2277	(25¢)	"E" Stamp	85.00	❏ 2411	25¢	Toscanini	36.00
❏ 2278	25¢	Flag	75.00	❏ 2412	25¢	House of Reps.	45.00
❏ 2286–35	22¢	Wildlife	95.00	❏ 2413	25¢	Senate	55.00
❏ 2336	22¢	Delaware	55.00	❏ 2414	25¢	Executive Br.	55.00
❏ 2337	22¢	Pennsylvania	55.00	❏ 2415	25¢	Supreme Court	55.00
❏ 2338	22¢	New Jersey	55.00	❏ 2416	25¢	South Dakota	55.00
❏ 2339	22¢	Georgia	45.00	❏ 2417	25¢	Gehrig	60.00
❏ 2340	22¢	Connecticut	50.00	❏ 2418	25¢	Hemingway	50.00
❏ 2341	22¢	Massachusetts	50.00	❏ 2419	$2.40	Moon Landing	185.00
❏ 2342	22¢	Maryland	65.00	❏ 2420	25¢	Letter Carriers	25.00
❏ 2343	22¢	South Carolina	65.00	❏ 2421	25¢	Bill of Rights	50.00
❏ 2344	22¢	New Hampshire	65.00	❏ 2422–25	25¢	Dinosaurs	65.00
❏ 2345	22¢	Virginia	65.00	❏ 2426	25¢	Southwest	35.00
❏ 2346	22¢	New York	65.00	❏ 2427	25¢	Madonna	50.00
❏ 2347	22¢	North Carolina	65.00	❏ 2428	25¢	Sleigh	50.00
❏ 2348	22¢	Rhode Island	65.00	❏ 2434	25¢	UPU	50.00
❏ 2349	22¢	Morocco	35.00	❏ 2439	25¢	Idaho	40.00
❏ 2350	22¢	Faulkner	50.00	❏ 2440	25¢	Love	40.00
❏ 2351–54	22¢	Lace	40.00	❏ 2442	25¢	Wells	45.00
❏ 2360	22¢	Constitution	50.00	❏ 2444	25¢	Wyoming	40.00
❏ 2361	22¢	CPAs	175.00	❏ 2445–49	25¢	Films	100.00
❏ 2367	22¢	Madonna	65.00	❏ 2449	25¢	Moore	30.00
❏ 2368	22¢	Ornament	85.00	❏ 2476	1¢	Kestrel	15.00
❏ 2369	22¢	Skier	40.00	❏ 2477	1¢	Kestrel	15.00
❏ 2370	22¢	Australia	32.00	❏ 2478	3¢	Bluebird	15.00
❏ 2371	22¢	Johnson	35.00	❏ 2479	19¢	Fawn	50.00
❏ 2372–75	22¢	Cats	45.00	❏ 2480	30¢	Cardinal	75.00

❑ 2481	45¢	Sunfish	125.00
❑ 2482	$2	Bobcat	125.00
❑ 2496	25¢	Olympians	42.00
❑ 2506–07	25¢	Micronesia	45.00
❑ 2508–11	25¢	Sea Mammals	42.00
❑ 2512	25¢	Grand Canyon	50.00
❑ 2513	25¢	Eisenhower	50.00
❑ 2514	25¢	Madonna	35.00
❑ 2515	25¢	Christmas Tree	45.00
❑ 2517	(29¢)	"F" Stamp	80.00
❑ 2521	(4¢)	Make Up Rate	18.00
❑ 2524	29¢	Tulip	80.00
❑ 2524A	29¢	Tulip	140.00
❑ 2531	29¢	Flags	140.00
❑ 2531A	29¢	Torch	80.00
❑ 2532	50¢	Switzerland	65.00
❑ 2533	29¢	Vermont	60.00
❑ 2534	29¢	Savings Bonds	50.00
❑ 2535	29¢	Love	50.00
❑ 2535A	29¢	Love	50.00
❑ 2537	52¢	Love Birds	85.00
❑ 2538	29¢	Saroyan	60.00
❑ 2539	$1	Olympic Rings	60.00
❑ 2540	$2.90	Eagle	175.00
❑ 2541	$9.95	Express Mail	500.00
❑ 2542	$14	Express Mail	750.00
❑ 2543	$2.90	Spacecraft	350.00
❑ 2544	$3	Space Shuttle	175.00
❑ 254A	$10.75	Space Shuttle	500.00
❑ 2550	29¢	Porter	60.00
❑ 2551	29¢	Desert Storm	55.00
❑ 2553–57	29¢	Olympics	55.00
❑ 2558	29¢	Numismatics	55.00
❑ 2559	29¢	WWar II, 1941	25.00
❑ 2560	29¢	Basketball	50.00
❑ 2561	29¢	D.C.	50.00
❑ 2567	29¢	Matzeliger	50.00
❑ 2579	(29¢)	Santa	35.00
❑ 2587	32¢	Polk	85.00
❑ 2590	$1	Burgoyne	50.00
❑ 2592	$5	Washington/Jackson	300.00
❑ 2611–15	29¢	Olympics	45.00
❑ 2616	29¢	Stamp Expo	35.00
❑ 2617	29¢	DuBois	55.00
❑ 2618	29¢	Love	55.00
❑ 2619	29¢	Baseball	60.00
❑ 2620–23	29¢	Columbus	45.00
❑ 2630	29¢	Stock Exchange	45.00
❑ 2631–24	29¢	Space	50.00
❑ 2635	29¢	Alaska Hiway	35.00
❑ 2636	29¢	Kentucky	50.00
❑ 2637–41	29¢	Olympics	50.00
❑ 2647–96	29¢	Wildflowers	50.00
❑ 2697	29¢	WW II, 1942	25.00
❑ 2698	29¢	Parker	60.00
❑ 2699	29¢	von Kármán	60.00
❑ 2700	29¢	Minerals	60.00
❑ 2704	29¢	Cabrillo	45.00
❑ 2711–14	29¢	Christmas	50.00
❑ 2720	29¢	Rooster	20.00
❑ 2721	29¢	Elvis	45.00
❑ 2722	29¢	Oklahoma!	35.00
❑ 2723	29¢	Williams	40.00
❑ 2723A	29¢	Williams	800.0
❑ 2724–30	29¢	Singers	50.00
❑ 2746	29¢	Julian	40.00
❑ 2747	29¢	Oregon Trail	55.00
❑ 2748	29¢	Univ. Games	55.00
❑ 2749	29¢	Grace Kelly	40.00
❑ 2750–53	29¢	Circus	50.00
❑ 2754	29¢	Cherokee Strip	20.00
❑ 2755	29¢	Acheson	42.00
❑ 2756–59	29¢	Horse Racing	42.00
❑ 2765	29¢	WWar II, 1943	40.00
❑ 2766	29¢	Louis	50.00
❑ 2771–74	29¢	Singers	35.00
❑ 2779–82	29¢	Postal Museum	35.00
❑ 2783–84	29¢	Deafness	22.00
❑ 2785–88	29¢	Literature	50.00
❑ 2789	29¢	Madonna	40.00
❑ 2791–94	29¢	Christmas	60.00
❑ 2804	29¢	Mariana Is.	25.00
❑ 2805	29¢	Columbus	50.00
❑ 2806	29¢	AIDS	50.00

❑ 2807–11	29¢	Olympics	25.00	❑ 2950	32¢	Florida	25.00
❑ 2812	29¢	Murrow	35.00	❑ 2951–54	32¢	Environment	22.00
❑ 2814C	29¢	Love	60.00	❑ 2955	32¢	Nixon	50.00
❑ 2815	52¢	Love	75.00	❑ 2956	32¢	Coleman	50.00
❑ 2816	29¢	Davis	35.00	❑ 2957	32¢	Love	50.00
❑ 2817	29¢	Year of Dog	35.00	❑ 2958	55¢	Love	75.00
❑ 2818	29¢	Buffalo Soldiers	20.00	❑ 2961–65	32¢	Sports	30.00
❑ 2819–28	29¢	Film Stars	35.00	❑ 2966	32¢	POW - MIA	30.00
❑ 2834	29¢	Soccer	25.00	❑ 2967	32¢	Marilyn	30.00
❑ 2835	40¢	Soccer	25.00	❑ 2968	32¢	Texas	25.00
❑ 2836	50¢	Soccer	35.00	❑ 2974	32¢	U.N.	20.00
❑ 2838	29¢	WW II, 1944	30.00	❑ 2975	32¢	Civil War	18.00
❑ 2839	29¢	Rockwell	50.00	❑ 2976–79	32¢	Carousel	25.00
❑ 2842	29¢	Moon	650.00	❑ 2980	32¢	Suffrage	35.00
❑ 2848	29¢	Meany	50.00	❑ 2981	32¢	WW II, 1945	35.00
❑ 2849–53	29¢	Singers	25.00	❑ 2982	32¢	Armstrong	35.00
❑ 2854–61	29¢	Singers	50.00	❑ 2983–92	32¢	Singers	35.00
❑ 2862	29¢	Thurber	50.00	❑ 2998	60¢	Rickenbacker	85.00
❑ 2863–66	29¢	Sea Wonders	50.00	❑ 2999	32¢	Palau	40.00
❑ 2867–68	29¢	Cranes	25.00	❑ 3000	32¢	Comics	30.00
❑ 2869	29¢	Legends	25.00	❑ 3001	32¢	Annapolis	30.00
❑ 2870	29¢	Legends	175.00	❑ 3002	32¢	Williams	30.00
❑ 2871	29¢	Madonna	45.00	❑ 3003	32¢	Christmas	40.00
❑ 2872	29¢	Stocking	45.00	❑ 3004–07	32¢	Christmas	45.00
❑ 2876	29¢	Year of Boar	20.00	❑ 3019–23	32¢	Autos	25.00
❑ 2877	(4¢)	Make-up Rate	20.00	❑ 3024	32¢	Utah	45.00
❑ 2878	(4¢)	Make-up Rate	20.00	❑ 3031	1¢	Kestrel	15.00
❑ 2879	(20¢)	"G" Stamp	75.00	❑ 3031A	1¢	Kestrel	15.00
❑ 2880	(20¢)	"G" Stamp	75.00	❑ 3032	2¢	Woodpecker	15.00
❑ 2881	(32¢)	"G" Stamp	250.00	❑ 3033	3¢	Blue Bird	15.00
❑ 2882	(32¢)	"G" Stamp	140.00	❑ 3036	$1	Red Fox	50.00
❑ 2897	32¢	Flag	140.00	❑ 3058	32¢	Just	25.00
❑ 2933	32¢	Hershey	80.00	❑ 3059	32¢	Smithsonian	25.00
❑ 2934	32¢	Farley	100.00	❑ 3060	32¢	Year of Rat	35.00
❑ 2935	32¢	Luce	25.00	❑ 3061–64	32¢	Scientists	25.00
❑ 2936	32¢	Wallace	25.00	❑ 3065	32¢	Scholarships	50.00
❑ 2938	46¢	Benedict	125.00	❑ 3066	50¢	Cochran	75.00
❑ 2940	55¢	Hamilton	135.00	❑ 3067	32¢	Marathon	20.00
❑ 2941	55¢	Morrill	45.00	❑ 3068	32¢	Olympics	20.00
❑ 2942	77¢	Breckinridge	45.00	❑ 3069	32¢	O'Keeffe	22.00
❑ 2943	78¢	Paul	200.00	❑ 3070	32¢	Tennessee	40.00
❑ 2948	(32¢)	Love	45.00	❑ 3072–76	32¢	Dance	22.00

❑ 3077–80	32¢	Prehistoric	25.00		❑ 3179	32¢	Year of Tiger	18.00
❑ 3081	32¢	Breast Cancer	35.00		❑ 3180	32¢	Skiing	25.00
❑ 3082	32¢	Dean	35.00		❑ 3181	32¢	Walker	25.00
❑ 3083–86	32¢	Folk Heroes	35.00		❑ 3182	32¢	1900s	16.00
❑ 3087	32¢	Olympics	20.00		❑ 3183	32¢	1910s	16.00
❑ 3088	32¢	Iowa	40.00		❑ 3184	32¢	1920s	14.00
❑ 3090	32¢	RFD	20.00		❑ 3185	32¢	1930s	14.00
❑ 3091–95	32¢	Riverboats	20.00		❑ 3186	33¢	1940s	17.00
❑ 3096–99	32¢	Musicians	25.00		❑ 3187	33¢	1950s	17.00
❑ 3100–03	32¢	Composers	25.00		❑ 3188	33¢	1960s	17.00
❑ 3104	23¢	Fitzgerald	40.00		❑ 3189	33¢	1970s	12.00
❑ 3105	32¢	Endangered	22.00		❑ 3190	33¢	1980s	18.00
❑ 3106	32¢	Computers	35.00		❑ 3191	33¢	1990s	18.00
❑ 3107	32¢	Madonna	40.00		❑ 3192	32¢	The Maine	22.00
❑ 3108–11	32¢	Christmas	50.00		❑ 3193–87	32¢	Flowers	16.00
❑ 3118	32¢	Hanukkah	16.00		❑ 3198–02	32¢	Calder	20.00
❑ 3120	32¢	Year of Ox	25.00		❑ 3203	32¢	Cinco de Mayo	18.00
❑ 3121	32¢	Davis	25.00		❑ 3209	1¢–$2	Trans-Mississippi	14.00
❑ 3125	32¢	Learning	25.00		❑ 3210	$1	Cattle in Storm	40.00
❑ 3130–31	32¢	Pacific 97	25.00		❑ 3211	32¢	Airlift	16.00
❑ 3134	32¢	Wilder	20.00		❑ 3212–19	32¢	Singers	24.00
❑ 3135	32¢	Wallenberg	20.00		❑ 3220	32¢	Spanish Settlement	24.00
❑ 3136	32¢	Dinosaurs	16.00		❑ 3221	32¢	Benét	24.00
❑ 3139	50¢	Pacific 97	16.00		❑ 3226	32¢	Hitchcock	20.00
❑ 3140	60¢	Pacific 97	20.00		❑ 3227	32¢	Organ Donors	20.00
❑ 3141	32¢	Marshall Plan	20.00		❑ 3230–34	32¢	Bright Eyes	25.00
❑ 3142	32¢	Aircraft	20.00		❑ 3235	32¢	Klondike	20.00
❑ 3147	32¢	Lombardi	24.00		❑ 3236	32¢	Art	16.00
❑ 3148	32¢	Bryant	24.00		❑ 3237	32¢	Ballet	20.00
❑ 3149	32¢	Warner	20.00		❑ 3238–42	32¢	Future Space	20.00
❑ 3150	32¢	Halas	20.00		❑ 3243	32¢	Giving	20.00
❑ 3151	32¢	Dolls	15.00		❑ 3249–52	32¢	Wreaths	20.00
❑ 3152	32¢	Bogart	20.00		❑ 3257	(1¢)	Weather Vane	8.00
❑ 3153	32¢	Stars & Strips	40.00		❑ 3258	(1¢)	Weather Vane	8.00
❑ 3154–57	32¢	Opera	25.00		❑ 3259	22¢	Uncle Sam	10.00
❑ 3158–65	32¢	Composers	25.00		❑ 3260	(33¢)	Hat	40.00
❑ 3166	32¢	Varela	25.00		❑ 3261	$3.20	Space Shuttle	225.00
❑ 3167	32¢	Air Force	16.00		❑ 3262	$11.75	Space Shuttle	750.00
❑ 3168–72	32¢	Monsters	22.00		❑ 3272	33¢	Year of Rabbit	24.00
❑ 3173	32¢	Flight	22.00		❑ 3273	33¢	Malcolm X	24.00
❑ 3174	32¢	Military Women	20.00		❑ 3276	33¢	Hospice	15.00
❑ 3175	32¢	Kwanzaa	42.00		❑ 3277	33¢	Flag	100.00

❑ 3286	33¢	Irish	20.00	❑ 3431	76¢	Caraway	35.00
❑ 3287	33¢	Lunt & Fontanne	20.00	❑ 3632	37¢	Ferber	25.00
❑ 3288–92	33¢	Arctic Animals	20.00	❑ 3438	33¢	California	18.00
❑ 3293	33¢	Desert	12.00	❑ 3439–43	33¢	Fish	17.00
❑ 3308	33¢	Rand	18.00	❑ 3444	33¢	Wolfe	17.00
❑ 3309	33¢	Cinco de Mayo	18.00	❑ 3445	33¢	White House	17.00
❑ 3314	33¢	Bartram	18.00	❑ 3446	33¢	Robinson	17.00
❑ 3315	33¢	Prostate Cancer	18.00	❑ 3448	(34¢)	Flag	20.00
❑ 3316	33¢	Gold Rush	18.00	❑ 3449	(34¢)	Flag	20.00
❑ 3317–20	33¢	Fish	18.00	❑ 3467	21¢	Buffalo	50.00
❑ 3321–24	33¢	Extreme Sports	18.00	❑ 3468	21¢	Buffalo	16.00
❑ 3325	33¢	Glass	18.00	❑ 3468A	23¢	Washington	18.00
❑ 3329	33¢	Cagney	18.00	❑ 3469	34¢	Flag	18.00
❑ 3330	33¢	Mitchell	32.00	❑ 3470	34¢	Flag	20.00
❑ 3331	33¢	Who Served	32.00	❑ 3471	55¢	Eagle	32.00
❑ 3332	45¢	U.P.U.	32.00	❑ 3471A	57¢	Eagle	32.00
❑ 3333–37	33¢	Trains	22.00	❑ 3472	$3.50	Capitol Dome	20.00
❑ 3338	33¢	Olmsted	22.00	❑ 3473	$12.25	Wash. Monument	550.00
❑ 3339–44	33¢	Composers	22.00	❑ 3499	55¢	Love	25.00
❑ 3345–50	33¢	Composers	22.00	❑ 3500	34¢	Year of Snake	20.00
❑ 3351	33¢	Insects	20.00	❑ 3501	34¢	Wilkins	20.00
❑ 3352	33¢	Hanukkah	20.00	❑ 3502	34¢	Illustrators	20.00
❑ 3354	33¢	NATO	20.00	❑ 3503	34¢	Diabetes	15.00
❑ 3356–59	33¢	Stag	20.00	❑ 3504	34¢	Nobel Prize	16.00
❑ 3369	33¢	New Year	20.00	❑ 3505		Inverts	15.00
❑ 3370	33¢	Year of Dragon	20.00	❑ 3506	34¢	Prairie	15.00
❑ 3371	33¢	Harris	16.00	❑ 3507	34¢	Snoopy	20.00
❑ 3372	33¢	Submarine	16.00	❑ 3508	34¢	Veterans	18.00
❑ 3378	33¢	Rain Forest	16.00	❑ 3509	34¢	Kahlo	18.00
❑ 3379–83	33¢	Nevelson	20.00	❑ 3510–19	34¢	Stadiums	18.00
❑ 3385–88	33¢	Hubble	20.00	❑ 3521	34¢	Bernstein	18.00
❑ 3389	33¢	Samoa	20.00	❑ 3523	34¢	Ball	18.00
❑ 3390	33¢	Library of Cong.	20.00	❑ 3524–27	34¢	Quilts	16.00
❑ 3393	33¢	War Heroes	20.00	❑ 3528–31	34¢	Carniverous	16.00
❑ 3397	33¢	Runners	20.00	❑ 3532	34¢	Eid	16.00
❑ 3398	33¢	Adoption	16.00	❑ 3533	34¢	Fermi	12.00
❑ 3399–02	33¢	Sports	16.00	❑ 3537–40	34¢	Christmas	18.00
❑ 3403	33¢	Flags	16.00	❑ 3545	34¢	Monroe	18.00
❑ 3408	33¢	Baseball	16.00	❑ 3546	34¢	Thanks	20.00
❑ 3414–17	33¢	Drawings	16.00	❑ 3547	34¢	Hanukkah	18.00
❑ 3420	10¢	Stillwell	16.00	❑ 3548	34¢	Kwanzaa	18.00
❑ 3426	33¢	Pepper	16.00	❑ 3551	57¢	Love	20.00

❑ 3552–55	34¢	Olympics	16.00	❑ 3672	37¢	Hanukkah SA	22.00
❑ 3556	34¢	Mentoring	16.00	❑ 3673	37¢	Kwanzaa SA	22.00
❑ 3557	34¢	Hughes	18.00	❑ 3674	37¢	Islamic Festival	22.00
❑ 3558	34¢	Birthday	18.00	❑ 3675	37¢	Madonna (pane of 20)	22.00
❑ 3559	34¢	Year of Horse	17.00	❑ 3676–79	37¢	Snowman	22.00
❑ 3560	34¢	West Point	17.00	❑ 3692	37¢	Cary Grant	22.00
❑ 3561–10	34¢	Greetings	35.00	❑ 3695	37¢	Happy Birthday	22.00
❑ 3611	34¢	Pine Forest	15.00	❑ 3746	37¢	Thurgood Marshall SA	22.00
❑ 3613	3¢	Star	15.00	❑ 3747	37¢	Year of the Ram SA	22.00
❑ 3614	3¢	Star	15.00	❑ 3748	37¢	Zora Neale Hurston SA	22.00
❑ 3646	60¢	Eagle	25.00				
❑ 3647	$3.85	Jefferson Memorial	175.00	❑ 3751	10¢	U.S. Clock	5.00
❑ 3648	$13.65	Capitol Dome	500.00	❑ 3757	1¢	Tiffany Lamp	40.00
❑ 3649	37¢	Photography	17.00	❑ 3771	80¢	Special Olympics	30.00
❑ 3650	37¢	Audubon	17.00	❑ 3773	37¢	Ohio Statehood	22.00
❑ 3651	37¢	Houdini	17.00	❑ 3774	37¢	Pelican Island	16.00
❑ 3652	37¢	Andy Warhol	17.00	❑ 3781	37¢	Cesar Chavez SA	20.00
❑ 3653–56	37¢	Teddy Bears	17.00	❑ 3782	37¢	Louisiana Purchase SA	15.00
❑ 3657	37¢	Love Pane of 20	30.00	❑ 3784	37¢	Purple Heart	20.00
❑ 3659	37¢	Ogden Nash SA	25.00	❑ 3785	37¢	Sea Coast	20.00
❑ 3660	37¢	Duke Kahanamoku	25.00	❑ 3786	37¢	Audrey Hepburn	20.00
❑ 3661–64	37¢	American Bats	25.00	❑ 3787–91	37¢	Cape Henry Lighthouse	20.00
❑ 3665–68	37¢	Nellie Bly	25.00				
❑ 3669	37¢	Irving Berlin	25.00	❑ 3803	37¢	Korean War	20.00
❑ 3670–71	37¢	Neuter and Spay	25.00	❑ 3812	37¢	Roy Acuff	20.00

SEMIPOSTAL STAMPS

❑ B1	(32¢+8¢)	Breast Cancer	30.00	❑ B2	(34¢+11¢)	Heroes of 2001	25.00

AIRMAIL

❑ C25	6¢	Transport	18.00	❑ C38	5¢	New York	32.00
❑ C26	8¢	Transport	18.00	❑ C39	6¢	DC-4	25.00
❑ C27	10¢	Transport	75.00	❑ C40	6¢	Alexandria	16.00
❑ C28	15¢	Transport	175.00	❑ C42	10¢	UPU	20.00
❑ C29	20¢	Transport	150.00	❑ C43	15¢	UPUI	28.00
❑ C30	30¢	Transport	150.00	❑ C44	25¢	UPUI	42.00
❑ C31	50¢	Transport	750.00	❑ C45	6¢	Wright Bros.	15.00
❑ C32	5¢	DC-4, large	15.00	❑ C46	80¢	Diamond Head	335.00
❑ C33	5¢	DC-4, small	18.00	❑ C47	6¢	Flight	16.00
❑ C34	10¢	Building	18.00	❑ C48	4¢	Eagle	16.00
❑ C35	15¢	N.Y. Skyline	30.00	❑ C49	6¢	Air Force	14.00
❑ C36	25¢	Golden Gate	60.00	❑ C50	5¢	Eagle	16.00

❑ C51	7¢	Jetliner, blue	22.00
❑ C53	7¢	Alaska	18.00
❑ C54	7¢	Balloon Jupiter	18.00
❑ C55	7¢	Hawaii	14.00
❑ C56	10¢	Pan Am Games	15.00
❑ C57	10¢	Liberty Bell	80.00
❑ C58	15¢	Statue of Liberty	35.00
❑ C59	25¢	Abraham Lincoln	35.00
❑ C60	7¢	Jetliner, carmine	25.00
❑ C62	13¢	Liberty Bell	25.00
❑ C63	15¢	Statue of Liberty	25.00
❑ C64	8¢	Jetliner-Capitol	25.00
❑ C66	15¢	Blair	35.00
❑ C67	6¢	Eagle	25.00
❑ C68	8¢	Amelia Earhart	25.00
❑ C69	8¢	Robert Goddard	25.00
❑ C70	8¢	Alaska Purchase	16.00
❑ C71	20¢	Columbia Jays	45.00
❑ C72	10¢	Runway of Stars	30.00
❑ C74	10¢	Biplane	18.00
❑ C75	20¢	USA & Jet	25.00
❑ C76	10¢	Moon Landing	18.00
❑ C77	9¢	Delta Wing	40.00
❑ C78	11¢	Jetliner	40.00
❑ C79	13¢	Winged Letter	40.00
❑ C80	17¢	Statue of Liberty	25.00
❑ C81	21¢	USA & Jet	35.00
❑ C84	11¢	City of Refugee	25.00
❑ C85	11¢	Skiers	20.00
❑ C86	11¢	Electronics	20.00
❑ C87	18¢	Statue of Liberty	25.00
❑ C88	26¢	Mt. Rushmore	42.00
❑ C89	25¢	Jetliner & Globes	42.00
❑ C90	31¢	Jetliner	50.00

❑ C91–92	31¢	Wright Bros.	125.00
❑ C93–94	21¢	Chanute	125.00
❑ C95–96	25¢	Post	175.00
❑ C97	31¢	High Jumper	60.00
❑ C98	40¢	Mazzei, perf 11	65.00
❑ C98A	40¢	Mazzei, perf 10½ x11½	55.00
❑ C99	28¢	Scott	65.00
❑ C100	35¢	Curtiss	50.00
❑ C101–4	28¢	Olympics	80.00
❑ C105–8	40¢	Olympics	80.00
❑ C109–12	35¢	Olympics	80.00
❑ C113	33¢	Verville	60.00
❑ C114	39¢	Sperry	65.00
❑ C115	44¢	Clipper	60.00
❑ C116	44¢	Serra	85.00
❑ C117	44¢	New Sweden	85.00
❑ C118	45¢	Langley	65.00
❑ C119	36¢	Sikorsky	55.00
❑ C120	45¢	French Revolution	50.00
❑ C121	45¢	Carved Figure	95.00
❑ C122–5	45¢	Space Travel	95.00
❑ C127	45¢	Tropical Beach	95.00
❑ C128	50¢	Quimby	95.00
❑ C129	40¢	Piper	95.00
❑ C130	50¢	Antarctic	95.00
❑ C131	50¢	Asia Crossing	95.00
❑ C132	40¢	Piper	100.00
❑ C133	48¢	Niagara Falls	25.00
❑ C134	40¢	Rio Grande	20.00
❑ C135	60¢	Grand Canyon	42.00
❑ C136	70¢	Nine Mile Prairie	42.00
❑ C137	80¢	Mount McKinley	42.00
❑ C138	60¢	Acadia National Park	25.00

SPECIAL DELIVERY

❑ E20	20¢	Letter, blue	40.00
❑ E21	30¢	Letter, maroon	40.00
❑ E22	45¢	Arrows	75.00
❑ E23	60¢	Arrows	80.00

CERTIFIED MAIL

❑ FA1	10¢	Letter Carrier	35.00

POSTAGE DUE

❑ J88	¼¢	Red & Black	400.00		❑ J97	10¢	Red & Black	40.00
❑ J89	1¢	Red & Black	14.00		❑ J98	30¢	Red & Black	120.00
❑ J90	2¢	Red & Black	14.00		❑ J99	50¢	Red & Black	125.00
❑ J91	3¢	Red & Black	15.00		❑ J100	$1	Red & Black	325.00
❑ J92	4¢	Red & Black	20.00		❑ J101	$5	Red & Black	1000.00
❑ J93	5¢	Red & Black	15.00		❑ J102	11¢	Red & Black	45.00
❑ J94	6¢	Red & Black	35.00		❑ J103	13¢	Red & Black	45.00
❑ J95	7¢	Red & Black	35.00		❑ J104	17¢	Red & Black	100.00
❑ J96	8¢	Red & Black	35.00					

OFFICIAL STAMPS

❑ O127	1¢	Great Seal	18.00		❑ O146	4¢	Great Seal	16.00
❑ O128	4¢	Great Seal	18.00		❑ O146A	10¢	Great Seal	25.00
❑ O129	13¢	Great Seal	45.00		❑ O147	19¢	Great Seal	65.00
❑ O130	17¢	Great Seal	65.00		❑ O148	23¢	Great Seal	75.00
❑ O132	$1	Great Seal	325.00		❑ O151	$1	Great Seal	450.00
❑ O133	$5	Great Seal	875.00		❑ O154	1¢	Great Seal	16.00
❑ O138	(14¢)	"D"	425.00		❑ O155	20¢	Great Seal	75.00
❑ O143	1¢	Great Seal	15.00		❑ O156	23¢	Great Seal	80.00

AMERICAN FIRST DAY COVERS
THE AMERICAN FIRST DAY COVER SOCIETY

The FIRST and ONLY not-for-profit, non-commercial, International Society devoted exclusively to First Day Covers and First Day Cover collecting.

FIRST DAYS IS THE AWARD-WINNING OFFICIAL PUBLICATION OF THE AMERICAN FIRST DAY COVER SOCIETY. FDC collecting is a hands-on hobby of personal involvement—much more than simple collecting. It encourages the individual collector to fully develop his range of interests so that his collection is a reflection of his personal tastes. FDCs will encourage your creativity to reach full expression by adapting cachets or cancellations or using combinations (related stamps). In this hobby uniqueness is the rule, not the exception.

BUT . . . *FIRST DAYS* IS AVAILABLE ONLY TO MEMBERS OF THE AFDCS. It's just ONE of the many benefits of membership. Whether you are interested in topical areas of collecting, working on serious research, or just learning more about the hobby in general, this is the organization for you.

AMERICAN FIRST DAY COVER SOCIETY

CHAPTERS

A complete list of all of the chapters of the American First Day Cover Society, along with names of the chapter representatives, is included in The Official Blackbook Price Guide to United States Postage Stamps. This list is found after this introduction to First Day Covers collecting and before the Glossary of First Day Cover Terms. If you see a chapter that meets in your area, or one that features the type of cover you collect, do not hesitate to contact the chapter representative for more information.

American First Day Cover Society chapters can be reached through the contact person listed, or you can contact the AFDCS chapter coordinator, Foster E. Miller, III, P.O. Box 44, Annapolis, MD 20701, e-mail: fmiller@pobox.net.

#1. Queen City Stamp & Cover Club: James Demos,
69 Liberty Corner Rd., Warren, NJ 07059

#2. Baltimore Philatelic Society, Inc.: Alice M. L. Robinson, 1224 N. Calvert St., Baltimore, MD 21202

#3. Motor City Stamp & Cover Club: Robert Quintero, 22608 Poplar Ct., Hazel Park, MI 48030

#4. ChicagoLand FDC Society: Randall Sherman, 1101 W. Columbia Ave. #212, Chicago, IL 60626

#5. W. Suburban Stamp Club of Plymouth: Editor, Newsletter,
P.O. Box 700049, Plymouth, MI 48170

#6. Harford County Stamp Club: Kenneth Rapple, P.O. Box 163, Bel Air, MD 21014

#7. Carroll County Philatelic Assoc.: Blair H. Law, 4510 Willow View St., Hampstead, MD 21074

#8. Robert C Graebner Chapter of AFDCS: Rollin Beiser, 13000 Evans, Ford Ct., Clifton, VA 20124

#9. Metropolitan FDC Society: Benjamin Green, 66-15 Thornton Pl, Rego Park, NY 11374

#10. FDC Collectors Club: Stephen Neulander, 951 Brookside Lane, Deerfield, IL 60015

#11. Coryell's Ferry Stamp Club: Mrs. Frank Davis, P.O. Box 52, Penns Park, PA 18943

#12. Ft. Findlay Stamp Club: Tom Foust, 5578 State Rt. 186, McComb, OH 45858

#13. Hazlet Stamp Club: Oscar Strandberg, 54 Crestview Dr, Middletown, NJ 07748

#14. Columbus Philatelic Club: Paul Gault, P.O. Box 20711, Columbus, OH 43220

#15. Autograph Chapter of AFDCS: George Haggas, P.O. Box 1463, Merchantville, NJ 08109

#17. Columbia Philatelic Society: Harold T. Babb, 341 Tram Rd., Columbia, SC 29210

#18. FDC Unit of Clifton Stamp Society: Andrew Boyajian, P.O. Box 229, Hasbrouck Heights, NJ 07604

#19. George Washington Masonic Stamp Club: Stan Longenecker, 930 Wood St., Mount Joy, PA 17552

#20. Hamilton Township Philatelic Society: John Ranto, 10 Cranbrook Rd., Hamilton, NJ 08690

#21. Joplin Stamp Club: Fred Roesel, 4225 East 25th St., Joplin, MO 64801

#22. Gulf Coast FDC Group: Monte Eiserman, 14359 Chadbourne, Houston, TX 77079

#23. Claude C. Ries Chapter of AFDCS: Rick Whyte, 2870 N. Town Ave., Apt. 137, Pomona, CA 91767

#24. The 7/1/71 Affair: Roy E. Mooney, P.O. Box 2539, Cleveland, GA 30528

#25. Central NY FDC Society: Rick Kase, P.O. Box 10833, Rochester, NY 14610

#26. Journalists, Authors and Poets on Stamps (JAPOS): Clete Delvaux, 1600 Rushwoods Ct., Green Bay, WI 59301

#27. Louisville FDC Society: Arthur S. Buchter, 5410 Cannonwood Ct., Louisville, KY 40229

#28. North Texas Chapter of AFDCS: Paul Benson, 201 Willow Creek Circle, Allen, TX 77079

#29. Long Island Cover and Autograph Society: Secretary LIC&AS, Box 2095, Port Washington, NY 11050

#30. American Ceremony Program Society: Monte Eiserman, 14359 Chadbourne, Houston, TX 77079

#31. Florida Chapter of AFDCS: George Athens, 3295 Datura Rd., Venice, FL 34293

#32. Ohio Cachetmakers Assoc.: Chris & Denise Lazaroff, 2967 Aylesbury St. NW, N. Canton, OH 44720

#33. Gateway to the West Chpt. of AFDCS: Art Rosenberg, 8686 Delmar Blvd., #2W, St. Louis, MO 63124

#35. Society of Philatelists & Numismatists: Joe R. Ramos, 1929 Millis St., Montebello, CA 90640

#36. Cachet Makers Assoc.: Chris Lazarolt, 2467 Aylesbury St., NW, N. Canton, OH 44720

#37. Maximum Card Study Unit: Gary Denis, P.O. Box 766, Patuxent River, MD 20670

#38. Rochester Philatelic Assoc.: Joe Doles, 105 Lawson Rd., Rochester, NY 14616

#39. Tucson Stamp Club: Alex Lutgendorf, P.O. Box 50603, Tucson, AZ 85703

#40. North Carolina Chapter of AFDCS: Eric Wile, 2202 Jane St., Greensboro, NC 27407

#41. Gay and Lesbian History on Stamps: Ed Centeno, P.O. Box 140942, Dallas, TX 75214

#42. Hand-Painted Cover Chapter of AFDCS: Alan Freedman, 48 Kent Rd., Hillsdale, NJ 07642

#43. Multnomah Children's Covers: Tommy Lee, 4572 Catalpa St., Los Angeles, CA 90032

#44. American Indian Philatelic Society: Dean Lilly, 5460 Margie Lane, Oak Forest, IL 60542

#45. Harry C. Ioor Chapter of AFDCS: Patrick Tudor, 920 N. Bolton Ave., Indianapolis, IN 46219

#46. Molly Pitcher Stamp Club: Gary Dubnik, 74 Cumberland Ave., Verona, NJ 07044

#47. National Duck Stamp Collectors Society: Secretary, P.O. Box 43, Harleysville, PA 19438

#48. Art Cover Exchange (ACE): Joseph Doles, 105 Lawson Rd., Rochester, NY 14616

#49. Waterbury Stamp Club: Laurent Corriveau, P.O. Box 581, Waterbury, CT 06720

#52. Dayton Stamp Club: Frank Shivly, 415 Far Hills Ave., Dayton, OH 45409

#53. Virtual Stamp Club: Lloyd de Vries, Box 561, Paramus, NJ 07653, e-mail: stamps@pobox.com

#54. Norwalk Stamp Club: Richard Hoffman, Box 267, Norwalk, CT 06856

#55. Junior Philatelists of America: Erik Thompsen, 25301 Emperial Drive, Eagle River, AK 99577

#56. American Society of Philatelic Pages and Panels: Gerald Blankenship, P.O. Box 475, Crosby, TX 77532

#57. Stamp Collector Club of Toledo: Frank Ellis, 1436 Abbott, Toledo, OH 43604

#58. U.S. Presidential Inaugural Philatelic Society: Ed Krohn, P.O. Box 357309, Gainesville, FL 32655

#59. Australian Society: Noei Almeida, P.O. Box 768, Dandenong 3173 Australia

#60. Ebony Society of Philatelic Events Reflection (ESPER): Eugene Robinson, 112–45 175th St., Jamaica, NY 11433

A GLOSSARY OF
FIRST DAY COVER TERMS

Compiled by FIRST DAYS Staff

Add-on—A cachet design added to a cover which was originally unca-cheted. An add-on cachet should be identified by maker and date so that it is clear that it is not contemporary with the cover. Unfortunately, many add-ons are not so identified.

Aerogramme—Postal stationery characterized by a single sheet which may be folded into an envelope, sealed, and then sent at a rate less than the airmail letter rate. Postage is usually but not always imprint-ed. Also known as aerogram.

AFDCS—American First Day Cover Society.

All-over cachet—A cachet design that covers most of or the entire face (front) of the envelope, as compared to one that occupies just the left side.

All-purpose cachet—A cachet with a general design that can be used for any stamp subject. It has no specific theme. Also, General Purpose.

Alternate cancel—Any First Day cancellation from the official First Day city, other than the official First Day of Issue postmarks supplied by the USPS. (These are sometimes referred to as semi-officials, or by the specific name of the cancel, such as plug, slogan, show, or ship cancels, etc.)

AMF—Air Mail Field. Found in many postmarks of postal facilities locat-ed in airports.

Autographed—An autographed envelope bears one or more signatures of individuals who are usually associated with the stamp. The auto-graph relationships may be the stamp subject, the designer, the local postmaster, dignitaries present at the dedication ceremony, etc. Authenticity and possible mechanical application of an autograph are significant considerations.

Auxiliary markings—Postal markings which are occasionally found on First Day Covers such as "Registered," "Insured," "Return to Sender," "Postage Due ——¢," etc.

B/4—Block of four stamps. Also B4.

Back stamp—The arrival mark of the destination city which usually appears on the reverse of the cover. Most registered covers are back-stamped on arrival.

Booklet pane—A sheetlet of stamps removed from a stamp booklet which may have one or more such panes. On FDC it is desirable to include the tab which is used to bind the pane into the booklet. This may not be possible with some modern issues.

Bullseye—also, bull's-eye. 1) The dial or circular portion of a postmark used by itself as a cancel. 2) Any circular postmark struck directly on the center of a stamp. (See Socked-on-the-nose.)

Cachet—Any textual or graphic design which has been applied to a cover usually, but not always, on the left side of the envelope. A cachet may be produced by any means—printed, rubber stamped, hand drawn, etc. A First Day cachet should be related specifically to the stamp on the cover.

Cachetmaker—One who designs and/or produces cacheted envelopes. Cachets may be identified by the artist's name, brand name, or manufacturing firm.

Cancel—The portion of a postmark which defaces or "kills" the stamp. Often loosely used interchangeably with "postmark."

CDS—Circular date stamp, ie. the dial or circular portion of the postmark.

Ceremony program—The printed program usually distributed by the Post Office or sponsoring organization at the First Day dedication of a new stamp. These are usually collected with the new stamp affixed and cancelled on the First Day.

Classic—The period prior to 1930 during which few First Day Covers were serviced and cachets were not common.

Coil—Stamps produced in rolls for use in vending machines. They are characterized by two opposite edges being straight or imperforate. A horizontal coil stamp is imperforate top and bottom and a vertical coil is straight-edged at the left and right sides.

Combo—One or more thematically related stamps affixed to a FDC. Also, combination cover.

Commemorative—A stamp, usually of large format, which is issued to salute or honor a person, event, state, organization, place, etc. Typically issued on an anniversary in a multiple of 10, 50, 100 years, etc. and produced in limited quantities. Contrasted with "definitive."

Commercial FDCs—FDCs sponsored by an individual, company, or organization used for promoting a service, product or as a gesture of goodwill.

Contract station—A sub-unit of a larger post office which is contracted to a private individual. Most contract stations are located in private business establishments.

Corner card—The imprint at the upper left corner of a cover which may be the return address or other identification of the sender.

Counterfeit—A stamp, postmark, or cachet created in direct imitation of a genuine item and intended to deceive. It is a Federal offense to counterfeit any postal marking or postal issue.

Cover—An envelope that has seen postal service or has a cancelled stamp on it, usually one with philatelic interest. May exemplify some segment of postal history or simply be a souvenir of an event or a place.

Crash cover—Any cover or FDC salvaged from the crash of a plane or vehicle in which it was carried. Usually bears postal markings explaining its damaged condition.

CXL—Abbreviation for "cancel." Also, cxl.

Definitive—Stamp issued for an indefinite period in an indefinite quantity to meet an ordinary postal rate. Designs do not usually honor a specific time dated event or person; most frequently in small format. Contrasted with "commemorative." Also known as "regular issue."

Designated First Day—The date officially announced by the Post Office for the sale of a new postal issue. Many issues prior to 1922 had no designated First Day. Covers cancelled prior to the designated dates are predates.

Dial—Circular portion of a postmark, usually containing the city, date and time. See bullseye.

Dual cancel—Two related or unrelated cancellations on a cover, each cancelling a stamp. One or both cancels may be for a First Day.

Duplex cancel—A metal handstamp containing both cancel and postmark in a single unit. Often found on FDCs before the mid-1930s.

EDC—Earliest documented cover. The earliest known postmark on a postal issue which had no designated First Day. Used interchangeably with EKU.

EFO—Errors, Freaks, and Oddities, i.e., stamps, cachets, cancellations, etc. that contain unintended mistakes or design faults.

EKU—Earliest known use. A designation for the earliest identified postmark on a stamp for which a first day of issue was not designated.

Electric eye (EE)—An electronic device which guides the perforating equipment during stamp manufacture. This is accomplished by heavy ink dashes in the selvage, which are used for detection and alignment. FDCs of EE stamps must have the selvage with dashes attached to the stamps.

Embossing—The process of impressing a design in relief into the paper of an envelope.

Engraved—A method of printing in which the lines of the design are cut into metal, which are recessed to retain the ink. The paper is forced under pressure into these lines to pick up the ink. Hence engraved cachets appear to have the design raised above the paper surface.

Error—A consistent abnormal variety created by a mistake in the production of a stamp or postmark. For example, the name of a city may be misspelled in the First Day cancel. Used in contrast to "freak."

Esoterica—Any item, other than a cover or envelope, that has been First Day cancelled that doesn't fit any of the regular collecting categories.

Event cover—A cacheted cover, not a FDC, prepared as a souvenir of a specific event or an anniversary of an event.

Event program—A list of events or speakers in any program related to the stamp release, such as a stamp show, any function at which a stamp is released, or any event honoring the same event as the stamp.

Fancy cancel—A cancellation which is or includes a design. The term is normally used for 19th-century cancels which were created by local postal officials according to personal whim. Also, see Pictorial.

Favor cancel—Any postal marking supplied as a favor or accommodation for a stamp collector.

FD—First Day.

FDC—First Day Cover. (FDCs—plural)

FDOI—First Day Of Issue. The slogan found in most First Day cancellations since Sc. 795, released in 1937.

FFC—First flight cover, ie. a cover flown on the inaugural flight of a new air route.

Filler—A stiff piece of paper, cardboard, or plastic found inside a First Day Cover. It provides necessary stiffness for a clearer cancellation. It also protects the cover from bending when it travels through the mail stream. Fillers, also termed stuffers, occasionally are imprinted with an advertising message or information pertaining to the stamp or cachet on the cover.

First cachet—The initial cachet commercially produced by a cachetmaker.

First Day—The day on which a stamp for the first time is officially sold by the Post Office.

First Day cover—Cover with a new stamp(s) or postal indicia, cancelled on the First Day.

Flag cancel—A cancellation used during the early 20th century incorporating a flag design. The stripes of the flag are the killer bars. Also, any more recent cancel with a similar design.

Flocked—A cachet production method in which powdered cloth is adhered to the envelope in the desired design.

Forgery—A fraudulently produced or altered philatelic item intended to deceive the collector.

Frank—A stamp, mark, or signature that shows payment of postage on a piece of mail. (A signature, with no stamp or paid marking, is called a Free Frank. Free as available to Congress and the President.)

Freak—An abnormal variety created by an unusual circumstance and not repeated with regularity. For example, a FDC may bear only a portion of a postmark because the cover was misfed into the cancelling machine. Used in contrast to "error."

General purpose (GP)—A cachet with a general design that is non-specific and may be used with any stamp subject. Also, All-purpose.

Hand cancel (HC)—A canceller which is applied to stamps individually and by hand. May be manufactured of plastic, rubber, or steel and is similar to a rubber stamp.

Hand-drawn (H/D)—A cachet applied to a cover by hand with pen, pencil, brush, chalk, or other art media. Each cachet is made individually and is an original.

Handmade (H/M)—A cachet applied to a cover by hand by adding seals, pasteups, collage, or similar materials. Each cachet is made individually and is an original.

Hand-painted (H/P) or Hand-colored (H/C)—A printed, hand-drawn or handmade cachet to which hand painting or hand coloring has been added.

HC, H/C, H/D, H/M, H/P—See preceding definitions.

HPO—Highway Post Office. The Post Office sorted mail on special motor vehicles in transit between cities. This system was in use from the late 1930s through the mid-1970s. FDCs were occasionally cancelled with HPO markings.

IA—Ink addressed. Refers to the method of addressing a cover.

Inaugural cover—A cover cancelled on the day that a president is sworn into office. Since 1957 the words INAUGURATION DAY have been incorporated into the cancel. The site was usually Washington, D.C., although other locations, like the President's city of birth, are now being designated. (In 1957 and 1985 the inauguration date fell on a Sunday. In both cases, covers of January 20, the private swearing-in ceremony, and January 21, the date of the public ceremony, both exist, and both are considered collectible.)

Indicia—An imprint on postal stationery indicating prepayment of postage. The plural is also "indicia."

Joint issue—Two or more stamps issued by different countries to commemorate the same event, topic, place, or person. Officially sanctioned joint issues are intentionally issued with the cooperation of the postal services of the countries involved.

Killer bars—The horizontal lines of a postmark which cancel the stamp. Since 1937 the FIRST DAY OF ISSUE slogan has appeared between the bars of most First Day cancels.

LA—Label addressed. Refers to the addressing method on a cover.

Last Day—The final day of a postal rate, post office operation, or similar occurrence. A cover cancelled on this day is referred to as a last day cover.

Lithography, or litho—A common method of printing stamps and cachets in which the design is transferred from a smooth plate by selective inks which wet only the design portion of the printing plate.

LL—Lower left. Refers to the plate number or marginal marking position on a sheet of stamps.

LR—Lower right. Refers to the marginal marking position.

LSASE—A legal-sized, stamped, self-addressed envelope. See SASE.

Luminescent—The condition of a stamp or postal stationery which has been treated with chemicals which are sensitive to and glow under ultraviolet (UV) light. This permits automatic cancelling equipment to detect the position of the postage on the cover and to orient it for rapid mechanical cancelling.

Machine cancel (MC)—A cancellation applied by an automatic cancelling device or machine.

Maximum card—A picture (post)card with a reproduction of the stamp or related subject from which the stamp was derived. Maximum card specialists prefer that the card and the stamp be as directly related as possible, but not be reproduced. The attempt is to achieve maximum agreement or concordance between the stamp subject and postcard. The stamp and cancel are usually placed on the illustrated side. This may be cancelled on the First Day of the stamp. See "Souvenir card."

Mellone catalog—A series of cachet catalogs for various time periods. They feature cachet illustrations with assigned code numbers for identification.

Mylar—Dupont's trademark for a durable plastic (polyester) film often recommended for storing stamps or covers because of its excellent chemical stability and the protection offered.

Nondenominated—Stamp or postal stationery without denomination or value in the design. These were created by the Post Office in anticipation of postal rate change when the exact rates could not be determined in advance.

Obliterator—Another term for the cancel portion of a postmark which defaces or obliterates the stamp.

OE—An abbreviation which indicates that a cover has been opened at the end or side.

Official—1) Of or related to the Federal government. USPS postmarks are official markings. 2) Stamps or stationery issued for use by government departments in the course of official business.

Official cachet—1) A cachet produced and applied by or for postal administrations. Official cachets are rare on U.S. FDCs but are common for many other countries. 2) Loosely used to refer to cachets authorized or sponsored by an organization closely associated with the issuance of a stamp, more properly called a sponsored cachet. The word "official" is abused by some cachetmakers.

Official FDC—Any First Day Cover with an official government postmark. This term is often misused for covers with sponsored cachets.

Offset—A printing method in which the design is transferred by ink from the image to another surface and then applied to the paper.

OT—An abbreviation indicating that a cover has been opened at the top.

PA—Pencil addressed. Refers to the method of cover addressing.

Patriotic or patriotic cachet—Design with patriotic or nationalistic theme, most often used to bolster public spirit during periods of war or national stress.

PB—Plate block. A group of stamps with the plate number in the selvage. May contain four or more stamps depending on the configuration of the printed numbers.

Peelable label—A self-stick label that can be easily removed from a cover without leaving adhesive or blemish. Used for addressing covers—later removed to create unaddressed covers.

Philatelic center—A post office window or station where most currently available stamps may be purchased by collectors. Created for the convenience of stamp collectors. Also postique.

Photocachet—A cachet consisting in part or entirely of a photograph.

Pictorial—A cancellation incorporating a pictorial design. Pictorial First Day cancels were used by the United States from 1958 to 1962 and are becoming more widespread on FDC issues of the 1980s and '90s. Many postiques each have a unique pictorial cancel. Many non-FD pictorial cancels are available nationwide, and are used for a limited time at special public or philatelic events.

Planty Catalogue—Catalog of U.S. cachets, for various year periods in individual volumes, assembled by Prof. Earl Planty. Planty identification designations are referred to as Planty Numbers.

Plug cancel—Colloquial name for a round, double circle marking, officially known as a validator stamp. The plug is chiefly used on postal receipts and registered envelopes. Also called a registry cancel or round-dater.

PNC—1) Plate Number Coil, ie. a coil stamp with a plate number thereon. 2) Philatelic-numismatic cover, ie. a cover with a cancelled stamp and a visible coin on the front, both thematically related. May be a FDC for the stamp.

POD—Post Office Department, the predecessor of the USPS. Also USPOD.

Polysleeve—Any of a variety of generally clear plastic sleeves, usually closed on two or three sides, to contain covers so they may be handled without soiling or damage.

Postage due—Stamps issued to indicate a penalty for insufficient postage. Postage due stamps are not used to pay postage, yet some issues are known on FDCs. These FDCs were cancelled inadvertently or by favor.

Postal card—A government produced postcard with an indicia indicating prepayment of postage.

Postal stationery—Postal cards, aerogrammes, and envelopes on which postage has been imprinted. Created as a convenience for the public so postage need not be applied.

Post-cancelled (post-dated, back-dated)—A cover which has been cancelled on a date later than that indicated on the postmark.

Postcard—A privately produced card usually bearing an illustration on one side and spaces for message, address, and postage on the other.

Postique—A special station or location at a post office where collectors may obtain currently available stamps. Each office usually has its own pictorial cancellation.

Postmark—A postal marking which indicates the time and point of origin of the mail to which it is applied. Often loosely used interchangeably with "Cancel."

PR—Pair of stamps.

Precancel—Stamps or stationery issued by the Post Office with words or lines printed thereon which prevent further use of the stamp. Precancelled stamps need not be cancelled again during mail handling. The standard First Day postmarks, however, are applied to FDCs of precancels.

Predate—A cover with a stamp cancelled earlier than the officially designated First Day of sale. Predates usually are created when stamps are sold prior to the official release date, contrary to postal regulations. Predates can exist only for issues with a designated First Day date.

Presentation album—Album containing a pane of a new stamp which is distributed to each dignitary at a First Day dedication ceremony. The album may have the recipient's name engraved on it. The first album is always for the President of the United States.

Presidentials—The 1938 series of definitive stamps featuring the Presidents of the United States.

Prexy—An information alternative term to designate the Presidential series of definitives.

Printed cachets—A cachet design type that is produced by printing, using any one of many methods.

Program—See Ceremony program.

Rag content—Pertains to the use of cotton fiber rather than wood pulp in the manufacture of envelopes. High rag content or 100 percent rag envelopes resist the ravages of time much better than do wood fiber covers, which contain processing chemicals that eventually discolor the paper and make the envelope more brittle.

Registry cancel—See Plug cancel.

Regular issue—Stamp issued for an indefinite period and quantity for ordinary postal use. See definitive.

RPO—Railway post office. A system once used by the POD to process mail in railroad cars enroute between cities. A distinctive cancel was used and FDCs exist with RPO postmarks.

RSA—Rubber-stamp addressed. A cover addressing method.

RSC—Rubber-stamp cachet.

Rubber stamps (R/S) cachet—A cachet applied to a cover using a rubber stamp. This method or device was very popular in the 1930s.

SASE—Self-addressed stamped envelope or SAE—self-addressed envelope. See also "LSASE."

Scott—Philatelic Publishing Company which produces Scott catalogs. A Scott (Sc.) number refers to a Scott catalog number to identify a stamp—a widely accepted practice.

Second-Day cover—A cover postmarked on the day following the First Day Of Issue. These were popular in the 1940s when the stamps were available at the Philatelic Agency in Washington, DC, on the second day.

Self-adhesive—A pre-gummed postage stamp on a peelable backing which requires no moisture for affixing to an envelope.

Selvage—The edges of a stamp pane beyond the perforations—including the portions that contain marginal markings as plate numbers, copyright notice, and other symbols/text. The plain selvage is usually removed from stamps when preparing FDCs, except for plate numbers and other collectible markings. Also spelled "selvedge."

Service—The act of affixing a stamp to and having it cancelled on a cover.

Servicer—One who performs the act of servicing. Frequently a person who does so on a commercial and large volume basis.

SGL—Single stamp. Also "sgl."

Ship cancel—A cancellation applied aboard a vessel—most frequently U.S. Navy although there are others. Ship cancels are fairly common but such strikes on FDCs are considered unusual because they represent a special effort in order to be obtained.

Show cancel—Special Post Office cancellation designed for and applied at a philatelic show or exhibition station.

Silk cachet—A cachet type with a pictorial design printed on a piece of fabric with a silky finish.

Slogan cancel—A cancellation with a message incorporated, such as—"Mail Early Before Christmas" or "Fight Tuberculosis."

Socked-on-the-nose (SOTN)—Designation for a stamp where the circle of the postmark falls exactly on the center. Another designation for "bullseye."

Souvenir card—A commemorative card, usually with reproductions of previously issued stamps and an inscription, issued by postal authorities in conjunction with a special philatelic event. The card or stamp units cannot be used for postal purposes but are often enhanced by collectors with an actual stamp and cancel.

Souvenir program—See Ceremony program.

Sponsor (cachet)—Individual or organization that has commissioned an established cachetmaker to prepare a special design in addition to the regular cachet for a particular issue. The term is sometimes used interchangeably with "cachetmaker."

Sponsored cachet—A cachet authorized or sponsored by an organization closely associated with the issuance of a stamp. See also "Official cachet," No. 2.

Station cancel—A cancellation applied at a temporary postal station established for a convention, exhibition, or other special event.

Stuffer—See Filler.

Tagged—Stamp or postal stationery which has had the postage area treated with a material sensitive to ultraviolet (UV) light, so that the cover can be mechanically oriented for canceling. Also luminescent.

Thermography—A printing method for producing raised designs by use of a special powder and heat. Often called, "poor man's embossing."

Tied—The cancellation overlaps the stamp, falling on both the postage and the cover thus affirming that the stamp was affixed prior to the postmarking. Also may be applied to non-postal labels or adhesives to show contemporaneous usage.

Toning—A deleterious condition of a cover resembling darkening or discoloration caused by excess gum at the edge of the stamp or a stain from the gum of the envelope flap. May also result from chemicals used in the production of inexpensive envelopes.

Trade name—A name or identification assigned to a cachet line by the producer. Example: Washington Press produces Artcraft Cachets.

UA—Unaddressed. A cover which does not have an address.

UL—Upper left. Refers to the position of stamp marginal markings.

Unaddressed (UA)—A cover which has no address.

Uncacheted—A cover which has no cachet design.

Unofficial cancel—A private, non-postal marking, usually resembling an official postmark, applied to a stamp or cover.

Unofficial FDC (UO)—A FDC cancelled with other than the official FIRST DAY OF ISSUE slogan cancel or official First Day pictorial cancelled supplied by the USPS for the First Day. For FDCs before the initial use of the FDOI slogan, this term refers to any city other than that which was officially designated. (There is much controversy among specialists and purists about this definition. Some dislike the use of the word "unofficial" as all postmarks are official cancellations of the USPS. Some would like to make a further distinction between stamps purchased in the official FD city, versus stamps sold in error on or before the FD in cities other than the FD city. Both of these are points well taken, but basically UOs are any FDC serviced in the city of issue or another location with any cancel other than the official FD cancel supplied by the USPS. A UO FDC must have the correct First Day date.)

UO—Unofficial First Day cover.

UR—Upper right. Refers to the position of the marginal markings on stamp selvage.

USPS—United States Postal Service, established in 1971.

Validator—See Plug.

FIRST DAY COVERS

NOTE: "D.C." indicates Washington, D.C., as the official city and date of issue. Other cities with significantly different values are also listed. When no city is indicated, the number of cities in which the stamps were issued is indicated.

Scott No.			Single	Block of 4
Uncacheted.				
❏ 551	½¢	Hale (D.C. & New Haven, CT, 4/4/25)	20.00	28.00
❏ 552	1¢	Franklin (D.C., 1/17/23)	25.00	45.00
❏ 552	1¢	Franklin (Philadelphia, PA)	55.00	60.00
❏ 553	1½¢	Harding (D.C., 3/19/25)	35.00	40.00
❏ 554	2¢	Washington (D.C., 1/15/23)	45.00	50.00
❏ 555	3¢	Lincoln (D.C., 2/12/23)	45.00	65.00
❏ 555	3¢	Lincoln (Hodgenville, KY)	200.00	350.00
❏ 556	4¢	Martha Washington (D.C., 1/15/23)	75.00	120.00
❏ 557	5¢	Roosevelt (D.C., 10/27/22)	120.00	180.00
❏ 557	5¢	Roosevelt (New York, NY)	275.00	425.00
❏ 557	5¢	Roosevelt (Oyster Bay, NY)	2000.00	—
❏ 558	6¢	Garfield (D.C., 11/20/22)	225.00	300.00
❏ 559	7¢	McKinley (D.C., 5/1/23)	195.00	255.00
❏ 559	7¢	McKinley (Niles, OH)	200.00	—
❏ 560	8¢	Grant (D.C., 5/1/23)	195.00	225.00
❏ 561	9¢	Jefferson (D.C., 1/15/23)	195.00	260.00
❏ 562	10¢	Monroe (D.C., 1/15/23)	175.00	260.00
❏ 563	11¢	Hayes (D.C., 10/4/22)	1000.00	3750.00
❏ 563	11¢	Hayes (Fremont, OH)	3200.00	—
❏ 564	12¢	Cleveland (D.C., Boston, MA, Caldwell, NJ, 3/20/23)	250.00	375.00
❏ 565	14¢	Indian (D.C., 5/1/23)	375.00	500.00
❏ 565	14¢	Indian (Muskogee, OK)	2500.00	6000.00
❏ 566	15¢	Statue of Liberty (D.C., 11/11/22)	550.00	850.00
❏ 567	20¢	Golden Gate (5/1/23)	600.00	1250.00
❏ 567	20¢	Golden Gate (San Francisco)	3750.00	—
❏ 568	25¢	Niagara Falls (D.C., 11/11/22)	650.00	1250.00
❏ 569	30¢	Bison (D.C., 3/20/23)	850.00	1500.00
❏ 570	50¢	Arlington (D.C., 11/11/22)	1600.00	—
❏ 571	$1	Lincoln Memorial (D.C., Springfield, IL 2/12/23)	8000.00	18,000.00
❏ 572	$2	U.S. Capitol (D.C., 3/20/23)	20,000.00	—

Scott No.			Single	Block of 4
❏ 573	$5	America (D.C., 3/20/23)	35000.00	—
❏ 576	1½¢	Harding (D.C., 4/4/25)	50.00	85.00
❏ 581	1¢	Franklin (D.C., 10/17/23)	725.00	—
❏ 582	1½¢	Harding (D.C., 3/19/25)	60.00	55.00
❏ 583a	2¢	Washington (booklet pane, D.C., 8/27/26)	1400.00	—
❏ 584	3¢	Lincoln (D.C., 8/1/25)	65.00	100.00
❏ 585	4¢	Martha Washington (D.C., 4/4/25)	65.00	100.00
❏ 586	5¢	Roosevelt (D.C., 4/4/25)	65.00	100.00
❏ 587	6¢	Garfield (D.C., 4/4/25)	65.00	100.00
❏ 588	7¢	McKinley (D.C., 5/29/26)	85.00	100.00
❏ 589	8¢	Grant (D.C., 5/29/26)	85.00	110.00
❏ 590	9¢	Jefferson (D.C., 5/29/26)	85.00	110.00
❏ 591	10¢	Monroe (D.C., 6/8/25)	100.00	150.00
❏ 597	1¢	Franklin (coil, D.C., 7/18/23)	750.00	—
❏ 598	1½¢	Harding (coil, D.C., 3/19/25)	500.00	—
❏ 599	2¢	Washington (coil, D.C., 1/15/23)	2800.00	—
❏ 600	3¢	Lincoln (coil, D.C., 5/10/24)	125.00	—
❏ 602	5¢	Roosevelt (coil, D.C., 3/5/24)	110.00	—
❏ 603	10¢	Monroe (coil, D.C., 2/1/24)	125.00	—
❏ 604	1¢	Franklin (coil, D.C., 7/19/24)	100.00	—
❏ 605	1½¢	Harding (coil, D.C., 5/9/25)	80.00	—
❏ 606	2¢	Washington (coil, D.C., 12/31/23)	150.00	—
❏ 610	2¢	Harding (D.C., Marion, OH 9/1/25)	40.00	60.00
❏ 611	2¢	Harding (imperf., D.C., 11/15/23)	140.00	165.00
❏ 612	2¢	Harding (perf. 10, D.C., 9/12/23)	140.00	165.00
❏ 614	1¢	Huguenot-Walloon (5/1/24)	50.00	70.00
❏ 615	2¢	Huguenot-Walloon (5/1/24)	50.00	75.00
❏ 616	5¢	Huguenot-Walloon (5/1/24)	75.00	125.00
❏ 614–616		Huguenot-Walloon, set on one cover (5/1/24),from any of the following cities: Albany, NY, Allentown, PA, Charleston, SC, Jacksonville, FL, Lancaster, PA, Mayport, FL, New Rochelle, NY, New York, NY, Philadelphia, PA, Reading, PA, and Washington, D.C.	150.00	—
❏ 617	1¢	Lexington-Concord (4/4/25)	40.00	65.00
❏ 618	2¢	Lexington-Concord (4/4/25)	40.00	65.00
❏ 619	5¢	Lexington-Concord (4/4/25)	70.00	100.00

Scott No.			Single	Block of 4
❏ 617–619		Lexington-Concord, set on one cover (4/4/25), from any of the following cities: Boston, MA, Cambridge, MA, Concord, MA, Lexington, MA, or Washington, D.C. Concord, MA sells for 25% more.	150.00	—
❏ 620	2¢	Norse-American (5/18/25)	20.00	50.00
❏ 621	5¢	Norse-American (5/18/25)	40.00	60.00
❏ 620–621		Norse-American, set on one cover (5/18/25) from any of the following cities: Angola, IN, Benson, MN, Decoran, IA, Minneapolis, MN, Northfield, MN, St. Paul, MN, or Washington, D.C.	60.00	100.00
❏ 622	13¢	Harrison	25.00	55.00
❏ 622	13¢	Harrison (Indianapolis, IN, 1/11/26)	25.00	55.00
❏ 622	13¢	Harrison (North Bend, OH, 1/11/26)	140.00	300.00
❏ 623	17¢	Wilson (New York, NY, Princeton, NJ, Staunton, VA, Washington, D.C., 12/28/25)	20.00	40.00
❏ 627	2¢	Sesquicentennial (Boston, MA, Philadelphia,PA, D.C., 5/10/26)	15.00	25.00
❏ 628	5¢	Erikson (Chicago, IL, Minneapolis, MN, New York, NY, D.C. 5/29/26)	22.00	25.00
❏ 629	2¢	White Plains (White Plains, NY, New York, NY, Philadelphia, PA Expo 10/18/26)	12.00	15.00
❏ 630	2¢	White Plains (complete sheet, 10/18/26)	1500.00	—
❏ 631	1½¢	Harding (D.C., 8/27/26)	55.00	75.00
❏ 632	1¢	Franklin (D.C., 6/10/27)	55.00	75.00
❏ 632a	1¢	Franklin booklet of 6 (D.C. 11/2/27)	3750.00	
❏ 633	1½¢	Harding (D.C., 5/17/27)	50.00	70.00
❏ 634	2¢	Washington (D.C., 12/10/26)	46.00	65.00
❏ 635	3¢	Lincoln (D.C., 2/3/27)	45.00	55.00
❏ 635a	3¢	Bright Violet (D.C., 2/7/34)	45.00	60.00
❏ 636	4¢	Martha Washington (D.C., 5/17/27)	45.00	65.00
❏ 637	5¢	Roosevelt (D.C., 3/24/27)	35.00	45.00
❏ 638	6¢	Garfield (D.C., 7/27/27)	45.00	60.00

Scott No.			Single	Block of 4
❑ 639	7¢	McKinley (D.C., 3/24/27)	45.00	50.00
❑ 640	8¢	Grant (D.C., 6/10/27)	50.00	75.00
❑ 641	9¢	Jefferson (D.C., 5/17/27)	60.00	50.00
❑ 642	10¢	Monroe (D.C., 2/3/27)	50.00	100.00
❑ 643	2¢	Vermont (Burlington, VT, D.C., 8/3/27)	14.00	18.00
❑ 644	2¢	Burgoyne (Albany, NY, Rome, NY, Syracuse, NY, Utica, NY, and D.C., 8/3/27)	14.00	18.00
❑ 645	2¢	Valley Forge (Cleveland Phil Sta., OH, Lancaster, PA, Norriston, PA, Philadelphia, PA, Valley Forge, PA, West Chester, PA, and D.C., 5/26/28)	5.00	8.00
❑ 646	2¢	Molly Pitcher (Freehold, NJ, Red Bank, NJ, D.C., 10/20/18)	6.00	15.00
❑ 647	2¢	Hawaii (Honolulu, HI, D.C., 8/13/28)	22.00	25.00
❑ 648	5¢	Hawaii (Honolulu, HI, D.C., 8/13/28)	22.00	—
❑ 647–648		Hawaii set on one cover (8/13/28)	40.00	65.00
❑ 649	2¢	Aero Conf. (D.C., 12/12/28)	8.00	12.00
❑ 650	5¢	Aero Conf. (D.C., 12/12/28)	10.00	14.00
❑ 649–650		Areo Conf. set on one cover (12/12/18)	12.00	20.00
❑ 651	2¢	Clark (Vincennes, IN, 2/25/29)	5.00	10.00
❑ 653	½¢	Hale (D.C., 5/25/29)	—	20.00
❑ 654	2¢	Electric Light (Menlopark, NJ, 6/5/29)	10.00	14.00
❑ 655	2¢	Electric Light (D.C., 6/11/29)	70.00	90.00
❑ 656	2¢	Electric Light (coil, 6/11/29)	125.00	—
❑ 657	2¢	Sullivan (16 different New York cities and D.C., 6/17/29)	4.00	8.00
❑ 658	1¢	Kansas (D.C., 5/1/29)	25.00	30.00
❑ 659	1½¢	Kansas (D.C., 5/1/29)	40.00	45.00
❑ 660	2¢	Kansas (D.C., 5/1/29)	40.00	45.00
❑ 661	3¢	Kansas (D.C., 5/1/29)	40.00	45.00
❑ 662	4¢	Kansas (D.C., 5/1/29)	65.00	85.00
❑ 663	5¢	Kansas (D.C., 5/1/29)	65.00	85.00
❑ 664	6¢	Kansas (D.C., 5/1/29)	150.00	100.00
❑ 665	7¢	Kansas (D.C., 5/1/29)	125.00	150.00
❑ 666	8¢	Kansas (D.C., 5/1/29)	125.00	150.00
❑ 667	9¢	Kansas (D.C., 5/1/29)	100.00	140.00
❑ 668	10¢	Kansas (D.C., 5/1/29)	100.00	140.00
❑ 658–668		Kansas set on one cover (D.C., 5/1/29)	1000.00	—

Scott No.			Single	Block of 4
❏ 669	1¢	Nebraska (D.C., 5/1/29)	50.00	60.00
❏ 670	1½¢	Nebraska (D.C., 5/1/29)	50.00	60.00
❏ 671	2¢	Nebraska (D.C., 5/1/29)	50.00	65.00
❏ 672	3¢	Nebraska (D.C., 5/1/29)	45.00	65.00
❏ 673	4¢	Nebraska (D.C., 5/1/29)	55.00	65.00
❏ 674	5¢	Nebraska (D.C., 5/1/29)	60.00	65.00
❏ 675	6¢	Nebraska (D.C., 5/1/29)	80.00	115.00
❏ 676	7¢	Nebraska (D.C., 5/1/29)	80.00	115.00
❏ 677	8¢	Nebraska (D.C., 5/1/29)	75.00	85.00
❏ 678	9¢	Nebraska (D.C., 5/1/29)	75.00	85.00
❏ 679	10¢	Nebraska (D.C., 5/1/29)	80.00	—
❏ 659–669		Nebraska set on one cover (D.C., 5/1/29)	1200.00	—
❏ 680	2¢	Fallen Timbers (5 cities 9/14/29)	5.00	10.00
❏ 681	2¢	Ohio River (7 cities 10/19/29)	5.00	10.00
❏ 682	2¢	Massachusetts Bay Colony (2 cities 4/8/30)	4.00	9.00
❏ 683	2¢	Carolina-Charleston (4/10/30)	4.00	9.00
❏ 684	1½¢	Harding Marion, OH(12/1/30)	7.00	9.00
❏ 685	4¢	Taft Cinncinnati, OH (6/4/30)	7.00	9.00
❏ 686	1½¢	Harding Marion, OH (coil, 12/1/30)	7.00	9.00
❏ 687	4¢	Taft (coil, D.C., 9/18/30)	30.00	—
❏ 688	2¢	Braddock (7/9/30)	6.00	9.00
❏ 689	2¢	Von Steuben	6.00	9.00
❏ 690	2¢	Pulaski (12 cities, 1/16/31)	6.00	9.00
❏ 692	11¢	Hayes (D.C., 9/4/31)	125.00	145.00
❏ 693	12¢	Cleveland (D.C., 8/25/31)	125.00	145.00
❏ 694	13¢	Harrison (D.C., 9/4/31)	125.00	145.00
❏ 695	14¢	Indian (D.C., 9/8/31)	125.00	145.00
❏ 696	15¢	Liberty (D.C., 8/27/31)	125.00	145.00
❏ 697	17¢	Wilson (D.C., 7/27/31)	150.00	145.00
❏ 698	20¢	Golden Gate (D.C., 9/8/31)	150.00	145.00
❏ 699	25¢	Niagara Falls (D.C., 7/27/31)	175.00	150.00
❏ 700	30¢	Bison (D.C., 9/8/31)	160.00	150.00
❏ 701	50¢	Arlington (D.C., 9/4/31)	250.00	300.00
❏ 702	2¢	Red Cross (2 cities 5/21/31)	6.00	9.00
❏ 703	2¢	Yorktown (2 cities, 10/19/31)	6.00	9.00
❏ 704	½¢	Olive Brown (D.C., 1/1/32)	—	9.00
❏ 705	1¢	Green (D.C., 1/1/32)	6.00	9.00

Scott No.			Single	Block of 4
❏ 706	1½¢	Brown (D.C., 1/1/32)	4.00	6.00
❏ 707	2¢	Carmine Rose (D.C., 1/1/32)	4.00	6.00
❏ 708	3¢	Deep Violet (D.C., 1/1/32)	4.00	6.00
❏ 709	4¢	Light Brown (D.C., 1/1/32)	4.00	6.00
❏ 710	5¢	Blue (D.C., 1/1/32)	4.00	6.00
❏ 711	6¢	Red Orange (D.C., 1/1/32)	4.00	6.00
❏ 712	7¢	Black (D.C., 1/1/32)	4.00	6.00
❏ 713	8¢	Olive Bistre (D.C., 1/1/32)	4.00	6.00
❏ 714	9¢	Pale Red (D.C., 1/1/32)	4.00	6.00
❏ 715	10¢	Orange Yellow (D.C., 1/1/32)	4.00	6.00
❏ 704–715		set on one cover	40.00	—
❏ 716	2¢	Olympic Winter Games (1/25/32)	4.00	5.25
❏ 717	2¢	Arbor Day (4/22/32)	4.00	5.25
❏ 718	3¢	Olympic Summer Games (6/15/32)	3.00	4.00
❏ 719	5¢	Olympic Summer Games (6/15/32)	5.00	6.00
❏ 718–719		Olympic Summer Games set on one cover	5.00	6.00
❏ 720	3¢	Washington (D.C., 6/16/32)	4.00	5.00
❏ 720b	3¢	Washington (booklet of 6, D.C., 7/25/32)	50.00	—
❏ 721	3¢	Washington (coil, D.C., 6/24/32)	5.25	—
❏ 722	3¢	Washington (coil, D.C., 10/12/32)	5.25	—
❏ 723	6¢	Garfield (coil, 8/18/32)	5.25	—
❏ 724	3¢	William Penn (3 cities, 10/24/32)	4.75	6.00
❏ 725	3¢	Daniel Webster (3 cities, 10/24/32)	4.75	6.00
❏ 726	3¢	Gen. Oglethorpe (2/12/32)	4.75	6.00
❏ 727	3¢	Peace Proclamation (4/19/32)	4.75	6.00
❏ 728	1¢	Century of Progress (5/25/32)	3.00	5.50
❏ 729	3¢	Century of Progress (5/25/32)	3.00	5.50
❏ 728–729		Century of Progress set on one cover	4.00	5.50
❏ 730	1¢	American Philatelic Society (full sheet)	80.00	—
❏ 730a	1¢	American Philatelic Society (8/25/33)	4.00	6.00
❏ 731	3¢	American Philatelic Society (full sheet)	85.00	—
❏ 731a	3¢	American Philatelic Society (8/25/33)	2.75	4.25
❏ 732	3¢	National Recovery Administration (D.C., 8/15/33)	2.75	4.25
❏ 733	3¢	Byrd Antarctic (D.C., 10/9/33)	5.00	8.00
❏ 734	5¢	Kosciuszko (6 cities, 10/13/33)	5.00	8.00
❏ 734	5¢	Kosciuszko (Pittsburg, PA)	5.00	6.00
❏ 735	3¢	National Exhibition (full sheet)	5.00	—

Scott No.			Single	Block of 4
❑ 735a	3¢	National Exhibition (2/10/34)	5.00	6.00
❑ 736	3¢	Maryland Tercentenary (3/23/34)	5.00	6.00
❑ 737	3¢	Mothers of America (D.C., 5/2/34)	5.00	6.00
❑ 738	3¢	Mothers of America (D.C., 5/2/34)	5.00	6.00
❑ 739	3¢	Wisconsin (7/9/34)	5.00	6.00
❑ 740	1¢	Parks, Yosemite (2 cities, 7/16/34)	5.00	6.00
❑ 741	2¢	Parks, Grand Canyon (2 cities, 7/24/34)	5.00	6.00
❑ 742	3¢	Parks, Mt. Rainier (2 cities, 8/3/34)	5.00	6.00
❑ 743	4¢	Parks, Mesa Verde (2 cities, 9/25/34)	5.00	6.00
❑ 744	5¢	Parks, Yellowstone (2 cities, 7/30/34)	5.00	6.00
❑ 745	6¢	Parks, Crater Lake (2 cities, 9/5/34)	5.00	6.00
❑ 746	7¢	Parks, Acadia (2 cities, 10/2/34)	5.00	6.00
❑ 747	8¢	Parks, Zion (2 cities, 9/18/34)	5.00	6.00
❑ 748	9¢	Parks, Glacier Park (2 cities, 8/27/34)	5.00	6.00
❑ 749	10¢	Parks, Smoky Mountains (2 cities, 10/8/34)	5.00	7.00
❑ 750	3¢	American Philatelic Society (full sheet)	38.00	—
❑ 750a	3¢	American Philatelic Society (8/28/34)	5.00	—
❑ 751	1¢	Trans-Mississippi Philatelic Expo, (full sheet)	25.00	—
❑ 751a	1¢	Trans-Mississippi Philatelic Expo. (10/10/34)	4.00	—
❑ 752	3¢	Peace Commemoration (D.C., 3/15/35)	7.00	8.00
❑ 753	3¢	Byrd (D.C., 3/15/35)	7.00	8.00
❑ 754	3¢	Mothers of America (D.C., 3/15/35)	7.00	8.00
❑ 755	3¢	Wisconsin (D.C., 3/15/35)	7.00	8.00
❑ 756	1¢	Parks, Yosemite (D.C., 3/15/35)	7.00	8.00
❑ 757	2¢	Parks, Grand Canyon (D.C., 3/15/35)	7.00	8.00
❑ 758	3¢	Parks, Mount Ranier (D.C., 3/15/35)	7.00	8.00
❑ 759	4¢	Parks, Mesa Verde (D.C., 3/15/35)	7.00	8.00
❑ 760	5¢	Parks, Yellowstone (D.C., 3/15/35)	7.00	8.00
❑ 761	6¢	Parks, Crater Lake (D.C., 3/15/35)	8.00	12.00
❑ 762	7¢	Parks, Acadia (D.C., 3/15/35)	8.00	12.00
❑ 763	8¢	Parks, Zion (D.C., 3/15/35)	8.00	12.00
❑ 764	9¢	Parks, Glacier Park (D.C., 3/15/35)	8.00	12.00
❑ 765	10¢	Parks, Smoky Mountains (D.C., 3/15/35)	8.00	12.00
❑ 766a	1¢	Century of Progress (D.C., 3/15/35)	8.00	12.00
❑ 767a	3¢	Century of Progress (D.C., 3/15/35)	8.00	12.00
❑ 768a	3¢	Byrd (D.C., 3/15/35)	8.00	12.00
❑ 769a	1¢	Parks, Yosemite (D.C., 3/15/35)	8.00	12.00

Scott No.			Single	Block of 4
❏ 770a	3¢	Parks, Mount Ranier (D.C., 3/15/35)	6.00	10.00
❏ 771	16¢	Airmail, special delivery (D.C., 3/15/35)	6.00	10.00

Cacheted Covers.

NOTE: For dates of issue, see **Uncacheted Covers** above.

❏ 610	2¢	Harding	800.00	—
❏ 617	1¢	Lexington-Concord	140.00	—
❏ 618	2¢	Lexington-Concord	140.00	—
❏ 619	5¢	Lexington-Concord	225.00	—
❏ 620–621		Norse American set on one cover	225.00	
❏ 623	17¢	Wilson	300.00	—
❏ 627	2¢	Sesquicentennial	80.00	—
❏ 628	5¢	Erikson	400.00	—
❏ 629	2¢	White Plains	75.00	—
❏ 630	2¢	White Plains (souvenir sheet) single	75.00	—
❏ 635a	3¢	Bright Violet	50.00	—
❏ 643	2¢	Vermont	50.00	100.00
❏ 644	2¢	Burgoyne	55.00	85.00
❏ 645	2¢	Valley Forge	50.00	75.00
❏ 646	2¢	Molly Pitcher	100.00	—
❏ 647	2¢	Hawaii	65.00	85.00
❏ 648	5¢	Hawaii	75.00	95.00
❏ 647–648		Hawaii set on one cover	125.00	—
❏ 649	2¢	Aero Conf.	60.00	85.00
❏ 650	5¢	Aero Conf.	60.00	60.00
❏ 649–650		Aero Conf. set on one cover	65.00	—
❏ 651	2¢	Clark	35.00	50.00
❏ 654	2¢	Electric Light	35.00	50.00
❏ 655	2¢	Electric Light	140.00	—
❏ 656	2¢	Electric Light (coil)	240.00	—
❏ 657	2¢	Sullivan, Auburn N.Y.	50.00	60.00
❏ 680	2¢	Fallen Timbers	50.00	60.00
❏ 681	2¢	Ohio River	50.00	60.00
❏ 682	2¢	Massachusetts Bay Colony	50.00	60.00
❏ 683	2¢	California-Charleston	50.00	60.00
❏ 684	1½¢	Harding	50.00	60.00
❏ 685	4¢	Taft	55.00	80.00
❏ 686	1½¢	Harding (coil)	55.00	80.00
❏ 687	4¢	Taft (coil)	85.00	100.00

Scott No.			Single	Block of 4
❏ 688	2¢	Braddock	45.00	50.00
❏ 689	2¢	Von Steuben	45.00	50.00
❏ 690	2¢	Pulaski	45.00	50.00
❏ 702	2¢	Red Cross	45.00	50.00
❏ 703	2¢	Yorktown	45.00	50.00
❏ 704	½¢	Olive Brown	20.00	30.00
❏ 705	1¢	Green	20.00	30.00
❏ 706	1½¢	Brown	20.00	30.00
❏ 707	2¢	Carmine Rose	20.00	30.00
❏ 708	3¢	Deep Violet	20.00	30.00
❏ 709	4¢	Light Brown	20.00	30.00
❏ 710	5¢	Blue	20.00	30.00
❏ 711	6¢	Red Orange	20.00	30.00
❏ 712	7¢	Black	20.00	30.00
❏ 713	8¢	Olive Bistre	20.00	30.00
❏ 714	9¢	Pale Red	20.00	30.00
❏ 715	10¢	Orange Yellow	20.00	30.00
❏ 704–715		Set on one cover	165.00	—
❏ 716	2¢	Olympic Winter Games	32.00	45.00
❏ 717	2¢	Arbor Day	32.00	45.00
❏ 718	3¢	Olympic Summer Games	32.00	45.00
❏ 719	5¢	Olympic Summer Games	32.00	45.00
❏ 718–719		Set on one cover	32.00	45.00
❏ 720	3¢	Washington	35.00	45.00
❏ 720b	3¢	Booklet pane of 6	180.00	—
❏ 721	3¢	Washington (coil)	45.00	—
❏ 722	3¢	Washington (coil)	45.00	—
❏ 723	6¢	Garfield (coil)	50.00	—
❏ 724	3¢	William Penn	28.00	35.00
❏ 725	3¢	Daniel Webster	28.00	35.00
❏ 726	3¢	Gen. Oglethorpe	28.00	35.00
❏ 727	3¢	Peace Proclamation	28.00	35.00
❏ 728	1¢	Century of Progress	28.00	35.00
❏ 729	3¢	Century of Progress	16.00	22.00
❏ 730	1¢	American Philatelic Society (full sheet)	150.00	—
❏ 730a	1¢	American Philatelic Society (single)	25.00	35.00
❏ 731	3¢	American Philatelic Society (full sheet)	160.00	—
❏ 731a	3¢	American Philatelic Society (single)	20.00	20.00
❏ 732	3¢	National Recovery Administration	20.00	35.00
❏ 733	3¢	Byrd Antarctic	30.00	35.00

Scott No.			Single	Block of 4
❏ 734	5¢	Kosciuszko	20.00	30.00
❏ 734b	5¢	Kosciuszko (Pittsburgh, PA)	50.00	60.00
❏ 735	3¢	National Exhibition (full sheet)	50.00	—
❏ 735a	3¢	National Exhibition (single)	18.00	—
❏ 736	3¢	Maryland Tercentenary	20.00	.30.00
❏ 737	3¢	Mothers of America	20.00	30.00
❏ 738	3¢	Mothers of America	20.00	30.00
❏ 739	2¢	Wisconsin	20.00	30.00
❏ 740	1¢	Parks, Yosemite	20.00	30.00
❏ 741	2¢	Parks, Grand Canyon	20.00	30.00
❏ 742	3¢	Parks, Mt. Ranier	20.00	30.00
❏ 743	4¢	Parks, Mesa Verde	20.00	30.00
❏ 744	5¢	Parks, Yellowstone	20.00	30.00
❏ 745	6¢	Parks, Crater Lake	18.00	25.00
❏ 746	7¢	Parks, Acadia	18.00	25.00
❏ 747	8¢	Parks, Zion	18.00	25.00
❏ 748	9¢	Parks, Glacier Park	18.00	25.00
❏ 749	10¢	Parks, Smoky Mountains	18.00	25.00
❏ 750	3¢	American Philatelic Society (full sheet)	50.00	—
❏ 750a	3¢	American Philatelic Society (single)	18.00	25.00
❏ 751	1¢	Trans-Mississippi Expo. (full sheet)	40.00	—
❏ 751a	1¢	Trans-Mississippi Expo. (single)	12.00	16.00
❏ 752	3¢	Peace Commemoration	35.00	45.00
❏ 753	3¢	Byrd	35.00	45.00
❏ 754	3¢	Mothers of America	35.00	45.00
❏ 755	3¢	Wisconsin Tercentenary	35.00	45.00
❏ 756	1¢	Parks, Yosemite	35.00	45.00
❏ 757	2¢	Parks, Grand Canyon	35.00	45.00
❏ 758	3¢	Parks, Mount Rainier	35.00	45.00
❏ 759	4¢	Parks, Mesa Verde	35.00	45.00
❏ 760	5¢	Parks, Yellowstone	35.00	45.00
❏ 761	6¢	Parks, Crater Lake	35.00	45.00
❏ 762	7¢	Parks, Acadia	35.00	45.00
❏ 763	8¢	Parks, Zion	35.00	45.00
❏ 764	9¢	Parks, Glacier Park	35.00	45.00
❏ 765	10¢	Parks, Smoky Mountains	35.00	45.00
❏ 766a	1¢	Century of Progress	45.00	60.00
❏ 767a	3¢	Century of Progress	45.00	60.00
❏ 768a	3¢	Byrd	45.00	60.00
❏ 769a	1¢	Parks, Yosemite	45.00	60.00

Scott No.			Single	Block of 4
☐ 770a	3¢	Parks, Mount Rainier	42.00	65.00
☐ 771	16¢	Airmail, special delivery	42.00	65.00

Scott No.			Single	Block	Plate Block
☐ 772	3¢	Connecticut Tercentenary	8.00	15.00	24.00
☐ 773	3¢	California Exposition	8.00	15.00	24.00
☐ 774	3¢	Boulder Dam	9.00	15.00	24.00
☐ 775	3¢	Michigan Centenary	9.00	15.00	24.00
☐ 776	3¢	Texas Centennial	10.00	15.00	24.00
☐ 777	3¢	Rhode Island Tercentenary	8.00	15.00	24.00
☐ 778	3¢	TIPEX	6.00	15.00	—
☐ 782	3¢	Arkansas Centennial	8.00	15.00	24.00
☐ 783	3¢	Oregon Territory	8.00	15.00	24.00
☐ 784	3¢	Susan B. Anthony	8.00	15.00	24.00
☐ 785	1¢	Army	5.00	12.00	22.00
☐ 786	2¢	Army	8.00	12.00	22.00
☐ 787	3¢	Army	8.00	12.00	22.00
☐ 788	4¢	Army	8.00	12.00	22.00
☐ 789	5¢	Army	8.00	12.00	22.00
☐ 790	1¢	Navy	8.00	12.00	22.00
☐ 791	2¢	Navy	8.00	12.00	22.00
☐ 792	3¢	Navy	8.00	12.00	22.00
☐ 793	4¢	Navy	8.00	12.00	22.00
☐ 794	5¢	Navy	8.00	12.00	22.00
☐ 795	3¢	Ordinance of 1787	8.00	9.00	15.00
☐ 796	5¢	Virginia Dare	8.00	9.00	15.00
☐ 797	10¢	Souvenir Sheet	8.00	—	—
☐ 798	3¢	Constitution	8.00	10.00	16.00
☐ 799	3¢	Hawaii	8.00	10.00	16.00
☐ 800	3¢	Alaska	8.00	10.00	16.00
☐ 801	3¢	Puerto Rico	8.00	10.00	16.00
☐ 802	3¢	Virgin Islands	8.00	10.00	16.00
☐ 803	½¢	Franklin	6.00	8.00	14.00
☐ 804	1¢	Washington	6.00	8.00	14.00
☐ 805	1½¢	Martha Washington	6.00	8.00	14.00
☐ 806	2¢	Adams	6.00	8.00	14.00
☐ 807	3¢	Jefferson	6.00	8.00	14.00

NOTE: Beginning with No. 795, first day covers bear the slogan cancellation "First Day Issue."

Scott No.			Single	Block	Plate Block
❑ 808	4¢	Madison	5.00	7.00	12.00
❑ 809	4½¢	White House	5.00	7.00	12.00
❑ 810	5¢	Monroe	5.00	7.00	12.00
❑ 811	6¢	Adams	5.00	7.00	12.00
❑ 812	7¢	Jackson	5.00	7.00	12.00
❑ 813	8¢	VanBuren	5.00	7.00	12.00
❑ 814	9¢	Harrison	5.00	7.00	12.00
❑ 815	10¢	Tyler	5.00	7.00	15.00
❑ 816	11¢	Polk	5.00	8.00	15.00
❑ 817	12¢	Taylor	5.00	8.00	15.00
❑ 818	13¢	Fillmore	5.00	8.00	15.00
❑ 819	14¢	Pierce	5.00	8.00	15.00
❑ 820	15¢	Buchanan	5.00	8.00	15.00
❑ 821	16¢	Lincoln	5.00	8.00	15.00
❑ 822	17¢	Johnson	6.00	8.00	14.00
❑ 823	18¢	Grant	6.00	8.00	14.00
❑ 824	19¢	Hayes	6.00	8.00	14.00
❑ 825	20¢	Garfield	6.00	8.00	14.00
❑ 826	21¢	Arthur	6.00	8.00	14.00
❑ 827	22¢	Cleveland	6.00	8.00	14.00
❑ 828	24¢	Harrison	6.00	8.00	14.00
❑ 829	25¢	McKinley	6.00	8.00	14.00
❑ 830	30¢	Roosevelt	6.00	10.00	14.00
❑ 831	50¢	Taft	12.00	18.00	25.00
❑ 832	$1	Wilson	40.00	80.00	125.00
❑ 832c	$1	Wilson	20.00	30.00	50.00
❑ 833	$2	Harding	110.00	150.00	225.00
❑ 834	$5	Coolidge	210.00	300.00	500.00
❑ 835	3¢	Constitution	8.00	15.00	20.00
❑ 836	3¢	Swedes and Finns	8.00	15.00	20.00
❑ 837	3¢	Northwest Sesquicentennial	8.00	15.00	20.00
❑ 838	3¢	Iowa	8.00	15.00	20.00
❑ 852	3¢	Golden Gate Expo	8.00	15.00	20.00
❑ 853	3¢	N.Y. World's Fair	8.00	15.00	20.00
❑ 854	3¢	Washington Inauguration	8.00	15.00	20.00
❑ 855	3¢	Baseball Centennial	20.00	30.00	45.00
❑ 856	3¢	Panama Canal	6.00	20.00	15.00
❑ 857	3¢	Printing Tercentenary	6.00	20.00	15.00
❑ 858	3¢	50th Statehood Anniversary	6.00	8.00	15.00
❑ 859	1¢	Washington Irving	4.00	6.00	8.00

Scott No.			Single	Block	Plate Block
❏ 860	2¢	James Fenimore Cooper	6.00	7.00	12.00
❏ 861	3¢	Ralph Waldo Emerson	6.00	7.00	12.00
❏ 862	5¢	Louisa May Alcott	6.00	7.00	12.00
❏ 863	10¢	Samuel L. Clemens	7.00	10.00	22.00
❏ 864	1¢	Henry W. Longfellow	4.00	5.00	14.00
❏ 865	2¢	John Greenleaf Whittier	4.00	5.00	14.00
❏ 866	3¢	James Russell Lowell	4.00	5.00	14.00
❏ 867	5¢	Walt Whitman	4.00	6.00	14.00
❏ 868	10¢	James Whitcomb Riley	6.00	6.00	20.00
❏ 869	1¢	Horace Mann	5.00	7.00	12.00
❏ 870	2¢	Mark Hopkins	5.00	7.00	12.00
❏ 871	3¢	Charles W. Eliot	5.00	7.00	12.00
❏ 872	5¢	Frances E. Willard	4.00	8.00	12.00
❏ 873	10¢	Booker T. Washington	8.00	12.00	25.00
❏ 874	1¢	John James Audubon	4.00	6.00	14.00
❏ 875	2¢	Dr. Crawford W. Long	4.00	6.00	14.00
❏ 876	3¢	Luther Burbank	4.00	6.00	14.00
❏ 877	5¢	Dr. Walter Reed	4.00	6.00	12.00
❏ 878	10¢	Jane Addams	5.00	10.00	20.00
❏ 879	1¢	Stephen Collins Foster	5.00	8.00	12.00
❏ 880	2¢	John Philip Sousa	5.00	8.00	12.00
❏ 881	3¢	Victor Herbert	5.00	8.00	12.00
❏ 882	5¢	Edward A. MacDowell	4.00	6.00	12.00
❏ 883	10¢	Ethelbert Nevin	7.00	10.00	20.00
❏ 884	1¢	Gilbert Charles Stuart	4.00	5.00	10.00
❏ 885	2¢	James A. McNeill Whistler	4.00	5.00	10.00
❏ 886	3¢	Augustus Saint-Gaudens	4.00	5.00	10.00
❏ 887	5¢	Daniel Chester French	4.00	5.00	14.00
❏ 888	10¢	Frederic Remington	6.00	8.00	20.00
❏ 889	1¢	Eli Whitney	5.00	8.00	15.00
❏ 890	2¢	Samuel F.B. Morse	5.00	8.00	15.00
❏ 891	3¢	Cyrus Hall McCormick	5.00	8.00	15.00
❏ 892	5¢	Elias Howe	4.00	8.00	20.00
❏ 893	10¢	Alexander Graham Bell	7.00	10.00	35.00
❏ 894	3¢	Pony Express	6.50	10.00	15.00
❏ 895	3¢	Pan American Union	6.50	10.00	15.00
❏ 896	3¢	Idaho Statehood	6.50	10.00	15.00
❏ 897	3¢	Wyoming Statehood	6.50	10.00	15.00
❏ 898	3¢	Coronado Expedition	6.50	10.00	15.00
❏ 899	1¢	Defense	6.50	10.00	15.00

Scott No.			Single	Block	Plate Block
❑ 900	2¢	Defense	7.00	8.00	16.00
❑ 901	3¢	Defense	7.00	8.00	16.00
❑ 899-901		Defense set on one cover	8.00	10.00	—
❑ 902	3¢	Thirteenth Amendment	8.00	10.00	16.00
❑ 903	3¢	Vermont Statehood	8.00	10.00	16.00
❑ 904	3¢	Kentucky Statehood	5.00	6.00	12.00
❑ 905	3¢	"Win the War"	5.00	8.00	12.00
❑ 906	5¢	Chinese Commemorative	8.00	12.00	18.00
❑ 907	2¢	United Nations	5.00	7.00	10.00
❑ 908	1¢	Four Freedoms	7.00	10.00	14.00
❑ 909	5¢	Poland	7.00	10.00	14.00
❑ 910	5¢	Czechoslovakia	7.00	10.00	14.00
❑ 911	5¢	Norway	7.00	10.00	14.00
❑ 912	5¢	Luxembourg	7.00	10.00	14.00
❑ 913	5¢	Netherlands	7.00	10.00	14.00
❑ 914	5¢	Belgium	7.00	10.00	14.00
❑ 915	5¢	France	7.00	10.00	14.00
❑ 916	5¢	Greece	7.00	10.00	14.00
❑ 917	5¢	Yugoslavia	7.00	10.00	14.00
❑ 918	5¢	Albania	7.00	10.00	14.00
❑ 919	5¢	Austria	7.00	10.00	14.00
❑ 920	5¢	Denmark	7.00	10.00	14.00
❑ 921	5¢	Korea	7.00	10.00	14.00
❑ 922	3¢	Railroad	7.00	10.00	10.00
❑ 923	3¢	Steamship	7.00	10.00	14.00
❑ 924	3¢	Telegraph	7.00	10.00	14.00
❑ 925	3¢	Philippines	7.00	10.00	12.00
❑ 926	3¢	Motion Picture	7.00	10.00	12.00
❑ 927	3¢	Florida	7.00	10.00	12.00
❑ 928	5¢	United Nations Conference	7.00	10.00	12.00
❑ 929	3¢	Iwo Jima	11.00	15.00	20.00
❑ 929, 934–936		Set on one cover	9.00	—	—
❑ 930	1¢	Roosevelt	5.00	8.00	12.00
❑ 931	2¢	Roosevelt	5.00	8.00	12.00
❑ 932	3¢	Roosevelt	5.00	8.00	12.00
❑ 933	5¢	Roosevelt	5.00	8.00	12.00
❑ 930–933		Roosevelt set on one cover	5.00	8.00	8.00
❑ 934	3¢	Army	5.00	8.00	8.00
❑ 935	3¢	Navy	5.00	8.00	8.00
❑ 936	3¢	Coast Guard	5.00	8.00	8.00

Scott No.			Single	Block	Plate Block
❏ 937	3¢	Alfred E. Smith	4.00	5.00	8.00
❏ 938	3¢	Texas	5.00	7.00	12.00
❏ 939	3¢	Merchant Marine	5.00	7.00	12.00
❏ 940	3¢	Honorable Discharge	5.00	7.00	12.00
❏ 941	3¢	Tennessee	5.00	7.00	11.00
❏ 942	3¢	Iowa	5.00	7.00	11.00
❏ 943	3¢	Smithsonian	5.00	7.00	11.00
❏ 944	3¢	Santa Fe	5.00	7.00	11.00
❏ 945	3¢	Thomas A. Edison	5.00	7.00	11.00
❏ 946	3¢	Joseph Pulitzer	5.00	7.00	11.00
❏ 947	3¢	Stamp Centenary	5.00	7.00	11.00
❏ 948	5¢,10¢	Centenary Exhibition Sheet	5.00	7.00	11.00
❏ 949	3¢	Doctors	5.00	7.00	11.00
❏ 950	3¢	Utah	5.00	7.00	11.00
❏ 951	3¢	"Constitution"	5.00	7.00	11.00
❏ 952	3¢	Everglades Park	5.00	7.00	11.00
❏ 953	3¢	Carver	5.00	7.00	11.00
❏ 954	3¢	California Gold	4.00	6.00	8.00
❏ 955	3¢	Mississippi Territory	4.00	6.00	8.00
❏ 956	3¢	Four Chaplains	4.00	6.00	8.00
❏ 957	3¢	Wisconsin Centennial	4.00	6.00	8.00
❏ 958	5¢	Swedish Pioneers	4.00	6.00	8.00
❏ 959	3¢	Women's Progress	4.00	6.00	8.00
❏ 960	3¢	William Allen White	4.00	6.00	8.00
❏ 961	3¢	U.S.-Canada Friendship	4.00	6.00	8.00
❏ 962	3¢	Francis Scott Key	4.00	6.00	8.00
❏ 963	3¢	Salute to Youth	4.00	6.00	8.00
❏ 964	3¢	Oregon Territory	4.00	6.00	8.00
❏ 965	3¢	Harlan Fiske Stone	4.00	6.00	8.00
❏ 966	3¢	Palomar Observatory	4.00	6.00	8.00
❏ 967	3¢	Clara Barton	4.00	6.00	8.00
❏ 968	3¢	Poultry Industry	4.00	6.00	8.00
❏ 969	3¢	Gold Star Mothers	4.00	6.00	8.00
❏ 970	3¢	Volunteer Fireman	4.00	8.00	12.00
❏ 971	3¢	Ft. Kearney, Nebraska	4.00	6.00	8.00
❏ 972	3¢	Indian Centennial	4.00	6.00	8.00
❏ 973	3¢	Rough Riders	4.00	6.00	8.00
❏ 974	3¢	Juliette Low	4.00	7.00	10.00
❏ 975	3¢	Will Rogers	4.00	6.00	8.00
❏ 976	3¢	Fort Bliss	4.00	6.00	8.00

Scott No.			Single	Block	Plate Block
❑ 977	3¢	Moina Michael	4.00	5.00	8.00
❑ 978	3¢	Gettysburg Address	4.00	8.00	8.00
❑ 979	3¢	American Turners Society	4.00	5.00	8.00
❑ 980	3¢	Joel Chandler Harris	4.00	5.00	8.00
❑ 981	3¢	Minnesota Territory	4.00	5.00	8.00
❑ 982	3¢	Washington and Lee University	4.00	5.00	8.00
❑ 983	3¢	Puerto Rico Election	4.00	5.00	8.00
❑ 984	3¢	Annapolis, Md.	4.00	5.00	8.00
❑ 985	3¢	G.A.R.	4.00	5.00	8.00
❑ 986	3¢	Edgar Allan Poe	4.00	5.00	8.00
❑ 987	3¢	American Bankers Association	4.00	5.00	8.00
❑ 988	3¢	Samuel Gompers	4.00	5.00	8.00
❑ 989	3¢	Freedom Statue	4.00	5.00	8.00
❑ 990	3¢	Executive	4.00	5.00	8.00
❑ 991	3¢	Judicial	4.00	5.00	8.00
❑ 992	3¢	Legislative	4.00	5.00	8.00
❑ 989–992		Capital set on one cover	4.00	5.00	8.00
❑ 993	3¢	Railroad Engineers	4.00	5.00	8.00
❑ 994	3¢	Kansas City Centenary	4.00	5.00	8.00
❑ 995	3¢	Boy Scout	4.00	8.00	12.00
❑ 996	3¢	Indiana Ter. Sesquicentennial	4.00	6.00	8.00
❑ 997	3¢	California Statehood	4.00	6.00	8.00
❑ 998	3¢	United Confederate Veterans	4.00	6.00	8.00
❑ 999	3¢	Nevada Centennial	4.00	6.00	8.00
❑ 1000	3¢	Landing of Cadillac	4.00	6.00	8.00
❑ 1001	3¢	Colorado Statehood	4.00	6.00	8.00
❑ 1002	3¢	American Chemical Society	4.00	6.00	8.00
❑ 1003	3¢	Battle of Brooklyn	4.00	6.00	8.00
❑ 1004	3¢	Betsy Ross	4.00	6.00	8.00
❑ 1005	3¢	4-H Clubs	4.00	6.00	8.00
❑ 1006	3¢	B & O Railroad	4.00	6.00	8.00
❑ 1007	3¢	American Automobile Assoc.	4.00	6.00	8.00
❑ 1008	3¢	NATO	4.00	6.00	8.00
❑ 1009	3¢	Grand Coulee Dam	4.00	6.00	8.00
❑ 1010	3¢	Lafayette	4.00	6.00	8.00
❑ 1011	3¢	Mt. Rushmore Memorial	4.00	6.00	8.00
❑ 1012	3¢	Civil Engineers	4.00	6.00	8.00
❑ 1013	3¢	Service Women	4.00	6.00	8.00
❑ 1014	3¢	Gutenberg Bible	4.00	6.00	8.00
❑ 1015	3¢	Newspaper Boys	4.00	6.00	8.00

Scott No.			Single	Block	Plate Block
❏ 1016	3¢	Red Cross	4.00	6.00	8.00
❏ 1017	3¢	National Guard	4.00	6.00	8.00
❏ 1018	3¢	Ohio Sesquicentennial	4.00	6.00	8.00
❏ 1019	3¢	Washington Territory	4.00	6.00	8.00
❏ 1020	3¢	Louisiana Purchase	4.00	6.00	8.00
❏ 1021	5¢	Opening of Japan	4.00	6.00	8.00
❏ 1022	3¢	American Bar Association	4.00	6.00	8.00
❏ 1023	3¢	Sagamore Hill	4.00	6.00	8.00
❏ 1024	3¢	Future Farmers	4.00	6.00	8.00
❏ 1025	3¢	Trucking Industry	4.00	6.00	8.00
❏ 1026	3¢	Gen. George S. Patton, Jr.	4.00	6.00	8.00
❏ 1027	3¢	New York City	4.00	6.00	8.00
❏ 1028	3¢	Gadsden Purchase	4.00	6.00	8.00
❏ 1029	3¢	Columbia University	4.00	6.00	8.00
❏ 1030	½¢	Franklin	—	3.50	5.00
❏ 1031	1¢	Washington	—	3.50	5.00
❏ 1031a	1¼¢	Palace of Governors	—	3.50	5.00
❏ 1032	1½¢	Mount Vernon	—	3.50	5.00
❏ 1033	2¢	Jefferson	—	3.50	5.00
❏ 1034	2½¢	Bunker Hill	—	3.50	5.00
❏ 1035	3¢	Statue of Liberty	4.00	5.00	7.00
❏ 1036	4¢	Lincoln	4.00	5.00	7.00
❏ 1037	4½¢	Hermitage	4.00	5.00	7.00
❏ 1038	5¢	Monroe	4.00	5.00	7.00
❏ 1039	6¢	Roosevelt	4.00	5.00	7.00
❏ 1040	7¢	Wilson	4.00	5.00	7.00
❏ 1041	8¢	Statue of Liberty	4.00	5.00	7.00
❏ 1042	8¢	Statue of Liberty	4.00	5.00	7.00
❏ 1042a	8¢	Pershing	4.00	5.25	8.00
❏ 1043	9¢	The Alamo	4.00	6.00	7.00
❏ 1044	10¢	Independence Hall	4.00	6.00	7.00
❏ 1045	12¢	Harrison	4.00	6.00	7.00
❏ 1046	15¢	John Jay	4.00	6.00	7.00
❏ 1047	20¢	Monticello	4.00	6.00	7.00
❏ 1048	25¢	Paul Revere	4.00	6.00	7.00
❏ 1049	30¢	Robert E. Lee	5.00	7.00	8.00
❏ 1050	40¢	John Marshall	5.00	8.00	10.00
❏ 1051	50¢	Susan Anthony	7.00	12.00	20.00
❏ 1052	$1	Patrick Henry	12.00	18.00	22.00
❏ 1053	$5	Alexander Hamilton	50.00	100.00	125.00

Scott No.			Single	Block	Plate Block
❏ 1054	1¢	Washington (coil)	3.00	—	—
❏ 1055	2¢	Jefferson (coil)	3.00	—	—
❏ 1056	2½¢	Bunker Hill (coil)	3.00	—	—
❏ 1057	3¢	Statue of Liberty (coil)	3.00	—	—
❏ 1058	4¢	Lincoln (coil)	3.00	—	—
❏ 1059	4½¢	The Hermitage (coil)	3.00	—	—
❏ 1059a	25¢	Paul Revere (coil)	3.00	—	—
❏ 1060	3¢	Nebraska Territory	3.00	5.00	6.00
❏ 1061	3¢	Kansas Territory	3.00	5.00	6.00
❏ 1062	3¢	George Eastman	3.00	5.00	6.00
❏ 1063	3¢	Lewis & Clark	3.00	5.00	6.00
❏ 1064	3¢	Pennsylvania Academy	3.00	5.00	6.00
❏ 1065	3¢	Land Grant Colleges	3.00	5.00	7.00
❏ 1066	8¢	Rotary International	3.25	5.00	7.00
❏ 1067	3¢	Armed Forces Reserve	2.50	5.00	7.00
❏ 1068	3¢	New Hampshire	2.50	5.50	7.00
❏ 1069	3¢	Soo Locks	2.50	5.50	7.00
❏ 1070	3¢	Atoms for Peace	2.50	5.50	7.00
❏ 1071	3¢	Fort Ticonderoga	2.50	5.50	7.00
❏ 1072	3¢	Andrew W. Mellon	2.50	5.50	7.00
❏ 1073	3¢	Benjamin Franklin	2.50	5.50	7.00
❏ 1074	3¢	Booker T. Washington	2.50	5.50	7.00
❏ 1075	3¢, 8¢	FIPEX Souvenir Sheet	10.00	—	—
❏ 1076	3¢	FIPEX	2.50	5.00	6.00
❏ 1077	3¢	Wildlife (Turkey)	2.50	5.00	6.00
❏ 1078	3¢	Wildlife (Antelope)	2.50	5.00	6.00
❏ 1079	3¢	Wildlife (Salmon)	2.50	5.00	6.00
❏ 1080	3¢	Pure Food and Drug Laws	2.50	5.00	6.00
❏ 1081	3¢	Wheatland	2.50	5.00	6.00
❏ 1082	3¢	Labor Day	2.50	5.00	6.00
❏ 1083	3¢	Nassau Hall	2.50	5.00	6.00
❏ 1084	3¢	Devil's Tower	2.50	5.00	6.00
❏ 1085	3¢	Children	2.50	5.00	6.00
❏ 1086	3¢	Alexander Hamilton	2.50	5.00	6.00
❏ 1087	3¢	Polio	2.50	5.00	7.00
❏ 1088	3¢	Coast & Geodetic Survey	2.50	4.00	7.00
❏ 1089	3¢	Architects	2.50	4.00	7.00
❏ 1090	3¢	Steel Industry	2.50	4.00	7.00
❏ 1091	3¢	Naval Review	2.50	4.00	7.00
❏ 1092	3¢	Oklahoma Statehood	2.50	4.00	7.00

Scott No.			Single	Block	Plate Block
❏ 1093	3¢	School Teachers	2.85	4.50	7.50
❏ 1094	4¢	Flag	2.85	4.50	7.50
❏ 1095	3¢	Shipbuilding	2.85	4.50	7.50
❏ 1096	8¢	Ramon Magsaysay	2.85	4.50	7.50
❏ 1097	3¢	Lafayette Bicentenary	2.85	4.50	7.50
❏ 1098	3¢	Wildlife (Whooping Crane)	2.85	4.50	7.50
❏ 1099	3¢	Religious Freedom	2.85	4.50	7.50
❏ 1100	3¢	Gardening Horticulture	2.85	4.50	7.50
❏ 1104	3¢	Brussels Exhibition	2.85	4.50	7.50
❏ 1105	3¢	James Monroe	2.85	4.50	7.50
❏ 1106	3¢	Minnesota Statehood	2.85	4.50	7.50
❏ 1107	3¢	International Geophysical Year	2.85	4.50	7.50
❏ 1108	3¢	Gunston Hall	2.85	4.50	7.50
❏ 1109	3¢	Mackinac Bridge	2.85	4.50	7.50
❏ 1110	4¢	Simon Bolivar	2.85	4.50	7.50
❏ 1111	8¢	Simon Bolivar	2.85	4.50	7.50
❏ 1110–1111		Bolivar set on one cover	2.85	4.50	7.50
❏ 1112	4¢	Atlantic Cable	2.25	4.50	7.50
❏ 1113	1¢	Lincoln Sesquicentennial	2.25	4.50	7.50
❏ 1114	3¢	Lincoln Sesquicentennial	2.25	4.50	7.50
❏ 1115	4¢	Lincoln-Douglas Debates	2.50	4.50	6.00
❏ 1116	4¢	Lincoln Sesquicentennial	2.50	4.50	6.00
❏ 1113–1116		Lincoln set on one cover	8.00	4.50	—
❏ 1117	4¢	Lajos Kossuth	2.50	4.50	6.00
❏ 1118	8¢	Lajos Kossuth	2.50	4.50	6.00
❏ 1117–1118		Kossuth set on one cover	2.50	—	—
❏ 1119	4¢	Freedom of Press	2.25	4.25	6.00
❏ 1120	4¢	Overland Mail	2.25	4.25	6.00
❏ 1121	4¢	Noah Webster	2.25	4.25	6.00
❏ 1122	4¢	Forest Conservation	2.25	4.25	6.00
❏ 1123	4¢	Fort Duquesne	2.25	4.25	6.00
❏ 1124	4¢	Oregon Statehood	2.25	4.25	6.00
❏ 1125	4¢	San Martin	2.25	4.25	6.00
❏ 1126	8¢	San Martin	2.25	4.25	6.00
❏ 1125–1126		San Martin set on one cover	2.25	4.25	6.00
❏ 1127	4¢	NATO	2.25	4.25	6.00
❏ 1128	4¢	Arctic Explorations	2.25	4.25	6.00
❏ 1129	8¢	World Trade	2.25	4.25	6.00
❏ 1130	4¢	Silver Centennial	2.25	4.25	6.00
❏ 1131	4¢	St. Lawrence Seaway	2.25	4.25	6.00

Scott No.			Single	Block	Plate Block
❏ 1132	4¢	Flag	2.25	4.25	5.00
❏ 1133	4¢	Soil Conservation	2.25	4.25	5.00
❏ 1134	4¢	Petroleum Industry	2.75	4.65	6.00
❏ 1135	4¢	Dental Health	2.75	4.65	6.00
❏ 1136	4¢	Reuter	2.75	4.65	5.50
❏ 1137	8¢	Reuter	2.75	4.65	5.50
❏ 1136–1137		Reuter set on one cover	4.00	4.65	5.50
❏ 1138	4¢	Dr. Ephraim McDowell	2.50	4.65	5.50
❏ 1139	4¢	Washington "Credo"	2.50	4.65	5.50
❏ 1140	4¢	Franklin "Credo"	2.50	4.65	5.50
❏ 1141	4¢	Jefferson "Credo"	2.50	4.65	5.75
❏ 1142	4¢	Francis Scott Key "Credo"	2.50	4.65	5.75
❏ 1143	4¢	Lincoln "Credo"	2.50	4.65	5.75
❏ 1144	4¢	Patrick Henry "Credo"	2.50	4.65	5.75
❏ 1145	4¢	Boy Scouts	2.75	4.65	5.75
❏ 1146	4¢	Olympic Winter Games	2.25	4.65	5.25
❏ 1147	4¢	Masaryk	2.25	4.65	5.50
❏ 1148	8¢	Masaryk	2.25	4.65	5.50
❏ 1147–1148		Masaryk set on one cover	3.00	4.65	—
❏ 1149	4¢	World Refugee Year	2.25	4.65	6.25
❏ 1150	4¢	Water Conservation	2.25	4.65	6.25
❏ 1151	4¢	SEATO	2.25	4.65	6.25
❏ 1152	4¢	American Woman	2.25	4.65	6.25
❏ 1153	4¢	50-Star Flag	2.25	4.65	6.25
❏ 1154	4¢	Pony Express Centennial	2.25	4.65	6.25
❏ 1155	4¢	Employ the Handicapped	2.25	4.65	6.25
❏ 1156	4¢	World Forestry Congress	2.25	4.65	6.25
❏ 1157	4¢	Mexican Independence	2.25	4.65	6.25
❏ 1158	4¢	U.S. Japan Treaty	2.25	4.65	6.25
❏ 1159	4¢	Paderewski	2.25	4.65	6.25
❏ 1160	8¢	Paderewski	2.25	4.65	6.25
❏ 1159–1160		Paderewski set on one cover	3.00	4.65	6.25
❏ 1161	4¢	Robert A. Taft	2.25	4.65	6.25
❏ 1162	4¢	Wheels of Freedom	2.25	4.65	6.25
❏ 1163	4¢	Boys' Clubs	2.25	4.65	6.25
❏ 1164	4¢	Automated P.O.	2.25	4.65	6.25
❏ 1165	4¢	Mannerheim	2.25	4.65	6.25
❏ 1166	8¢	Mannerheim	2.25	4.65	6.25
❏ 1165–1166		Mannerheim set on one cover	3.00	4.65	6.25
❏ 1167	4¢	Camp Fire Girls	2.25	4.65	6.25

Scott No.			Single	Block	Plate Block
❑ 1168	4¢	Garibaldi	2.25	4.25	6.25
❑ 1169	8¢	Garibaldi	2.25	4.25	6.25
❑ 1168–1169		Garibaldi set on one cover	3.00	4.25	6.25
❑ 1170	4¢	Senator George	2.25	4.25	6.25
❑ 1171	4¢	Andrew Carnegie	2.25	4.25	6.25
❑ 1172	4¢	John Foster Dulles	2.25	4.25	6.25
❑ 1173	4¢	Echo I	2.25	4.25	6.25
❑ 1174	4¢	Gandhi	2.25	4.25	6.25
❑ 1175	8¢	Gandhi	2.25	4.25	6.25
❑ 1174–1175		Gandhi set on one cover	4.00	—	6.25
❑ 1176	4¢	Range Conservation	2.25	4.00	6.25
❑ 1177	4¢	Horace Greeley	2.25	4.00	6.25
❑ 1178	4¢	Fort Sumter	3.75	5.00	6.25
❑ 1179	4¢	Battle of Shiloh	3.75	5.00	6.25
❑ 1180	5¢	Battle of Gettysburg	3.75	5.00	6.25
❑ 1181	5¢	Battle of Wilderness	3.75	5.00	6.25
❑ 1182	5¢	Appomattox	3.75	5.00	6.25
❑ 1179–1182		Set on one cover	12.00	—	6.25
❑ 1183	4¢	Kansas Statehood	2.75	5.00	6.25
❑ 1184	4¢	Senator Norris	3.00	4.00	6.25
❑ 1185	4¢	Naval Aviation	3.00	3.40	6.25
❑ 1186	4¢	Workmen's Compensation	3.00	3.40	6.25
❑ 1187	4¢	Frederic Remington	3.00	3.40	6.25
❑ 1188	4¢	China Republic	4.50	6.00	8.00
❑ 1189	4¢	Naismith	8.00	10.00	12.00
❑ 1190	4¢	Nursing	8.50	12.00	18.00
❑ 1191	4¢	New Mexico Statehood	2.50	4.00	5.00
❑ 1192	4¢	Arizona Statehood	2.50	4.00	5.00
❑ 1193	4¢	Project Mercury	3.50	5.50	7.50
❑ 1194	4¢	Malaria Eradication	2.50	4.25	6.25
❑ 1195	4¢	Charles Evans Hughes	2.50	4.25	6.25
❑ 1196	4¢	Seattle World's Fair	2.50	4.25	6.25
❑ 1197	4¢	Louisiana Statehood	2.50	4.25	6.25
❑ 1198	4¢	Homestead Act	2.50	4.25	6.25
❑ 1199	4¢	Girl Scouts	3.50	5.00	7.00
❑ 1200	4¢	Brien McMahon	2.25	4.00	6.00
❑ 1201	4¢	Apprenticeship	2.25	4.00	6.00
❑ 1202	4¢	Sam Rayburn	2.25	4.00	6.00
❑ 1203	4¢	Dag Hammarskjold	2.25	4.00	6.00
❑ 1204	4¢	Hammarskjold "Error"	5.00	8.00	10.00

Scott No.			Single	Block	Plate Block
❏ 1205	4¢	Christmas	2.25	4.25	5.75
❏ 1206	4¢	Higher Education	2.25	4.25	5.75
❏ 1207	4¢	Winslow Homer	2.25	4.25	5.75
❏ 1208	4¢	Flag	2.25	4.25	5.75
❏ 1209	1¢	Jackson	2.25	4.25	5.75
❏ 1213	5¢	Washington	2.25	4.25	5.75
❏ 1225	1¢	Jackson (coil)	2.25	—	—
❏ 1229	5¢	Washington (coil)	2.25	—	—
❏ 1230	5¢	Carolina Charter	2.25	4.25	5.75
❏ 1231	5¢	Food for Peace	2.25	4.25	5.75
❏ 1232	5¢	West Virginia Statehood	2.25	4.25	5.75
❏ 1233	5¢	Emancipation Proclamation	2.25	4.25	5.75
❏ 1234	5¢	Alliance for Progress	2.25	4.25	5.75
❏ 1235	5¢	Cordell Hull	2.25	4.25	5.75
❏ 1236	5¢	Eleanor Roosevelt	2.25	4.25	5.75
❏ 1237	5¢	Science	2.25	4.25	5.75
❏ 1238	5¢	City Mail Delivery	2.25	4.25	5.75
❏ 1239	5¢	Red Cross	2.25	4.25	5.75
❏ 1240	5¢	Christmas	2.25	4.25	5.75
❏ 1241	5¢	Audubon	2.25	4.25	5.75
❏ 1242	5¢	Sam Houston	2.25	4.25	5.75
❏ 1243	5¢	Charles Russell	2.25	4.25	5.75
❏ 1244	5¢	N.Y. World's Fair	2.25	4.25	5.75
❏ 1245	5¢	John Muir	2.25	4.25	5.75
❏ 1246	5¢	John F. Kennedy	2.25	4.25	5.75
❏ 1247	5¢	New Jersey Tercentenary	2.25	4.25	5.75
❏ 1248	5¢	Nevada Statehood	2.25	4.25	5.75
❏ 1249	5¢	Register & Vote	2.25	4.25	5.75
❏ 1250	5¢	Shakespeare	2.25	4.25	5.75
❏ 1251	5¢	Drs. Mayo	5.00	6.00	8.00
❏ 1252	5¢	American Music	3.00	4.15	6.00
❏ 1253	5¢	Homemakers	2.25	3.50	5.50
❏ 1254–57	5¢	Christmas	2.25	5.00	9.00
❏ 1258	5¢	Verrazano Narrows Bridge	2.25	5.00	6.25
❏ 1259	5¢	Fine Arts	2.25	5.00	6.25
❏ 1260	5¢	Amateur Radio	2.25	5.00	6.25
❏ 1261	5¢	Battle of New Orleans	2.25	5.00	6.25
❏ 1262	5¢	Physical Fitness	2.25	5.00	6.25
❏ 1263	5¢	Cancer Crusade	2.25	5.00	7.00
❏ 1264	5¢	Churchill	2.25	4.00	5.00

Scott No.			Single	Block	Plate Block
❑ 1265	5¢	Magna Carta	2.25	4.25	5.75
❑ 1266	5¢	Int'l. Cooperation Year	2.25	4.25	5.75
❑ 1267	5¢	Salvation Army	2.25	4.25	5.75
❑ 1268	5¢	Dante	2.25	4.25	5.75
❑ 1269	5¢	Herbert Hoover	2.25	4.25	5.75
❑ 1270	5¢	Robert Fulton	2.25	4.25	5.75
❑ 1271	5¢	Florida Settlement	2.25	4.25	5.75
❑ 1272	5¢	Traffic Safety	2.25	4.25	5.75
❑ 1273	5¢	Copley	2.25	4.25	5.75
❑ 1274	11¢	Int'l. Telecommunication Union	2.25	3.50	6.25
❑ 1275	5¢	Adlai Stevenson	2.25	3.50	6.25
❑ 1276	5¢	Christmas	2.25	3.50	6.25
❑ 1278	1¢	Jefferson	2.25	3.50	6.25
❑ 1279	1¼¢	Gallatin	2.25	3.50	6.25
❑ 1280	2¢	Wright	2.25	3.50	6.25
❑ 1281	3¢	Parkman	2.25	3.50	6.25
❑ 1282	4¢	Lincoln	2.25	3.50	6.25
❑ 1283	5¢	Washington	2.25	3.50	6.25
❑ 1283b	5¢	Washington	2.25	3.50	6.25
❑ 1284	6¢	Roosevelt	2.25	3.50	6.25
❑ 1285	8¢	Einstein	2.25	3.50	6.25
❑ 1286	10¢	Jackson	2.25	4.00	6.25
❑ 1286a	12¢	Ford	2.25	4.00	6.25
❑ 1287	13¢	Kennedy	2.25	5.00	8.00
❑ 1288	15¢	Holmes	2.50	3.75	5.00
❑ 1289	20¢	Marshall	2.50	4.00	7.00
❑ 1290	25¢	Douglas	2.50	4.00	7.00
❑ 1291	30¢	Dewey	2.75	4.50	7.00
❑ 1292	40¢	Paine	4.00	7.00	10.00
❑ 1293	50¢	Stone	4.00	10.00	14.00
❑ 1294	$1	O'Neill	4.50	10.00	14.00
❑ 1295	$5	Moore	50.00	85.00	140.00
❑ 1304	5¢	Washington (coil)	—	2.00 (pr)	5.00 (lp)
❑ 1305	6¢	Roosevelt (coil)	—	2.00 (pr)	5.00 (lp)
❑ 1305c	$1	O'Neill (coil)	—	2.00 (pr)	5.00 (lp)
❑ 1306	5¢	Migratory Bird Treaty	4.00	5.25	6.25
❑ 1307	5¢	Humane Treatment of Animals	4.00	5.25	6.25
❑ 1308	5¢	Indiana Statehood	2.00	4.00	6.25
❑ 1309	5¢	Circus	4.00	5.00	6.25
❑ 1310	5¢	SIPEX	2.00	4.00	5.00

Scott No.			Single	Block	Plate Block
❏ 1311	5¢	SIPEX (sheet)	3.25	4.00	5.25
❏ 1312	5¢	Bill of Rights	3.25	4.00	5.25
❏ 1313	5¢	Polish Millennium	3.25	4.00	5.25
❏ 1314	5¢	National Park Service	3.25	4.00	5.25
❏ 1315	5¢	Marine Corps Reserve	2.25	3.50	5.25
❏ 1316	5¢	Gen'l. Fed. of Women's Clubs	2.25	3.50	5.25
❏ 1317	5¢	Johnny Appleseed	2.25	3.50	5.25
❏ 1318	5¢	Beautification of America	2.25	3.50	5.25
❏ 1319	5¢	Great River Road	2.25	3.50	5.25
❏ 1320	5¢	Savings Bonds	2.25	3.50	5.25
❏ 1321	5¢	Christmas	2.25	3.50	5.25
❏ 1322	5¢	Mary Cassatt	2.25	3.50	5.25
❏ 1323	5¢	National Grange	2.25	3.50	5.25
❏ 1324	5¢	Canada Centenary	2.25	3.50	5.25
❏ 1325	5¢	Erie Canal	2.25	3.50	5.25
❏ 1326	5¢	Search for Peace	2.25	3.50	5.25
❏ 1327	5¢	Thoreau	2.25	3.50	5.25
❏ 1328	5¢	Nebraska Statehood	2.25	3.50	5.25
❏ 1329	5¢	Voice of America	2.25	3.50	5.25
❏ 1330	5¢	Davy Crockett	2.25	3.50	5.25
❏ 1331–32	5¢	Space Accomplishments	12.00	24.00 (pr)	28.00
❏ 1333	5¢	Urban Planning	2.25	3.50	5.25
❏ 1334	5¢	Finland Independence	2.25	3.50	5.25
❏ 1335	5¢	Thomas Eakins	2.25	3.50	5.25
❏ 1336	5¢	Christmas	2.25	3.50	5.25
❏ 1337	5¢	Mississippi Statehood	2.25	3.50	5.25
❏ 1338	6¢	Flag	2.25	3.50	5.25
❏ 1339	6¢	Illinois Statehood	2.25	3.50	5.25
❏ 1340	6¢	Hemis Fair '68	2.25	3.50	5.25
❏ 1341	$1	Airlift	7.75	14.50	20.00
❏ 1342	6¢	Youth-Elks	2.00	4.00	5.00
❏ 1343	6¢	Law and Order	3.50	5.00	8.25
❏ 1344	6¢	Register and Vote	3.00	5.00	7.00
❏ 1345–54	6¢	Historic Flags (on one cover)	10.00	—	16.00
❏ 1345–54		Set on 10 covers	35.00	—	—
❏ 1355	6¢	Disney	12.00	14.00	26.00
❏ 1356	6¢	Marquette	3.00	4.25	6.00
❏ 1357	6¢	Daniel Boone	3.00	4.25	6.00
❏ 1358	6¢	Arkansas River	3.00	4.25	6.00

Scott No.			Single	Block	Plate Block
❏ 1359	6¢	Leif Erikson	2.75	4.00	6.00
❏ 1360	6¢	Cherokee Strip	2.75	4.00	6.00
❏ 1361	6¢	John Trumbull	2.75	4.00	6.00
❏ 1362	6¢	Waterfowl Conservation	2.75	5.00	5.25
❏ 1363	6¢	Christmas	2.75	5.00	5.25
❏ 1364	6¢	American Indian	2.75	5.00	5.65
❏ 1365–68	6¢	Beautification of America	2.75	8.00	12.00
❏ 1369	6¢	American Legion	2.75	6.00	7.00
❏ 1370	6¢	Grandma Moses	2.75	6.00	7.00
❏ 1371	6¢	Apollo 8	4.00	7.00	12.00

NOTE: From No. 1372 to date, most first day covers have a value of $2.00 to $2.50 for single stamps, $3.00 to $4.50 for blocks of four and $4.50 to $5.50 for plate blocks of four.

STAMP COLLECTORS'
TERMINOLOGY

Adhesives—A term given to stamps that have gummed backs and are intended to be pasted on articles and items that are to be mailed.

Aerophilately—The collecting of airmail or any form of stamps related to mail carried by air.

Airmail—Any mail carried by air.

Albino—An uncolored embossed impression of a stamp generally found on envelopes.

Approvals—Stamps sent to collectors. They are examined by the collector, who selects stamps to purchase and returns balance with payment for the stamps he retained.

Arrow Block—An arrow-like mark found on blocks of stamps in the selvage. This mark is used as a guide for cutting or perforating stamps.

As-is—A term used when selling a stamp. It means no representation is given as to its condition or authenticity. Buyers should beware.

Backprint—Any printing that may appear on reverse of stamp.

Backstamp—The postmark on the back of a letter indicating what time or date the letter arrived at the post office.

Bantams—A miniature stamp given to a war economy issue of stamps from South Africa.

Batonne—Watermarked paper used in printing stamps.

Bicolored—A two-color printed stamp.

Bisect—A stamp that could be used by cutting in half and at half the face value.

Block—A term used for a series of four or more stamps attached at least two high and two across.

Bourse—A meeting or convention of stamp collectors and dealers where stamps are bought, sold, and traded.

Cachet—A design printed on the face of an envelope, generally celebrating the commemoration of a new postage stamp issue. Generally called a first-day cover.

Cancellation—A marking placed on the face of a stamp to show that it has been used.

Cancelled to Order—A stamp cancelled by the government without being used. Generally remainder stamps or special issues. Common practice of Russian nations.

Centering—The manner in which the design of a stamp is printed and centered upon the stamp blank. A perfectly centered stamp would have equal margins on all sides.

Classic—A popular, unique, highly desired, or very artistic stamp. Not necessarily a rare stamp, but one sought after by the collector. Generally used only for nineteenth-century issues.

Coils—Stamps sold in rolls for use in vending machines.

Commemorative—A stamp issued to commemorate or celebrate a special event.

Crease—A fold or wrinkle in a stamp.

Cut Square—An embossed staple removed from the envelope by cutting.

Dead Country—A country no longer issuing stamps.

Demonetized—A stamp no longer valid for use.

Error—A stamp printed or produced with a major design or color defect.

Essay—Preliminary design for a postage stamp.

Face Value—The value of a stamp indicated on the face or surface of the stamp.

Frank—A marking on the face of an envelope indicating the free and legal use of postage. Generally for government use.

Fugitive Inks—A special ink used to print stamps, which can be rubbed or washed off easily, to eliminate erasures and forgeries.

General Collector—One who collects all kinds of issues and all types of stamps from different countries.

Granite Paper—A type of paper containing colored fibers to prevent forgery.

Gum—The adhesive coating on the back of a stamp.

Handstamped—A stamp that has been handcancelled.

Hinge—A specially gummed piece of glassine paper used to attach a stamp to the album page.

Imperforate—A stamp without perforations.

Inverted—Where one portion of a stamp's design is inverted or upside down from the remainder of the design.

Local Stamps—Stamps that are only valid in a limited area.

Margin—The unprinted area around a stamp.

Miniature Sheet—A smaller-than-usual sheet of stamps.

Mint Condition—A stamp in original condition as it left the postal printing office.

Mirror Print—A stamp error printed in reverse as though looking at a regular stamp reflected in a mirror.

Multicolored—A stamp printed in three or more colors.

Never Hinged—A stamp in original mint condition never hinged in an album.

Off Paper—A used stamp that has been removed from the envelope to which it was attached.

On Paper—A used stamp still attached to the envelope.

Original Gum—A stamp with the same or original adhesive that was applied in the manufacturing process.

Pair—Two stamps unseparated.

Pen Cancellation—A stamp cancelled by pen or pencil.

Perforation Gauge—A printed chart containing various sizes of perforation holes used in determining the type or size of perforation of a stamp.

Perforations—Holes punched along stamp designs allowing stamps to be easily separated.

Philatelist—One who collects stamps.

Pictorial Stamps—Stamps that bear large pictures of animals, birds, flowers, etc.

Plate Block Number—The printing plate number used to identify a block of four or more stamps taken from a sheet of stamps.

Postally Used—A stamp that has been properly used and cancelled.

Precancels—A stamp that has been cancelled in advance. Generally used on bulk mail.

Reissue—A new printing of an old stamp that has been out of circulation.

Revenue Stamp—A label or stamp affixed to an item as evidence of tax payment.

Seals—An adhesive label that looks like a stamp, used for various fund-raising campaigns.

Se-tenant—Two or more stamps joined together, each having a different design or value.

Sheet—A page of stamps as they are printed, usually separated before distribution to post offices.

Soaking—Removing used stamps from paper to which they are attached by soaking in water. (NOTE: Colored cancels may cause staining to other stamps.)

Souvenir Sheet—One or more specially designed stamps printed by the government in celebration of a special stamp.

Splice—The splice made between rolls of paper in the printing operation. Stamps printed on this splice are generally discarded.

Tete-Beche—A pair of stamps printed together so that the images point in opposite vertical directions.

Transit Mark—A mark made by an intermediate post office between the originating and final destination post office.

Typeset Stamp—A stamp printed with regular printer's type, as opposed to engraved, lithographed, etc.

Ungummed—Stamps printed without an adhesive back.

Unhinged—A stamp that has never been mounted with the use of a hinge.

Unperforated—A stamp produced without perforations.

Vignette—The central design portion of a stamp.

Want List—A list of stamps a collector needs to fill gaps in his collection.

Watermark—A mark put into paper by the manufacturer, not readily seen by the naked eye.

Wrapper—A strip of paper with adhesive on one end, used for wrapping bundles of mail. Especially in Great Britain, it refers to any bit of paper to which a used stamp is still attached.

EQUIPMENT

To collect stamps properly a collector will need some "tools of the trade." These need not be expensive and need not all be bought at the very outset. That might, in fact, be the worst thing to do. Many a beginning collector has spent his budget on equipment, only to have little or nothing left for stamps and then loses interest in the hobby.

It may be economical in the long run to buy the finest quality accessories, but few collectors, just starting out, have a clear idea of what they will and will not be needing. It is just as easy to make impulse purchases of accessories as of stamps and just as unwise. Equipment must be purchased on the basis of what sort of collection is being built now, rather than on what the collection may be in the future. There is no shame in working up from an elementary album.

Starter Kits. Starter or beginner outfits are sold in just about every variety shop, drugstore, etc. These come in attractive boxes and contain a juvenile or beginner's album; some stamps, which may be on paper and in need of removal; a packet of gummed hinges; tongs; a pocket stockbook or file; and often other items such as a perforation gauge, booklet on stamp collecting, magnifier, and watermark detector. These kits are specially suited to young collectors and can provide a good philatelic education.

Albums. When the hobby began, more than a century ago, collectors mounted their stamps in whatever albums were at hand. Scrapbooks, school exercise tablets, and diaries all were used, as well as homemade albums. Today a number of firms specialize in printing albums of all kinds for philatelists, ranging from softbounds for the cautious type to huge multi-volume sets that cost hundreds of dollars. There are general worldwide albums, country albums, U.N. albums, and albums for mint sheets, covers, and every other conceivable variety of philatelic material. Choose your album according to the specialty you intend to pursue. It is not necessary, however, to buy a printed album at all. Many collectors feel there is not enough room for creativity in a printed album and prefer to use a binder with unprinted sheets. This allows items to be arranged at will on the page, rather than following the publisher's format, and for a personal write-up to be added. Rod-type binders will prove more durable and satisfactory than ring binders for heavy collections. The pages of an album should not be too thin, unless only one side is used. The presence of tiny crisscrossing lines (quadrilled sheets) is intended as an aid to correct alignment. Once items have been mounted and written up, these lines are scarcely visible and do not interfere with the attractiveness of the page.

Hinges. These are small rectangular pieces of lightweight paper, usually clear or semiopaque, gummed and folded. One side is moistened and affixed to the back of the stamp and the other to the album page. Hinges are sold in packets of 1,000 and are very inexpensive. Though they are by far the most popular device for mounting stamps, the hobbyist has his choice of a number of other products if hinges are not satisfactory to him. These include cello mounts, which encase the stamp in clear sheeting and have a black background to provide a kind of frame. These are self-sticking. Their cost is much higher than hinges. The chief advantage of cello mounts is that they prevent injuries to the stamp and eliminate the moistening necessary in using hinges; however, they add considerably to the weight of each page, making flipping through an album less convenient, and become detached from the page more readily than hinges.

Glassine Interleaving. These are sheets made of thin semitransparent glassine paper, the same used to make envelopes in which stamps are stored. They come punched to fit albums of standard size and are designed to be placed between each set of sheets, to prevent stamps on one page from becoming entangled with those on the facing page. Glassine interleaving is not necessary if cello mounts are used, but any collection mounted with conventional hinges should be interleaved. The cost is small. Glassine interleaving is sold in packets of 100 sheets.

Magnifier. A magnifier is a necessary tool for most stamp collectors, excepting those who specialize in first-day covers or other items that would not likely require study by magnification. There are numerous types and grades on the market, ranging in price from about $1 to more than $20. The quality of magnifier to buy should be governed by the extent to which it is likely to be used, and the collector's dependence upon it for identification and study. A collector of plate varieties ought to have the best magnifier he can afford and carry it whenever visiting dealers, shows, or anywhere that he may wish to examine specimens. A good magnifier is also necessary for a specialist in grilled stamps and for collectors of Civil War and other nineteenth-century covers. Those with built-in illumination are best in these circumstances.

Tongs. Beginners have a habit of picking up stamps with their fingers, which can cause injuries, smudges, and grease stains. Efficient handling of tongs is not difficult to learn, and the sooner the better. Do not resort to ordinary tweezers, but get a pair of philatelic tongs which are specially shaped and of sufficiently large size to be easily manipulated.

Perforation Gauge. A very necessary, inexpensive article, as the identification of many stamps depends upon a correct measuring of their perforations.

TEN LOW-COST WAYS TO START COLLECTING STAMPS

Courtesy of the
American Philatelic Society.

If you have recently started collecting stamps, or are thinking about start-ing, you may be wondering if the hobby is expensive. Can you enjoy it with limited financial resources? What if you have no money at all for the hobby?

One of the biggest questions any stamp collector faces is where to find stamps inexpensively. If you intend to save stamps of the United States or the world and want to save used as well as unused stamps, the opportunities are really great. Not all collections consist mainly of unused stamps that you buy in the post office. Used stamps are worth saving, have value, and they may cost you nothing.

Many stamp collectors save only used stamps. Others save both used and unused ones. Others save stamps only from one country or one part of the world. Some collectors save stamps by "topic," for example, stamps that depict horses or trains or birds. There are any number of dif-ferent types of collections.

1. All postally used stamps started out being received in someone's mailbox, at no cost to the person receiving them. The first place to search for stamps, then, is your own mailbox. Don't be discouraged when you notice that many senders use postage meters or the imprint "Bulk Rate Postage Paid" on their envelopes to enjoy a better postal rate or to keep from affixing stamps. Also, when people do use real stamps, they often use the same common small ones.

You can begin to change this by asking people who write to you to use commemorative stamps on their mail. These are normally the larger stamps issued to honor famous people, places, or events. These stamps are printed in lesser quantities than the common smaller (definitive) stamps and usually are of much more interest to collectors. Many people will remember to ask for commemorative stamps at the post office when mailing letters to you or your family if you let them know you are a stamp collector. Also, if you write away for offers that require postage or a self-addressed, stamped envelope, you can put commemoratives on your return envelope, knowing that they will come back to you later.

2. Neighbors, friends, and relatives are another good source of stamps. The majority of people just throw away stamps when they receive them on mail and are only too happy to save them for someone who appreciates them. You may even know someone who gets letters from other countries who can save these stamps, too. Always be on the lookout for potentially good stamp contacts, and don't be afraid to ask them to go through their mail for you before they throw away all the envelopes.

3. Office mail may be even better. You may know someone who works in an office that gets a lot of mail. Out of 100 letters a day, there may be ten or twenty good stamps that are being thrown away. Many businesses get a lot of foreign mail and regularly throw away stamps that have interest and/or value to a collector.

4. Ask friends and coworkers to save envelopes with stamps for you. Youngsters can ask parents if they have any old letters, which may have stamps on the envelopes. When taking stamps off envelopes, always tear off the corner so that there is paper all around the stamp, and the stamp and all its perforations are undamaged. Anyone who is saving stamps for you should be told that this is the way to do it; otherwise, he/she may try to peel the stamp off the envelope. This will cause thin spots or tears, both of which ruin a stamp's appearance and lessen its value to collectors. If you run across envelopes that are very old or have postal markings that may be of particular interest, it is best to save the entire envelope until you can find out if the stamp is worth more attached to the cover.

Now that you have stamps on paper, what do you do with them? The most common way to get stamps off paper is to soak them in cool water, then dry them on paper. To understand more about soaking stamps, refer to the following section, beginning on p. 621.

There is a lot to learn about stamps as you get more and more of them. For example, different shades of color may exist on stamps with the same design, or they may have different perforation measurements (number of holes per side). Major varieties of stamps and "catalog values" are listed in stamp catalogs, which are available in most libraries. The most common one, the Scott Standard Postage Stamp Catalogue, has a very good section in front that explains how stamps are made and how to tell varieties apart, as well as how to use the catalog. Having access to a catalog in a nearby library is very useful until you decide if you want one of your own.

5. Longtime collectors may be another source of stamps. Usually a person who has been a collector for a number of years has developed many sources for stamps. The collector may have thousands of duplicates, some of which may be very inexpensive while others may have more value. Often older collectors are willing to help new philatelists get started by giving them stamps, or at least providing packets of stamps much more cheaply than can be purchased in stores or by mail.

6. Many stamp companies advertise free stamps. However, these ads must be read carefully before you send away for anything. Usually these ads offer "approvals," which means they will send you the free stamps advertised, plus an assortment of other stamps which you may either buy or return. By sending for the free stamps, you have already agreed that you will return the other stamps within a reasonable period of time if you do not buy anything. Usually you must pay the return postage. This is a convenient way to buy stamps from your own home.

7. Stamp clubs are another place to get stamps. A club may offer stamps as prizes, or have inexpensive stamps you can afford to buy.

Some stamp clubs sponsor junior clubs that meet at schools or the local YMCA or community center. If you are fortunate enough to have one of these in your area, it can be a great source of both stamps and advice.

8. One way to increase your sources for stamps and also have a lot of fun is to help start a local club, if one does not already exist. All it takes are four or five other stamp collectors who are interested in getting together to learn about and trade stamps and ideas.

9. Obtaining a pen pal in another country is a very good way to get stamps from that country. His or her extra stamps may seem really common in that country, but over here they are much scarcer. Your own stamps may look fairly common to you, but he or she is sure to appreciate them.

10. Trading off your duplicate stamps can be a lot of fun. Even if you don't know many collectors where you live, stamps are so lightweight that they can easily be traded by mail. Check out the stamp newspapers and magazines available at your local library for classified ads that list stamp trades. You may find, for example, that another collector will send you 100 large foreign stamps if you send 100 U.S. commemoratives. Usually schools do not subscribe to any of the periodical stamp publications, so you will have to go to your public library. (Many stamp publications also offer to send one free sample issue if you request it, because they are always looking for potential new subscribers.)

Collecting stamps need not be an expensive hobby. Thousands of stamps are issued every year, and while some of them cost many dollars, others cost just a few cents each. Nobody expects you to try to save every stamp that exists, and the key to enjoying philately is to save whatever you enjoy the most! With free stamps and a few inexpensive accessories, such as a small album and a package of stamp hinges, even collectors with little money can have a great time. Don't forget to mention stamps, stamp albums, and hinges before your birthday or Christmas! Also remember that a great many inexpensive stamps in the past have turned into more valuable stamps over the years.

THREE TIPS FOR STAMP COLLECTORS:

Soaking Stamps,
Choosing an Album, and Using Tongs.

Courtesy of the American Philatelic Society.

• TIP 1: SOAKING STAMPS

BEFORE SOAKING

Set aside any stamps on colored paper, or on paper with a colored backing. Pick out any stamps with colored cancellations, especially with red or purple ink.

Set aside any dark-colored stamps, stamps on poor-quality paper, or with strange-looking inks that might dissolve in the water and stain other stamps being soaked, etc. Any "problem" stamps must be handled carefully later, one at a time.

Trim the envelope paper close to the stamp, being careful not to cut the perforated edges or otherwise damage the stamp.

SOAKING THE STAMPS

Use a shallow bowl and fill it with several inches of cool-to-lukewarm water. (Never use hot water.) Float the stamps with the picture side up. Make sure the stamps have room to float and do not stick to one another. Don't soak too many at one time.

Let the stamps float until the glue dissolves and the stamps slide easily off the paper. Paper is very weak when it is wet and it's easy to tear a wet stamp if you handle it roughly. Be patient, and let the water do its work!

Rinse the back of the stamp gently in fresh water to make sure all the glue is off. Change the water in the soaking bowl often to make sure it is clean.

Place the stamps to dry on paper towels or old newspapers. (Don't use the Sunday comics! The colored inks might stick to the wet stamps.) It's a good idea to use your stamp tongs (see p. 624) to lift the wet stamps, instead of using your fingers. Lay the stamps in a single layer, and so they are not touching one another.

Let the stamps dry on their own. They may curl a little or look wrinkled, but don't worry about that. When they are completely dry, lift them with your tongs and put them in a phone book or a dictionary or some other book. (Special "stamp drying books" also can be purchased.) It's important not to put the stamps in a book until they are completely dry. After a few days, they should be nice and flat, and you can put them in your collection.

STAMPS ON COLORED PAPER OR WITH COLORED-INK CANCELS

Cut away all the excess envelope paper without harming the edges of the stamp.

Fill a shallow dish with cool water (cooler than you would usually use for soaking) and float the stamp face up. If the water becomes stained before the stamp is free from the paper, empty it out and use clean water, to prevent the stamp from being stained.

Dry as before.

DIRTY OR STAINED STAMPS

These can be soaked carefully in a small amount of undiluted liquid dish-washing detergent (not dishwasher detergent), then rinsed in clean cool water.

Very badly stained stamps can be washed gently in a weak solution of water and a bit of enzyme laundry detergent. Careful! This can work too well and remove the printing ink!

SELF-ADHESIVE STAMPS

Some self-adhesive stamps have a special, water-soluble backing, and they can be soaked off envelopes. You just need extra patience, as they may have to soak for an hour or more before they will separate from the backing paper. In general, U.S. self-adhesive stamps from about 1990 and later can be soaked with water; earlier ones cannot. If you don't want to try soaking, just trim the paper closely around a self-adhesive stamp on cover, and then mount it in your collection with a stamp mount.

• TIP 2: CHOOSING AN ALBUM

You've raided the mailbox, rummaged in the wastebasket in the post office lobby, and pestered your friends to save their envelopes. Now that you have all these philatelic goodies, where will you put them?

True, an ordinary shoebox gives storage space, but you should want a nicer home for your treasures—a place to display your material, not just store it. And, on the practical side, stamps and covers (envelopes with stamps on them, used in the mail) kept in a shoebox or paper folder risk damage from dirt or creases, losing value as well as beauty.

Since the first known commercial stamp album was published in 1862, the stamp hobby has grown tremendously, and many types of albums have become available.

When buying a home for your collection, here are some things to think about:

It may be your first album, but it probably will not be your last or only one. Your first album may be a kind of experiment, unless you already have seen someone else's album and think that kind would be right for you too. You also may have tried homemade pages and got some ideas of what you would want in a standard album.

If you are buying an album in person, rather than by mail, listen to the seller's advice, but don't be fully convinced by claims that one or another album is "the best." An album may be by a famous maker, and expensive, but that doesn't make it "the best" one for you. Be a careful shopper; consider all the factors—appearance, price, format—and make the best choice. Good beginners' albums are available that are not too expensive, are fully illustrated to show which stamp goes where, and may even contain extra information, such as maps and facts about the countries.

Certain styles of albums can present problems. For example, if an album is designed for stamps to be mounted on the front and back of each page, when the book is closed, the stamps can become tangled with one another on the facing pages. Opening the book may tear the mounted stamps apart. If you are looking at an album with this page format and don't like that aspect, but do like other things about the album, buy some good-quality plastic sheets to insert between the pages, and prevent the tangles.

You may choose not to buy a top-of-the-line album because of cost, but do be willing to pay for some quality. An album with pages of flimsy paper will not stand up to the stress of increasing numbers of stamps as you fill the album. An album with torn, falling-out pages is not much better than the old shoebox.

Homemade pages can be experimented with before album-shopping or may even become your permanent storage choice. Some options include a notebook or looseleaf binder of plain paper, though longtime, safest storage of your stamps should be on acid-free paper. If you have an unusual specialty, or enjoy unique arrangements, no standard album may ever suit your needs, and homemade will be best.

Blank, acid-free album pages punched for three-hole binders are widely available. It is easy to assemble a safe, stable home for your personalized collection, if you don't need or want the kind of structured format that standard albums provide. Makers of custom pages and albums advertise regularly in the philatelic press.

Buying an album is not so different from buying anything else: Think before and during the purchase; buy as wisely as you can and not over your budget; and don't be too discouraged if your first acquisition turns out to be less than perfect. You will always need places for temporary storage as you continue in the hobby. Old albums never go to waste!

• TIP 3: USING TONGS

Philatelic tongs (not to be confused with the tweezers in the medicine cabinet) are must-have items for every stamp collector. Get into the habit early of using your tongs every time you work with your stamps. They will act as clean extensions of your fingers and keep dirt, skin oil, and other harmful things from getting on your philatelic paper.

It's important to use tongs correctly and carefully. As with knives, scissors, and other helpful tools, tongs used carelessly are harmful rather than helpful. Cut some plain paper into stamp-sized pieces and practice using your tongs, watching what happens as you change the angle, pressure, and method of using them.

Grip a bit of paper strongly with the pointy-end style of tongs and watch what happens. If that were a favorite stamp, would you have wanted that hole poked in the middle of it? Keep experimenting, and you will find that it's not difficult to hold a stamp firmly but gently with tongs.

There are several common styles of tongs to suit your preference and for special purposes.

Some have very pointed ends; they touch only a tiny part of the stamp, but there is the risk of poking holes through it. Working with extra-long tongs (five or six inches) with small pointed tips requires a lot of dexterity, and while experts may prefer them, they may not be comfortable or necessary for "everyday" stamp work.

The rounded, spatula-type style known as the "spade" are good, general-purpose tongs. A squared-off version of the spade also is commonly available, though the rather sharp corners present the same kind of risk as the thin, pointy tongs. One handy style is angled, with a bend near the tips that makes it easier to remove stamps from watermark or soaking trays, or to insert and remove stamps from stockbooks or mounts.

Tongs cost anywhere from a couple of dollars to quite a few for some of the imported, high-quality models. A special gift for a philatelist would be some gold-plated tongs, which are not hard to find, believe it or not! Tongs can be found anywhere stamp supplies are sold; check under "Accessories" in the philatelic press ads.

Tongs are among the least expensive and most essential stamp-hobby needs. You may even want to have several different kinds on hand—instead of your hands! Your stamps will appreciate it.

BUYING STAMPS

There are many ways to buy stamps: packets, poundage mixtures, approvals, new issue services, auctions, and a number of others. To buy wisely, a collector must get to know the language of philately and the techniques used by dealers and auctioneers in selling stamps.

Packets of all different worldwide stamps are sold in graduated sizes from 1,000 up to 50,000. True to their word, they contain no duplicates. The stamps come from all parts of the world and date from the 1800s to the present. Both mint and used are included. When you buy larger quantities of most things, a discount is offered; with stamp packets, it works in reverse. The larger the packet, the higher its price per stamp. This is because the smaller packets are filled almost exclusively with low-grade material.

Packets are suitable only as a collection base. A collector should never count on them to build his entire collection. The contents of one worldwide packet are much like that of another. Country jackets are sold in smaller sizes, but there are certain drawbacks with packets.

1. Most packets contain some cancelled-to-order stamps, which are not very desirable for a collection. These are stamps released with postmarks already on them, and are classified as used but have never gone through the mail. Eastern Europe and Russia are responsible for many C.T.O.s.

2. The advertised value of packets bears little relation to the actual value. Packet makers call attention to the catalog values of their stamps, based on prices listed in standard reference works. The lowest sum at which a stamp can be listed in these books is 2¢; therefore, a packet of 1,000 automatically has a minimum catalog value of $20. If the retail price is $3 this seems like a terrific buy when, in fact, most of those thousand stamps are so common they are almost worthless.

Poundage mixtures are very different than packets. Here the stamps are all postally used (no C.T.O.s) and still attached to small fragments of envelopes or parcel wrappings. Rather than sold by count, poundage mixtures are priced by the pound or ounce and quite often by kilos. Price varies depending on the grade, and the grade depends on where the mixture was assembled. Bank mixtures are considered the best, as banks receive a steady flow of foreign registered mail. Mission mixtures are also highly rated. Of course, the mixture should be sealed and unpicked. Unless a mixture is advertised as unpicked, the high values have been removed. The best poundage mixtures are sold only by mail. Those available in shops are of medium or low quality. Whatever the grade, poundage mixtures can be counted on to contain duplicates.

If you want to collect the stamps of a certain country, you can leave a standing order for its new releases with a new-issue service. Whenever that government puts out stamps, they will be sent to the collector along with a bill. Usually the service will supply only mint copies. The price charged is not the face value, but the face value with a surcharge added to meet the costs of importing, handling, and the like. New issue services are satisfactory only if the collector is positive he wants all the country's stamps, no matter what. Remember that its issues could include semi-postals, long and maybe expensive sets, and extra high values.

By far the most popular way to buy stamps is via approvals. There is nothing new about approvals, as they go back to the Victorian era. Not all services are alike, though. Some offer sets, while others sell penny approvals. Then there are remainder approvals, advanced approvals, and seconds on approval. Penny approvals are really a thing of the past, though the term is still used. Before inflation, dealers would send a stockbook containing several thousand stamps, all priced at a penny each. If all the stamps were kept, the collector got a discount plus the book! Today the same sort of service can be found, but instead of 1¢ per stamp, the price is anywhere from 3¢ to 10¢. Remainder approvals are made up from collection remainders. Rather than dismount and sort stamps from incoming collections, the approval merchant saves himself time by sending them out right on the album pages. The collector receives leaves from someone else's collection with stamps mounted just as he arranged them. Seconds on approval are slightly defective specimens of scarce stamps, which would cost more if perfect. Advanced approvals are designed for specialized collectors who know exactly what they want and have a fairly substantial stamp budget.

In choosing an approval service you should know the ground rules of approval buying and not be unduly influenced by promotional offers. Most approval merchants allow the selections to be kept for ten days to two weeks. The unbought stamps are then returned along with payment for those kept. As soon as the selection is received back, another is mailed. This will go on, regardless of how much or how little is bought, until the company is notified to refrain from sending further selections. The reputable services will always stop when told.

Approval ads range from splashy full-pagers in the stamp publications to small three-line classified announcements in magazines and newspapers. Most firms catering to beginners offer loss leaders, or stamps on which they take a loss for the sake of getting new customers. If an approval dealer offers 100 pictorials for a dime, it is obvious he is losing money on that transaction, as 10¢ will not even pay the postage. It is very tempting to order these premiums. Remember that when ordering approvals. What sort of service is it? Will it offer the kind of stamps desired? Will prices be high to pay for the loss leaders? Be careful of confusing advertisements. Sometimes the premium offers seem to promise more than they actually do. A rare, early stamp may be pictured. Of course you do not receive the stamp, but merely a modern commemorative picturing it.

Auction Sales. Stamp auctions are held all over the country and account for millions of dollars in sales annually. Buying at auction is exciting and can be economical. Many sleepers turn up—stamps that can be bought at less than their actual value. To be a good auction buyer, the philatelist must know stamps and their prices pretty well, and know the ropes of auctions. An obvious drawback of auctions is that purchases are not returnable. A dealer will take back a stamp that proves not to a collector's liking, but an auctioneer will not. Also, auctioneers require immediate payment while a dealer may extend credit.

Stamps sold at auction come from private collections and the stocks of dealers; not necessarily defunct dealers, but those who want to get shelf space. Because they were brought together from a variety of sources, the nature and condition will vary. In catalog descriptions the full book value will be given for each stamp, but of course defective stamps will sell for much less than these figures. A bidder must calculate how much less. Other lots which can be difficult for the bidder to evaluate are those containing more than one stamp. Sometimes a superb specimen will be lotted along with a defective one. Then there are bulk lots which contain odds and ends from collections and such. It is usual in auctioning a collection for the better stamps to be removed and sold separately. The remainder is then offered in a single lot, which may consist of thousands or even tens of thousands of stamps. By all means examine lots before bidding. A period of inspection is always allowed before each sale, usually for several days. There may or may not be an inspection on sale day. If the bidder is not able to make a personal examination but must bid on strength of the catalog description, he should scale his bids for bulk lots much lower than for single stamp lots. He might bid $50 on a single stamp lot with a catalog value of $100, if the condition is listed as top-notch, but to bid one-half catalog value on a bulk lot would not be very wise. These lots are not scrutinized very carefully by the auctioneers and some stamps are bound to be disappointing. There may be some heavily canceled, creased, torn, etc. Also, there will very likely be duplication. A bid of one-fifth the catalog value on a bulk lot is considered high. Often a one-tenth bid is successful.

The mechanics of stamp auctions may strike the beginner as complicated. They are run no differently than other auctions. All material to be sold is lotted by the auctioneer; that is, broken down into lots or units and bidding is by lot. Everything in the lot must be bid on, even if just one of the stamps is desired. The motive of bulk lotting is to save time and give each lot a fair sales value.

Before the sale a catalog is published listing all the lots, describing the contents and sometimes picturing the better items. Catalogs are in the mail about 30 days before the sale date. If a bid is to be mailed, it must be sent early. Bids that arrive after the sale are disqualified, even if they would have been successful.

When the bid is received it is entered into a bidbook, along with the bidder's name and address. On sale day each lot opens on the floor at one level above the second-highest mail bid. Say the two highest mail bids are $30 and $20. The floor bidding would begin at $25. If the two highest bids are $100 and $500, the opening bid would probably be $150. The larger the amounts involved, the bigger will be the advances. The auctioneer will not accept an advance of $5 on a $500 lot; but on low-value lots even dollar advances are sometimes made. Then it becomes a contest of floor versus book. The auctioneer acts as an agent, bidding for the absentee until his limit is reached. If the floor tops him, he has lost. If the floor does not get as high as his bid, he wins the lot at one advance over the highest floor bid.

When a collector buys stamps by mail from a dealer, he should choose one who belongs to the American Stamp Dealers' Association or A.S.D.A. The emblem is carried in their ads.

HOW TO ORDER STAMPS "TOLL-FREE" FROM THE USPS

You can now order stamps, toll-free, from the USPS by calling the Philatelic Fulfillment Service Center located in Kansas City, Missouri, 1-800-782-6724. Listening to a computerized voice, you can choose from six options using a touch-tone phone: 1) ordering stamps, 2) catalog requests, subscription programs information, 3) customer assistance, 4) personalized envelopes, post offices and official mail agencies. This is a very useful service. It is recommended that you first order one of the catalogs, "Stamps, Etc." or "Not Just Stamps," in order to correctly place your order for stamps.

SELLING STAMPS

Almost every collector becomes a stamp seller sooner or later. Duplicates are inevitably accumulated, no matter how careful one may be in avoiding them. Then there are the G and VG stamps that have been replaced with F and VF specimens, and have become duplicates by intent. In addition to duplicates, a more advanced collector is likely to have stamps that are not duplicates but for which he has no further use. These will be odds and ends, sometimes quite valuable ones, that once suited the nature of his collection but are now out of place. Collectors' tastes change. The result is a stockpile of stamps that can be converted back to cash.

The alternative to selling the stamps you no longer need or want is trading them with a collector who does want them, and taking his unwanted stamps in return. All stamp clubs hold trading sessions. Larger national stamp societies operate trade-by-mail services for their members. The APS (American Philatelic Society) keeps $8,000,000 worth of stamps constantly circulating in its trading books or "circuit" books. Trading can be an excellent way of disposing of surplus stamps. In most cases it takes a bit longer than selling. Another potential drawback, especially if you are not a club member, is finding the right person with the right stamps.

The nature and value of the material involved may help in deciding whether to sell outright or trade. Also, there are your own personal considerations. If you're not going to continue in the stamp hobby, or need cash for some purpose other than stamp buying, trading is hardly suitable. Likewise, if you have developed an interest in some very exotic group of stamps or other philatelic items it may be impossible to find someone to trade with.

Once you have decided to sell, if indeed you do make that decision, the matter revolves upon how. To a stamp shop? To another collector? Through an auction house? Possibly by running your own advertisements and issuing price lists, if you have enough stamps and spare time to make this worthwhile?

While some individuals have an absolute horror at the prospect of selling anything, stamp collectors tend to enjoy selling. It is difficult to say why. Some enjoy it so much they keep right on selling stamps, as a business, long after their original objective is achieved. Nearly all professional stamp dealers were collectors before entering the trade.

Selling your stamps outright to a dealer, especially a local dealer whom you can personally visit, is not necessarily the most financially rewarding but it is quick and very problem-free. Of course it helps if the dealer knows you and it's even better if he knows some of your stamps. Dealers have no objection to repurchasing stamps they've sold to you. You will find that the dealers encourage their customers to sell to them just as much as they encourage them to buy. The dealers are really anxious to get your stamps if you have good salable material from popular countries. In fact most dealers would prefer buying from the public rather than any other source.

The collector selling stamps to a dealer has to be reasonable in his expectations. A dealer may not be able to use all the stamps you have. It is simply not smart business for a dealer to invest money in something he may not be able to sell. So, if you have esoteric or highly specialized items for sale, it might be necessary to find a specialist who deals in those particular areas rather than selling to a neighborhood stamp shop.

The local stamp shop will almost certainly want to buy anything you can offer in the way of medium-to-better-grade U.S. stamps of all kinds, including the so-called "back of the book" items. He may not want plate blocks or full sheets of commemoratives issued within the past 20 years. Most dealers are well supplied with material of this nature and have opportunities to buy more of it every day. The same is true of first-day covers, with a few exceptions, issued from the 1960s to the present. The dealers either have these items abundantly or can get them from a wholesaler at rock-bottom prices. They would rather buy stamps that are a bit harder to get from the wholesalers, or for which the wholesalers charge higher prices. On the whole you will meet with a favorable reception when offering U.S. stamps to a local dealer. With foreign stamps it becomes another matter: what do you have and how flexible are you in price? Nearly all the stamp shops in this country do stock foreign stamps to one extent or another. They do not, as a rule, attempt to carry comprehensive or specialized stocks of them. In the average shop you will discover that the selection of general foreign consists of a combination of modern mint sets, topicals, souvenir sheets, packets which come from the wholesaler, and a small sprinkling of older material, usually pre-1900. The price range of this older material will be $5 to $50. Non-specialist collectors of foreign stamps buy this type of item and that is essentially who the local shop caters to. When a local dealer buys rare foreign stamps or a large foreign collection, it is not for himself. He buys with the intent of passing them along to another dealer who has the right customers lined up. He acts only as a middleman or go-between. Therefore the price you receive for better-grade foreign stamps tends to be lower than for better-grade U.S., which the dealer buys for his own use.

What is a fair price to get for your stamps? This is always difficult to say, as many variable factors are involved. Consider their condition. Think in terms of what the dealer could reasonably hope to charge for them at retail and stand a good chance of selling them. Some of your stamps may have to be discounted because of no gum, poor centering, bent perfs, hinge remnants, repairs, or other problems. But even if your stamps are primarily F or VF, a dealer cannot pay book values for them. If you check his selling prices on his specimens of those same stamps, you can usually count on receiving from 40 to 50 percent of those prices. Considering the discount made from book values by the dealer in pricing his stock, your payment may work out to about 25 percent of book values. For rare U.S. stamps in top condition you can do better than 25 percent, but on most stamps sold to a dealer this is considered a fair offer. Keep in mind that the difference between a dealer's buying and selling prices is not just "profit margin." Most of the markup goes toward operating costs, for without this markup, there would be no stamp dealers.

WHAT IS AN ERROR, FREAK,
OR ODDITY?

In an attempt to answer the questions above, an article, "Listing of Existing EFO Variations According to Group," by Mr. John M. Hotchner, was published originally in the June 1982 issue of *The EFO Collector,* the quarterly journal of the Errors, Freaks, Oddities Collectors Club. Resulting correspondence and experience in the EFO field, plus selected portions of Mr. Hotchner's article, are contained herein to attempt to provide some guidance as to what constitutes an error, freak, or oddity.

Nothing makes a philatelist's head turn so fast as an obvious error in an issued stamp. Many of philately's true blue-chip errors are from the early days. The United States 1869 inverts on the fifteen-cent, twenty-four-cent and thirty-cent values, Spain's 1851 two-real value in a six-real blue sheet, New South Wales stamps of the 1850s and '60s with the wrong watermark, etc.

Why? Most stamps of this era had relatively small printings compared to today's. In addition, they were used with little thought given to looking for or saving errors or misprints of lesser significance. Most of the varieties that have been found were used, and exist in very small quantities. Incidentally, this is a very good reason for one to keep one's eye open, for there remains a possibility that classic errors can still be found in old albums or accumulations.

In the early days of philately, collectors gathered EFOs (errors, freaks, oddities) to dress up their country or topical collections. Many modern collectors continue to collect EFOs in that fashion. There has, however, been a recent increase in collecting and studying EFOs as a specialty area.

Modern-day specialization has been fostered by the greatly increased awareness of and search for EFO material. This is a search which is often rewarded because of the increasing complexity of modern production equipment and the continuing pressure to reduce cost.

The lack of commonly accepted definitions of EFO terms has been an impediment to the growth of EFO philately. In the absence of a clear sense of what EFOs include, philatelists, in large numbers, have found the area complex and difficult. It has been hard to understand how values developed, so collectors merely kept what they came across, but rarely sought out EFO material unless it was listed in a catalog.

Catalog listing is, of course, reserved for errors. Catalog-listed errors get space in albums. Thus, recognized errors tend to have an increased value because collectors search for them because they like to fill their empty album spaces. Without a catalog listing, the remainder of EFO material tended to wallow in a valley of conflicting and confusing opinion and wildly varying prices. Also, if an item lacks catalog recognition, one might call the item a "freak," "oddity," or "variety."

The answer to an often-asked question regarding EFOs—"Aren't they expensive?"—is that while some EFOs are valued in the thousands of dollars, others cost no more than a regular used stamp. In fact, it is quite possible for one to find a spectacular EFO item in one's own mailbox. You have probably heard of collectors who bought stamps or postal stationery at their local post office only to find something wrong with the purchase. Think of some of the people who used their find before they realized they had an EFO item. Knowledge is the key to recognizing EFO material when you find it.

The best possible source of information and education can be obtained by becoming a member of a philatelic organization such as the American Philatelic Society (APS), The American Topical Association (ATA), etc.; by joining specialty groups such as the Bureau Issues Association (BIA), The Errors, Freaks, Oddities Collectors Club (EFOCC), etc.; by subscribing to publications such as Linn's, Meekels, *Stamp Collector,* etc.; by joining libraries such as the Cardinal Spellman Museum, the Western Philatelic Library, etc. Through these organizations and publications, one will obtain knowledge so that one can differentiate between what a postal entity designs and what is the produced product.

The following is the best tool, to date, to attempt to type EFO material that is at variance from the intended design.

ERRORS

To be classed as such, an item must be completely missing a production step, i.e. the item must be completely missing a color, completely missing required perforations, contain an inverted design step, etc. Other examples might be:

- Perforations entirely missing between stamps—one or more sides.
- Perforations fully doubled or tripled.
- Perforations of wrong gauge applied.
- Items unintentionally printed on paper watermarked for another issue, or not watermarked at all.

FREAKS

To be classed as such, an item might have a lesser degree of production problem, or problems that are partial and not repeatable. Examples might be:

- Perforations shifted into the design portion of an issue.
- Overinking, underinking, smeared inking.
- Foldovers, foldunders, creases creating crazy perforations.
- Printer's waste (by definition, "Unlawfully Salvaged"). This category would include rejection markings that indicate material that should have been destroyed.
- Gutter snipes (less than a full stamp on one side).

ODDITIES

"Oddities" or, as European collectors seem to favor, "Varieties" include unusual issuances. Examples might be:

- Stamps printed on backs of stamps.
- Usages (bisects).
- Essays, proofs, specimens.
- Cancel/meter varieties.
- Unusual local overprints.
- Double transfers, layout lines, position dots.
- Pre–first-day-of-issue cancels.

The bottom line is any item, be it freak, error, oddity, or variety, can be collected as a specialty, or a collector can try to obtain an example of each. Some collectors will restrict their collecting to one country, or even one major issue within a country. Others simply accumulate and enjoy anything they come across with no particular rhyme-or-reasoned order.

The Errors, Freaks, Oddities Collectors Club has an international membership, quarterly publication and mail auction, heir's assistance program, study groups, etc. Annual dues are $16 USD North America, Europe $30 USD. Sample copy of The EFO Collector is $3 USD, or mint postage. EFOCC, P.O. Box 1126, Kingsland, GA 31548-1126; (912) 729-1573; FAX: (912) 729-1585; e-mail—cwouscg@aol.com.

PUBLICATIONS—
LINN'S STAMP NEWS

Linn's Stamp News is a magazine-size full-color newspaper for stamp and postal history collectors. It has been published continuously as a weekly since 1928. *Linn's* is the largest weekly publication in the stamp hobby.

Linn's carries news stories about new stamp issues of the United States, Canada and other countries; outstanding auctions and realizations; new discoveries of errors and other valuable stamps and covers; and developments in the U.S. Postal Service. It also contains the regular columns Asia, Great Britain, World Classics, U.S. Notes, Modern First-Day Covers, Kitchen Table Philately, Stamp Market Tips, Topics and Themes, World of New Issues, Computers and Stamps, Latin America, Who's Who on U.S. Stamps, Modern U.S. Mail, Postmark Pursuit, Cradle of Civilization, The Insider, and Postal History.

Regular departments include the Collectors Forum (question and answer page), Readers' Opinions (letters page), Refresher Course (collecting workshops for new and not-so-new collectors), Stamp Events Calendar, U.S. Stamp Market Index, Auction Calendar, the Editor's Column, Collecting Made Easy, Puzzle and Trickies.

Linn's U.S. Stamp Program is published each week and includes a schedule of U.S. new issues for the year, with details and USPS ordering numbers for each issue.

Stamp programs for Canada and the United Nations are also published regularly.

Linn's editorial staff comprises the best journalistic talent, from professional reportage to knowledge of stamp collecting. *Linn's* columnists and freelancers are among the best informed and well-connected people in the hobby.

Linn's contains full-page, display and classified ads from all areas of the collecting community: from the most prestigious auction houses the world over to individual collectors who want to sell or trade their duplicates—and everyone in between.

Linn's averages 64 pages a week. An annual subscription is $45.95.

Collectors can take advantage of a special offer of just $9.99 for a one-year digital edition subscription. To view a sample of *Linn's* digital edition, visit *Linn's* web site at www.linns.com. The web site also offers a How-To feature, reference information, special features, weekly headlines, marketplace, stamp quiz, the new issue of the week, stamp wallpaper for computers, and more.

Linn's also operates the online retail database Linn's Zillions of Stamps (www.zillionsofstamps.com), which allows collectors the convenience of shopping for U.S. and worldwide stamps, covers, and supplies at one online address.

THE NATIONAL POSTAL MUSEUM

On July 30, 1993, the National Postal Museum opened its doors to the public, marking the creation of a new Smithsonian Institution museum, and making way for the nation's first major museum devoted to postal history and philately.

In what is a sophisticated and highly interactive museum, the National Postal Museum in Washington, D.C., features exhibitions that tell the history of the nation's mail service, from the Colonial era and the Pony Express to the art of letters and the beauty and lore of stamps.

"The theme of the museum is 'America's history is in the mail.' We are presenting American history from a new perspective," says James H. Bruns, former director of the National Postal Museum. "The museum is intended to inspire appreciation for a system that affects our lives every day. The history of America's mail service is the history of our success as a nation. The museum tells an upbeat and endearing story of American ingenuity and remarkable progress."

The Postal Museum is located at First Street and Massachusetts Avenue N.E. on the lower level of the former Washington City Post Office Building, which is on Capitol Hill next to Union Station. The museum houses and displays the nation's stamp and postal history collection, the largest and most comprehensive of its kind in the world.

"Not only is America's history in the mail, its future is in the mail, too," says William J. Henderson, former Chief Executive Officer and Postmaster General of the U.S. Postal Service. "We want people to understand the role the Postal Service has played for more than two centuries in helping our nation grow and prosper, and the important social and economic role the mail continues to play for the United States."

The museum occupies approximately 75,000 square feet, with more than 25,000 square feet devoted to exhibit space. It also features a Library Research Center, a Discovery Room for educational programs, a museum shop, and a philatelic sales center. The Library Research Center, available to the public by appointment, is among the largest postal history and philatelic research centers in the world, with more than 40,000 volumes and manuscripts. The museum also houses collections, conservation facilities, and curatorial and administrative offices.

HISTORY

The National Postal Museum was made possible by an agreement between the Smithsonian and the United States Postal Service. The museum was established after lengthy negotiations about relocating the Smithsonian's vast postal history and philatelic collection of more than 16 million stamps, covers, and artifacts. Previously housed on the third and fourth floors of the National Museum of American History, the collection lacked adequate exhibit, storage, and research space in that location.

On November 6, 1990, the Smithsonian Institution and the U.S. Postal Service signed an agreement in which the Postal Service would provide the site and approximately $15.4 million for start-up and construction costs and the Smithsonian would administer the museum and its staff.

The National Postal Museum is funded by both the Postal Service and the Smithsonian, as well as by money raised from endowments and ongoing fund-raising campaigns. The Smithsonian contribution to the new museum has been the same as that spent on the collection when it was at the Museum of American History. The more than $3 million raised from private organizations through March 1993 went toward the installation of the new and expanding exhibits. Private funds continue to be used to develop and expand exhibits.

THE COLLECTION

The National Philatelic Collection was established at the Smithsonian in 1886 with the donation of a sheet of 10-cent Confederate postage stamps. Generous gifts from individuals and foreign governments, transfers from government agencies and purchases have increased the collection to today's total of more than 16 million items.

From 1908 until 1963, the collection was housed in the Smithsonian's Arts and Industries Building on the National Mall. In 1964, the collection was moved to the National Museum of American History where it was expanded to include postal history and stamp production. In addition to the stamp collection, the museum has postal stationery covers, postal history material that predates stamps, vehicles used to transport the mail, mailboxes, meters, greeting cards, and letters.

EXHIBITIONS

More than 50,000 stamps and objects, and 400 graphics are on display throughout the museum's five major exhibit galleries that explore different facets of mail communication and history. The galleries include:

MOVING THE MAIL

Faced with the challenge of moving the mail quickly, the postal service looked to trains, automobiles, airplanes, and buses to deliver the mail, all of which are the focus of the museum's 90-foot-high Atrium gallery. After the Civil War, postal officials began to take advantage of railway trains for moving and sorting the mail. Sorting the mail while it was being carried between towns was a revolutionary approach to mail delivery, involving generations of devoted postal employees who worked as railway mail clerks.

Airmail service was established between New York, Philadelphia, and Washington, D.C., in 1918 with the remarkable pioneering flights of pilots Torrey Webb, James Edgerton, H. Paul Culver, and George Boyle. Airmail service was the base from which America's commercial aviation industry developed.

Some of the most ambitious movers of the mail were not aviators, railway mail clerks, or even postal employees. They are the star route contractors, who have delivered mail with everything from mules to motorcycles, including the 1850s Concord-style stagecoach on display in the museum.

THE ART OF CARDS AND LETTERS

While other galleries focus on systems of mail service, this gallery emphasizes letters. A cherished art form, letters are windows into history, used throughout museum displays to relate personal stories of survival, success, and tragedy. Through an array of wartime correspondence from World War I to Desert Storm, as well as objects and a video, one section highlights the struggle of soldiers and their loved ones to maintain ties during war. Changing exhibits in this gallery concentrate on the important stories letters tell of families and friends bound by these missives over land and across time.

BINDING THE NATION

The museum's first gallery provides an overview of the events in America from colonial times through the 19th century, stressing the importance of written communication in the young nation. As early as 1673, regular mail was carried between New York and Boston following Indian trails. That route, once known as the King's Best Highway, is now U.S. Route 1.

Benjamin Franklin, a colonial postmaster for the British government, played a key role in establishing mail service in the colonies, as well as in forging a strong link between colonial publishers and the postal service. Many newspapers that relied heavily on information carried in the mail customarily adopted the word "Post" into their title. Newspapers were so important to the dissemination of information to the people that they were granted cheaper postage rates.

By 1800, mail was carried over more than 9,000 miles of postal roads. The challenge of developing mail service over long distances is the central theme of "The Expanding Nation," which features the famed Pony Express. At an interactive video station, visitors can create their own postal route.

CUSTOMERS AND COMMUNITIES

By the turn of the 20th century, nearly 10,000 letter carriers worked in over 400 cities. The nation's population was expanding at top speed, and with it, the nation's mail volume and the need for personal mail delivery. This gallery focuses on the modern changes in mail service introduced at the turn of the century.

Crowded cities inspired postal officials to experiment with a variety of mail delivery systems, such as the impressive but ultimately impractical underground pneumatic tubes. Home delivery of mail began in the cities during the Civil War, when postal officials decided it was inhumane to require soldiers' families to receive death notices at post office windows.

As rural Americans watched city residents receive free home delivery, they began to demand equal treatment. This was the start of Rural Free Delivery. Facets of Rural Free Delivery and its important and often heartwarming role in the fabric of the nation is explored with photographs, mail vehicles, and a variety of rural mailboxes.

The history of the vast direct mail industry is the subject of a special interactive gallery. Through the use of sophisticated technology, the exhibition "What's in the Mail for You!" uses touch screen panels, three-dimensional projections, video workstations, holograms, and computer interactives to tell the story of the mailing industry and its function as a major means of commerce in America. This hands-on exhibit allows visitors to create a mailer and "target" customers; related exhibit topics look at different mail marketing techniques, the key to a successful mail campaign, and the success stories of well-known mail order entrepreneurs like L.L. Bean.

STAMPS AND STORIES

Among some 20 million stamp collectors in the United States, many are casual collectors, while others work at the hobby with a devotion to detail and scholarship unmatched by other pastimes. This gallery is for all collectors, as well as for those who know little about the renowned hobby of philately. The history of the stamp begins in 1840, when Great Britain issued the first gummed postage stamp. Since then stamps of every subject, shape, and design have been produced for consumer use or as collectibles.

Serving not only as proof of postage, stamps are also miniature works of art, keepsakes, and rare treasures—as well as the workhorses of the automated postal system. Some stamps tell stories, while others contain secrets and hidden meanings.

Some of the highlights of the gallery are priceless rarities from the museum's vast collection, including inverted stamps and scarce covers. Videos address questions of how and why stamps were invented, and how they are printed. A selection of more than 55,000 stamps is on display, and will be rotated every six months.

Within the exhibit galleries are more than 30 interactive areas, including, for example, video games that invite visitors to choose the best mail route between various cities in the 1800s, or deliver mail in a DeHavilland biplane. The museum features 17 video presentations, with topics ranging from America's railway mail clerks, the star route contractors, early letter carriers, and transportation technology, to stories about mail-train wrecks and robberies, and postal workers.

THE JEANETTE CANTRELL RUDY GALLERY

In this 800-square-foot gallery, a major exhibition devoted to federal duck stamps, entitled "Artistic License: The Duck Stamp Story," opened in Spring 1996. Made possible by a generous donation from Jeanette Cantrell Rudy of Nashville, TN., the exhibition explores the history of duck stamps, their contribution to the conservation of America's waterways, and the extraordinary craftsmanship that goes into their creation. A selection of rare duck stamps is on display, drawn from the collections of Mrs. Rudy and from the National Postal Museum.

TOURS

One-hour highlights tours are offered daily at 11 a.m. and 1 p.m. The National Postal Museum's Education Office will arrange guided tours for school and camp groups from September through May. Group leaders should call (202) 633-5534 (Voice) or (202) 633-9849 (TTY) for more information.

MUSEUM DESIGNED SPECIFICALLY TO HOUSE UNIQUE COLLECTION

The National Postal Museum was designed by the firm of Florance Eichbaum Esocoff King Architects. Chief among the objectives for designing the museum was the desire to create a maximum-security facility to protect the Smithsonian's priceless stamp collection, while at the same time creating an aesthetically rich setting that will attract visitors and encourage exploration of the museum's themes of postal history and philately.

The new museum's centerpiece is a 90-foot-high atrium that projects through the center of the quadrangle-shaped City Post Office Building.

Three airmail planes hang from steel girders inside the atrium, which has a glass ceiling 1.5 inches thick. The entire atrium area houses mail transportation vehicles and related displays; however, enough space on the atrium's marble floor remains for visitors to observe the intricate envelope and stamp design within the floor's tiles.

The museum is equipped with an array of sophisticated surveillance and safety equipment. The museum's research facilities, including the 6,000-square-foot Library Research Center, are meant to enhance the work and study of visiting researchers and scholars. The library features a specimen study room, an audio-visual viewing room, and a separate library of rare books.

HISTORIC BUILDING ENHANCES MUSEUM'S MESSAGE

The Washington City Post Office Building was built between 1911 and 1914 to serve as the District's central post office facility. Designed by architect Daniel Burnham, architect of Union Station, the City Post Office Building was built next door to the elegant train station in order to expedite the distribution of incoming mail to the nation's capital.

Completely renovated and restored to its original appearance, the City Post Office Building houses the National Postal Museum as well as a full-service post office and several federal agencies. The museum is located in what was once the building's mail processing and distribution center. An impressively ornate historic marble lobby, formerly the main service area of the City Post Office Building, will now serve as the foyer to the National Postal Museum. The Beaux Arts–style building is eligible for listing in the National Register of Historic Places.

EDUCATION PROGRAMS AND CHANGING EXHIBITIONS

The National Postal Museum offers a series of educational outreach activities. Through scheduled events in the museum's Discovery Center, individuals from preschool age to adult are invited to participate in events that aim to enhance the information presented in exhibits. Activities range from learning more about the art of stamps, postal transportation, automation, and mail delivery to letter writing and the analysis of historic letters. The museum also engages in school and community collaborative projects.

LIBRARY RESEARCH CENTER

With its more than 40,000 volumes and manuscripts, the museum's Library Research Center is among the world's largest philatelic and postal history research facilities. The 6,000-square-foot library features a rare-book reading room, an audiovisual room, research cubbies, and a workroom for viewing items from the collection. The library also offers current philatelic and postal magazines and newsletters as well as U.S.

Postal Service publications and annual reports. The center is operated by the Smithsonian Institution Libraries. It is open to the public by appointment from 10 a.m. to 4 p.m., Monday through Friday. For more information, call (202) 633-5544.

PUBLICATIONS

The official newsletter of the National Postal Museum is a quarterly, titled *EnRoute,* and is available by becoming a member of the National Postal Museum for $25.00 annually. A six-month calendar of events and membership information is offered by request by calling (202) 633-5544.

STAFF

The museum staff includes fifty-two full-time professional positions.

THE JUNIOR PHILATELISTS OF AMERICA

ABOUT THE JPA

There are many stamp organizations in North America today—national, state, and local. The major societies are naturally operated by and for adult collectors. Young people may be allowed to join, but usually are not given an active role.

In the JPA, the situation is different. It is a group run by and for young people, age eighteen and under. Junior members operate services, write for the publication, serve on study groups and committees, and elect their own officers.

The JPA is a dynamic organization; the Officers and Board of the JPA are willing to listen to each and every idea of the membership. Please tell us what you want to see in the JPA. After all, as a member, it is your organization.

Open to Collectors of All Ages—Beginners or Advanced. There's no minimum age for JPA membership. We welcome the youngest and newest collector as well as the advanced philatelist. Everyone can benefit from JPA services and publications!

BENEFITS OF MEMBERSHIP

- You'll be part of an exciting organization that is bringing change and excitement to stamp collecting.

- The opportunity to participate in all of the JPA's activities and our bimonthly magazine, *The Philatelic Observer*.

- Access to the JPA's services, including Pen Pals, Stamp Identification, American Philatelic Research Library access, and periodic stamp auctions.

- The JPA Study Groups are a great way to meet up with other members interested in the same types of stamps as you are interested in.

- As soon as you join you will receive a "Goodie Packet" filled with stamps, a membership card, more information on JPA services, and other great free stuff that varies from month to month.

- Every two months all members receive a copy of *The Philatelic Observer,* which is filled with interesting articles from JPA members as well as prominent stamp collectors.

SERVICES AVAILABLE TO MEMBERS OF THE JPA

Awards Committee

Contact Central Office to request awards for your stamp show/ exhibition (JPA, P.O Box 2625, Albany, OR 97321). For more information, contact Central Office.

Educational Projects

Teachers and Stamp Club Leaders, we have stamps and stamp collecting information available for use in clubs and classrooms.

Library Services

The American Philatelic Research Library is open to JPA members. Others may browse the library to find books that can be checked out at their local library. Look in the latest *Philatelic Observer* for the person to contact to access the library.

MEMBERSHIP APPLICATION AND DUES

JPA dues are quite reasonable, set with a young person's budget in mind. For more information on dues and membership contact the JPA.

Junior Philatelists of America
P.O. Box 850
Boalsburg, PA 16827-0850
Website: www.jpastamps.org.

Pen Pals Service

Looking for a Pen Pal somewhere in the world? Send your name, JPA No., and what type of Pen Pal you are looking for to the Pen Pal Chairman.

Recruiting Committee

Help recruit more members to keep the JPA growing! You could even earn next year's dues free! Contact Central Office for Membership Applications and share the JPA's Web site with your friends.

Public Relations

Do you have a Hobbies or Collectibles section in your local paper? Find out how to get the word out about the JPA.

The Philatelic Observer

The JPA's very own award-winning newsletter is sent to all members every two months! It's filled with information, games, and stories from and about other members! For a sample copy of *The Philatelic Observer*, send $1.

Pamphlets

JPA pamphlets are available free of charge from JPA Central Office, P.O. Box 2625, Albany, OR 97321 for members and nonmembers alike. Please send an SASE.

Stamp Identification

Simply send a photocopy of any stamp you can't identify along with an SASE to the address in the front of the *Observer.*

Welcoming Committee

Do you need help on writing "Welcome Letters" to new JPA members? Look in the front of your *Observer* to see who to contact.

Member E-mail Address Directory

Keep up-to-date with Collin Rickman. Contact him with your JPA No. and e-mail address to be added or removed. Members' e-mail addresses are not included unless they have asked to be included.

STAMP CLUSTERS

Welcome to the Junior Philatelists of America's Stamp Clusters Program! We are glad you've decided to learn more about the program. This handbook has been developed to give you a guided tour into the fun and excitement of participating in one or more JPA study groups. Stamp Clusters are actually a means to learn more about your collecting interests and possible ways to increase your collection through stamp trading and auctions. There is no actual studying required, just an interest in sharing your knowledge, or a desire to learn more about the stamps you collect, and more fun adventures with your collection. There are no special requirements to join any Stamp Clusters other than being a JPA member. It does not matter how long you have been a member, your age, or your knowledge about a particular subject. Even foreign members can join Stamp Clusters. There are no additional dues required to participate in any Stamp Clusters and you need no special equipment. All you need is an interest in learning more about the stamps you collect.

You may even join more than one Cluster. You will be able to explore and participate in such activities as

- Contests and games
- Auctions
- Columnist for *The Philatelic Observer*
- Pen pals
- Adult mentors
- Chairing a Stamp Cluster
- Creating new Stamp Clusters
- Exhibiting your stamps

Many fun opportunities await you when you join a Stamp Cluster. You find that members are excited about the stamps they collect and want to share their enthusiasm and knowledge with other JPA members.

What Stamp Clusters Are Currently Available?

- Asian Stamp Cluster

Do you have an interest in the Orient? How about the East Indies? Or the Himalayas? Then join the Asian Stamp Cluster! Our purpose is to try and learn what little bits we can of the world's largest land mass, from the Ural Mountains to the Pacific Ocean. It's an open forum about Asia, where we all can talk about the countries, topics, and other things that we want to talk about.

- Canadian Stamp Cluster

The Canadian Stamp Cluster is finally out of the grave and back in full motion. If you want to join this fun and informational group, please send me a request! Expect articles, information, and a contest or two. If anyone signing up could write an article on Canadian stamps, that would be great. Look in the *Observer* for Tyson's address.

- European Stamp Cluster

Do you collect European stamps and would like to join a free group that gives you the opportunity to participate in contests, quizzes, and write articles for *The Philatelic Observer*? If your answer is yes and you are a JPA member, the European Stamp Cluster is for you.

- First Day Cover Stamp Cluster

If you're a member of the JPA, then why not join the FDCSC?
The FDCSC (First Day Cover Stamp Cluster) specializes in the study of First Day Covers. Even if you don't collect FDCs, they're a lot of fun to learn about—why not give it a shot? Who knows . . . you may even learn so much about FDCs that you'll want to start collecting them, too!

• Historical Stamp Cluster

Learn about the history of the world in a fun way, the Historical Stamp Cluster! Going back in time by the method of philately, we can see the World War (etc.) all over again, by games, puzzles, a newsletter, and much, much, more! Do you want to join? Or do you have a question or a comment?

• Topical Stamp Cluster

If you are a JPA member and enjoy any topic of stamps, then this is the Stamp Cluster for you! In our bimonthly newsletter, the *Variety,* we have a certain topic that the members help decide! There are also contests, prizes, etc., and this is all free!

• U.S. Stamp Cluster

Join the U.S. Stamp Cluster, and see what all the fuss is about! Keep up-to-date on U.S. stamp news with the full-color newsletter *The American Essence.* Participate in group discussions, quizzes, contests. Build your collection with the trading circuit and classified ads, plus take part in activities and earn prizes.

• Women on Stamps Cluster

Do you collect famous women on stamps—or is this a subject that interests you? Join this Stamp Cluster and the fun is just beginning! Learn more about the famous women found on stamps all over the world while having fun with all sorts of games and quizzes.

How Long Can I Stay in a Stamp Cluster?

All questions, comments, or concerns concerning the JPA Cluster Program should be directed to Alison Turtledove (alcyone175@aol.com), Second V.P.

Participation in any given Stamp Cluster is solely up to the individual JPA member. Not all members will be interested in participating in a Stamp Cluster. There are no time constraints on any member of the JPA. We hope that you'll enjoy the activities provided in the Stamp Cluster program so much that you will participate indefinitely.

How Do I Get More Information about Joining a Study Cluster?

The Philatelic Observer contains a listing of current Stamp Clusters along with the name and address of the Chairperson. Simply contact the Chairperson for the Stamp Cluster you are interested in joining. For general information about the Stamp Clusters, contact the JPA Second Vice President.

How Do Stamp Clusters Correspond?

The Stamp Cluster Chair can provide you with a list of names and addresses of the members in your Stamp Cluster. Correspondence is usually carried on directly between members of that particular Stamp

Cluster or through articles and columns in the *Observer*. Your Stamp Cluster Chair's address can be found on the inside front cover of the *Observer*. (Please include a #10 SASE.)

How to Start a New Stamp Cluster

While the current Stamp Cluster program covers many popular areas of stamp collecting, there are undoubtedly JPA members who collect stamps that don't fit into any one of the established groups. Any active member may emerge as the leader of the proposed Stamp Cluster. This member should have significant contact with other interested JPA members. A formal request is sent to the President and Second Vice President (Coordinator of the Stamp Clusters) by postal mail. This request should include the proposed name of the cluster; proposed Chairperson's name, age, address, and JPA No.; and the names, addresses, and JPA Nos. of other interested members. A brief statement on how this Stamp Cluster will benefit JPA should be included in your submission. Upon approval for the new Cluster and the appointment of the Chair by the President, a new Cluster can be formed.

What Activities Are Offered in the Observer?

Most of the activities of a Stamp Cluster center around the concepts of education, encouragement, and the fellowship of stamp collecting.

The Philatelic Observer—Allows Stamp Cluster members and Adult Supporting Mentors the opportunity to submit articles and columns relating to their Stamp Cluster topic. Through these columns and articles you will be able to participate in such activities as

- Auctions
- Contests
- Educational articles
- Games
- Stamp Cluster quizzes

Columnist for the Observer—Ideas for columns and articles may be submitted to the Stamp Cluster Chair or the editor of the *Observer*. You should furnish both the Chair and the editor a copy of your article or column. It is not mandatory to write for the newsletter, but if you have an interesting subject to share, why not give it a try? The Stamp Cluster Chairperson can provide you with information for resources relating to your Stamp Cluster topic when participating as a columnist for the *Observer*.

Stamp Cluster Quizzes—Generally follow an article or column pertaining to an individual Stamp Cluster. These quizzes may be submitted to the Stamp Cluster Chairperson either by the writer of an article or by any member of a group. Directions for participation are always included, and usually a philatelic prize is offered to the winner. (Winners of such quizzes and contests are usually listed in Recent Winners.)

Contests—Related to a particular area of study may take any form such as an essay, stamp design, cacheted covers, etc. Ideas for contests may be submitted by members of a Stamp Cluster to the Chairperson. These contests may also be sponsored by a member of the Advisory Council, the Educational Director, an Adult Advisor, or another philatelic society.

Games—Featured on the "Fun Page," may be submitted to the editor of the *Observer* or to the Stamp Cluster Chair. Word search and crossword puzzles, logic problems, cryptograms, and matching games are very popular with many of the readers.

Auctions—Relating to specific Stamp Cluster interests usually take the form of a mini lot auction. These auctions generally contain ten or less items. Auction lots usually consist of donated materials and are generally sponsored by the Educational Director or by an adult advisor to a particular Stamp Cluster. All junior members of JPA may bid on lots featured. The instructions for any type of auction will appear in the *Observer* preceding the auction lots. Money received from the successful bidders of these auctions is used to support and improve the JPA programs.

Newsletters—Many Stamp Clusters have their own newsletters. These newsletters may be circulated by the Stamp Cluster Chair.

What Other Activities Are Offered?

Recruit new members to any Stamp Cluster by writing a welcome letter to new members. Often new members will list their collecting interests, which will give you an opportunity to include them in your Stamp Cluster. If you need more information about recruiting new members to your Stamp Cluster, contact your Stamp Cluster Chairperson.

Pen Pals—Matching your collecting interests may be available through the Pen Pals Service. The coordinator of the Pen Pals Service often receives inquiries from youth groups in other countries requesting pen pals for their youth. To find out more information about JPA's Pen Pal Service, write to the coordinator listed in the Departments and Services Directory.

Contests sponsored by other philatelic societies or periodicals may occasionally appear in *The Philatelic Observer*. These contests may take the form of essays, mini exhibits, or quizzes. All JPA members are encouraged to participate in these contests.

The Stamp Cluster Chair can provide you with a list of names and addresses of the other members of the Stamp Cluster if you wish to establish a pen pal just within the Stamp Cluster you belong to.

Is There Assistance for a Stamp Cluster?

Write to the Second Vice President for assistance with all aspects of your Stamp Cluster. Assistance available to your Cluster and/or individual members can include, but is not limited to, the following:

- Sample letters
- Adult supporting member mentors
- Auctions, contests, and quizzes
- Pen pal service
- Library services, including research support for columnists
- Information about foreign postal administrations
- Information about other societies specializing in your Cluster's interests
- Adult mentors for exhibiting

Additional assistance can be obtained from the Board of Directors and JPA Officers. Their addresses can be found in the Departments and Services Directory located in the *Observer*.

How Do You Become a Stamp Cluster Chair?

The Chairperson of a Stamp Cluster is appointed by the JPA President and works directly with the Second Vice President, who is the coordinator of the Stamp Clusters. Vacancies are announced in the *Observer*. Since JPA members live all over the United States and in other countries, the majority of Stamp Cluster contact will be made through the *Observer* and through letter writing. A candidate for a Chairperson position should have good communication and organizational skills. The Chairperson of each Stamp Cluster is the leader and coordinator of the activities of the Cluster. They are responsible for Clusters' activity updates, recruiting new members, trading programs, and establishing relationships with adult supporting member mentors.

Chairperson Stamp Cluster Kit—Currently in the works for and will be available exclusively to a Stamp Cluster Chair. The kit is a user-friendly tool to help organize and guide Chairs with their responsibilities and Cluster's activities. Each Chair will be responsible for the care and updating of this resource kit.

How Can I Get Exhibiting Help from a Stamp Cluster?

A Stamp Cluster is a great place to start when you are interested in exhibiting. The Stamp Cluster Chair can match you with an adult supporting member mentor who can advise you on the exhibiting process, inform you about the entry process, and even critique your exhibit.

How Can Adult Supporting Members Get Involved with JPA Stamp Clusters?

Adult supporting members are the most valuable resource to any Stamp Cluster. Many adults have many years of expertise and knowledge about philately. They may participate by

- Answering questions of individuals or Stamp Cluster Chairs
- Assisting a Stamp Cluster Chair with mailing lists and updating the Chair's resource kit
- Submitting articles or columns for publication
- Assisting with contests
- Developing and/or coordinating auctions with the Stamp Cluster Chairperson or the Educational Director
- Designing games or puzzles
- Facilitating trading or exchange programs
- Mentoring individual members with an exhibiting project

The best way to support youth in philately is to get involved. The Stamp Cluster Mentorship allows you to actively participate in youth philately within your own boundaries and sharing your expertise in a particular area of philately.

Any adult supporting member interested in getting involved and nurturing future philatelists should contact the Membership Services Department, which coordinates adult supporting member mentorships with the Second Vice President. Their names and addresses can be found in the Departments and Services Directory located in the *Observer*.

THE AMERICAN
PHILATELIC SOCIETY

Founded in 1886 the American Philatelic Society (APS) is a nonprofit association for stamp collectors, which seeks to promote the hobby and serve its members. The 37,000+ member organization is run by a full-time staff of 33 and is guided by a volunteer Board of Directors elected by the members.

Whether you are a beginning collector or have collected for years, the APS offers many services and educational opportunities to enhance your collecting enjoyment—including a subscription to *The American Philatelist*. The full-color one hundred page monthly magazine features articles written by members on all aspects of stamp collecting, information on U.S. news issues, hobby related websites, Society news, a calendar of upcoming stamp shows and exhibitions around the world.

The APS Sales Division provides an opportunity for collectors to buy or sell stamps from each other through the mail. Members may request "circuits" of stamps or covers from more than 160 categories of countries and topics. The items are priced by the submitting members, and most range from under $1 to $20. The APS also offers items for sale at our online StampsStore, www.stampstore.org. Anyone may browse the 300,000+ items, but buying and/or selling is a privilege of membership. The online store features some rarities and more expensive stamps in addition to the many modestly priced items.

Another popular service offered by the APS is the insurance program, which allows for the purchase of $8,500 in coverage for only $25 per year. Unlike most riders to homeowner policies, the standard Society insurance includes no deductible and requires no appraisal or inventory (except for individual items valued at $25,000 or more).

In addition to the APS, the American Philatelic Center, located in Bellefonte, Pennsylvania, also houses the American Philatelic Research Library (APRL). The APRL is the largest public philatelic library in the United States with more than two miles of books, catalogues, auction listings, journals, dealer price lists, indexes, research papers of famous collectors, and other materials. The materials in the library are supplemented by the Society's Reference Collection of genuine and fake postage stamps.

More than 6,000 items are submitted for authentication to the Society's Expertizing service each year. For as little as $25 an item, a member can receive a guaranteed opinion on the genuineness of their stamp or cover. This Society service has been a forerunner in the use of technological equipment employing the use of a Crimescope and other scientific analysis to assist personal expert evaluation.

Other APS services include estate advice, a translation service, an annual stamp show, a website at www.stamps.org to assist all collectors, even nonmembers, and much more!

MEMBERSHIP INFORMATION

Membership dues are just $45 per year. Our membership year runs from January 1 through December 31. New members applying will have their first year's dues prorated based on the quarter in which their application is received. A one-time $3 application fee is required.

More information on the American Philatelic Society is available from www.stamps.org, or by calling 814-933-3803 or writing to APS Dept. BB, 100 Match Factory Place, Bellefonte, PA 16823.

We Invite you to join in the fun!

LOCAL STAMP CLUBS

Numerous local stamp clubs exist all across the country, far too many to mention individually. Most hold regular meetings, often featuring presentations or slide programs by established collectors, and many permit trading sessions, an activity enjoyed by all. Newcomers, especially, find local stamp clubs useful in enriching their understanding and appreciation of the hobby. Some, either individually or in concert with other local clubs, sponsor annual stamp shows that feature exhibits as well as a dealer bourse.

Many local clubs are chapters of the American Philatelic Society. The APS Chapter Activities Committee serves as a focal point for services available to local stamp clubs. The committee publishes a quarterly newsletter, sponsors a publications contest, and conducts other programs for local clubs. APS chapters may schedule APS Sales Division circuits and philatelic slide programs produced by the Society exclusively for use by chapters for their meetings. Information about local APS chapters can be obtained from the APS, 100 Match Factory Place, Bellefonte, PA 16823; (814) 933-3803; or on the APS Web site www.stamps.org.

Information about local clubs that are not APS chapters often can be obtained by checking with a local stamp dealer or clerk in the nearest Postal Service philatelic center.

HOUSE OF COLLECTIBLES SERIES

Title	ISBN	Price	Author
The Official® Price Guides to			
Antique Jewelry, 7th ed.	9780609809136	$27.95	Kaplan
Clocks	9780609809730	$19.95	Korz
Collecting Books, 6th ed.	9780375722936	$21.95	Tedford/Goudey
Collector Knives, 15th ed.	9780375722806	$21.95	Price
Disney Collectibles, 2nd ed.	9780375722622	$29.95	Hake
Dolls	9780375720369	$20.00	Van Patten
Glassware, 4th ed.	9780375721823	$24.95	Pickvet
Hislop's International Fine Art, 2nd ed.	9780375722141	$24.95	Hislop
Mickey Mouse Collectibles	9780375723070	$12.95	Hake
Mint Errors, 7th ed.	9780375722158	$21.95	Herbert
Overstreet Comic Book Companion, 11th ed.	9780375723087	$12.99	Overstreet
Overstreet Comic Book Grading Guide, 3rd ed.	9780375721069	$24.95	Overstreet
Overstreet Comic Books, 39th ed.	9780375723117	$29.95	Overstreet
Overstreet Indian Arrowheads, 11th ed.	9780375723124	$29.99	Overstreet
Pop Culture Memorabilia	9780375722820	$34.95	Hake
Records, 18th ed.	9780375722363	$26.95	Osborne
Star Wars Memorabilia	9780375720758	$17.95	Beckett
The Official® Guides to			
Coin Collector's Survival Manual, 6th ed.	9780375723056	$22.95	Travers
One-Minute Coin Expert, 6th ed.	9780375720406	$14.95	Travers
Scott Travers' Top 88 Coins to Buy and Sell	9780375722219	$13.95	Travers
The Official® Beckett Sports Cards Price Guides			
Baseball Cards 2010, 30th ed.	9780375723360	$8.99	Beckett
Basketball Cards 2010, 19th ed.	9780375723285	$8.99	Beckett
Football Cards 2010, 29th ed.	9780375723278	$8.99	Beckett

The Blackbooks!

The leading authorities on U.S. coins, U.S. paper money, U.S. postage stamps, and world coins!

All national bestsellers, these dynamic books are the *proven* annual guides for collectors in these fields!

- **Coins**—Every U.S. coin evaluated . . . features the American Numismatic Association Official Grading System
- **Paper Money**—Every government-issued note covered
- **World Coins**—Features the most popular and collectible foreign coins from forty-eight countries around the world
- **Postage Stamps**—Brings the current value of each U.S. postage stamp along with its illustration on every page

BUY IT ● USE IT ● BECOME AN EXPERT™

Available from House of Collectibles in bookstores everywhere!